GW00456566

Thank you to the following people for their invaluable contributions: Castleford Tigers Head Coach Daryl Powell and Director of Rugby Jon Wells, Hampshire's Director of Cricket Giles White, Leicester Tigers' Defence Coach Mike Ford, former US Submarine Commander L. David Marquet, designer Wayne Hemingway and businessman Gerald Ratner.

I would also like to thank Dave Davies at Blue Frontier for bringing my rough sketches of the cover and the diagrams to life, through his design input.

~~~

Once again, I would like to give massive thanks to James Kerr for his time and his inspirational book "Legacy" for starting this whole journey. Reading "Legacy" remains the game changer for me.

~~~

As this is a work of opinion, any references to real people, places or events may include factual inaccuracies, adaptations or omissions. If that is the case, I apologise unreservedly for any offence or upset caused.

~~~

This book is dedicated to Piggy, Rocky, Coochie and George.

~~~

GET WIN READY

MASTER THE WINNING CONTROLLABLES

SIMON J. RHODES

CONTENTS

INTRODUCTION

Everyone starts a new book with a sense of anticipation. And everyone wants to finish that book with a sense of satisfaction. All books should pose their readers a challenging problem or scenario to resolve. Then they should go on to offer a credible and compelling solution. This is as true of a novel as it is a business book. Offering a solution to a problem is a worthwhile basis for a book. So, which problem am I trying to solve?

Too many individuals and teams underperform, year on year, competition by competition. Too many chances of winning are lost by a lack of preparedness, disengagement from the core purpose, misalignment of resources, poor decision-making, closed mindsets and many more utterly avoidable reasons. Each time a win is blown, it's a missed opportunity. Avoidable losses shouldn't happen and they certainly shouldn't be repeated. That's because every person and every team can make themselves ready to win. Under-performing teams can develop into high-performing ones. And very often, improvements can be made quickly and without spending much money.

There are some common themes that we can all benefit from. By seeking insights from winners and losers in business, sport, politics, the military and the wider world, I have tried to discover how winning is really done. That is the problem I set out to solve in the book and I will go on to explain the solution. I have included some notable contributions from Daryl Powell, Gerald Ratner, Giles White, L. David Marquet, Wayne Hemingway and Mike Ford, for which I am very grateful.

~~~~~

First a little about me. I was born in Castleford in 1968. My birthplace was chosen for me, but I have chosen my affinity with the place ever since. I feel a strong connection because I was born in the town, before the maternity unit was closed and before Castleford people started being born in Pontefract. My affinity is also partly because of the town's rugby league team. These reasons might seem trivial or immaterial to you, but what's important is that they matter to me. Whatever the reasons, my birthplace still matters to me over fifty years later, even though I live at the other end of the country. There is an emotional pull from my birthplace which hasn't faded. Our favourite places influence what we feel and often where we compete. Our favourite places can lift our spirits and drive our actions.

Growing up in the late 1970's I wanted to play for Manchester United. Why? I'd watched them on television and I must have said I liked them, because I was given a Man United kit for Christmas when I was ten. I wore it outside it in the garden, pretending to be United's new star striker Joe Jordan. I remember feeling absolutely gutted when Alan Sunderland scored the winning goal for Arsenal in 89th minute of the 1979 F.A. Cup Final. But, a few years later, when I was about thirteen years old, I had a football epiphany. I realised that supporting Manchester United wasn't right for me. I lived far closer to Leeds than Manchester. I had a Leeds postcode. I had absolutely no connection to Manchester, other than my out of date shirt, shorts and socks. They didn't fit me anymore and nor did Manchester United. It dawned on me that I had chosen the wrong team to support. In an ironic role reversal with my football hero Joe Jordan, I transferred myself from Manchester United to Leeds United. This was perhaps the first kind of fundamental change I'd made in my life and I haven't changed that back. We are all inherently tribal, whether we like sport or not.

Working out which tribes we belong to is an important part of growing up and something we need to bear in mind throughout life. We need to feel comfortable in our tribes, rather than out of place. That means changing or adding tribes when we need to. We don't just have one tribe. In the right environment, we can experience a tribal comfort and passion elsewhere. Finding the right place to do our work is hugely important. That's because we always do our best work in our best tribes.

Before I made my 'United' transfer, I had already made another more important commitment. This time it was to rugby league. My parents were both regulars at Castleford and my brother Jason and I went along with them, long before I got into football. But it wasn't until I was eleven that I really started to go for myself. As a family we went to every home game and plenty of away matches too. We also got to meet up with friends there[1]. I have also dragged plenty of other friends to watch Cas matches over the years. The atmosphere at 'the Jungle' is intense and emotional. Being there with other people I care about, always makes that viewing experience richer. Our people matter to us and to our success. We are rarely truly happy on our own. It's even rarer that we are truly successful on our own. We do our best work, with people and organisations that we care about.

---

[1] I can clearly remember standing behind the posts and celebrating Castleford tries with my next door neighbour Jeremy Atkinson and his Dad. We shared a pride in the same community, but our shared passion for Cas was even stronger.

When I wasn't playing football, the 1970's involved playing 'soldiers' quite a lot. Despite the glamour of General Custer and his 7th Cavalry, whenever I played 'Cowboys and Indians²' I always wanted the Native Americans to win. My toy soldiers agreed. I preferred their reason for fighting, the defence of each other and their homeland. Those Native Americans felt more like the sort of people I wanted to be part of. So I chose their side. All the sides we choose have a big influence on us throughout life. All of that playing 'soldiers' must have had an effect on my brother Jason as he ended up joining the Army. I obviously liked the principle of defending social injustice as I decided to become a lawyer. Our choices were very different. Collectively, one after another, all of our choices create our direction in life. Amongst all of our decisions, our career choices dictate the arenas in which we compete and the skills we need to acquire to be successful.

It wasn't just playing 'soldiers' that forged my legal career. My teenage years were spent watching Crown Court³ and dreaming of become a criminal barrister. I wanted to defend the innocent and say "Yes M'lud" in a wise and dignified manner. The excitement that I got from that programme gave me something to aim for. When the time came to choose a career, I didn't become a barrister, but I did get to achieve my legal dream. Fired up by the chance to protect the rights of employees and defend the good work of decent employers, I chose to become an employment solicitor instead. Through commitment, collaboration and plenty of hard work I have a lot of cases in the Employment Tribunal. My legal dream was achieved, just in a different way. Our hopes and dreams matter. Having dreams, gives us the motivation to do things we otherwise might never do. Dreams keep us moving when our feet begin to tire.

"You are never too old to set another goal or dream a new dream"⁴

In 1991, when I was about twenty-three, I vividly remember watching the Great British Men's 4 x 400 metres relay team compete in the World Championships Final. David Coleman was commentating. We had a very good team, which included the 400 metres silver medal winner Roger Black. We had a good chance of a relay team medal. Based on running times, the Americans had a significantly faster team. If we ran at our best we could win silver, which would have been a relative success. The Americans were the previous winners of the event and they

---

² Native Americans.
³ An ITV daytime drama about criminal trials in the Crown Court, which ran from 1972 to 1984.
⁴ C.S. Lewis, author of the Narnia series.

had won the same event at the last two Olympics games as well. To beat them we had to produce something exceptional.

In a change to standard operating procedures, the team decided that our fastest man, Roger Black, should run the first leg. Normally the faster runner always runs last. Although Roger had established a lead by the time he handed over to Derek Redmond, that lead had gone by the time our final runner Kris Akabusi began his leg. The tactical gamble hadn't paid off. Starting three metres behind Antonio Pettigrew, the 400 metres World Champion, Kris Akabusi was at a massive disadvantage. Even Roger Black couldn't catch him in the 400 metres final. Kris was the 400m hurdles Bronze medal winner, running against the fastest 400 metres runner in the World and he had to come from behind to win.

When Kris passed Antonio Pettigrew in the home straight, my heart leapt. When he crossed the finish line in first, I shouted for joy. It was a sensational performance. It proved that teams could produce amazing performances against the odds. About ten years later, I was lucky enough to see Kris and Roger on stage together, commentating 'live' to an audience on that race. They talked about how they'd agreed as a team that Roger would run first; and how they all believed in that approach. Then Kris explained how he had managed to psych-out Antonio Pettigrew, by talking to him as he chased him round the track. How did he have the breath and energy? Kris found his greatest performance when his team really needed it. About ten years after that, I was asked to co-host a business awards ceremony with Roger Black. When that 1991 event played on the big screen, the audience reacted as if it were live. Special performances like that can inspire the next ones.

In 2005, after several years at other law firms, I joined Trethowans solicitors. I held a series of management roles, until in 2009 I was asked to become the firm's Managing Partner (and afterwards its Senior Partner). When I joined the firm our turnover was under £6 million and our profile was pretty limited. In fact it was so limited that we referred to ourselves as a "hidden secret". As I write this, Trethowans LLP is now an £18 million turnover law firm that is well-regarded, well-ranked by the legal guides and punches above its weight. Growing the business through a recession and the run up to Brexit has been immensely challenging, but it has also been very rewarding in a rounded sense. The experience of leadership has taught me a lot. I definitely haven't got every decision right, but I have always tried to learn something from every decision and every outcome. Our opportunities to make decisions and our chances to show leadership give us new chances to be successful.

As an employment lawyer for over twenty five years, I've acted for all shapes and sizes of employer, from national brand names to NHS trusts, from charities to local government, from professional partnerships to local businesses. Employers and employees don't involve lawyers unless something is amiss. I have worked on hundreds of cases where teams are under-performing, businesses are failing and working relationships are broken. I have seen and learned a great deal about failure. I have always wanted to understand why that was happening. What should have been done differently? How could those failures have been turned into successes? There's always learning to be done. Our failures teach us at least as much as our successes, if not more. A loss is never a final judgement, it's a greater opportunity to be more successful next time. How often do we learn enough from our losses and failures? The honest answer is seldom.

> *"The important thing is to learn a lesson every time you lose.*
> *Life is a learning process and you have to try to learn what's best*
> *for you. Let me tell you, life is not fun when you're banging*
> *your head against a brick wall all the time"*[5]

During my career I have spent considerable time working with others outside my day job, building and working within voluntary collaborations. I have chaired a group focusing on economic growth called 'Future Southampton', helped to start the process that gave Southampton a Business Improvement District, chaired three environmental conferences, served as a trustee at the Southampton Cultural Development Trust, served as a Southampton Board member at Hampshire Chamber of Commerce, created the concept for the 'Salisbury Big Business Event' and co-run it for six years, created the concept for the 'Solent Business Growth Summit' and co-run it for four years, helped to try and get a Hampshire-wide skills initiative started, created the concept for a Solent skills initiative and worked on its development, judged at the South Wiltshire Business Awards, judged at the South Coast Business of the Year Awards; and co-hosted and co-presented the South Coast Business of the Year Awards. I wasn't paid for any of this time, but that was never my reason for getting involved. The possibility of building something for the benefit of the wider community has kept pulling me back in, to try something else. Not all of these initiatives were rip-roaring successes, it has to be said. But I keep on learning and I keep on trying.

---

[5] Seven times tennis Grand Slam Champion John McEnroe (three of those Championships were at Wimbledon).

There are so many reasons why an initiative succeeds, why one partially succeeds or why one fails entirely. Many of these reasons are outside our control. My experience of facing those kind of reasons has taught me not to fight the impossible battles. My experiences have also taught me about the importance of a shared mission and the need for alignment. I have learned a huge amount about myself and about other people from experiencing each of those situations. Our choice of relationships and collaborations matters enormously to our chances of being successful. A key question for us all, is in which tribes can we do our best work?

In recent years, I have helped a number of other businesses, professional sports teams and schools from the outside, acting as a sounding-board or mentor for their leaders. Sometimes that has been on mutual basis. These conversations have given me an insight into winning that I would otherwise never have experienced. The stories and insights that we get from others make us more likely to win. I have shared a series of stories and insights throughout this book. Some are from my own experience, many more are from other people's. I hope they are helpful.

My life so far has been a game of two halves. I was born to one Northern and one Southern parent. I have lived half my life in the North of England and half in the South. I have been an insider and an outsider in business, building from within and without. I have spent part of my time building my own organisations; and part of my time building collaborations between other organisations. Living this split-life has made me appreciate more people, more tribes and more joint-working. The variety of life on offer has made me less tribal in the insular, closed-minded sense and more Super-tribal (where tribes come together as one to achieve a common purpose[6]). We are one hundred percent better together.

"The way a team plays as a whole determines its success.
You may have the greatest bunch of individual stars in the world,
but if they don't play together, the club won't be worth a dime"[7]

I love building teams and I love building partnerships, alliances and Super-tribes even more. Why? The bigger the pool of people and skills you have to harness together, the greater the mission you can achieve. The corollary is also true. The fewer people and resources available to you, the less chance of success you have.

---

[6] This is the subject of my books 'Build Your Super-tribe' and 'Lead Your Super-tribe.
[7] George Herman 'Babe' Ruth Jr, winner of 7 World Series with Boston Red Sox (3) and the New York Yankees (4).

Progressing from being a lone individual, to being part of a tribe matters enormously to winning. Turning your tribe into a Super-tribe gives you even greater chance of succeeding.

~~~~

I will just tell you one quick, personal story before I get into the book properly. When my daughter Libby was in Infant School, she ran in her School Sports' Day. The race was about sixty metres long and she was looking forward to it. I just wanted her to have fun and enjoy the competition.

When she crossed the finishing line, she was third out of ten, only a stride or two behind first place. Standing on the side-line I should have felt pride, but I felt a sense of disappointment. Please don't judge me quite yet. You see the reason Libby finished third was because of me. My disappointment was with myself. Just before the race had begun, I had shouted across to wish her good luck. She saw me and starting waving back. We shared a happy smile. The gun went off and we were both still smiling and waving to each other.

> *"Preparation, I have often said,*
> *is rightly two-thirds of any venture"*[8]

I could see that all the other children were sprinting away. So, I started a different type of waving and urged Libby to start running. When she realised what had happened, she started to give chase. The other boys and girls had a head start on her but she gave it absolutely everything. She did her very best to catch the others. By the time she crossed the line she'd got herself up into third.

It was only a school sports' day, but I am still proud of Libby because she did her absolute best in the circumstances. But over ten years on I still feel a bit of disappointment in myself that I prevented her from winning. Of course she might not have won the race, but my action took away her chance of winning. Libby was naturally fast and ready to race until she became distracted. She lost her concentration just when she needed it. Looking back, I learned a fundamental thing about winning that day and it's stayed with me. If you aren't ready to win, you won't. Whatever you're trying to succeed in may change. But the art of being

---

[8] Aviation pioneer Amelia Earhart, who became the first woman to complete a non-stop transatlantic flight in 1932.

ready to succeed doesn't. In short, becoming 'win ready' matters enormously to winning. It can make all the difference.

~~~~~

Success lessons come in many forms and many sources. Some come from business and the world of work, others from sport and competitive games. We need to embrace them all. We learn the most from competitions that have similar challenges but different insights and solutions. What we need are situations with useful parallels and transferable learnings. The more we're made to think, the better we think.

Some people use the expression 'Stay ready so you don't have to get ready.' The point being that if you are ready to go all the time, you don't need to do any last minute preparation. But that's not right. Everyone needs to get ready first, before they are able to 'stay ready' afterwards. And everyone needs at least a moment of priming. So, more accurately, that phrase should be 'Get win ready and stay win ready.' And that's what this book is about.

1. WHAT IS 'WIN READY'?

1.1 THAT'S HOW WINNING IS DONE

'Rocky Balboa' is the fifth film in Sylvester Stallone's 'Rocky' franchise. It's not a cinematic high point, but it contains a very insightful monologue. In the film, Rocky has a grown-up son called Robert who hears that his father is about to return to the boxing ring aged 61. Hugely concerned, Robert immediately seeks his father out. When he finds him, Robert doesn't express any concern for this father's health. He doesn't remind him of what he's achieved and ask "Isn't that enough?" Instead he complains about how being 'Rocky's son' is holding him back and making him look like a joke. Rocky is understandably hurt, but he doesn't get angry. Instead, Rocky Balboa offers his son a life-lesson in resilience.

"The time came for you to be your own man and take on the World and you did. But somewhere along the line you changed. You stopped being you. You let people stick a finger in your face and tell you you're no good. And when things got hard, you started looking for something to blame. Like a big shadow. Let me tell you something you already know. The World ain't all sunshine and rainbows. It's a very mean and nasty place and I don't care how tough you are, it will beat you to your knees and keep you there permanently if you let it. You, me, or nobody is gonna hit as hard as life. But it ain't about how hard you hit. It's about how hard you can get hit and keep moving forward. How much you can take and keep moving forward. That's how winning is done.

Now, if you know what you're worth, then go out and get what you're worth. But you gotta be willing to take the hits, and not pointing fingers saying you ain't where you wanna be because of him, or her, or anybody. Cowards do that and that ain't you. You're better than that! I'm always gonna love you, no matter what. No matter what happens. You're my son and you're my blood. You're the best thing in my life. But until you start believing in yourself, you ain't gonna have a life."

This form of 'tough love' may have been helpful to Rocky's fictional son. It certainly gave him a lesson about life. However, despite claiming to, Rocky's words did not explain how winning is really done. Whilst mental strength is certainly a factor, winning depends on many more elements than that.

~~~~~

In a competitive environment, no one can guarantee themselves or their team a win. And yet, when any competition begins, some people and some teams are already more likely to win than others. Why is that? If everyone starts on a level playing field, how can anyone be ahead of the game before the competition even begins? It's because some people and teams are more ready to win than their opponents. Being win ready means being in the best possible position to win whatever competition you're involved in.

In business, there are always this year's targets and KPI's[9] to be hit. You have to do the numbers to be successful. You have to do the numbers to keep your job. So business preparation is often too narrowly focused on hitting the numbers, not building the organisation for the long term. When success happens, there are pay rises, commissions, bonuses and LTIPs[10] to be given out. Not training, investment or time off to refresh. And what follows? Higher targets or reduced resources or both. Business goals tend to be short-term and so do its rewards. Does that approach make businesses more ready to win? Possibly yes if the numbers imposed from the top are all that matters. But success has to be judged more broadly than that. Focusing too hard on the numbers on a spreadsheet excludes the human issues and the people who delivered those numbers. Short-termism can reduce engagement and therefore your chances of winning in the years ahead. So there has to be investment in the future as well as the present.

In the military, there are battles and wars to be fought and enemies to be defeated. In turn there are victories to be won, bravery to be glorified and medals to be awarded. In the UK, the real cost of having an army reduces year on year. More is constantly expected for less. As things stand, all of the British Army could fit inside Wembley Stadium. That's not very reassuring. Size is one factor in success, but the bigger question is "Is the British Army win ready?" The answer is "Barely". Everyone has their own opinion about how many soldiers, guns and bombs any country should have. Some would say none at all. Ideally it would be none. But if you have an army, you need it to be win ready, every single time it's needed.

"There are no secrets to success. It is the result of preparation, hard work, and learning from failure"[11]

---

[9] Key Performance Indicators.
[10] Long Term Incentive Plans.
[11] Retired US Army General Colin Powell.

In sport, there are competitions of all kinds to be won. They include league championships, play-offs, knock-out cup competitions and events where you have to try and finish in first place. When sporting competitions are won, there are cups, trophies, plates, jackets, awards and medals to be presented. Teams have to try and win all this year's competitions as well as preparing for next year's and the year after's. That's almost impossible to do with equal focus.

In many other walks of life there are no trophies, no bonuses and not even a well done or thank you. But winning isn't always about standing on a podium or being praised and glorified. Sometimes winning is about quietly succeeding underneath the radar. Sometimes winning is simply about not losing. Other times, the cost of winning means there is no celebrating to be done. But, whatever the circumstances are, winning matters. Winning always matters.

Finishing first or 'top' is the aim in any competition, but sometimes achieving a form of relative success is all that's possible. When you achieve as much as you possibly can, that is your winning. This can happen when you're under-resourced, inexperienced or facing the nightmare scenario where every option has a negative and costly outcome. In this type of situation, success will be relative. That might mean finishing mid-table and being pleased with that. Or it might mean choosing, planning for and delivering the least bad option for everyone.

Not every competition results in immediate glory. Sometimes you need to finish last in order to get the wake-up call that you need for your development. Without that kick up the backside, you might not win next year. Everyone likes to be safely inside their comfort zone, but it's when the pressure is truly on that the best learning takes place. Think back to an occasion when you and your team were under real pressure. How did you and your team react to it? How did the combined pressures of responsibility, accountability and fear (of making mistakes) impact on your performance? Did they stifle your decision-making? Did your communication break down? Did the external stressors impede your internal analysis? Did the pressure produce inaction (analysis paralysis) and mistakes that you desperately wanted to avoid? Or did you fight back and thrive?

"Pressure makes diamonds much harder than stone
And they only get finer as each day goes on" [12]

---

[12] 'Pressure makes diamonds' by Don Williams.

Wherever you finish in a competition, there are learnings for next time. Competing is what teaches us how to compete. You do have to be in it to win it. Writing off the last year at a stroke and starting again is wasteful. To coin an old phrase, it's like 'Throwing out the baby with the bathwater'. Always hold a complete review. No upper level of management or sensitive subject should be off-limits. End of competition reviews are often too shallow, politically pre-ordained, or avoided altogether. Reviews are essential to understand how winning is done. Trying to assess what's need to win an event, without learning from previous attempts is going to be very difficult.

To be effective, reviews have to be wide-ranging, open, respectful and deep (WORD). They need to analyse all aspects of the past performance, seek further internal and external input to learn more; and go on to reach conclusions. The key question is "With hindsight, what would you have changed to increase your chances of winning?" Even the team that finishes first can learn from reviewing its own performance. Winning again next year is never guaranteed and it's unlikely without learning from how you won it.

Reviews should always make recommendations for change. By estimating the implementation cost and time, as well as their likely impact), a review should be able to prioritise those recommended changes. Once your review report is ready, it's for the organisation as a whole to implement the changes needed. The better your retrospective reviews become, the better your active decision-making becomes. The past both informs the present and improves it.

Each year's experience can get you and your team closer to success next time. Collectively, by learning all the lessons, year after year, you can prepare yourself and your team for winning. Development is rarely caused by a "eureka" moment. Development is a learning and layering process. That's how winning is done.

1.2 WHAT IS WINNING?

Sometimes measuring success is easy. If a competition only offers one trophy, then there is only one winner. If there are three medals, then there are three winners placed in ranking order. But sometimes are more 'winners' than just the Champions of a league competition. What about the team that finished in mid-table with the lowest resources in the league? Didn't it 'win' too? What about the team that avoided relegation despite a crippling injury crisis? What about the team who was robbed of the title by a terrible referring or VAR decision? Didn't they have some kind of success?

Winning doesn't only mean crossing the line in first place, collecting a trophy or being presented with a medal. Winning is about achieving your goals, whatever they may be. That could mean closing out your first big sale, setting up your own business, securing a promotion at work, getting a new job that pays more or coming first in a competition. Winning can also mean gaining respect. Or it could be sticking to your values, when you're under pressure to give them up. Winning is about facing up to a competitive challenge and coming out on top. Winning is always mission dependent. One mission's win might be another mission's failure.

Measuring success is often difficult, as not every goal or outcome is easily measurable. For example, if a competition doesn't award any trophies, medals or titles, how do you decide who has been successful? Even when there are elements which are measurable, they don't always tell the whole story. Statistics don't often reflect the context or the human stories behind the data. Sometimes winning isn't obvious. You have to look at the data and the story behind the data.

Take the Ambulance Service. We would all agree that the Ambulance Services does a vital and challenging job. Without it, many tens of thousands more people would die. The Ambulance Technicians and other medical staff are the experts. We need to allow them to go their jobs to the best of their ability. They need to be empowered to do their best job, not pressurised into achieving artificial data targets. So how would you measure a successful ambulance call? Do the available statistics tell the whole story?

The Ambulance Services has a series of timescales to meet, as well as many other NHS standards. One time target is based on the time it takes from receiving a 999 call to the vehicle arriving at the patient's location. This target is a key priority for Ambulance Services, so they have sometimes sent more than one vehicle to the same location in order to meet that NHS time target. That doesn't seem right. That second ambulance could have been sent to another call. The correct decision surely depends on the prevailing circumstances at the time. If the traffic in the area is quiet and the service's ambulances are well-maintained, why send two of them? The question is perhaps best left to the Ambulance Service control team to decide, rather than focusing on a national target?

The Ambulances Services have four categories of ambulance call. The average response times required for each category is set by The NHS England 'New Ambulance Standards.

The four categories are:

Category 1: Life threatening: The average response time required is 7 minutes.
Category 2: Emergency: The average response time required is 18 minutes.
Category 3: Urgent call: The average response time required is 120 minutes at least 90% of the time.
Category 4: Less urgent call: The average response time required is 180 minutes at least 90% of the time.

The likely time difference between a Category 1 and a Category 4 call allocation is huge. The accuracy of the categorisation of 999 calls is therefore critically important. Putting a call into the wrong category could mean the difference between life and death. Is the accuracy of this category allocation process measured? I couldn't find any measure for this.[13] How thorough is this category allocation process, when call-handlers are under pressure to take as many calls as possible? The call volume is measured. The mean (average) and median (50th centile) length of each emergency call have to be reported. But the effect of category allocation, doesn't seem to be measured. Which elements should be measured to ensure success?

"My favourite things in life don't cost any money. It's really clear that the most precious resource we all have is time"[14]

In a growing and ageing population, the number of calls climbs ever higher every year. Having a process, a checklist and training will all help, but the call handler has to be able to make the call on category allocation. That brings increasing pressure on operators to free up the telephone lines even faster. But being fast doesn't necessarily mean being accurate, reassuring or compassionate. Being fast doesn't necessarily mean you get satisfied patients or satisfied staff. That brings us back to the question of what is a successful call? Surely it can't be measured just in response time.

---

[13] That's not to say that it doesn't exist.
[14] Steve Jobs, co-founder of Apple with Steve Wozniak.

Ambulance crews also work to the 'golden hour' principle, which is the aim to get definitive care for any patient within 60 minutes of the time of injury. This is because the risk of death significantly increases after this point. There is clear medical logic to this principle, but judging anyone on this measure alone would ignore all the uncontrollable variations in weather conditions, remoteness, vehicle access and the number of injured patients. It also ignores the time for other emergency responders to arrive, such as the Fire and Rescue Service, who may need to cut out the patient from a vehicle, before he she or they can be treated.

There is also the 'platinum 10 minutes' principle, which considers that seriously injured patients should have no more than 10 minutes of emergency 'scene-time stabilisation' prior to their transport to receive definitive care at a trauma centre (hospital). Meeting this principle is only partly in the control of an ambulance crew. The actual time it takes will depend on all the variables already mentioned, as well as the age and size of the patient; and the nature and extent of their injuries.

Then there's another time test. After an ambulance reaches its allocated hospital, a patient should wait no more than 30 minutes between arrival and handover to a clinician. This statistic is not within an ambulance crew's control. It depends on which hospital they are sent to and how busy it is. Some crews are left waiting far longer than they should be, because the hospital is too busy for the available resources. The crew is then stuck and unable to help any other injured patients, because they can't be released back into the community.

Each of these time targets have a purpose. Each one helps to reveal a trend; and ongoing measurement of them can reveal changes in those trends. But do they tell us what is a successful ambulance call? The answer is 'partly'. All these statistics are time related, which is a measurement of quantity rather than quality. Winning surely involves an evaluation of both. The way the Ambulance crew did its job should count massively. You only have to watch the BBC's uplifting 'Ambulance' television programme to see the wonderful skill and bedside manner on display. The time data matters, but within 'success' surely people's experiences and feelings matter too? Other statistics can be measured, which could really help monitor the success of the service. They could include patient satisfaction and feedback from a friend, colleague or loved one accompanying the patient.

"Intrinsic value is not measured by how much money you make, it's measured by the size of the problem you solve"[15]

The Ambulance Services does an amazing job. There aren't enough ambulances or call handlers to manage demand. There aren't enough hospital cubicles, beds or staff to cope with demand. It's an impossible job that's getting increasingly less possible. And yet, they cope. Despite that, each regional service can expect criticism if any of their target times aren't met. That may be due to an unmanageable volume of calls, a lack of budget and resources or any other uncontrollable factor that made their success impossible. This broader kind of assessment needs to be done for every evaluation of success. We shouldn't try and distil any form of 'success' to a single, arbitrary statistic. When you decide how to measure success, you need to review it in its context. Ask how you can best measure success in the round. Start with the wide series of outcomes that winning brings and measure them all, not just who gets the trophy or how long the task took.

So how do you approach this thorny issue of measuring success? With a specific mission in mind, you can assess success based on the outcomes you want to see achieved and the outcomes you want to avoid. Winning is therefore made up of a mixture of achievements and avoidances. However, that's not all about the statistics, there are wider outcomes than just points in a league season or arrival times at a patient's location.

Success all starts with the right mission. What is the main goal you're working towards? Have you achieved it? In the case of the Ambulance Services isn't the main goal improving patient lives? In that case, timescales are only one aspect of that success. A winning service might currently be deemed a failing service by an arbitrary target and that's not fair. We need to find a way of assessing a rounded form of success.

1.3 HOW DO YOU KNOW YOU'RE WINNING?

With so many ways to define success, how can be sure whether we're winning or losing? We all need to know which target we're shooting at. Until we can describe what 'winning' is we can't prepare for it.

---

[15] Author Joseph Jordan.

There is a saying in the art world that "A painting is never finished, it is merely abandoned."[16] The logic being that a painting is only 'finished' when the artist decides it is, not because there is a set end point. A painting can be made of one brush stroke or hundreds. A canvass can be painted on once or dozens of times. It is the artist's own subjective view that matters. When does the painter want to stop? When is that artist satisfied?

A similar decision-making process takes place with all kinds of creative processes. Before the process begins, not even the artist knows exactly what the end result will look like. The question to ask, is the same question that exists for every type of quest or exercise. When is our mission complete?

To answer that question, you need to define success before the mission starts. That way you know what your task has to achieve. By described the outcomes you want, you can precisely deliver them. As a result, you can tell when you're finished. If you're a painter and you're painting from a photograph you've taken, or a scene you can see live, you know what your painting should look like. A successful painting would strongly resemble that photograph or scene; and an unsuccessful painting wouldn't, unless it's deliberately surrealist. However, if a painter paints from scratch, with no instructions or guide, there is no agreed 'end'. Success, in that case, would become much more subjective and difficult to assess. What would you paint? When would you stop? Without a definition of success, all kinds of missions lose momentum, turn off-track, or get abandoned before they can be completed.

Without a definition of success to work to, we can't focus our efforts on achieving it. Without knowing what constitutes a win, we can't fire ourselves up to become winners. Without a fixed set of goalposts to aim at, we can't start trying to score. Once we have a mission, we have to define what its success looks like. Then we can move on to how to win.

~~~~~

Too many organisations fail to define success. And many organisations that do define success, fail to involve all their stakeholders in establishing that definition. Unless a mission is agreed, it isn't agreed. And that means it isn't accepted. Without sufficient engagement from its people, any organisation's mission is likely to fail. That's why success should never be determined by closed-minded

---

[16] Leonardo da Vinci.

people with unreasonable expectations. Why not? Because that type of organisation is unlikely to ever deliver that definition of success, despite the fact that organisation might actually be winning.

When we are planning a mission, the first step is to decide 'Who defines what winning means?' Who gets to define what 'success' means for you or your organisation? In business, whether there's been a good financial year is decided by the owners and funders. Are they happy with the profits and dividends for the financial year? Are they content with the balance sheet position? Did they get the return on their investment that they wanted?

In sport, those decision-makers are likely to be the club's owners, sponsors and supporters. Without their money and support a club cannot run. Are they happy with the season? Did they get the league position and trophies they were hoping for? Each organisation's decision-makers get to decide what they think and what they expect. But if that decision is taken in a vacuum, it might not be the right assessment.

The second step is to make that decision-making process inclusive. Whoever gets to decide shouldn't do it alone. Defining success needs to be an inclusive assessment involving the whole organisation and its stakeholders. Everyone has to buy into a mission, or it's likely to fail. Unless a team cares about the outcome of its mission, it won't ever deliver it. An organisation's purpose has to be meaningful and motivating to all its stakeholders. All questions about winning should invite a joint approach, even though the decision-makers have the ultimate power. Inclusive questions include: What can we achieve together? What's possible if we all do our jobs really well? How much further can we push ourselves? Using an inclusive approach will produce greater buy-in and therefore a greater performance. Once success is defined, everyone has to buy-in to the mission. No one can stand back if you're going to become winners.

"I attribute my success to this: I never gave or took any excuses"[17]

If you were in a sales team which was given a target of selling £750,000 worth of products next year, your first thought would probably be "Can we deliver that?" If you felt the team could sell that much, you might accept the target and the fact that the target was imposed on you. Why? Because the target would feel realistic and achievable. However, if instead of being issued with an arbitrary target, your

---

[17] Florence Nightingale.

team was asked what it thought, you are more likely to buy into whatever target you end up with. That's especially true if your views have had a clear effect on that target. For example, if your team had suggested annual sales of £700,000 and your team given £725,000, you might accept that target because it's pretty close to what you asked for. Being pushed a bit more than you'd like is common in business, which is fine as long as that new figure of £725,000 is achievable.

Thirdly, the success defining process needs to be objective. That requires a questioning approach. What achievements are good enough to be deemed a 'win'? Have we checked whether what's being proposed is achievable? Have we asked what additional resources the team needs, to deliver these additional sales? Winning shouldn't be too easy. Success has to be aspirational, mission critical and driving the organisation towards something better. But it also has to be realistic and achievable.

It would be very frustrating to be given a target of £750,000 if you and your sales colleagues weren't asked for your input, or if you expressly warned that you can only deliver £600,000 as a maximum. The imposition of an unachievable target on you, could make you give up before you've even started. Facing impossible odds eats away at a team's belief until all hope is lost. To be successful, we need to believe that we can be a success. Without the hope of succeeding, people tend to give up on trying. We want to be a winner, not a loser. Being successful feels motivating and exciting. Achieving goals feels rewarding and worth the effort we've invested. We try much harder when we can become winners. By creating a cycle of winning, we can create a series of winners. Setting realistic targets and goals is a key part of getting that right.

"The only place where success comes before work is in the dictionary"[18]

Fourthly, organisations should approach goal-setting as a way to create success. Making goals realistic, inclusive and objective (RIO) should make them more achievable, avoiding a cycle of impossible tasks, disengaged staff and repeated failures. Hopeless failing becomes so demotivating that it routinely reduces the chances of success, on every possible measure. In the armed forces, the success defining process is generally better than in business and sport. A military mission always has clear objectives. A review is always carried out afterwards. The

---

[18] Credited to American football coach Vince Lombardi; and to Vidal Sassoon, who in the 1960's modernised a 1920's hairstyle to create the iconic 'Bob'.

questioning is short and direct. For example 'Were our objectives achieved?' If they were, the mission was a success and those forces won. If the objectives weren't achieved, then the mission didn't succeed. By keeping things specific and focused, success can be objectively defined. It's just that, very often, it isn't.

Fifthly, those people and that process needs to specifically define success. It has to be crystal clear and specific enough. To use an example, your mission might be to become 'Chess Champion' in your local pub. What does that involve? For the purposes of the example, it might mean winning five consecutive matches, including a final. If that's the case, then the full definition of success means 'Becoming Chess Champion at the Queen's Head, by winning five consecutive chess matches.'

The final step is to break the definition of success down into its constituent parts. By defining each element of success individually, we can be specific about what success means for us. That's done by choosing the Measurables (the elements we need to achieve for success) and the Measures (the amounts of them that constitute success). Our Measurables must relate directly back to the mission (or why bother measuring them?). Our Measures must be a simple way of assessing whether enough has been achieved yet (or you won't know if you're winning).

So, in our local chess tournament example, we each need to win five chess matches out of five in order to become the champion. Our Measurable is therefore '5 matches won'; and our Measure is 'counting 1 win for each match that we win'. Once we have this data, we know exactly what you'll need to achieve. We need to win all five matches in order to be successful and we know how to assess our progress.

~~~~~

If instead of being an individual chess player, we're part of a sales team, then we need to define success in the same way. That leaves us with the process of working out what we should measure and how much of each element amounts we need for success. If we've done something similar before, then our Measurables and Measures could be based on our own past performances. As targets rarely go down, we could potentially base them on our past achievements and scale them up for our new higher targets. We could also look at the performance of other teams (if we have their data) to see what they did to produce the targets they achieved. If another team has achieved the same targets as we are being set, then its data will be extremely useful.

So in a sales environment, the measurables we should include will have a simple headline level (the Overall Sales Total) and the levels underneath that help us to measure and achieve that overall total. Those sub-levels will include: Individual Product (or Service) Sales (so we know what quantity needs to be sold of each product and service), Total Sales Per Quarter (to help rate seasonal fluctuations), Average Customer Contacts Per Sale (to see how hard we have to work), Average Time from First Contact to Sale (to see how urgently we need to begin), Average Sales Per Team Member (so we can see how many people we need and how much each person needs to deliver) and Sales Cost (how much investment each sale costs).

When we're considering how much we need to sell, it's important to measure Average Sale Volume as well. That tells us how much we sell each time, on average. That will help us to find where our sales sweet-spots might be. If there is a popular volume for our products or services we need to understand why, to help feed future sales. We could package up to deals to fit our popular sales volumes. Average Sales Price Per Unit is an important measurable too. That's because we need to know how much we're really selling our products or services for.

These measurables can tell us whether or not we're on track to achieve our mission. They can help to keep us focused on what matters to success, but they don't directly help us to win. For that, we also need to measure the things that make sales happen. They include getting feedback on why our customers chose us (Why I buy) and why our other prospects didn't make a purchase from us (Why I don't buy). We have to know what makes the biggest difference to making sales, to inform and improve our own sales process. Customer Satisfaction is therefore a key measurable that counts towards achieving success. So is staff engagement. If we don't measure these, we won't sell as much as we could.

In addition to these, there will be other elements that we need to achieve for our mission. Any factor that significantly contributes towards winning; and can be measured, should become a measurable.

~~~~~

King Æthelred II was King of England in the late first century. His mission would have been to rule over a peaceful, wealthy and happy Kingdom until his death and then pass his Kingdom onto his children, then grandchildren and so on, until a dynasty has been established.

One measurable would have been keeping his Kingdom safe from invasion. With this in mind, King Æthelred II paid huge tributes to the Danish Vikings in response to every threat of invasion. Each time these 'Danegeld 'payments secured a peaceful resolution. However buying-off the Danes came at a great cost to England. During the years in between the Viking threats, England thrived, unperturbed about the prospect of war.

In 1013, the Danish threats gave way to invasion and Vikings landed in huge numbers on the eastern coast of England. Unprepared for war through poor advice, Æthelred fled to Normandy and England fell to Sweyn Forkbeard, who became King of England. Now known as 'Æthelred the Unready' the King's mission failed and he lost his kingdom. After the first Viking threat (if not before), England should have spent the tribute money on preparing a vast army to defend herself.

Two years later, after King Sweyn had died, Æthelred II returned to England. Acting with more planning and patience, Æthelred II re-established his right to rule and became King once again, until his death two years later. However, because of the new Danish influence that he had allowed, Æthelred failed to establish a dynasty to follow him. In fact, King Sweyn's son Cnut became King after Æthelred, who we know better as King Canute.

~~~~~

We shouldn't begin any mission before first defining what 'winning' it means. Winning doesn't have a 'one size fits all' approach. It has to be tailored for the situation. Defining winning doesn't just mean having one single goal. That's too narrow. We shouldn't set targets that require us to repeatedly over-achieve in order to be successful. Defining winning requires us to be more thoughtful than that. We need a realistic and achievable purpose and a range of outcomes.

Everyone and everything has limitations. Find out what they are and work within them. Don't require anyone to exceed them in order to be successful. Don't rely on a 'perfect' performance to complete the mission. Winning preparation demands a lot more than big targets or unrealistic hope. That's a guaranteed way to disappointment. Don't set such high expectations that a winning performance ends up feeling like a losing one.

"When you aim for perfection, you discover it's a moving target" [19]

Too many line-managers expect their people and team to do better than they actually can. If a sales team's quarterly figures have never exceeded £250,000 then why give them a £300,000 target? Senior management may be demanding 'more' but on what basis is it achievable? Greater success needs a greater performance, which in turn requires a greater opportunity. What has changed to justify these greater expectations of success?

There are plenty of ways in which the opportunity could have increased. There are plenty of ways in which a team can improve its performance. Have any of these been put in place? They include an extra product or service line to sell, an improvement to the quality or functionality of the existing products and services, an increase in the available marketing budget, more latitude on pricing and the deals that can be offered, being allocated a bigger market or territory to sell into, the recruitment of more people to help with sales, receiving better product/services and sales training, being given additional incentives and benefits to motivate the sales team. Without one or more of these improvements in opportunity why would a team's performance suddenly increase?

We need to rate success in a fair, achievable and realistic way. We need to cater for multiple outcomes and define what each one means. Winning is a relative term and requires a relative approach. This will give us clarity over what winning means and the consequences of it. Firstly then, we need to decide what absolute success is. Then what qualified success is, followed by what qualified failure is; and finally, what absolute failure is. That gives us the four quartiles of success. Then once we know where we're aiming for, we can set realistic expectations of success within that framework. This can be set out in a diagram and applied to any mission.

---

[19] American author George Fisher.

WHAT IS WINNING?

MISSION FAILS IN EVERY RESPECT

CORE MISSION FAILS BUT WITH SOME ASPECTS OF SUCCESS

CORE MISSION ACHIEVED BUT WITH SOME ASPECTS OF FAILURE

MISSION ACHIEVED IN ALL RESPECTS
(ABSOLUTE SUCCESS)

(QUALIFIED SUCCESS)

(QUALIFIED FAILURE)

(ABSOLUTE FAILURE)

EXPECTED RESULT
(MINIMUM SUCCESS DEMANDED)

1.4 WINNING STANDARDS

Before we can win any competition, we need to understand what it takes to win it. Armed with the necessary insight and awareness, we can focus on what's needed and get ourselves win ready. However, without that insight, we lack the essential knowledge for winning. Without that awareness, we'll make too many mistakes and misjudgments to win. This is why it's so difficult to go straight from being a novice to a champion. As a novice, we don't know how to win and we haven't prepared ourselves for winning.

We have to assess and learn the relevant winning standards, before we can reach them. We need to gain the necessary experience and expertise, by analysing and assessing what winning really takes. We need to set winning standards that will deliver us success and then we need to go about achieving them.

Winning Standards can be applied to any form of competition, whether you're competing against other people or just competing against yourself. To apply a set of standards to anything, you need to know what outcomes to apply them to. That involves breaking down your mission into all its component elements. What are you trying to achieve? What needs to happen for you to complete it? What mission outcomes are required, for it to be successful?

For example, a mission to produce a new vaccine will require several winning outcomes. A successful vaccine has to produce sufficient protection against the virus concerned. It also has to produce that effect quickly enough and cheaply enough. It has to be easily stored and transported; and it has to work without any unacceptable side-effects. Each one of those winning outcomes has winning standards that have to be reached.

It is vitally important, for everyone involved, to know and understand the mission in hand. That means getting into as much detail as the mission requires you to. Once every targeted outcome of the mission is clear, we need to work out how to produce each of those outcomes. That's done by working backwards from each completed outcome, to understand which steps lead up to that summit.

Without goalposts to aim for, how do we know where to shoot?

Some missions involve short-term, repetitive or one-off events, such as selling houses or stacking supermarket shelves. In these kinds of missions, the winning outcomes are likely to be limited and the mission focus is likely to be narrow. In these simpler missions, there may be useful, existing data available, to shed light on what's needed to achieve success. That data might be internal or external. Using the shelf-stacking example, that data might include how many shelves there, how many cans there are; and how many cans will fit on each shelf.

Some other kinds of mission involve medium-term plans or multiple connected events, such as putting on a music festival or winning a knock-out cup competition. These can require greater consideration of what's needed, in order to produce success. They are also likely to require more winning outcomes and a wider range of successes than single event missions. More data and more analysis will help to create a clear path to the winning outcomes.

Finally, some other missions are long-term, sustainability projects. These may need multiple outcomes and measurements over a number of projects or years. The more extensive the mission, the less likely that it has been done in the same way before. If there is no past data to work with, then new analysis will be needed. Which winning outcomes are needed for your mission?

~~~~~

During the World War II, the Allies were losing far too many bombers over occupied France and Germany. The Allies couldn't build them fast enough to replace the planes being shot down. Bomber Command knew somehow that it had to keep more aeroplanes in the air, in order to win the war. The challenge or 'mission' was to get more RAF bombers home safely.

The most effective solution was to add armour plating. But adding too much weight would make the planes consume too much fuel, fly too slowly and possibly even struggle to take-off. Too much weight would stop them from completing their missions. The whole plane couldn't be reinforced. The critical question was where should that armour be concentrated?

The Allies had a pattern of data available from the returning planes. Virtually no plane had returned without flak damage and the heaviest damage was always to the fuselage, the outer wings and the tail. So, the obvious solution to was to provide greater protection where the flak had made the most impact, namely the fuselage, outer wings and tail. But Bomber Command was in danger of answering the wrong question, of completing the wrong mission.

The planes that made it back, had made it back. Adding additional armour to those three areas, wouldn't make any difference because those planes would still make it back. The Allies needed to focus on the planes which had been shot down. Where had they been hit? Nobody knew exactly. The answer would come from questioning the obvious logic, from a diversity of thinking.

Abraham Wald and the team at the Strategic Review Group in New York, spent World War II tackling problems like these with logic. The SRG team was able to see the problem from a difference perspective. The Allies were viewing the data they had with a survivorship bias. They were applying an error of logic, by focusing on the planes that made it back to base and overlooking those that hadn't. Abraham Wald's team concluded that the planes which had been shot down must have been hit elsewhere, or they too would have returned with the same pattern of flak damage. So the reinforcement work needed to be to the areas that hadn't been hit on the returning planes. As a result, the engines in particular were reinforced and more bombers returned home from their missions. By focusing on the right controllable, Bomber Command had an answer to the right question. Not all controllables are winning ones. We need to see the wood for the trees and focus on the winning controllables.

~~~~~

When dealing with any challenge, we need to concentrate on our mission and the winning outcomes it needs. Then we need to work backwards, to calculate how we can best achieve them. As we've seen, asking the right questions is a critical element of that. Too often a fear of embarrassment prevents us from asking, or truthfully answering, the big questions. Poor communication often holds us back from winning and that's usually down to poor working relationships. We have to get past that and build trust, respect, friendship, caring and devotion.

Winning outcomes and winning standards are best set in an environment where everyone is willing and able to ask questions and to answer them. The more information that's hidden or withheld, the less chance you've got of making an accurate assessment. The more that your questioning skirts over the real issues, the less chance you've got of establishing what it really takes to win. Setting winning standards requires a combination of diverse thinking and an open environment to think out loud in.

~~~~~

Every element of every mission requires the same level of winning performance. If one element fails, the whole mission may fail. For example, if your mission is to win a motor race and you build a fast, reliable petrol car, you will be a good position. You may have achieved the necessary car-building standard. But, if you then fill your racing car with an inexperienced driver, or even worse with diesel instead of petrol, you definitely won't win that race. Every element counts. Every element requires its own winning standard to be set and achieved. Using the same racing analogy, if you know what racing time will win you the race, you can work backwards to calculate the average speed you need to win. Working back from that average speed, you can work out what size engine, weight of car, compound of tyres, level of driver and type of fuel you need to achieve that average speed. Each element feeds backwards off the winning standard that matters the most, the time it takes to win a race.

The need to apply a winning standard to every element of your mission, applies to every kind of mission. If a chef creates a spectacular recipe for a beautiful meal but then orders the wrong ingredients, that chef will produce a different meal entirely. That wasn't the meal that was planned, it might not be as enjoyable; and it might not even be edible. Every complex mission needs a set of individual winning standards to be created and achieved.

In most things in life, the outcomes that you get reflect the inputs that you gave. The more driven you are to meet a set of standards, the more likely you will achieve them. You have to know what each element is and you have to be able to calculate its winning standard. By setting winning standards for your mission, you are far more likely to complete that mission successfully.

~~~~~

To follow this through in a worked example, let's say for the sake of argument that we are an English Championship football club that wants to gain promotion to the Premier League. Our summary mission is therefore 'Being promoted to the Premier League'. Our mission is Promotion. Success means getting promoted. Therefore to be winners we have to be promoted. Everyone at our club can understand that and get behind it. But that's just the mission headline. It begs two questions. What will that actually take to achieve? Is that mission realistic for us?

As I write, there are two ways to achieve our promotion mission. The first is to gain automatic promotion (by finishing first or second in the Championship during the normal league season) or if we can't manage that, the second way is to secure the final promotion place is through winning the end of season play-offs. They are the only ways to win promotion. Our mission has been understood. We know what outcome we need. What inputs does that take?

The only way to ensure that we get promotion is to finish in those top two places. We don't want to rely on the uncertainties of three play-off matches. We might end up having to get promotion through the play-offs, but we should set our standards higher. We should set them at achieving automatic promotion. That will mean finishing the season in first or second place, higher than 18 other clubs who all have exactly the same mission as us.

Starting out on any mission without first assessing what it will take is foolhardy. We need to establish which elements (Measurables) will get us the promotion we want. What do we need to achieve? We obviously need to measure our League Position. That's the most obvious measurable. How do we do that? Well there is an official league table, so we can look it up on the BBC website or in multiple other places. If instead, we were on a commercial business mission, there would be management accounts or a sales dashboard for us to review.

How do we know if we are on track to securing the promotion we want? If we are in the top two at any time during the season, we are on our way to achieving automatic promotion (absolute success). If we are in the four play-off places below them (from 3rd to 6th) then we are on track to make the play-offs. That isn't the big win we want, but it's certainly not failing. By being in the play-off positions, we are achieving a relative or qualified form of success.

So if 3rd to 6th is a qualified success, then what is failing? Well, if we are placed anywhere below the top six positions, having played the same number of games as everyone else, we are failing to succeed in our mission.

"We create a standard for how we want to do things and everybody's got to buy into that standard or you really can't have any team chemistry. Mediocre people don't like high-achievers and high-achievers don't like mediocre people"[20]

---

[20] Nick Saban, Head American Football Coach at the University of Alabama. At the time of writing, Wikipedia credits Nick with a college football record of 246 wins, 65 losses and one tie (draw). That's a win percentage of 78.8%.

League position is the headline measurable, but it shouldn't be the only thing we monitor. Our league position is based on the total points we've achieved from the matches so far. The more points we get from our matches, the more likely we'll finish in first or second place. Our Total Points for the season is therefore another element we should measure (a measurable). This statistic is also included in the official Championship table. We can easily see how we are doing. If our mission didn't have a dashboard to review, we would need to create one. In our football analogy, we can see exactly where we stand compared to all our Championship competitors. In business we don't get that sort of access to our competitor's performance levels. We can only compare published accounts, public shareholder distributions and public profit warnings. But we still have to try.

Being in the top two positions is no guarantee of promotion until it's mathematically impossible for two other teams to finish ahead of us. That could still happen very late in the season, perhaps in the very last round of games. Measuring our League Position and Total Points will give us a relative idea of how we're doing and will help to keep us focused. But it won't actively help us to secure first or second position when the season ends.

How do we know after say ten games, whether we are 'on track' and likely to stay there? Are our Total Points going to end up being enough? What is enough? We need to know what 'enough' means and the current Championship table can't tell us that. We need to look to other data for this information. We need to work out what winning promotion really takes.

The data of past success can form the basis for setting our own standards. We can use the missions of the past to help set the standards we need today. Can we distil our mission into a single question that gives us the winning standards we need? In this case, yes we can. 'What Total Points were achieved by every team winning automatic promotion over the last ten years?' The data from the last ten years should be enough to go on.

We can use those numbers to measure what winning actually requires in practice. That data will help us to measure our success. We merely need to look up twenty numbers (the Total Points for the top two finishers in each of the last ten official Championship tables). The data from past seasons can help us to set the standards we need to set ourselves to gain promotion (the Past Promotion Standards). By reviewing that data, we can calculate what's going to be needed for us to win promotion. We can calculate the winning standard for Total Points.

~~~~

We need to plan for success based on the numbers that will really gain us promotion. We need to use the past promotion standards of other teams. Other than League Position and Total Points, what else should be a measurable? As our mission is a long one, we need to use a series of shorter milestone goals to keep us going. What about Average Points Per Game? We can use the averages of the past to set ourselves targets and expectations for each match we play. If we divide the Total Points figures earned by those twenty successful teams, by the 38 games they played, we will get an Average Points Per Game figure for each of those promoted teams.

Using those averages we can set ourselves a game by game target to keep us focused on promotion. After every game, the official Championship table is updated. We can measure our new League Position, Total Points and Average Points Per Game from the information in the table. Comparing our actual performance for each measurable against our winning standard for it, tells us whether or not we are doing enough.

Find out exactly what you need to achieve.
Then work backwards to plan for it

We need to search for all the data that's available to us. Which data sets (measurables) really matter to winning our competition? What we measure is what we strive for, so we should only measure what helps us to win. We have to stop measuring anything that draws our focus away from what really matters to winning. Just like the Ambulance Service, we need to focus all our efforts on the right measurables. What other data will help our football team to gain promotion?

Goals Scored and Goals Conceded are two other measurables that we should use. Why? Because both of these directly impact on winning games; and winning games directly contributes to our mission of gaining promotion. A third addition should be Goal Difference (the difference between Goals Scored and Goals Conceded). Fortunately, we can see all these three measurables on the official Championship table as well. So far, all the data we want is publicly available. So far, so easy.

The headline statistics and data aren't always enough though. What about the inputs behind them, that matter to winning, but which aren't measured in the official league table? What about minutes lost to red cards? The longer our team plays without a player, the more likely we are to lose matches and therefore miss out on promotion. So that should be a measurable too. That's not on the official Championship table, so our own measurables dashboard needs to add that in.

The fewer minutes you get from your best players the less likely you are to win promotion. So what about time away from playing due to injury (in the form of a Total Squad Time Off Injured measurable; and one for each player)? This should be a measurable too. These measurables will give our strength and conditioning team, medical staff and physios targets to work to. Everyone needs to be fairly challenged and measured on their contributions towards the mission. That's important for both inclusion and delivery. You might worry that this will create a higher risk of rushing someone back too soon after injury (to lower the Time Off measurables). But everyone knows that a reoccurrence of the same injury will mean even more time off. This process should actually reduce the pressure to rush anyone back too soon. It creates the need for balance and objective decision-making. The official Championship table doesn't include this data, so our measurables dashboard needs to add this in too.

If something makes a significant contribution to winning, we should try and measure it. Once we have all the measurables we need, we need to work out how to measure (i.e. count) them. In our football case there is a numerical figure for all of our measurables. That won't always be the case. Distilling every part of the mission into a number form helps us to make easy comparisons. However, if we can't use numbers, then we need to agree a set of standard concepts and terms instead. However it's done, we need to be able to measure our current performance against our winning standards. We have to know whether we are winning or not. If we want to win, we can't afford to drop our standards.

"Keep your heels, head and standards high"[21]

Having agreed our measurables and the numbers we measure them by, we've made a great start. The uncertainty around defining success is often what stops organisations from trying to define it. But failing to define success is failing. We need to be clear and realistic about what our mission needs to deliver. That's why we need winning standards.

---

[21] Gabrielle Bonheur "Coco" Chanel, the founder of the Chanel brand.

That brings us back to the biggest question. What does success look like? Is it automatic promotion? Is it the lower aim of promotion (however we get there)? Is making the play-offs a kind of success, even if we don't get promoted? Or is the idea of promotion a pipe dream, should success really be set at just avoiding relegation?

Winning is usually seen as an absolute concept, but winning is relative depending on the situation. So, as I've mentioned, defining winning as a single arbitrary goal isn't rounded or realistic enough. We need to accept that relative or qualified success can still be success. To give us a range of performance outcomes, we need to establish four bands of success before our mission starts. They take a relative approach to success, building on:

Absolute Success
Qualified Success
Qualified Failure
Absolute Failure

For each mission, we have to decide where to put the four bands of success. At what level do you consider something a win, a successful mission? We have to base these bands on the best mission data available if any such data exists. Unless this is the very first time that a mission has been attempted (in which case we need an alternative estimating approach) we can use the data from successful past missions (such as the past promotion standards) and assess it against our circumstances. Then we can agree the winning standards for our mission.

Once the four bands of success and failure are in place, we can add a fifth and final band, the Expected Minimum. This is set at the lowest level of expected performance. This Expected Minimum should be added last, somewhere realistic amongst the other four bands. The four success and failure bands should be based on what the mission needs. In this football case that's based on the past promotion standards. They should get us promotion, if we perform at that level.

This process should make the placement of our success bands an informed selection, not just an aspirational one. That means that the decision about what's our Expected Minimum should in turn become an informed decision. The expected minimum we face, should drive us toward a high but achievable standard. Don't set that expected minimum too high, or you'll be commiserating over failure, when you should be celebrating success. Don't set it too low it either, as what you settle for is what you'll get. It needs to be at the 'Goldilocks' sweet-spot (not too hard, but not too easy).

After all those five bands of success are in place, every player, physio and Manager knows exactly where they stand. We all know what we need to achieve to be successful. Using these bands of success will also reveal how reasonable our decision-maker's expectations are. In our case, we want promotion. That's our mission. We don't have to aim to be the best ever Championship team, we just have to be good enough to win promotion.

> *Expecting perfection in an imperfect World,*
> *is setting too high a bar for anyone to achieve*

Our owners and supporters will be expecting some form of success. We need to manage their expectations to the same level as ours. So, if the maximum Total Points or Goals Scored over the last ten years were set by a club twice the size of ours, with far more money, they are not fair comparisons to set us for the season. The question should be 'What are fair expectations for us?' Agreeing what success looks like has to be a fair and inclusive process. Internal and external communication from the club should help to set one expected minimum. The expected minimums of the owners, coaches, players and supporters should ideally all tally up. Credit has to be given for every win.

> *"It's important to recognise the small successes"*[22]

Achieving a qualified success should still be a 'success' if that's all that's realistically achievable for us. Overachieving is, by definition, beating the expectations placed on you. Unless you have better players and resources than every other club, achieving automatic promotion (absolute success) should be an overachievement, not an expected one. Another team's loss might be a great win for yours and vice versa.

We shouldn't have to repeatedly overachieve in order to be a 'success'. If we have to overachieve to be successful, it's a sign that the expected minimum is unrealistic, or put another way, the resources we've been given are insufficient for the expectations placed on us. If that's the case, the expected minimum should be

---

[22] Rafael Nadal, winner of 20 Grand Slam tennis titles (as I write this). If Rafa wins one more he will have overtaken Roger Federer's record haul.

adjusted down, or more investment is needed. Our owners then have a choice. Will they increase the available resources or will they reduce their expectations?

If, after a fair discussion about resources, our mission is agreed to be promotion, then we need to set our winning standards to try and secure that promotion. After setting automatic promotion as what constitutes absolute success, we also need to set what qualified success means for us.

If our mission is promotion, then achieving qualified success needs to be at least getting us into the play-offs, if not getting promotion through the play-off route. In overall mission terms, we might set the winning standards for our promotion-chasing Championship football team as follows.

WHAT IS WINNING?
PROMOTION

THE EXPECTED MINIMUM
(PROMOTION THROUGH THE PLAYOFFS)

* e.g. Finishing between 3rd and 6th but losing in the play-off final

~~~~~

We've defined what success and failure mean on a headline basis for us and our mission. That gives clarity on our mission and our Expected Minimum is promotion. Once that's been considered and confirmed, we need the club's full support to achieve that goal. Promotion isn't just the Manager or Head Coach's responsibility. The mission is the whole club's mission, so every stakeholder in the club has to fully commit to that. Every stakeholder has to go 'all in' on the mission.

As a club, we need the finances, stadium, training facilities, players, coaches, medics, conditioners, physios, merchandise, community links, sales team, risk management and reward structures in place to achieve promotion. Every stakeholder has to contribute what's needed from them individually and collectively.

On top of that, someone has got to manage the project as a whole. One person needs overall control of the mission. Delegation of skills is essential, but without someone to lead the mission, we are unlikely to achieve it. Who is that person? It's probably the club's Chief Executive or Managing Director who will have the overview and authority to take the necessary decisions. But does that person have the skills and experience to lead the project to a successful conclusion? Does that person have the respect of all the 'teams' within the club? Every project leader needs a Super-tribe approach. It can't be someone who is heavily partisan or biased to the owning, playing or the commercial side.

Once we have our mission and our leader, we need to allocate responsibility for each element of the mission and work together to achieve it. Having responsibility for something is all well and good, but do we know what's needed? How do we know what level of performance is required in each area? We need to do well enough to achieve the mission. We need to understand every element our mission demands and we need winning standards for every element. We need to set an aspirational tone to our definition of success, but we also need to add a heavy dose of realism.

"I think goals should never be easy, they should force you to work, even if they are uncomfortable at the time"[23]

It's vital to remember that everyone has to play a part in success. Owners and commercial executives can't just lay all those expectations on the Manager and coaching team. To that end, it's crucial to give everyone a role and a responsibility in achieving success. If all the players, coaches, directors and owners have winning standards to meet, they can't sit back. Every single stakeholder is needed. The more people who are helping, the more will get done.

~~~~~

If the commercial and playing sides of a club are at loggerheads, success is much less likely. That's the same with different teams and divisions in a manufacturing or sales environment. The mission has to have a bigger call and focus than any organizational history, politics, or personalities. We need a Super-tribe mentality to win, rather than a local, tribal mentality. We need a joined up mission plan that involves everyone and absolves no one. We need to all share the inputs so that we can all share the outputs.

---

[23] Michael Phelps, American swimmer and the most successful and the most decorated Olympian of all time with 28 medals, including 23 Gold Medals.

SHARED CLUB INPUTS AND OUTPUTS

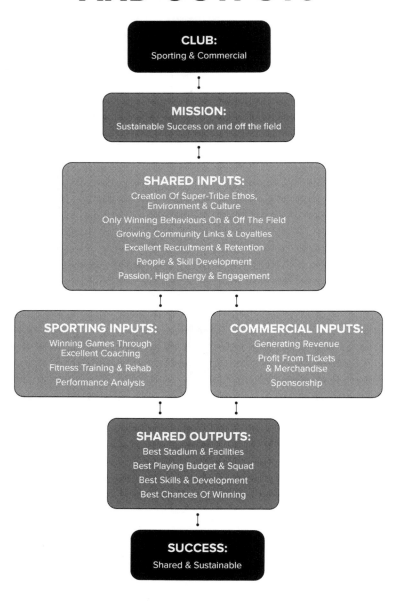

CLUB:
Sporting & Commercial

MISSION:
Sustainable Success on and off the field

SHARED INPUTS:
Creation Of Super-Tribe Ethos, Environment & Culture
Only Winning Behaviours On & Off The Field
Growing Community Links & Loyalties
Excellent Recruitment & Retention
People & Skill Development
Passion, High Energy & Engagement

SPORTING INPUTS:
Winning Games Through Excellent Coaching
Fitness Training & Rehab
Performance Analysis

COMMERCIAL INPUTS:
Generating Revenue
Profit From Tickets & Merchandise
Sponsorship

SHARED OUTPUTS:
Best Stadium & Facilities
Best Playing Budget & Squad
Best Skills & Development
Best Chances Of Winning

SUCCESS:
Shared & Sustainable

To apply winning standards to our promotion campaign, we need to set out all our measurables (the elements we will measure) and apply the past promotion standards to produce the winning standards we need. In short, we need do some maths.

Let's take our Total Points, which is perhaps our most important winning standard. We cannot afford to guess what's needed, especially as this is a path that's been travelled before many times. We can get insight from all the past journeys. What do the past promotion standards from the last ten years tell us?

The highest Total Points of the 20 promoted clubs over the last ten years was Leicester City with 102 points in 2013/14. The lowest Total Points that secured automatic promotion was Cardiff City with 79 in 2012/13. That's a huge range of 23 points. We need to look at this in more detail, to assess what success really looks like.

When we add all the Total Points of the 20 promoted clubs we get 1,806. The mean average of those twenty clubs 90.3 points. The median points figure sits between four clubs on 89 points and two on 90 points. 89.5 points is the middle total of those 20 clubs. These statistics point us towards a single figure. It looks like we'll need to earn 90 points from our 38 games to secure automatic promotion.

To test this figure, let's look at what's needed in a different way. What Total Points did all the third placed teams get? They all missed out on automatic promotion so we have to do better than every single one of them did.

The lowest Total Points of a team finishing in third place was 77 points. But that total was an outlier, because all the other 9 teams had points totals in the 80's. The highest of those totals was 89 points in 2015/16. No third placed team in the last ten years has amassed 90 points or more.

So using this data, we know that if accumulate 90 points we will almost certainly be promoted automatically. So, our winning standards have to bear this in mind. To achieve 90 points, we need to get enough points from each of our 38 games. Our Average Points Per Game standard will have to be 90 points divided by 38 games (which is 2.37 points a game). With only 3 points available per game, that shows us how well will have to do. We will have to win the vast majority of our games to get promotion. That is a very tough ask indeed.

This mission will be a massive challenge of skill, consistency and endurance. After all it is won over 38 games of at least 90 minutes for at least 11 players, plus all the minutes put into every match briefing, training session and social get together. Every minute and every behaviour counts, for every single person. Promotion is won over an extensive series of tasks over an extensive period. It's like putting all the 11,000 glass panes into Irvine Seller's Shard building and then doing it all over again. We cannot aim too low. We cannot settle for losing standards. Or we are highly likely to miss out.

"Many of life's failures are people who did not realise how close they were to success when they gave up"[24]

With at least 90 points needed to be sure of promotion, we have to ask ourselves 'Is 90 points realistic for our club?' If that isn't realistic, we need to go right back to our mission. Is it achievable? What else do we need to make it there? If there are not more resources available, we might need to re-set our expected minimum.

~~~~~

Let's not forget that there are two ways to secure promotion. We could also make it up through the play-offs. We also know that finishing in sixth place is enough to make the end of season play-offs. So, to prepare for a mission of promotion, we need to look at what it takes to make the top six places. During the last ten years, the highest points total for a side finishing in sixth was 78 points and the lowest was 68.

We should also look at 7th place too, as that's the first league position to definitely miss out on promotion. What points did the ten 7th placed teams achieve? The highest total achieved was 78 points (losing out on goal difference by 4 goals) and the lowest total was 68. They are the same figures as 6th. That tells us that the difference between getting into the play-offs and missing out can be extremely tight. We ideally want to be well above that part of the table.

Using all of our top two and top six information, we can create a Total Points Winning Standard for our mission of promotion. Our expected minimum, for the regular season, would be making the play-offs. I have put this into a diagram, so that our headline Winning Standards are clear.

---

[24] Thomas Edison, the inventor of the first commercially usable light bulb.

TOTAL POINTS WINNING STANDARD (PROMOTION)

67 OR FEWER POINTS (WE ALMOST CERTAINLY WON'T MAKE THE PLAY-OFFS, BUT WE ALSO MIGHT NOT)

68 TO 78 POINTS (WE MIGHT MAKE THE PLAY-OFFS IF WE DON'T MAKE AUTOMATIC PROMOTION)

79 TO 89 POINTS (WE SHOULD AT LEAST MAKE THE PLAY-OFFS)

90 OR MORE POINTS
(AS WE SHOULD GET AUTOMATIC PROMOTION)
(ABSOLUTE SUCCESS)

(QUALIFIED SUCCESS)

(QUALIFIED FAILURE)

(ABSOLUTE FAILURE)

THE EXPECTED MINIMUM
79 POINTS (AS THAT SHOULD GUARANTEE
THE PLAY-OFFS AT LEAST)

Once we've got the full season winning standards in place, we have our headline goal. To make sure we stay on track, we could also do this same exercise again for other stages of the season (e.g. at the start of New Year's Day). How were those 20 teams doing at that stage? Having early assessment points like this can help to keep you on track. If we have the software to help measure our progress, we could even measure it on a match by match basis.

The more we know what's needed to complete our mission, the more we can plan for it. Once we have the winning standards for our Total Points, we need to move on and set winning standards for the supporting actions that will secure at least 79 points and ideally 90 or more. What do we have to achieve to get to 90 points? By turning the available data into winning standards, we can closely monitor our progress and measure ourselves against those standards.

In this football example, there will be official figures for the number of Goals Scored, Goals Conceded and Goal Difference achieved by all of the thirty teams that were promoted. We can use these three data sets to set winning standards for each of those contributing areas. If we score as many goals and concede as few, we should be on track.

Setting expectations helps everyone (from owners to managers to physios to players) to understand what they need to be achieving. That helps to offer a range of success to be achieved and to keep standards consistently high. It also helps us to ask for exactly what we need to achieve their part of the mission. Comparing our past performances against the winning standards we need to hit, will show us how far off we've been. How many goals did we score last season? How many less than the winning standard was that? What do we need to do to score that many more goals? Once we've worked that our we need to action it, or we won't achieve that winning standard.

If any promotion winning standard is unrealistic for us, we need more help. That could mean signing a proven goal scorer to increase our Goals Scored, or signing a proven goalkeeper to reduce our Goals Conceded[25]. Setting and using these key measures is insightful, but data alone is worthless. The winning standards are a tool not a solution. They should lead to better decision-making. They should help to aim for the right level. What do we need to do better to win promotion?

---

[25] Although, that fact that they've performed well in a different environment might not make them good at our club.

We need to test our capability. Is promotion a realistic mission next season? Are we capable of winning promotion with these people and resources? Are we realistically capable of scoring all those goals, or conceding so few? Will we really win all the points needed to finish in the top two? We need to look closely at our resources (including stadium capacity, players, coaches, physios, and medical and rehab facilities). Are they good enough? Do we need better in order to perform better? If promotion is too much to expect of us, we can still keep the same mission, but the owners should lower their expected minimum to a more realistic finish.

Once we have clarified the Mission and our Winning Standards, we know what we are looking to achieve. Now we can focus on how to get ready to achieve that success. What can we do to improve our chances of winning? Even if we are likely to do achieve Absolute Success we cannot relax. We need to work on what will make that more likely.

"The trouble with not having a goal is that you can spend your life running up and down the field and never score"[26]

If even a qualified success seems unlikely, we need to change some things before we begin. Do we need a new manager or coaching team? That's for the owners to determine. The manager and coaches should be able to assess what else is needed. Do we need to buy new players? Do we need a modern gym, better physio room or a 4G training pitch? Or alternatively, should we be more realistic and change the mission to one we are likely to achieve?

Once we have our success framework (our Mission and Winning Standards) and our resources (players, coaches etc.) we need to work on the controllables that can influence the most positive inputs. By working on our team's philosophy, skills, techniques, tactical awareness diet, strength, match fitness and teamwork (at least) we can increase our chances of winning promotion. We need to set winning standards for everything that makes the difference between winning and losing.

~~~~~

Another advantage of this Winning Standards approach is that every team member's responsibilities, expectations and rewards can be set by reference to it.

---

[26] American author Bill Copeland.

Everyone involved with the club should be fairly rewarded. Missing out on a league position bonus that was always unachievable is unfair and demotivating. Even worse, sacking a Manager for not securing automatic promotion, when it was never realistic, would be totally unfair.

Every employee should have his or her pay and benefits linked to the mission. If we win, every stakeholder should win. No one should miss out. If we lose, no one should be paid mega-money. Bonuses that related to the performance of the whole organisation tend to process more successful missions, than separate individual schemes.

Using our example of a promotion chasing football team, our Manager's reward structure ought to be linked to that mission. Why not have a direct link? That would work well if the expectations and the related rewards are fair. That type of reward structure might look something like this.

MANAGER'S EXPECTATIONS AND REWARDS (PROMOTION)

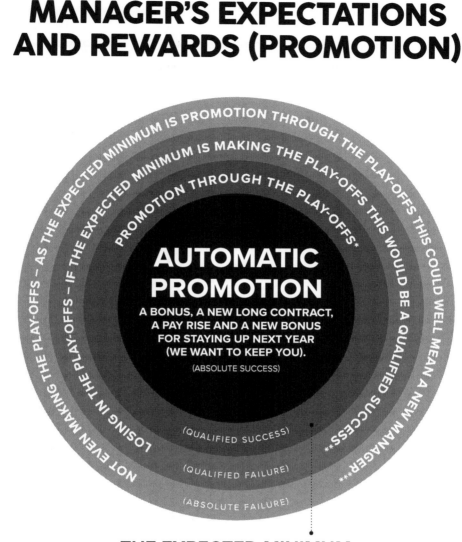

PROMOTION THROUGH THE PLAY-OFFS – AS THE EXPECTED MINIMUM IS PROMOTION THROUGH THE PLAY-OFFS THIS COULD WELL MEAN A NEW MANAGER***

PROMOTION THROUGH THE PLAY-OFFS – IF THE EXPECTED MINIMUM IS MAKING THE PLAY-OFFS THIS WOULD BE A QUALIFIED SUCCESS**

PROMOTION THROUGH THE PLAY-OFFS*

NOT EVEN MAKING THE PLAY-OFFS – LOSING IN THE PLAY-OFFS

AUTOMATIC PROMOTION

A BONUS, A NEW LONG CONTRACT, A PAY RISE AND A NEW BONUS FOR STAYING UP NEXT YEAR (WE WANT TO KEEP YOU).

(ABSOLUTE SUCCESS)

(QUALIFIED SUCCESS)

(QUALIFIED FAILURE)

(ABSOLUTE FAILURE)

THE EXPECTED MINIMUM
PROMOTION THROUGH THE PLAY-OFFS

* A bonus, a contract for next year with a pay rise and a new bonus for staying-up built in (let's see how you do).

** However, if the Expected Minimum is promotion through the play-offs (as it is for us) then this is a qualified failure. It might mean a change of manager. If the manager stays on it may only mean a contract for next year with the chance of a bonus if promotion is achieved (you have one more chance).

*** (Unless major things happened beyond your control, we need to make a change).

~~~~~

Having winning standards creates winning behaviours, which in turn creates a winning organisation. Setting off without any winning standards is heading out into the unknown, working on estimates and gut reactions. Without winning standards to work towards we'll be taken by surprise, often when it's too late to adapt. Without assessing what it really takes to win, how can we possibly prepare for winning? We need to know exactly what winning requires, so that we can plan meticulously for it. Well-prepared winning standards set the levels we have to reach. That knowledge gives us a clear head start, on at least some of our competitors. Then, we just work backwards from those winning standards to establish the structures, resources, teams and techniques that we need in place to reach them.

The logic is simple. If our winning standards are accurate, then delivering them will give us the outcomes we want. All we have to do is work out which resources and which actions produce those winning standards. Which people do we need? Where and when do we need them? Which resources and facilities do we need? Where and when do we need them? Which logistics (such as offices, performance areas, warehouses and supply chains) do we need? Where and when do we need them? Every stakeholder can offer different forms of help, whether that's planning, leadership or delivery. Using all their skills and insights, we can ensure our organisation the success it's chasing. We need to ensure that every stakeholder is fully engaged and actively contributing.

Many actions will need to be carried out. Planning for them all is essential. Allocating sufficient responsibility, authority, training, people, budgets, winning standards and timescales will aid the delivery of those actions enormously. Monitoring progress is essential too. Keeping up to date progress charts, using diagramming and data visualisation tools, will keep everyone focused on the same page. We get to get as many decisions right as humanly possible, especially the big ones under pressure.

Using a facile point as an illustration, if we only sign eight players for our Championship football team, we'd be lucky to win any matches, let alone gain promotion. If all eight of those players were goalkeepers we'd be in an even worse position. If none of those eight goalkeepers were very good, then we might as well prepare for relegation now. And that's before you analyse the coaching, training, strength & conditioning and medical people and facilities. Every recruitment and purchasing decision should link back to the relevant winning standards. We need to assess and gather together all of the necessary elements to deliver our winning standards, including the funding we need to pay for it all. We need to know exactly what needs to be delivered, so we can align our mission, philosophy, environment, values, culture, positioning, people, facilities and other resources to support our mission.

As a football team aiming for promotion, our shopping list is exhaustive. We can waste incredible amounts of money if we are not careful and methodical. Every time we assess our plans and resources, we have to ask ourselves one question. 'What do we need to reach our winning standards?' That's what we need to go out and get. If we always provide ourselves with less, we will always reduce our chances of winning.

We'll certainly need a large modern stadium to play in, a squad of the 25 players[27] with all the skills and experience for promotion, a coaching team with the experience needed to gain promotion, a recruitment team that picks the players to fit the winning standards, a medical team with deep experience of football injuries, a strength and conditioning team that knows exactly how to get our team fit enough, a team of performance analysts who can help guide training, an skilled commercial team to provide a fantastic match day experience; and sell a wide range of high-quality, value for money club merchandise. We'll also need a board of directors who can run the club effectively and efficiently within its means. We'll also need people with the skills to build relationships between all our stakeholders, including the game's controlling bodies and our local authority.

The list goes on and on. Every decision has an impact, creating an impression. It's often the smallest decisions that give away the level of an organisation's commitment, whether it's choosing cheap toilet rolls, or cheap tea bags instead of Yorkshire Tea[28]. Every decision creates momentum or stalls it. Every decision moves us nearer to achieving the winning standards, or it takes us further away from them. How good is your organisation's decision-making? That probably depends on what your winning standards are.

~~~~~

Outside of sport, there are many different sectors with their own forms of challenge and competition. Education poses a very complex set of challenges. The

---

[27] In 2020/21, the English Football League introduced a maximum 25 man squad (8 of whom have to be 'home grown').

[28] Other tea bags are available, but I wouldn't recommend them.

school of Eton is perceived to be a World leading school and its alumni include many highly successful people. They include nineteen British Prime Ministers, Ian Fleming, George Orwell, Prince William and Bear Grylls. Eton's mission statement is broad in its ambitions. "In educating the whole child, Eton School inspires creative, confident thinkers who have an enduring passion for learning and are poised to contribute to the world." The UK's state system is every bit as ambitious, with many more hurdles to be overcome. The successes of the state system are far less easy to see, but they are all the more remarkable.

One primary school in Hampshire describes its purpose as "to educate the whole child. By educating each child emotionally, physically and spiritually as well as academically, we will prepare them for the future. By doing this, we will equip our children with the life skills to become confident, caring citizens who can play a positive and active role in modern society." It goes on to describe its vision for the school as being "a positive, nurturing and happy school community, based on kindness, honesty and respect for ourselves, each other and for our environment. We will all strive to be successful lifelong learners by developing inquisitiveness, independence and resilience. We will all strive for excellence in everything that we do. We will all be brave, resilient learners, prepared to take learning risks and learn from our mistakes." That's a bold and sustainable commitment, lasting year after year, well into the future. In terms of analysis, that mission is, in itself, too large to assess without breaking it down into the specific outcomes that it's designed to produce; and working out how they can be properly measured.

If that kind of mission is being achieved in any school year, then the school is on track and great credit is due. But that has to be a way of ensuring that a mission is on track. OFSTED school inspections are brief, sporadic and rarely see the whole picture. This important issue of scrutiny begs two questions. What specific outcomes should have been achieved by the end of the Summer Term? What do we need to measure, to check if those outcomes are actually being achieved?

Every primary school has a widespread and challenging brief. The outcomes that a primary school needs to produce will need to reflect all those challenges. They will probably include: whether the school stays within its allocated budgets, whether it can provide adequate staffing and learning resources in every classroom for every pupil, the level of teacher and pupil wellbeing, the maintenance of all the school buildings, the results of each police and social services intervention on every affected child's education prospects; and how every Year 6 child performs in their SATS results. There will be many more besides. Running a school is an enormous job.

And that's before all the variables and uncontrollables kick in. Every child, every cohort of children, every teacher and every school location is different. In the state system, there are no selection criteria. There is no way of putting up the 'school fees' to buy in more staffing or resources. It is what it is. There are a wide variety of socio-economic variables and their impact on a school can be massive. So the expectations of success need to be realistic, achievable and set in each particular school's own context.

Which uncontrollables does a school have to contend with? The limitations of budgets, physical class sizes and access to outside playing areas are just some of those uncontrollables. All of them will affect the success outcomes. Other uncontrollables will include the number of pupils at the school with special educational needs; and the level of disruptions caused by staff and pupil absence (which could be due to multiple independent reasons, or for a collective reason such as the COVID-19 pandemic).

Therefore, when defining success for a school, the qualified and absolute criteria for both success and failure need to be applied to that school's own specific circumstances. OFSTED sets the criteria for its inspections of schools. They are universal. Its expectations need to be realistic and achievable for each individual school. There needs to be sufficient latitude to allow for that. The expectations of the Governors and parents need to be realistic too.

A school can help itself by producing the four bands of success for each key measurable (such as the Year 6 SATS results). These will need to take into account all of the statutory and professional standards. Compliance with these regulatory requirements is a key starting point. But there is still some flexibility as to the outcomes the school can choose to take on. Having clear outcomes to aim for and the measures to assess their progress, will help the Head Teacher, Senior Leadership Group and the School's Governors to monitor progress against those outcomes.

Once the success bands are ready, the school needs to agree a realistic and achievable 'expected minimum' for each measurable outcome. That clarity will help the Governors to carry out the important governance function that they are duty bound to provide, without putting undue pressure on the Head Teacher and school staff. The expected minimums will need to be reviewed for each different cohort. In more challenging years, those expectations might be set lower, but they should never be too low for the mission.

Running a school is a highly complex job. It requires every single stakeholder to perform their personal role and wider obligations to a high standard. Those stakeholders include: the Head Teacher, the Senior Leadership Group, the Governors, the parents, the pupils themselves, OFSTED, the local authority, the Department for Education, Social Services and the Police.

With so many important stakeholders in a school and with so little control over so many of them, it is entirely fair for the school to qualify any minimum expectations with what all those other stakeholders need to do. If any stakeholder doesn't perform their role to the standards required, then the expected minimum achievements will need to be reassessed and modified if needs be. Any expectations must always be set fairly and remain fair.

1.5 WHICH OF TWO APPROACHES TO WINNING?

Once you have set your winning standards, you need to decide which of two approaches to winning you're going to take. The first one is to be the best whilst playing fair and within the rules. The second approach is to cheat and keep cheating until you win. By breaking every rule you can, you can hugely increase your chances of finishing first.

But before this idea goes any further, we need to stop it firmly in its tracks. Cheating is never an option when you talk about winning. Never. Why not? Because cheating is by definition losing and that's the diametric opposite of winning. Every competition has laws, rules and regulations. They set the legal framework for being allowed to compete. Within business there are laws on corporate governance, employment, corruption, cartels, price-fixing, fraud, data protection and miss-selling amongst many others. They all govern what's allowed and what isn't. Breaches of some of those rules can lead to a fine, a claim for compensation or a very long prison term.

Rules govern every type of competition. The Geneva Convention governs military conflict. Breaches of it can end up before a war crimes tribunal (and also lead to a very long prison term). Every sport has its own laws of the game and a team of referees to enforce them. Board games like chess and draughts have clear rules, as do Monopoly and Cluedo. These restrictions and limitations frame and control how each competition works. Why do we have rules? Because they establish what competition we're part of and they create a clear (if not completely level) playing field within it.

"You have to learn the rules of the game, and then you have to play better than anyone else"[29]

As a competitor, it is not your job to ignore the rules. It is your job to find the best ways to win within those rules. Winning comes from staying within the 'laws' of the competition and being the best. Beating everyone else, without cheating, is what creates a win. Otherwise, you are not taking part in the same competition. As soon as you step outside the rules, you step outside the competition itself. If you're not in it, you can't win it. Cheating is not a way to win, it's the easiest way to lose. As a result, we need to discard that option entirely and start again with our two approaches to winning. But just before we do, let's remember what an incredible sporting icon we thought Lance Armstrong was; and what he turned out to be.

"I have never doped ... I have competed as an endurance athlete for 25 years with no spike in performance, passed more than 500 drug tests and never failed one."[30]

"All the fault and all the blame here falls on me. I viewed this situation as one big lie that I repeated a lot of times. I made my decisions. They are my mistakes, and I am sitting here today to acknowledge that and to say I'm sorry for that"[31]

Every time you break the rules, you step outside the competition. That's a pressure you can do without. Worrying about getting caught creates a stressful distraction that gets in the way of winning. Doubt replaces strength of purpose. Will I be caught? Will I lose my job? Will we be thrown out of the competition? Cheating always casts a dark shadow on our mental state, an impediment to winning. And when we're suspected (let alone caught) it casts a permanent shadow on our reputation and that of our club. Cheating implicates others in your team and leaves their careers and reputations at risk. Cheating is an exceptionally selfish losing behaviour.

Even if a cheat doesn't get caught, they still know they cheated. Cheating eats away inside us until it's revealed and then it shames us. Cheating robs a 'winner'

---

[29] Albert Einstein.
[30] Lance Armstrong in June 2012.
[31] Lance Armstrong in January 2013.

of actually winning. Even when no one finds out we've cheated, we still remember that we had to cheat to win. We know. Our flashbacks remind us that despite the cheers and applause, we really lost. Cheating robs us of the unbridled joy of winning. Every 'Congratulations' you receive has a hollow, lifeless ring to it. We are left broken by our failure to 'win' fairly. Cheating is not a winning option. Finishing second to a cheat is the real winning. A qualified win will always beat a cheating victory.

Whatever short-term gains cheating might bring, they come at a longer, heavier cost. Speaking about why he took drugs before the 1988 Olympic Games, Canadian sprinter Ben Johnson explained "I said to myself, why should I do this clean when everybody else is cheating? That's unfair". Convincing himself that everyone else was at it, Ben began to take a series of unknown drugs which changed his body shape and sprinting speed. Ben 'won' Bronze medal at the 1984 Olympics in a time of 10.22 seconds. He knew it wasn't fast enough to guarantee finishing first. Four years later, at the 1988 Seoul Olympics, Ben went on to win Gold in the Men's 100 metres final, beating Carl Lewis by a stunning 1.3 seconds. His time was a World Record 9.79 seconds. Ben was briefly on top of the World.

A few days later Ben Johnson tested negative for stanozolol and his Gold medal was stripped from him. Then the public vitriol started and a clinical depression hit him. For over thirty years Ben has struggled to justify himself and his decision. His mental health and relationships have been adversely affected ever since. Speaking in 2010, Ben reflected on that fateful decision to take drugs. "When I was racing it was like I was blindfolded. But I can see now. I wouldn't have gone that way if I could see what I see now. I would have taken another road."[32]

~~~~~

Cheating is therefore not one of the two genuine approaches to winning. The two approaches to winning are actually about how we tackle the process of winning. The first approach is to become the best team at interpreting and performing the current conventions and techniques. By operating the same skills and techniques as everyone else, but performing them better than everyone else does, we can become the very best. However, this approach faces the fiercest possible competition. I call it mainstreaming because almost every opponent will be trying something similar. It requires a life of exceptional dedication and application. It is a game of very, very small margins.

---

[32] Quotes taken from an interview by Donald McRae in the Guardian.

The second way to win is to find a higher level of performance entirely. This approach means challenging, improving and replacing the existing conventions and techniques, whilst always staying within the laws, rules, and regulations. This is done by stripping every single element back to its fundamentals and reimagining how each thing can be done better. I call this method slipstreaming because it's all about making advances that shoot you ahead of everyone else in the competition.

Winners get out of the mainstream and into a slipstream

In this book there are examples of attempts to win by both mainstreaming and slipstreaming. As we'll see, if you can find a new way to do something fundamentally better (which doesn't break any law, rule or regulation) you will dramatically improve your chances of winning.

Despite the fact that there are two quite different approaches to winning, there is one common methodology which underpins both approaches. This became clear from all the information and insights that I've experienced, collected and analysed. That common methodology is about controlling the winning controllables.

1.6 REMOVE THE UNCONTROLLABLES

We need to accept that we've got little or no control over the fixed elements in life. For example, we can't suddenly decide that there are fifty dates in a month, ten months in a year or twenty-five hours in a day. There's no chance of convincing the rest of the World to adopt those kind of changes. So, as that won't happen, we need to accept the calendar as it is. Likewise, we can't just decide that it will be sunny tomorrow. The weather is what meteorology makes it. Again, we need to accept that choosing the weather isn't in our power, it's beyond our control.

The same limitations apply to geography. Japan is a series of islands in the Pacific. Limited in space, it is a densely populated country with no room for expansion. That has limited its economic growth and its quality of life. The amount of land that's suitable for agriculture is insufficient to feed Japan's large population. As a result, Japan is dependent on importing its food. Japan also lacks many of the raw materials needed for industry and energy, such as oil, coal, iron ore, copper, aluminium and wood. As a result, Japan has produced nuclear power, to gain some control over its energy demands, with all the risks that entails.

Japan's geography also poses an ever present threat. Japan sits very close to the meeting point of four of the Earth's tectonic plates[33]. These parts of the earth's crust are in an endless pattern of moving together, locking up and separating. As part of the tectonic movement under the Pacific Ocean, the Pacific plate is gradually pushing itself underneath the North American plate at a rate of about ten centimetres a year[34]. Although that doesn't sound much, the clashing together of these plates creates enormous pressure. As they move and separate, that pressure suddenly and violently releases. The more they interlock, the more pressure is released when they separate. As a result, Japan suffers from regular earthquakes. On 11 March 2011, just over forty miles off Tōhoku, the Earth's crust ruptured. The rupture was estimated to be 180 miles long. The violent separation created a tsunami, which crashed into Japan and killed approximately 20,000 people. Japan cannot move its location. Its geography is fixed. Japan has to adapt to it and live with it.

"You can't control the cards you're dealt,
just how you play the hand"[35]

In contrast, Russia does not have the same seismic or geographic challenges. Russia is the biggest country in the World, with wide open spaces, as well as sea and land borders for trade. Russia also benefits from being the richest country in natural resources in the World, with commercially abundant supplies of oil, natural gas, timber and valuable minerals such as gold, silver, diamonds, mercury, lead, zinc, copper, bauxite, nickel and tin. In addition, Russia has access to huge volumes of fresh water. The Russian lake of Baikal in Southern Siberia alone holds approximately 22% of the World's freshwater. As a result of its geography, Russia has many controllable assets.

Japan can feel justifiably frustrated by its geographical limitations. But without drastic action, such as invasion or reclaiming land from the sea, Japan's boundaries are uncontrollable. Railing at the unfairness of its location won't change anything for the better. Japan has to adapt to its geography and make the very most of it. No country has it all its own way. Even Russia is faced with uncontrollables. The vast distances that have to be travelled and the bitter Siberian cold are just two of them.

---

[33] Namely the Pacific, North American, Eurasian and Filipino.
[34] According to the U.S. Geophysicist John Bellini.
[35] Randy Pausch, a former Professor of Computer Science and Design.

The truth that we have to accept is that we cannot have everything the way we want it. Not everything is perfect or possible. Some things in life are permanent and immovable. Despite being told that we can achieve everything that we set our minds to, the truth is different. The sentiment can be motivating, but it's not practical or realistic. Acknowledging the truth of life is the first step towards focusing on the elements that we can influence and control.

In any task, remove the uncontrollables. Don't fight them

If something is fixed, it is settled and not open to our influence or control. So there is no point trying to force it to change. There's no point spending any time railing against the way things are either. That's just wasted energy. Although we cannot change what's fixed in life, neither can our competitors. While they stop and complain, we can be getting ahead. Whilst they try to control the uncontrollables, we can be focusing on the elements that we can control.

Whilst we cannot predict the future, we can imagine and speculate about future events, until we have 'predicted' possible scenarios that we can plan for. This process allows us to anticipate the potential challenges ahead. By scenario planning, we can plan for predictable events (the 'known knowns'). We can even partially plan for Black Swan events, like the COVID-19 crisis of 2020 (by turning them from 'unknown unknowns' into 'known unknowns'[36] through extensive scenario planning). Controlling the controllables gets us Win Ready.

~~~~

Sometimes where there's a failure, there is a single reason for it, that's beyond your control. Sometimes that single reason can come out of left field as a complete shock, giving us no time to adjust or respond. However, far more often, a failure comes from a combination of uncontrollable and controllable reasons. And often the controllable reasons could have made all the difference.

Take the sinking of the Titanic. Everyone knows the Titanic sank because it hit an iceberg. But that's only one part of the story. It is widely accepted that there were at least ten controllable mistakes that could have saved the Titanic[37].

Let's start with the biggest uncontrollable, the iceberg. The iceberg struck by the

---

[36] Made famous in a 2002 speech by US Secretary of Defence Donald Rumsfeld.
[37] My research included watching the documentary "10 Mistakes that sank the Titanic" on Channel 5.

Titanic had travelled all the way from Greenland. Weighed down by heavy snow the iceberg came away from its ice-shelf and drifted Southwards into the Atlantic Ocean. And there it floated. The Titanic crew had zero control over its departure from the iceshelf or the ocean streams that took it there. However, in an ocean of 106.5 million square miles, there was no inevitability about the Titanic sailing straight into it. No ship would deliberately sail into an iceberg. So what else made the collision happen? Which controllables could have been managed differently?

The Titanic was built as one of three sister ships. On 20 September 1911, one of those sister-ships, the Olympic, was sailing in the Solent. Operating in a narrow channel, the Olympic accidentally cut-across a Navy warship called HMS Hawk and the two collided. That collision could certainly have been avoided. One of the Olympic's water-tight bulk-heads immediately took on water. But despite the heavy impact the water didn't spread further into the ship. The ship's bulk-head design contained the water in one section, allowing the Olympic to stay afloat. That was a delight to the White Star Line's owners. Their hopes for these three flagships instantly became beliefs and snowballed into a myth. These ships were now proven to be "unsinkable". The success of this incident created a strong sense of complacency.

"There is no danger that Titanic will sink. The boat is unsinkable and nothing but inconvenience will be suffered by the passengers"[38]

The man at the helm of the Olympic was called Captain Smith and he was the whole fleet's Commodore. Captain Smith was destined to take that sense of complacency with him when he became the Titanic's Captain.

"I cannot imagine any condition which would cause a ship to founder. I cannot conceive of any vital disaster happening to this vessel. Modern ship building has gone beyond that"[39]

After the Olympic's accident, she needed to be docked and repaired. As an already operational and fully booked-up ship, the Olympic's repairs were prioritised in Belfast's dockyard. This delayed the Titanic's maiden voyage by three weeks, which put it into April 1912, the beginning of the iciest season in the North Atlantic. Unfortunately 1912 turned out to be a particularly icy season, as

---

[38] Phillip Franklin, White Star Line Vice-President.
[39] Captain Smith reportedly said this before the Titanic's maiden voyage.

the warm winter of 1911 had produced approximately four hundred icebergs, three or four times as many as normal. The Labrador current and then the Gulf Stream directed all these icebergs through into the North Atlantic shipping lanes. The number of icebergs was therefore another uncontrollable. But the avoidable accident to the Olympic and the resulting delay in Belfast added enormously to the Titanic's risk.

Another uncontrollable was the fact that the iceberg had melted at the top, making it appear far smaller than it actually was and leaving a wide and jagged ridge underneath the water. The vast majority of its estimated one million tonne mass was hidden below the surface. That posed an obvious potential threat, that was masked from view. But what mattered more was that the Titanic was so poorly prepared for it.

It also didn't help that Captain Smith was in charge. As we know, his mindset wasn't one of safety, respect and diligence, it was one of complacency. Over the years, Captain Smith has become very popular with the wealthiest cruise passengers, earning his nickname "The Millionaires' Captain". At the time of the collision, Captain Smith was entertaining wealthy guests. As well as being a great host, Captain Smith was also known for sailing his ships fast, so that they never arrived late. The Titanic was no exception. An average speed of 18 knots would have got the Titanic to New York in seven days as planned. But when the Titanic hit her iceberg, she was travelling at 22 knots. Sailing through an enormous ice field at 22 knots was, with hindsight, travelling far too fast. So why did that happen?

There were several controllable reasons. By going faster at the beginning of a journey a Captain created time in hand, in case of meeting fog later on, which always necessitated a much slower speed. So, most Captains tended to travel faster than they needed to, in case they were forced to slow down later on in the journey. In addition to pushing his ship onward to stay ahead of time, Captain Smith was also under pressure to avoid any adverse publicity. This maiden voyage was an international event. Turning up late would have been commercially disastrous. Personally, Captain Smith wanted the glory of an early arrival. He was speeding the Titanic along to reach its dock by sunrise on the seventh day. That would give it a glamorous, early entrance into New York for all the 'A list' American passengers on board. That would make him an even bigger name. These artificial time pressures of time narrowed the Captain's focus and impacted on his decision-making.

There was another risk burning away on departure. The Titanic ran on steam power, generated from six hundred tonnes of coal a day. The packed coal bunkers got very hot. As the Titanic sailed out of Southampton, the bunker in boiler room five was on fire. The fire probably had probably begun on the earlier journey from Belfast to Southampton. The crew knew, but the passengers and the dignitaries on the quayside weren't told. The voyage should have been delayed, to put the fire out, but it wasn't. The pressures of time and reputation trumped the need for safety. That was a controllable mistake.

The only way to put the fire out was to rake out the burning coal and put it into the furnaces, so it could finish burning safely. The rush to leave Southampton meant that the raking had to be done as the ship steamed on towards New York. The clearing exercise proved horribly difficult as the bunker fire really took hold. In the end, the whole of the bunker had to be emptied out with shovels. The fire was eventually put out ten days after it started. During that long period, the steel bunker had been subjected to temperatures between 500 and 1,000 degrees, which warped its rear wall. This turned out to be disastrous as the bunker's rear wall was part of a water-tight bulk-head, like the one that had saved her sister the Olympic. The warping of the rear steel wall broke the bulk-head's water-tight seal. Nobody realised until it was too late.

"Learn from other people's mistakes"[40]

In 1912, wireless radio was new. The Titanic had it, but it was operated by Marconi operatives not the ship's crew. Marconi wanted to generate the maximum income it could from sending and receiving passenger messages. Instead of keeping the channel free for safety warnings, the paid-for messages to and from the passengers kept the single operator fully occupied. There was a process for dealing with urgent messages. Any messages marked 'MSG' contained a priority warning and had to go straight to the Captain. That system was working well during the day on the 14th April. But some point during late afternoon or early evening the Marconi system went down. It took six or seven hours to fix it, by which time the Marconi operator, Jack Phillips was inundated with passenger messages. Having only one radio, having only one operator and allowing Marconi to run the radio independently were all controllable mistakes.

At 9.52pm on the 14th April 1912, a warning message came in from the SS Mesaba which was a few hours ahead of the Titanic and on a very similar course towards New York. The Marconi operator, Jack Phillips either didn't receive the

---

[40] Tai Lopez, professional internet marketer.

58

message or misplaced it. The MSG prefix was never added to the message and it never reached Captain Smith. That message would have included an incredibly helpful warning "...saw much heavy pack ice and great number large icebergs." A controllable part of the Titanic's warning system had failed its 2,224 passengers and crew.

An even starker warning was on offer from a ship called the SS Californian at about 10.30pm. Again this radio message never reached Captain Smith. It came through as the Titanic was trying to contact Cape Race, four hundred miles away. The Titanic's radio signal had been turned right up to create enough range to reach Newfoundland and so when the message from the nearby Californian came through it must have sounded absolutely deafening. The Titanic's response was an instant "Be quiet old man". The Titanic then cut the Californian off. The operator on the Californian must have been irritated, as it seems he went off to bed without trying again. Ten minutes later the Titanic hit the iceberg. Had it not been interrupted, the message from the Californian would have said that it had stopped its engines and was waiting until sunrise before travelling onwards. The ice had stopped it in its tracks. The Titanic carried on it journey at a speed of 22 knots. Cutting off the Californian was another controllable mistake.

The Titanic had a manned Crow's Nest on her forward mast. The two men in it, Reginald Lee and Frederick Fleet were good choices for the job as they had good experience from working on other ships. It was their job to stare out into the horizon with their naked eyes to look for possible icebergs. If they thought they could see one, they then used a pair of binoculars to check more closely. Unfortunately, the only available pair of crew binoculars was locked inside the Second Officer's cabin. The Second Officer had been replaced late on in Southampton, by Captain Smith's number two from the Olympic. It seems that when the original Second Officer left, he took the key to his cabin with him. The binoculars were therefore inside the locked cabin and not in the Crow's Nest where they were needed. No one thought to forcibly open the cabin door and get them out. Leaving them in there was a controllable mistake.

"Winners blame themselves and look where they can improve"[41]

On the night of the 14th April 1912, there was a high pressure atmosphere, meaning that the air was very clear and the starlight was very bright. That was helpful, as it

---

[41] Former Dutch international footballer Robin Van Persie.

meant that the visibility and sound were excellent. With such good visibility, the Titanic could sail on at 22 knots an hour. The crew could surely spot any icebergs in time. This complacency came at an enormous cost. Unbeknown to the Crow's Nest crew, the high pressure atmosphere was in fact bending the light, distorting their view. It created a miraging haze behind the iceberg, only revealing its presence significantly later than normal. Without binoculars and at a speed of 22 knots, Reginald and Frederick couldn't see it early enough, or well enough.

At 11.39pm the iceberg was suddenly spotted very close up and the warning bell was struck. The First Officer, Andrew Murdoch immediately attempted evasive action, including turning the ship left and then right. This manoeuvre also involved stopping and then reversing the engines. But at the point when the engines were switched off, the power to the central propeller was instantly lost. That propeller could have powered a greater turning circle for the rudder, pushing the Titanic away to safety. Switching off the engines meant the collision became inevitable. Opting for the wrong manoeuvre so close to an iceberg was another controllable mistake.

The decision to turn the ship also caused more damage than a head-on crash would have done. As a result, the Titanic hit and scraped the mass of iceberg along its side underneath the water. That could have been avoided. The blow felt like a glancing one, so there was no immediate reaction amongst the passengers. The crew didn't immediately assess the impact or call for an evacuation. Valuable time was lost. It took forty-seven minutes after the accident before the Titanic used its radio to call for help. This was yet another controllable mistake and not the last.

"Come at once, we have struck a berg. It's a CQD old man"[42]

All these mistakes might not have sunk her, but they certainly contributed to the collision. The fatal blow was an weakness in the Titanic's hull construction. As the water was freezing that night, the Titanic needed steel rivets, inserted by a hydraulic riveting machine, to hold her together. What she had was iron rivets which had been hammered in by hand. Why? As the bow section of the Titanic was curved, she couldn't fit into the Belfast yard to allow the hydraulic riveting machine to be used. So the decision had been taken to use iron rivets which could

---

[42] The message sent by Jack Phillips the Wireless Operator. CQD was the forerunner to the signal S.O.S. used since.

be hammered in by hand. In the freezing conditions and on contact with the iceberg, those iron rivets failed. Choosing the wrong yard for the ship was a controllable mistake. Choosing to go ahead with iron rivets was another. The Titanic started taking on water.

Like her sister-ship the Olympic, the sixteen bulk-head compartments were designed to limit the spread of that water. If the bulk-heads had held, the Titanic would not have sunk. The water would have been contained and she could still have made New York. But the bulk-heads weren't tall enough to stop all the flooding. They were made deliberately shallower to give passengers more access to other areas of the ship. Favouring passenger convenience over safety was yet another controllable mistake. When the water came rushing in, the flawed ship's design was found out. The fact that the fire damage to the boiler room five bulk-head had created a bulk-head weakness certainly didn't help either.

At 12.40am the water started pouring into the upper decks. At the same time, many passengers started opening their portholes to see what was going on. As the ship sank the open portholes let in more water. This was another controllable error that accelerated the sinking process.

There were approximately 1,200 lifeboat spaces for the 2,224 crew and passengers. That will seem utterly unacceptable to in the 21st century. Having 1,200 lifeboat spaces was unusual in 1912, but ironically in a good way. At that time, everyone assumed another ship would rescue you, so most cruise ships had far fewer lifeboat spaces than the Titanic. In fact, the Titanic had more lifeboat spaces than any other ship. The bigger problem was that the nearest ship that could take people out of the lifeboats, and allow them to go back for more passengers, was the SS Californian. She didn't respond to calls for help, as her operator had gone to bed after being told to be quiet by Jack Phillips. Switching its radio off overnight was a controllable mistake that the SS Californian contributed to the disaster. As the Titanic started to sink, there was no help on hand.

"Striking the water was like a thousand knives being driven into one's body. The temperature was twenty-eight degrees, four degrees below freezing"[43]

---

[43] The Titanic's Second Officer, Charles Lightoller (who was on the bridge when the iceberg was struck, who jumped off the ship and who was the last person taken on board the SS Carpathia).

Rocket flares were sent out. The SS Californian saw them from its position ten miles away, but it didn't recognise them as being a distress signal. There was no system of flares at the time. The SS Californian must have thought it was a party. No one turned the radio back on to check the Titanic was okay and the radio controller was fast asleep. These were more controllable mistakes.

The closest ship to get the message and respond was the Carpathia. She was fifty-eight miles away but immediately set-off to help. One hour and thirty minutes later the Carpathia arrived, but by then over 1,500 of the 2,224 passengers and crew on board had died. One of them was radio operator Jack Phillips who remained at his radio post until the end.

At 2.20am on the 15th April 1912, the Titanic finally sank.

"I thought her unsinkable and I based my opinion on the best expert advice"[44]

The disaster was the product of a series of controllable and uncontrollable factors. The uncontrollables posed a deadly threat, but the human failure to manage the controllables was what turned a potential for disaster into a reality. The White Star Line and the Titanic crew couldn't change the melting of the ice-caps, the weather that evening or sweep away the icebergs ahead of them, but they could have made the ship and its journey much safer. Controlling the controllables is what turns a failure into a success

~~~~~

Accepting that we cannot control what's fixed and pre-determined, we are left with whatever's left over. Within the infinite pile of everything else, there are many variable elements. Those elements are flexible and open to influence and capable of change. They could all be useful, but they won't all be useful for your competition. Not all of the variables matter to winning. The skill to winning is to be able to pick out which controllables we need to control for our mission.

Every event, project and competition has a different combination of controllables. Only some of them make a fundamental contribution to winning. We need to work out which ones matter the most. Then we can concentrate on those variables

---

[44] Phillip Franklin, White Star Line Vice-President.

that really affect our chances of success. If we do that better than everyone else, we will increase our chances of winning enormously. Everyone and every organisation can make themselves win ready if they control their winning controllables. Those controllables might be the elements that go into making a successful sales pitch, scoring a goal or putting out a fire.

Amongst all of the possible controllables, there seem to be eleven that always seems to matter to winning. There are many other controllables that might matter in different circumstances, but these eleven are so fundamental that they apply across all competitions and challenges. They are: Mission, Philosophy, Culture and Values, People and Alignment, Mindset, Preparation and Positioning, Skills and Techniques, Science and Technology, Super-tribe thinking, Strength and Firepower; and Finishing. Just before we get onto these eleven variables, we need to start at our beginning.

Takeaway thoughts:

- Winning is about achieving your goals whatever they may be
- Define success and which measurables you're going to be measuring
- Think shared inputs and shared outputs
- Set the winning standards for your mission
- Define Absolute Success, Qualified Success, Qualified Failure and Absolute Failure
- Agree the Expected Minimum
- Link your rewards to your winning standards
- Don't cheat
- Understand the uncontrollables

2. NATURE AND NURTURE

2.1 GENETICS PLAY A PART

Our genetics place some limitations on what we're capable of. Martin Osborne Johnson CBE played in the second row for Leicester Tigers and England. Martin Johnson is 2.01 metres (6 ft 7") tall and in his playing days he weighed 119 kilograms (18 stones 9 pounds). Based on his genetics, Martin Johnson was probably never going to be a very good jockey. In 2003, and on his 84th and final international cap, Martin captained England to win the Rugby Union World Cup.

Our genetics don't prevent us from winning. They place some limitations on us that we need to discover and understand. But they never stop us from becoming winners. The more we limit ourselves, the less we will achieve. We need to believe in our own ability to win, regardless of our genetic code. We need to defy our limitations, at least until we hit our genetic ceiling, if we ever truly do. We shouldn't judge anyone else based our own preconceptions either.

According to Laureano Ruiz, the former Barcelona youth team coach, before Johan Cruyff became the Barcelona Manager "There was a sign on the door of the coaches' room which said 'If you're offering us a youth player who's less than 1.8 metres tall turn around and go home."[45] Luckily for Barcelona, Johan Cruyff immediately changed that self-limiting philosophy. Suddenly, height became irrelevant. Talent was all that mattered.

"Even the smallest person can change the course of the future"[46]

It's rather a good job too, as Lionel Messi is 1.7 metres tall, so is Xavi and so is Andrés Iniesta. The three of them went on to become Barcelona legends, because of that change. Lionel Messi has scored close to 700 goals and won over thirty trophies at the club. In fact Lionel is considered by many to be the greatest footballer of all time. At 1.7 metres tall Barcelona nearly missed out on three of its greatest ever players. Ability is more than a single physical or mental statistic. Artificially ruling someone out, based on a single arbitrary statistic talent, is a losing decision.

---

[45] Taken from "Take the ball, pass the ball: The making of the greatest team In the World".
[46] Galadriel from 'The Fellowship of the Ring'.

~~~~~

We are all born with a unique blend of physical and mental characteristics. No two people are ever born the same. Even identical twins aren't identical. We are born with the individual attributes we get. We can't choose how dexterous, intelligent or strong we'll be. We can't grow more height or bigger hands in middle age. We can't buy ourselves a software upgrade. Our genetic cards are dealt for us and we all have to play the hand we've been dealt. This truth provides us with three key steps towards achieving success.

1. Accept 'we are what we are' is the first part of developing a winning mentality. Denying what nature has given to us, or bemoaning what nature hasn't given to us, will always limit our development.

2. Understand our natural limitations and push them to their maximum limits to get the best out of ourselves. Working out where we can and can't still develop is therefore critical to our self-improvement. What can we improve? What do we need to focus on?

3. Be utterly determined to become the best version of ourselves that we can be. We can improve a great deal about ourselves if we want to. Skill development, technical expertise and self-improvement are all controllables.

To raise our winning abilities, we first have to answer four questions:

- What do I need to be capable of in order to succeed (What are the Winning Abilities)? – Analyse every physical and mental attribute, skill and technique that's required; and list all the necessary items and levels required to win.

- Where am I on each scale (How do I measure up)? – Compare yourself and your team against the Winning Abilities. Where are the matches and where are the skills gaps?

- Do I want to win enough to develop all the skills gaps up to the level required (Am I up for it) ? – Work through your motivation to succeed and test it against what you'll have to sacrifice for it. Do you still want to 'win'?

- How can I develop each attribute, skill and technique (What do I need to learn, practice and develop)? – Work through what you need to do to reach all the Winning Abilities required.

If you really understand what's needed to win the competition you're in, you will have an enormous head start. Test your understanding. Push this process extremely hard. Dig deeper. Find out everything you need to win. Every competition requires different skills, techniques and abilities. We each need to work out what winning abilities we need in our job and in our other roles. If you're a manager or other leader, you'll also need to work out what winning abilities your team or organisation needs.

Once you know how your organisation rates against the winning abilities, you'll have a set of goals to aim for. You can then design and set up the training and development programme needed to close those gaps. By picking people who are mentally and physically resilient you have more chance of reaching those goals. This winning abilities analysis should always get you and your team closer to winning. Across all forms of competition, there are too many forms of self-improvement to list. They can be very varied.

"Being a gentleman is nothing to do with one's accent. It's about being at ease in one's skin. As Hemingway said "There is nothing noble in being superior to your fellow man. True nobility is being superior to your former self."[47]

Whinging about how someone is smarter or faster than you, won't make you smarter or faster than them. Moaning about how someone can jump over more hurdles than you than you won't make you jump more. That wasted energy could have been spent on developing your own skills and stamina instead. Working out where improvements can be made and making them are winning behaviours. Whinging and moaning are losing behaviours.

We can't all be a Grand National winning jockey, a British Chess Champion or win Strictly Come Dancing, but we can all become better riders, chess players and dancers if we commit to our own self-development. Given good enough health and fitness, we can all make continual improvements to our skills, positioning and techniques, however small. There is often fierce competition around us to win anything, but the biggest competition we face is from within. You can only become what you can be. But you can become the best possible version of that. If you don't commit to continuous self-improvement, you are not making yourself win ready.

---

[47] Kingsman: The Secret Service.

~~~~~

Nature gives us the starting point for our lives. But it doesn't determine how we finish. That is for us to decide. Once nature deals our hand, we have to play it to the best of our ability. How? That's for us to figure out, using our strengths and the strengths of fellow tribe and Super-tribe members. We will develop faster and better if we learn from others. We shouldn't blame our nature or genetics for failing to take our opportunities.

> *"Punctured bicycle*
> *On a hillside desolate*
> *Will nature make a man of me yet?"* [48]

That's just wasted energy. It's up to us to take control of what we can. Instead we should take the time to understand what's needed to win. Work out what point you're starting from. Then commit to becoming the best version of you and your team that you can be. You can always close your winning abilities gap.

2.2   PREDISPOSITIONS AND OPPORTUNITIES

Our genetic start gives us a series of predispositions. How high we can reach, how fast we can run and how many exams we can pass are just three examples. But are they really pre-dispositions? Are they fixed? The answer is only partly. Our genetic and physical make-up does impose maximum limits on our potential, but our genes don't shape our future. Their basic level doesn't determine our lives, only their absolute maximum level does. That leaves us free to control how close to our maximum limits we get. That's up to us. The strength of our commitment to our own personal development is therefore a winning controllable. It's perhaps the key variable in how much of our potential we fulfil. We all start from a different starting place, but we can all have success. How much success and what kind of success is up to us.

---

[48] This Charming Man, by the Smiths.

"Whether you come from a council estate or a country estate, your success will be determined by your own confidence and fortitude. Success is only meaningful and enjoyable if it feels like your own,"[49]

Our focus should be on closing the gap between where we are and our maximum potential. In life there are competitions everywhere. Each one requires its own winning abilities. Our maximum potential might allow us to reach them. Or it may not. We have to work that out. To do that, we have to take our opportunities for learning and development when they come. Taking our opportunities is another winning controllable.

~~~~~

Football coach Colin Harvey gave Wayne Rooney his first opportunity to play professional football. Colin must have seen something very special in the young Wayne that meant he'd go out on such a limb for him. The issue was that Wayne was only 14 years old and still in school. The team he was picked for was Everton under 19's.

Buoyed by the extraordinary belief shown in him, Wayne had more reason than the other players to try and prove himself. Appreciative of what Everton and Colin Harvey were doing for him, Wayne Rooney gave absolutely everything for his coach and his club. Wayne's performances were spent trying to repay that faith in him; and take his opportunity. If the development process had been a more standard one, then at the time he was 18, Wayne might have been making his debut for Everton's under 19's. Instead, Wayne Rooney was playing first team football for Everton and earning himself a life-changing move to Manchester United.

In an article in the Sunday Times[50], Wayne Rooney explained how he grabbed his opportunity. "From 14, I changed my mindset. I'd go from school to football training and then straight to boxing training after that. My whole focus was on becoming a player. But I knew lads who couldn't make that commitment, who said "I'm good enough to make it anyway". Well they didn't." Wayne developed his decision-making and maximised his potential. Wayne is much smarter than some have given him credit for.

---

[49] Two quotes, back to back, from Michelle Obama.
[50] In April 2020.

"Winning isn't everything, but wanting it is"[51]

Wayne Rooney didn't just impress at 14 years old, he went on to become Manchester United's leading goal-scorer with 253 goals, winning five Premier League titles, a Champions League and an F.A. Cup amongst other trophies with the club. Wayne also went on to play for England. In fact, he earned himself 120 caps, making him second in appearances only to Peter Shilton (with the record of 125). Wayne was (and remains) England's youngest ever goal-scorer at seventeen. Wayne added to that debut goal and went on to become England's all-time leading goal-scorer with 53 goals. Wayne's dedication to his career and his endurance has set him apart from virtually everyone else.

Wayne Rooney's incredibly strong levels of personal commitment have allowed him to take the opportunities that have come his way. That all started with the opportunity he was given at 14. Despite his obvious ability, Wayne is quick to credit the help and support he has received along the way. Wayne has the awareness and humility to understand that he couldn't have achieved any of his career highlights on his own. Wayne's understanding of what success takes, will be a big benefit in his management career.

"Making it is about commitment, self-motivation
and getting help from parents and coaches like Colin.
It's about so much more than ability"[52]

~~~~~

In 1982, Major Chris Keeble was serving as second in command of the second Paratroop Regiment (known as 2 PARA) when the regiment was deployed to the Falkland Islands. Major Keeble immediately set about establishing and implementing a training programme to get the Battalion combat ready. While Lieutenant Colonel 'H' Jones was in the Ascension Islands, linking in with 3 Commando Brigade, Chris Keeble was operating in charge of the Battalion for nearly a month before its arrival in the Falkland Islands.

---

[51] Golf legend, Arnold Palmer.
[52] Wayne Rooney.

Like every other commissioned officer, Chris had received the same Sandhurst training programme. He was no more trained to be a successful officer, than any other.

At the battle of Goose Green, Chris's Commanding Officer, Lieutenant Colonel 'H' Jones, was killed charging an enemy machine gun post single-handed. That event must have come as a shock and a massive setback. As a Major, Chris was the next in command. In a single moment, Chris became the leader of the Battalion, just at the time that its attack on the Argentinian position broke down. It was a crucial point in the battle and the war. The Battalion had lost sixteen percent of its strength to casualties, it was running short of ammunition and it had been without sleep for 40 hours. This was a huge opportunity for Chris, but it came at a hugely stressful time.

It was Major Chris Keeble's turn to show what kind of leader he was. How good was his state of balance and his decision-making? Would he be ready to take his opportunity? Kneeling alone in prayer, Chris put his hands together and sought guidance as to what to do. Under extreme pressure, with the whole World watching, Chris conceived the idea of a psychological ploy. His idea was to release of several Argentine prisoners of war, sending them in the direction of their Goose Green garrison with a vital message for their commanders. The message was a demand for the garrison's surrender. The psychological ploy was the threat that went with that demand. The threat was of a large-scale assault by the British forces (which wasn't imminent), supported by heavy artillery (which wasn't available). The Argentine soldiers were given the message and sent on their way. They didn't know the threat was a ploy and they took it back to their Goose Green garrison as Major Keeble intended.

The plan was high-risk. Chris had just given the Argentinian's more men to fight his depleted battalion with. If they chose to stay and fight, then even more of his men would die. But if they surrendered, many lives would be saved. The contents of the message he sent was key, but so was the way he delivered it to the prisoners he released. The message had to be absolutely compelling and expertly delivered. Then it was a waiting game, one of patience. What would the Argentinians do?

Faced with the threat of an over-whelming assault and likely death, the Argentinian commander surrendered the garrison to 2 PARA without further fighting. This ploy undoubtedly saved lives on both sides. This was a win without loss.

Lieutenant Colonel 'H' Jones was posthumously awarded the Victoria Cross for his extraordinary bravery. Major Chris Keeble was awarded the Distinguished Service Order. The DSO is "an operational gallantry award given for highly successful command and leadership during active operations". At his medal ceremony, Chris was asked about what happened and he modestly replied "The victory, however, was H's. The inspiration of 2 PARA came from him, and my role was merely to act on his behalf in his absence. For that I am the caretaker of an enamelled bit of metal, which I carry on behalf of every man in 2 PARA, especially the junior non-commissioned officers and the soldiers."[53]

Major Chris Keeble took his opportunity to show what kind of leader he was, securing victory without further bloodshed and then praising everyone else afterwards. Promotion to Lieutenant Colonel followed, as did command of 15 PARA, before Chris became a senior staff officer at HQ Allied Forces Central Europe. After leaving the British Army, Chris went on to run a Management Consultancy that advised on how to 'balance the ethic of business performance and peoples' flourishing'.

When his opportunities came, Chris Keeble took them with both hands. His religion and his army training gave him the appreciation of life and the people he was dealing with. They also gave him balance in his decision-making and the endurance to see his plan through. Chris had to acquire the skills he needed and then tap into them when the time came. Under immense pressure he did just that. We can all develop the skills we need to achieve our wins and then employ them when they are needed.

~~~

Confident people seem to be more successful than people who lack confidence. There is a basis of truth to this. Having confidence allows you to spot opportunities faster, grab them quicker and take them better. Confidence is a winning controllable. Confidence is not limited by your genetics, you can develop it. If you want to spot and grab more opportunities, you just need to build up your confidence. That is more easily said and done, than you might think.

Most of us are fairly confident when we're operating safely inside our comfort zone. However, that level of confidence naturally drops every time we step outside it. We know our own limits; and when we reach them we feel

---

[53] Information from Paradata.org.uk.

uncomfortable and stressed. The smaller our comfort zone is, the more often we find ourselves outside it and operating under stress. Being at ease allows us to be at our best. Being at peace with our decisions allows us to make them and follow them through.

"When peace like a river attendeth my way
When sorrows like sea billows roll
Whatever my lot he has taught me to say
It is well, it is well with my soul"[54]

Working under intense pressure adversely affects our performance, including our ability to appreciate what's around us. Under stress we are predisposed towards a fight or flight response and our decision-making suffers. Pressure also adversely affects our state of inner balance and our endurance. If we can reduce that stress we can improve our performance. By holding our nerve we can usually operate at a higher level than we thought we could. We just need to take a step outside our comfort zone every day.

Each individual act of bravery helps to build our confidence and improve our decision-making under pressure. The more we step outside our comfort zone, the bigger that comfort zone grows. The bigger it is, the less stress we suffer and the better we perform.

"I'm through accepting limits
'Cuz someone says they're so
Some things I cannot change
But till I try, I'll never know!"[55]

Despite the appearance of confidence, even the most apparently 'confident' people feel the same nerves as everyone else. They just control them better. Some people appear more confident for that reason alone. They simply hold themselves together better. We assume that confidence is a natural gift that other people are blessed with and that we can't possess. But it's not inherited, it's developed. More confident people are just a bit further along the road to growing their comfort zone. Inside they feel the same strains as everyone else.

---

[54] From 'It is well with my soul'.
[55] From the song 'Defying Gravity' from the musical Wicked.

No one enjoys being too far outside their comfort zone for too long. But by taking baby steps every day, we can extend our comfort zone in many directions. By developing our mental control and resilience we can push ourselves into a pressure situation, breathe deeply and hold our nerve. The power to stand firm doesn't come from a genetic predisposition, it's a learned trait. Confidence is a balloon we inflate by stepping outside our comfort zone. The more often we step outside our comfort zone, the more pressure we can endure the next time.

Expanding our ability to cope gives us a greater belief in our own abilities. That belief makes it more likely that we'll make it outside our (larger) comfort zone the next time an opportunity arises.

"I lack confidence, but I've been so lucky the way jobs have come to me, and I'm so grateful for them. I know how many brilliant actors there are out there who aren't getting the chances. While the work is there, I will grab it with both hands. It could all end tomorrow. You never know what's around the corner"[56]

The more we appreciate the opportunities we get, the more we will try and take them. Focusing on the chance of success, rather than the size of the challenge, can reverse our thinking long enough for us to get stuck in. Once we've committed ourselves, we are well placed to get the job done. Appreciating our opportunities enough to take them is a winning controllable. Winning teams are usually the teams who really value the opportunities that they've been given.

~~~~~

A predisposition to winning is an incredibly helpful starting point. But winning is about more than genetics or breeding. When several highly-rated horse and jockey combinations race against each other, there is a competition. However good they all are, only one horse and jockey get to win it. Winning races involves far more than breeding or buying a good horse.

Choosing the best combination of horse and jockey is a crucial decision. As are the decisions about diet, training and rest. Even more fundamental, picking the type of racing is a hugely important early decision. Is it point to point, flat racing or National Hunt racing over jumps? If it's National Hunt, will your horse race over hurdles, run steeplechases or race in National Hunt flat races (known as

---

[56] Theatre and television actress Sheridan Smith.

Bumpers). There are pro's and con's to each option. Making good decisions is an essential part of winning.

Once you've chosen the type of racing you've still got more questions to answer. What's the right level for your horse? Is that a juvenile race, a novice's, handicap or a graded race? What's the best length of race? Racing runs from 5 furlongs (just over half a mile) up to two and half miles. For flat racing, which surface is best? Is it grass or All Weather? At which course should you run? Some run left to right and some right to left. Some are very flat and some are more undulating. What type of ground does your horse favour? The ground can be from Firm (via Good, Good to Soft and Soft) all the way to Heavy. There is knowledge, experience and skill that can help with all these decisions. If you don't have it, you can bring in people who do. Working out what's important, is assessing the winning controllables.

Your horse's breeding should help you to answer some of these questions. Many horses are predisposed in a similar way to their sire (father) and dam (mother). Some of the very top horses have gone on to produce generations of winners. However, many don't. Just like people, some horses never reach their potential. A horse's family tree give us an indication of it's likely performance level, but nothing more. Skilled trainers have to investigate each horse's abilities individually. In this regard, the daily work out on the gallops is a vital time for in assessing speed and stamina. Then all of the breeding and training data can feed into the decision-making process. Which types of race should this horse run in? Which racecourses favour us most? Which jockey should be on board? Like every other competition, horse racing is about blending all the available information to give you the best chance of winning.

Once your horse starts racing for the year, there's more investigation and learning to be done. What form is your horse showing? Which jockey seems to produce the best performances? Which race tactics work best? What seems to make the difference between winning and losing?

Even if you get all the preparation decisions right, what happens on the day is another challenge. Your horse's race is directly influenced by the preparation you do. If your horse is win ready, it has a potential chance to win. That prospect is of course affected by how all of the other horses run. Amongst all the jostling for places and spaces, a jockey has got to trust in their horse's preparation. Alone in the saddle, with no earpiece or microphone to use for advice, a jockey has to create an opportunity to win the race; and then go on and take it.

"For me it was Steve Davis walking in the snooker hall...it's about making sure that when you've had that luck you maximise it, that you grasp that opportunity and give it everything"[57]

Lanfranco "Frankie" Dettori is probably the most successful flat racing jockey of all time. Frankie climbed the racing ladder by working extremely hard and learning his trade over the years. As a result of his performances, he was spotted early and he had his first winner aged sixteen. Frankie has gone on to win 19 British Classic races, 250 Group One races, 5 Prix De L'Arc de Triomphe; and he has ridden over 3,000 winners in total. In 1996, Frankie won every one of the seven races on the same card at Royal Ascot. That has never been done before or since. Ever since the age of sixteen, Frankie Dettori has repeatedly created opportunities to win horse races and he has managed to take over three thousand of them. However, using the over-simplified approach "Book Frankie Dettori to ride" is not a well-balanced or win ready philosophy.

In flat racing, the King George and Queen Elizabeth Stakes at Ascot is probably the most prestigious race in the UK; and arguably the World. It's where the year's first four Classic[58] winners can take on the best of the older horses. The 'King George' is a very high-value[59], high-pressure, high-quality race. In 2011, Frankie Dettori was given the opportunity to ride a horse called Rewilding. Having previously won the race in 1995, 1998, 1999 and 2004, Frankie understood what was needed to win. By building up his experience and resilience at tracks across the World, Frankie had developed the skills to win races at the highest level. To him, this was just another big race. Frankie was very optimistic about his chances on board the highly-rated prospect Rewilding. When asked, he answered a journalist's question with the statement "I can't wait!"

Up against Rewilding was a highly-rated horse called Nathaniel, sired by a previous Derby winner called Galileo. Nathaniel was the only three year old horse in the race, with the disadvantage of youth against him. Whilst he hadn't run in the race before, his sire Galileo had won the King George in 2001. Nathaniel's breeding therefore gave him a genetic predisposition to winning the race, but only he could run it. Nathaniel's owners wanted to test out that chance at the highest level.

---

[57] Barry Hearn, in Business Leader South East Magazine July-August 2020.
[58] There are five classics: The Derby, The Oaks, The 2,000 Guineas, The 1,000 Guineas and the St. Leger.
[59] The 2019 (pre-COVID-19) first prize was £708,875. By contrast, the prize money for the 2020 running of The Derby was £283,550.

Frankie's horse Rewilding had less distinguished breeding, but Rewilding had more race experience than Nathaniel; and he also had Frankie Dettori on board.

As the 2011 King George and Queen Elizabeth Stakes developed, Frankie chose to position Rewilding at the back of the field. Holding him up was a race tactic to suit the horse. The plan was to let Rewilding run freely with about two furlongs left to go. When the time came, Frankie urged Rewilding to gallop at full pace and the race was on. Coming from the back of the field, Rewilding had more ground left to cover than the leaders, but he also had more energy left in the tank. As Rewilding picked up speed, Frankie must have felt very confident.

Suddenly, Rewilding veered off to the left, stumbled and fell, throwing Frankie onto the turf. The incident was shocking and highly unusual on the flat. Tragically, Rewilding suffered a broken leg and had to be humanely euthanised. It was a very sad and a crushing blow for everyone connected with the horse. Unchallenged by Rewilding, Nathaniel ran home in first, winning the 2011 King George.

Frankie was understandably very upset. But being a jockey, he had to carry on racing. The following year, Frankie had another opportunity to ride in the King George and Queen Elizabeth Stakes. Perhaps subconsciously affected by the events of 2011, Frankie and his horse didn't win. The next four years rolled by and Frankie couldn't get another win in the King George for love nor money. But he didn't give up. He didn't make excuses. He carried on riding, race after race, trying his hardest. A winning attitude never concedes defeat. It has an inner resilience.

"Fall down seven times and stand up eight"[60]

Six years after riding Rewilding, Frankie Dettori was given the opportunity to ride Enable in the 2017 running of the King George. Having not won the race since 2004, some thirteen years earlier, Frankie must have been hopeful, without being over-confident. He had yet another great horse to ride, but once again there was no guarantee of a victory. Rated very highly, Enable was one of the first crop of foals sired by the 2011 winner Nathaniel. Ironically, Frankie was about to ride a daughter of the horse that beat him in 2011.

Like Nathaniel before her, Enable was predisposed to run well over a mile and a half. She had already won the 2017 fillies' Oaks at Epsom proving that she had ability at that distance. However, as a filly, she had the challenge of facing older

---

[60] A Japanese proverb.

male horses like Ulysses and Highland Reel (both sired by Galileo, just like Nathaniel had been). It was a hotly-anticipated race, because of the similar breeding lines behind the runners. Several horses were predisposed to run well. Enable was one of them. Her connections had an opportunity to win the most prestigious flat race in the World. Would they be able to take it?

With two furlongs to go, Maverick Wave was leading, with Ulysses and Highland Reel well-placed. Unlike 2011, Frankie was riding with different tactics to the ones he had on Rewilding. Positioning Enable just behind Maverick Wave in second place, they stayed up towards the front of the group. Then when he was ready, Frankie allowed Enable to open-up her running and go for home. As she did, the other horses responded too. Frankie desperately wanted to win the race again.

"I was like... I am not having that feeling again. I am not having it at the Olympics in London. In the last 200m I just felt like I had been through that pain before so many times in training. This was my one opportunity to have that moment across the line. I had to do it"[61]

Enable picked up speed and ran on strongly. There was no veering off to the side and Frankie stayed firmly on board. Enable held-off Ulysses by four and half lengths to come home in first. It was a beautifully timed and balanced ride. Two years later, Enable and Frankie came back and won it again. After the 2019 win, Frankie said "She's an amazing horse in every way: ability, courageous, uncomplicated."

Enable's connections took the opportunity to put Enable and Frankie Dettori together. They chose a race that suited Enable's breeding and speed. Her trainer, John Gosden and his yard team put together the right diet and training plan for the race. The trainer and jockey agreed the best racing tactics to use. Frankie's big race experience gave him an understanding of the size and nature of the challenge. Frankie listened well and took on board the advice and guidance of the trainer. Enable had been trained to have the mental and physical stamina to endure. Frankie's big race experience also gave him the skill to manage the horse during the race. Everyone appreciated the abilities of everyone else.

---

[61] Dame Jessica Ennis-Hill after winning the Heptathlon Gold at the London 2012 Olympics.

The decisions made before and during the race secured the win. These highly-positive collaborations between all the connections made the horse and jockey win ready. Then when it came to the race build-up, Frankie stayed calm, making the right decisions during the race. As a result of all this, the horse and jockey delivered, twice.

~~~~~

As Maslow confirmed, social belonging matters to almost all of us. We are predisposed to living and working with other people. There is greater safety, increased chances of eating well and the bonds we build through human interaction are good for our self-esteem.

"The most stable and therefore the most healthy self-esteem is based on deserved respect from others, rather than on external fame or celebrity and unwarranted adulation"[62]

We feel better when others acknowledge our worth. We perform better when others acknowledge our worth. As a result, working as part of a team comes naturally and willingly to us. That is unless the experience is spoiled for us. Never praising someone's work will depress their self-esteem and reduce their performance levels. To get the best out of a team of people, we need to positively tap into this predisposition to bond. A sense of social belonging is good for us and for our team. If we can engineer a culture of mutual respect then it's a multiple win situation.

Gareth Malone is well-known for creating new choirs, by bringing together a group of strangers and building a social bond between them. Throughout his various BBC television series, time and again Gareth has helped those strangers to lose their social inhibitions and produce a strong vocal harmony. Gareth clearly understands the social bonds involved.

---

[62] Abraham Maslow.

"Archaeological evidence shows that humans have been making music for tens of thousands of years. Singing bonds people together, exercises a range of muscles and makes you feel happy. The camaraderie of communal singing is of benefit to people - you don't get that when listening to a CD no matter what style of music. You don't even get it in karaoke, because that's focused on individual performances. It's mostly at football matches and religious gatherings that people sing en masse with no thought of their own ability. I think it's important that people feel free to sing and that there is somewhere for them to be heard. People can feel very isolated and singing is an excellent way to combat that."[63]

As humans, we don't just like to be together, we have an inner need to be together. It drives us to find social belonging. That makes the forming of teams and organisations inevitable. Not every team is set up for success though. The best kinds of teams produce the best conditions for human performance. The best teams create a sense of social belonging where every stakeholder wins. When a team has become a tribe, it has reached the point of differentiation, where everyone in it wins. When a tribe becomes part of a Super-tribe it offers every tribe member an environment that allows them to feel their best. In a tribe or Super-tribe, everyone wins.

~~~~~

A predisposition doesn't have to be genetic. We are influenced by many people and many situations, but especially by the people we trust the most. Experiencing challenging circumstances during our childhood can predispose us to winning or losing in later life. Being exposed to negativity and defeatism from our parents, teachers or other key influencers can adversely affect our chances of success in life. That is unless we change our future. Hearing stories about other people overcoming their own adversity can become powerful metaphors for positive change. Our fear of failing doesn't have to stop us. Our fear can be reduced and overcome. Togetherness is built from overcoming the same adversity. Great teams face their fears and adversities together.

---

[63] A BBC interview with Gareth Malone.

"The great thing about playing team sport is you win and lose together, and the pain is never as bad when you share it"[64]

Losing teams, lose as individuals and rarely win. Winning teams lose as a team, with a shared responsibility for putting it right again and so, go on to win. Winning teams create an environment which supports all their people through past, present and future challenges. They create a bond of mutual trust and they do not break it. They don't fake an idea of unity, they continually try to foster a genuine feeling of unity. Winning teams are open and honest about issues, in a way that's constructive and not destructive. They don't exploit each other's vulnerabilities, they support them. Winning teams come together to agree what's best for the team, trusting in each other's commitment and confidentiality. In that kind of positive environment, team members don't mind admitting to limitations or vulnerabilities, because it allows others to understand them and help them improve their skills and abilities.

Losing teams create a shallow imitation of unity that's superficial and brittle. Differences of opinion are brushed under the rug. Disagreement is avoided, because the team isn't strong enough to cope with any real conflict. Losing team members compete more with each other than they do with the competition. They lie, cheat and let their colleagues take the hit for them. They ask for their own goals and rewards before they ask about the team. Instead of putting their shoulders to the wheel, they slope them so that every criticism roles away. In a losing team, team members don't sacrifice themselves, they sacrifice everyone and everything else before that.

These two states of performance are so different in their dynamics. Winning teams somehow find the way to move from a position of individual self-interest to one of group-interest (mission focus). They speak passionately about the mission. They tell positive stories to inspire and motivate their colleagues. They adapt fearful thinking into optimism. They exchange winning behaviours for losing ones. They move forward as 'one for all', not as 'everyone for themselves'.

This may sound very challenging, but no matter what's happened in the past, losers can become winners. That's why so many supposed under-performers go on to thrive at a new organisation. A reinvention of a team can create a new start.

---

[64] Brian O'Driscoll.

Winning teams create themselves a predisposition to win. They get themselves win ready.

2.3   EDUCATION THE ENABLER

When I was about fifteen I played chess for my school. I honestly can't remember why, as I wasn't that good. We had to play two games back to back against a local school. My first opponent was probably about the same level as me. It was tough going. I eventually won, but it took me a long time to grind it out. My patience eventually wore him down. I remember having to concentrate really hard. But as soon as he started to look bored, I knew I'd got him. When it was all over, I was excited to have the perfect winning record of one win from one game. All I had to do was win my second game to maintain my record.

As my first game had been longer than everyone else's, I had to start playing again almost immediately. I refocused myself and made my first move. Full of confidence, I now knew I could outlast any of their team. However long it took, I wouldn't give in. I was ready for a long war of attrition. Within two moves I'd lost. Afterwards, the other boy was kind enough to show me "Fool's Mate" and what I should have done to prevent it. Losing that quickly was very embarrassing. The fact it's called "Fool's Mate" didn't help reduce my embarrassment either. Those two matches turned out to be my only games for the school and I retired with a 50% win rate. What I'd learned was that I needed to dedicate myself to the game to be good at it. I needed to learn the theory; and practice often to improve my game, or I could be embarrassed again.

"I never lose. Either I win or I learn"[65]

As it turns out, many of the opening few moves in chess have great names, like 'The Sicilian Defence' and 'The Caro Kann'. Many player study these match phases like an academic subject. Many games are effectively won and lost in the first few moves without you realising it (as I discovered). The difference in skill can be vast. Chess Grand Masters can calculate fifteen to twenty moves ahead. That's working out and remembering their own moves and the possible responses by their opponent, for up to twenty moves ahead. That's astonishing. When I played my school matches, I couldn't even think two moves ahead.

---

[65] Nelson Mandela.

My chess experience taught me about the need for dedicated study and also how the winning moves of "Fool's Mate" work. I won't ever lose to that combination again. Every loss can teach you how to avoid it next time. So much of our development comes from a perceived failure. Chess is a game to be learned and committed to memory. The more you teach yourself, the better you get at it. The same is true for most disciplines in life. You have to study and practice any task to become good at it, let alone become a Grand Master. A life of practice is a life of continuous improvement.

> *"Let us never consider ourselves finished nurses.*
> *We must be learning all our lives"[66]*

Unless you're a well-known player on the chess circuit, you have no idea how good an opponent will be. By the same token, no one can know how good you'll be in advance. There are few give away signs to spot a great opponent. That means you can underestimate someone. The only way to prepare is to assume that you're facing a great opponent every single game.

~~~~~

Everyone is capable of changing and bettering themselves. The more we understand and the more we study, the greater our potential becomes. Throughout our lives we can grow our skills and abilities and also our potential skills and abilities. We can continually push our boundaries and maximums. It all stems from learning. A commitment to lifelong education is the surest way to grow our potential.

> *"Education is the passport to the future, for tomorrow*
> *belongs to those who prepare for it today"[67]*

There have never been more ways to learn new things. There has never been more information immediately available to us. With instruction and guidance, we can pretty much learn how to do anything, however challenging or difficult it seems. The information is out there. All we have to do is turn the pages or tap and swipe.

Many successful people have achieved their success through lifelong learning. Delia Smith CH CBE has written twenty-four cookbooks from 1971 to 2009,

---

[66] Florence Nightingale.
[67] Malcolm X.

which have sold nearly as many million copies between them. Delia is famous for being a television cook and a cookery writer. Delia is less well known for being a voracious reader. But that's what has kept her fresh and relevant. "I have always read all the latest cookery books and magazines, from all over the World"[68] Even the biggest selling writers read, to continue their own development.

~~~~~

Trying to become better is the challenge. We shouldn't fear the thought of finding our boundaries. Our limitations are not a weakness, they are just our current limits and current abilities. Learning and practicing give us the opportunities to reach our boundaries and then extend them. 'Push Yourself' is an often used phrase. It means pushing ourselves to places outside our comfort zone. We can't do that all day every day as it's too stressful, but we can do it regularly enough to continually develop ourselves. Learning how to do new things, or how to do old things better, are examples of pushing ourselves and expanding our horizons. Education isn't just about reading books, education comes in many forms.

"Education is the most powerful weapon
which you can use to change the world"[69]

We can continually modernise and change the way we operate. We can develop our personal characteristics and increase our winning behaviours. All we have to do is learn them, practice them and apply them. It's a matter of commitment.

"Being a gentleman has nothing to do with the circumstances of
one's birth. Being a gentleman is something one learns"[70]

Unfortunately we don't tend to be as open to learning new things as we could be. Perhaps it's because we are inundated with information. Perhaps it's because our minds are too busy and too full to properly listen to other people. We don't tend read enough either. That's a shame, as both reading and listening absorb useful information and involve us in constant learning.

"The more you learn, the more you learn"[71]

---

[68] Delia Smith CH CBE.
[69] Nelson Mandela.
[70] Kingsman: The Secret Service
[71] Billionaire business tycoon Warren Buffett.

Reading comes in many forms. It doesn't have to involve weighty novels, lengthy textbooks or broadsheet newspapers. Even bite sized snippets from magazines and social media posts can contain insights and lessons that we can benefit from.

"The more that you read, the more things you will know.
The more that you learn, the more places you'll go"[72]

The more relevant information we know, the better prepared we are. As preparation is the key to success, we should continually learn more and more, to make ourselves better prepared.

~~~~

Sir. Anthony Peter McCoy MBE rode a World Record 4,385 winners during his National Hunt career. 'AP' was Champion Jockey a World Record twenty times. Those statistics are beyond extraordinary, especially taking into account all the falls and injuries he suffered every year. What's even more impressive, is that those twenty championships came as a consecutive twenty year winning streak between 1995/96 and 2014/15. No one managed to beat him to the Championship for twenty years. What an extraordinary feat of endurance. AP is definitely the most successful jump jockey of all time.

Unlike Frankie Dettori[73], AP McCoy was tall for a jockey at 1.78 metres (5 ft 10"). That meant he had a daily battle to keep his weight down. His racing weight reportedly had to be a stone and a half below his natural state. Managing his weight for racing was a technique that AP had to master through incredible abstinence and dietary self-discipline. That wasn't the only skill he needed to acquire. AP McCoy had to learn how to become a champion jump jockey. That process happened at the stables of Jim Bolger.

AP's training there was the same every day. It was a routine process designed to teach all the young riders resilience and self-discipline. It started with mucking out the horses at dawn, followed by riding out the first of three or four groups of horses between 7.30 and 8.30am. Other than a short tea break, the riding-out went on from 7.30am until 12.00pm.

---

[72] Dr. Seuss.
[73] Frankie is 1.63 metres tall (5 ft 4").

Then the yard had to be cleaned until it was "spotless" before the trainees could have their lunch. The afternoon was spent brushing the horses and tidying up until 5.30pm. It was the same six days a week. Sometimes it was the seventh too, if according to AP "you'd done something you shouldn't".

AP openly acknowledges the importance of this regime on his success. "I found it too much at first, it felt more like joining the army than being a trainee jockey, but my time there was the absolute making of me. The good habits I learned from Jim were not just what I needed at a crucial time in my professional development, they stayed with me throughout my riding career."

If you want to have enduring success, it pays to build up the personal skills that give you competence and independence. Personal resilience will see you through the tough times. Sticking to a positive routine, come rain or shine, is a good example of building the resilience needed. Self-discipline is a winning controllable. We can become more self-disciplined by creating and following good routines. Then we will become a self-starter, someone with the drive to do what's needed every single day. When you're not reliant on other people to get you going, you have the self-discipline needed to be successful. Unless you're a self-starter you're not win ready.

2.4 WINNING BEHAVIOURS

Everything that we do shapes our lives and impacts on everything and everyone around us. The things that we don't do, our omissions, shape our lives and those of others in exactly the same way. Our decisions and actions belong to us and us alone. We have to take complete responsibility for ourselves. If we lead a team or organisation of any kind, we also have to take responsibility for that as well.

That does not mean that we have it easy. We live in a volatile, uncertain, complex and ambiguous (VUCA) World. So our actions and omissions can be heavily influenced and affected by the people and events going on around us. There are

---

[74] The quotes are taken from A.P. McCoy's autobiography 'Winner: My Racing Life'.

endless distractions that can pull our focus away. In competition, the situation is even worse. Some of the distractions we face will be the deliberate tactics of our competitors. But we cannot give up our control. Amongst all the confusion and cacophony around us, it is up to us to find the self-control needed to stick to our job and deliver our greatest performance.

It is too easy to blame other people and our circumstances for our own bad choices. Whatever happens, our behaviours are always our own responsibility. They are under our physical and mental control. Grasping that gets us started. A sense of personal responsibility is the key to maximising our winning behaviours and for minimising our losing ones. Aiming to be in control of all of our own behaviours is aspirational but achievable. Claiming to be in control of everyone else's behaviours is delusional and impossible. Understanding what we can and can't control is of fundamental importance.

"Control is an illusion, you infantile egomaniac. Nobody knows what's gonna happen next: not on a freeway, not in an airplane, not inside our own bodies and certainly not on a racetrack with forty other infantile egomaniacs"[75]

Accepting responsibility for our actions and omissions has to be genuine and meaningful. Are you prepared to take complete responsibility for all of your actions and omissions? Does the rest of your team feel the same way about theirs? Is everyone focusing on their own decision-making and making it the best it can be?

As our behaviours matter, in one respect or another, we need to understand their consequences and how to control them. We need to think about what we do more analytically. Everyone needs at least some help to improve. We all have triggers that make us emotional. We all have fears that prevent us from acting. We all lack experience in something. Some of us just need guidance to step back onto the right path. Others don't want to think differently. They need more help. Some don't have the self-awareness to understand how they're behaving. We can recognise that in other people, but not always in ourselves. We all need help. Appreciating that allows us to absorb constructive feedback. If we lose our humility, we lose our ability to help ourselves. Which of your team members need help and what kind of help? And what kind of help do you need?

~~~~

---

[75] Dr. Claire Lewicki (Nicole Kidman) to Cole Trickle (Tom Cruise) in 'Days of Thunder'.

We do things routinely every day, many of them are on auto-pilot without conscious thought. Changing those behaviours is really hard. The only way to address them is allow other people to help us re-set. By being open-book, we can strip back what we do and analyse whether each behaviour is working positively or negatively for us. Some people have good self-awareness, but they lack the self-control to stop themselves doing the wrong things. Some of them repeatedly make the wrong choices, especially when under pressure. What patterns do your team members fall into? How can you help them change their patterns of behaviour for the better, through practice and scenario planning? For deeply ingrained behaviours, Neuro-Linguistic Programming (NLP) and other support methods can help to effect positive change.

It is not our titles or qualifications that reveal who we are.
It's the choices we make

Within any competition some situations will repeat themselves. In fact, some situations repeat themselves predictably often, to the point that they become patterns. Winners are able to consciously and subconsciously analyse what those patterns are. They can work out what triggers them. Winners ask questions such as:

What patterns can we find?
How can we predict the beginning of each pattern?
When this pattern begins, what normally happens afterwards?

Some patterns may be obvious, but many require a forensic analysis of the data. Winners adapt to those patterns better than their opponents. Taking selling as our context, there must be study data available to predict sales results, based on using differing topics of conversation to try and complete the sale. For example, asking a potential customer about their 'family' must have an impact on whether a sale takes place and how much is sold. A pattern of similar discussion will typically follow. Where does that usually lead? Which topics of conversation increase the chances of a sale? Using words like 'happiness' must surely help the chances of making a sale. Which topics reduce the prospects of a sale? There must be words to avoid, like 'expensive' and 'unreliable'. How useful would it be to know what helps and what hinders a sale?

Within that scenario, there's also a question of timing. Does the prospect of a successful sale change if you ask about the customer's 'family' or mention 'happiness' early or late on in the sales process? If you can find out what typically happens in each case you will have predictable patterns to use or reject. If it helps

87

more to mention 'family' early and 'happiness' later on, then knowing that makes you ready to increase your sales. Once you've collected and analysed the data, you can employ the best combination of patterns to sell your products or services.

In sport there are patterns too. They reflect what tends to happen following certain events and scenarios. For example, having a player sent off during a game, must reduce your team's chances of winning. There must be data available to show that. Having two players sent off must reduce those chances even more. What change in win percentage does each event have? Knowing that will help you prepare for those eventualities.

The earlier in the competition that a loss-influencing event (LIE) happens (like a sending-off in sport) the lower that team's likely success percentage becomes. The reverse is also true. If it's a competitor that suffers the loss-influencing event, then by default your success percentage goes up. Why is that the case? It's because of the pattern of activities that typically follows that kind of loss-influencing event. What pattern tends to follow a sending-off, for example? With one fewer player, the affected team typically adopts a more defensive formation. With less of an attacking focus, teams with a player sent-off typically score fewer goals. Teams with players sent off typically win fewer games than when they play the full match with a full team. Logic says this must all be true. But what does the data say?

At the time of writing, Arsenal have had to finish 90 of their games in the Premier League after receiving a red card. The results of those 90 games were 34 wins (38%), 27 draws (30%) and 29 losses (32%). How does that compare to when they haven't had a player sent-of? Overall, Arsenal have played 1,085 Premier League games, winning 583 (54%), drawing 275 (25%) and losing 227 (21%) of those games[76]. The difference between a 38% and a 54% winning percentage is huge. The more data analysis you can do the better.

Studying likely patterns after LIE events, working out how best to adapt to them and practicing dealing with them can give you a winning advantage. Actively playing for them can change things even more. If, for example, having a player sent off in the first half took a team's average winning percentage down from say 40% to say 20%, you could actively try and exploit that, without any need for cheating. If your team's players ran into the opposition's penalty area more often, it would force

---

[76] This data is for all games. It includes the 90 matches player after having a player sent-off. The winning percentage for matches when no player was sent-off will therefore be a little higher. The difference is already large enough to illustrate the point.

the opposition to tackle your players under pressure. That would increase the chances of the opposition's players conceding yellow and red cards (and therefore getting sent off). You would also be more likely to win free-kicks and penalties, by running into the penalty area more often. Those events would create more opportunities for your team to score the winning goal. By controlling the events that create positive patterns, you can reduce the number of mistakes you make and increase your team's chances of winning. Staying calm and learning as you go are vital to making progress.

> *"I am not perfect and I have made a lot of mistakes. Being an entrepreneur is incredibly lonely. There were many hurdles along the way. From starting out, to making it, and almost losing it, to fighting back, to nearly losing it all again. There have been extreme highs and extreme lows"*[77]

There are plenty of other events that could turn a sporting match. The positive ones are win influencing events (WIE). Scoring the first goal[78] probably increases your chances of winning too. Does the data back that up? The difference it makes to your winning chances might be less than your opponent having a player sent-off, but it will create a pattern that increases your team's chances of winning. Scoring first makes your opponent attack you more, to try and get back into the game. That probably leaves more space for you to counter-attack in. If you know that a particular event often creates a helpful pattern, you could focus your efforts on creating that win influencing event over and over again. You might decide to put a disproportionate effort into scoring an early goal, in every match, if it helps winning enough.

According to an online platform called Hockey-Graphs, scoring first in the National Hockey League gave a 2016 NHL team a 67% chance of winning. Even more interestingly, the team that scored second also had a 67% chance of winning. The logic is that the second score either means one team leading by 2 scores to 0, or it has reversed the momentum to get back to 1 score all. Getting two scores up seems to be far more important that one score up. According to this same site, a 2016 NHL team that was losing 2 scores to 0, only had a 19% chance of winning from that position. Getting 2 v 0 ahead in the NHL can create a very strong chance of winning. Is that the same for competition? And how did the teams losing 2 v 0 come back to win 19% of the time? What patterns did they adopt?

---

[77] Baroness Michelle Mone OBE.
[78] Or point, or try etc..

Studying data on the impact of win influencing and loss influencing events can help you and your team to focus on creating WIE events for your team and avoiding LIE events. Equally it might help you to create LIE events for the opposition and avoid giving them WIE events. Understanding what impact an event or incident has (i.e. what pattern it tends to create) allows you to assess if it's worth trying to prevent it, ignore it or actively make happen. If no relevant data sets or patterns exist, you can study and analyse your own team's patterns. Repeating positive patterns becomes a winning behaviour. Repeating negative ones becomes a losing behaviour. What patterns can you master?

~~~~~

We don't challenge the status quo as often as we should. We tend to go with the flow. We suffer from habituation, which is a 'decrease in response to a stimulus after repeated presentations'. Essentially speaking, we put up with what we're used to. That means that we tolerate losing behaviours and losing standards too easily. We need to challenge ourselves and our team to re-imagine how things need to be done, try new things and see if they help us find our form of success.

Winning teams agree what they will accept and what they will not accept. These are controllables that we need to master. Winning teams agree what they will put up with in order to secure the mission objectives; and equally what they won't put up with because it gets in the way of achieving the mission. These are a set of tolerances. Winning teams have them and they stick to them.

A set of winning tolerances is broader than a set of winning behaviours alone. Each team's winning tolerances will be different. They need to be focused on your mission, philosophy and values. Below is an example of what a set of winning tolerances could look like. This set may be utterly wrong for your organisation and its stakeholders. What do you tolerate and what don't you tolerate? Do each of your tolerances and intolerances contribute to your mission and comply with your values?

THE WINNING TOLERANCES

BE TOLERANT AND INTOLERANT OF THE RIGHT THINGS

BEING UNPREPARED, LOSING BEHAVIOURS, TOO MUCH RED HEART OR BLUE HEAD, A NEGATIVE ATTITUDE • WE DO NOT TOLERATE CHEATING[3], UNCERTAINTY,

CONTINUAL CHANGE & INNOVATION, WINNING BEHAVIOURS, THE WAIT FOR OPPORTUNITIES, RISK[1], THE INDIVIDUALITY OF OTHERS[2] • WE TOLERATE SACRIFICE, LIFE OUTSIDE OUR COMFORT ZONE, CONFLICT[4],

[1] As long as risk is measured, scenario planned and covered.

[2] Individuality all our fellow stakeholders, as long as it doesn't jeopardise the organisation's mission, philosophy or values.

[3] Whether that's cheating yourself, your team or the competition

[4] Whether that's inner conflict or outer conflict, or between missions, values or people

Ultimately everyone needs to focus their own efforts onto the behaviours that make them successful individuals and successful team players (Winning Behaviours). In sharp contrast, everyone needs to minimise the behaviours that hold success back (Losing Behaviours). Any losing behaviours need to be identified and replaced by winning ones.

Our behaviours matter, because whatever we do, or don't do, has consequences for us and our team. If we try an unplanned move that isn't in our team's playbook, our colleagues around us will flounder. If we give away a goal, our whole team will suffer. Every person needs to be aware of their responsibilities to their teammates. That means working hard for them as well as for ourselves. By accepting feedback, we can learn the direct and indirect consequences of our behaviours. Then we can think more carefully about our behavioural choices. We can control the consequences of our actions and omissions more easily, if we know what they are.

Leaders and teammates can stimulate behavioural improvements in their teams and organisations, by explaining how each winning behaviour helps the team. Praising what helps the team, increases the chances of getting the same behaviour next time. This is even more effective where live examples are used to illustrate the point. This form of nudging will increase the number and effect of winning behaviours.

Leaders can also reduce the prevalence of losing behaviours, by explaining how each losing behaviour harms the team or organisation. Linking a player's action to an unwanted outcome, increases the chances of getting a different behaviour next time. Understanding the impact and effect of our actions can persuade us to make positive changes. If we are not sure what to do, or how to improve, there are always people to ask. Pride can stop us reaching out, but we all know what comes after pride. Every team member should look to their teammates who set higher standards and have more winning behaviours than they do. They can try and emulate them.

"Viggo Mortensen had the biggest impact on me in terms of approach, dedication, intention, and artistic outlook, and I'm nowhere close to how good he is as an artist, and I wouldn't even put myself in the same category as an actor"[79]

For every winning behaviour there is an opposing 'losing' behaviour. Those losing behaviours are negative forces which reduce our chances of success. We need to avoid them. For example, a winning behaviour could be 'Excellent communication of instructions to others'. The opposite losing behaviour could be 'Non-existent, confusing or negative communication to others'. By explaining the positive impact of the former and the negative impact of the latter, a person's behaviours can be altered.

As well as winning and losing behaviours there are neutral behaviours. They neither help nor hinder our team. They can't help us to get the win and they may not damage our chances of winning, but if we can turn them into winning behaviours instead, we can move ourselves closer to winning. Every team should establish what its Team Winning Behaviours are. As part of that exercise, be careful not to accept any neutral behaviours. The question to ask is 'Does this help us achieve our mission, do nothing, or hinder us?' If a behaviour doesn't help you, why is an acceptable behaviour?

Start with what you want to win, analyse what gets you closer to winning and what takes you further away from success. Then discuss, debate and draft a set of agreed Team Winning Behaviours. Those Winning Behaviours need to avoid any losing or neutral behaviours. Explaining how each losing behaviour hurts the team will help to stop people from doing it. Explaining how each neutral behaviour can become a winning one can benefit the team.

You can set out in your Team Winning Behaviours, which losing and neutral behaviours need to be avoided. The more clarity you have, the better.

~~~~~

Owners and managers shouldn't just expect winning behaviours from their team. That's not leadership and it's not even management. Leaders should establish and

---

[79] Orlando Bloom, who worked with Viggo Mortensen on 'The Lord of the Rings' as Legolas and Aragorn.

develop a culture and environment which produces winning behaviours. They should recruit people who exhibit and show a passion for winning behaviours. They should build a tribe[80] where every stakeholder helps and every stakeholder benefits. These supportive actions will naturally increase winning behaviours and reduce losing ones. What can be done?

Firstly, by recruiting people with good characters, you can hugely increase the number and frequency of winning behaviours in your team. Tolerating team members with poor characters, tolerates the losing behaviours that go with them. Far too many work interviews concentrate on past working history (which is of limited value), qualifications (which should have been checked already) and skills (which should be tested separately in a practical setting). The impact of character is often under-valued and is certainly under-tested. Often, where there's a role to fill, there's an efficiency pressure to fill it quickly. That creates a rushed starting point, which asks "Is there any reason to say no, or can we just hire them?" That question should be completely reversed. Your organisation's culture should be protected better than that. Instead you should ask yourself "Why should we let this person in?"

~~~~~

Whilst people operate through a wide range of traits and characteristics, there are five core characteristics that consistently tend to generate winning behaviours. None of them come from our genetic make-up. We aren't born with them or predisposed to have them. These five characteristics are all learned, practiced and developed. If you recruit, promote and reward these characteristics, you will continually increase your organisation's use of them. If you actively train and develop them, you will continually increase your team's chances of success. These five traits are the A to E of winning character. Recruit for them and develop them.

Appreciation. This is an appreciation of what you already have, what's around you and what others do for you. It's also an appreciation of what improvements you still have to make as a person. Another word for this might be humility. Appreciation is a mindset that can be strengthened through practice and experience.

Balance. This is the application of even-handedness and fairness across every stakeholder. It's the balancing of effort put in, to reward taken out, for every team member. It's the physical balance between building maximum fitness and

---

[80] I cover how in 'Build Your Super-tribe' and 'Lead Your Super-tribe'.

maintaining a state of calm readiness. It's the mental balancing and agility involved in powering a driving Red Heart and a controlling Blue Head[81]. It's also the balancing of team dynamics so that everyone is highly engaged and high-performing. Balance is a personal and leadership skill that can be learned and developed.

Collaboration. This could also be described as co-operation or partnering. It's the acceptance that you cannot achieve anything much on your own. It's the process of actively seeking collaborations with other people for mutual benefit; and it's the ability to turn your collaborations into winning ones. Collaboration is a skill that can be practiced, improved and developed.

Decision-making. It's the ability to choose exactly what to do and when to do it. It's being tactically astute, taking everyone with you; and perfecting the art of great timing. It's about knowing how to best interpret the competition rules in order to achieve the mission. It's about remaining cool under intense pressure, despite all the external influences and internal doubts. Decision-making is a skill that can be honed and developed.

Endurance. It's having the capability to make it to the winning post in first. It's having the ability to endure any challenge (however long and arduous the journey may be) and finish it strongly. It's also about being mission focused, tolerant of others and selfless. Another word for this might be resilience. Endurance is a skill that can be increased and expanded.

"Don't dream of winning, train for it"[82]

As we've seen, these five A to E characteristics are not based on genetics or predispositions. They are all controllable mindsets. Learning skills takes a willingness to learn and an enduring effort to continually improve them. All these five characteristics can be observed, adopted and adapted. They all improve with practice. That practice increases excellence. These are also strong leadership traits. When applied they will set a good example for others to follow. They can help to bring people and tribes together. They can push a person or a team into a winning position.

---

[81] There is more later, about the relationship between Red Heart and Blue Head.
[82] Mo Farah.

Secondly, as individuals we are all capable of a wide range of characteristics, traits and behaviours. Influencing which ones we choose to use is usually within our organisation's control. Depending on how engaged or disengaged a team member is, their feelings and behaviours will be very different. They might be actively engaged or apathetic, patient or impatient, humble or selfish. They might feel empowered or frustrated, included or rejected, embarrassed or proud. It all depends on how their organisation is treating them. Are their physiological, economic and social needs being met? Most organisations will meet some of those needs, sometimes, but not all of them. Some other organisations won't meet any of them, at any time. If there's no match, there's a mismatch. Mismatches result in losing behaviours and weak performance. By providing a mission, philosophy and culture that matches up to the needs of its people, an organisation can maximise its chances of winning.

So how can an organisation maximise the winning behaviours and minimise the losing ones? Any team or organisation will elicit far more winning behaviours from its people, if it is discharging these eight primary obligations:

1. The mission is clear, meaningful and inclusive; and every stakeholder benefits.
2. Working conditions are safe, ergonomic, modern, comfortable and clean.
3. All the necessary resources are quickly available, fit for purpose; and operate well.
4. Everyone's pay, rewards and treatment are fair and motivating.
5. All opportunities are based on merit (rather than favouritism); and discrimination has no place.
6. Training, development and supervision are constantly provided and actively encouraged.
7. Communication is clear, consistent, inclusive; and motivating.
8. Values & Winning Behaviours are mission focused, help everyone equally; and are fairly enforced.

Provide the eight or leave success to fate

Some will take more time and effort than others, but they are all deliverable. Get all of these eight primary obligations right and your organisation will be far more capable of winning. Failing to provide any of them will reduce the winning behaviours your organisation can generate.

~~~~~

After Liverpool narrowly lost out on the Premier League title by one point in 2018/19, they could have kicked-on or folded. In fact they came back very strongly the following season. Shortly after Liverpool had won that 2019/20 Premier League, James Milner was interviewed on the BBC's 'Match of the Day. He explained how they'd turned it around.

"We've proven that we were fuelled by disappointment and learning and going again the next year. I'm sure the hunger will stay there. We just want to be successful." As a pair of characteristics, learning and hunger are a good combination for positive change and development. Learning and hunger are winning behaviours. What behaviours does your organisation exhibit?

As well as expanding our winning behaviours, we also need to reduce our losing ones. Both processes involve re-focusing on the mission. Every behaviour should start with that. Losing behaviours can be reduced by a change in personal commitment and that normally comes from a clear and motivating mission and an improving organisational culture. Behavioural change is more likely to be successful when it's supported by rules and laws which are actively enforced.

For example, let's take behaviours that cause damage and injuries. There seem to be an ever increasing number of concussions and head injuries in rugby. Sport is supposed to be good for us. It has to be made as safe as realistically possible. Head injuries are particularly horrific. No one wants a player to suffer a concussion and yet that has become more prevalent. Bigger players with bigger hits are doing bigger damage.

Everyone loses out when a player is injured. Firstly, the player suffers pain and disorientation as a minimum. His or her game is over and the player will miss at least one game afterwards, through concussion protocols. But much worse, some rugby players go on to suffer life changing effects from concussion, especially when concussions are repeated. Personality changes can come from head injuries, causing severe difficulties with family relationships and working ones. Those effects needs to be minimised.

The player who caused the injury loses out too. It can't feel good to hurt someone. That guilt impacts on the offending player's state of mind and playing effectiveness. That player may also give away a penalty or get sent-off, causing their team to lose points, if not the game. They may also get banned for more games or get fined. Every player has to learn to control their own behaviours, the good and the bad. We are all responsible for our own acts and omissions.

"Every individual has to become their own captain. They've all got to understand that they have a big duty to be disciplined"[83]

High tackles in rugby are losing behaviours. The frequency and impact of them has to be reduced. As a result of concerns about concussion rates, World Rugby attempted to reduce the number of high tackles at the 2019 Rugby World Cup. It introduced a rule change designed to reduce the height of legal tackles. Those changes were seen as controversial by some, but they were a necessary step. Rugby Union is a great sport, but life outside rugby is much more important than that. Did the experiment work?

Dr. Éanna Falvey Chief Medical Officer for World Rugby (Union) was interviewed about it during the documentary 'Shane Williams: Rugby, Concussion and Me'. Dr. Falvey replied "The risk of concussion is much higher when the tackler tackles high. The person most at risk of concussion is the tackler, not the ball carrier... If we don't lower the height it's very difficult for us to lower the risk. We've seen that when a tackler tackles high-up, they're four and a half times more likely to have a head injury, if they tackle above the armpit. We saw that when there's foul play involved these risks go way higher again. We see that nearly three quarters of the head injury events occur in a tackle. We were able to show a significant reduction in the concussion rate during the World Cup, almost 40% in comparison across all international tournaments. If we use laws and we employ them properly and we get everybody on board, you can use the law to change behaviour."

The experiment worked. The focus of that competition's refereeing allowed for a dramatic reduction in incidents. We can change the rules to change the behaviours.

Takeaway thoughts:
- Push your natural limitations to their maximum limits
- Be completely determined to improve and better yourself
- Focus on closing the gap between where you are and your maximum potential
- Every act of bravery builds your self-confidence
- Time spent outside your comfort zone improves decision-making under pressure
- A commitment to lifelong education is the surest way to grow your potential
- Be tolerant and intolerant of the right things
- Adopt the winning behaviours that your mission needs
- Stop the losing behaviours that prevent success

[83] Former Wigan and Great Britain international rugby league player, Ellery Hanley.

3. BECOMING WIN READY

What kind of win ready you need to be, depends on what competition you're trying to win and what your winning outcomes are. Whatever the competition, getting ready to win it involves some challenging questioning and periods of reflection. Unless you passionately want to win, you won't ever be win ready. Until you understand what winning takes, you won't be win ready. Winning requires a never ending cycle of team-wide analysis. What does winning mean to us? How much do we really want this? What can we improve? What are we missing? How can we be better prepared?

Whatever type of competition it is, achieving anything significant involves a series of multiple actions, multiple omissions and multiple influencing factors. Each input and output affects the outcome in one way or another. Some of these contributing factors are fixed, whilst some are flexible and open to change. If you take away the elements that are fixed (and therefore beyond your control), you are left with the flexible and variable factors (that you can act on, influence and change).

As soon as you strip away (and stop worrying about) the fixed, uncontrollable elements, you can concentrate all your efforts on the elements that you can positively change, the controllable ones. This simple philosophy of focusing on the winning controllables can have the biggest impact on winning. There are five steps:

When facing any challenge, we first need to work out which factors will affect success in our competition? Secondly, we need to split those factors into two camps, which factors are uncontrollable? and which factors are controllable? Thirdly, we need to prioritise the controllables based on which controllables will make the most difference to winning? This helps us to narrow our sights and focus our efforts for competitive advantage. Fourthly, we need to what are the costs and benefits of all those options? Which ones will cost too much? Which one swill take too long? Which can't we do without help? Which options will use up too many resources? Which ones can't we afford? This stage helps us to rule out unrealistic actions and rule in deliverable improvements. Fifthly, with all that knowledge, we can choose which controllables are our winning ones? They are the ones to focus on; and action. By prioritising our actions, we can bring our impact where it's needed most.

Which factors will affect success in our competition?
Which factors are uncontrollable?
and Which factors are controllable?
Which controllables will make the most difference to winning?
What are the costs and benefits of all those options?
Which controllables are our winning ones?

By focusing all your inputs on the winning controllables, all your efforts will positively affect the outputs. What steps will make winning more likely? Which people can be persuaded to become more engaged, more energetic and more eager to help? Which conventions and techniques can be reimagined and improved? Which resources can be used more expertly or more creatively?

Taking a simple example, if you can't reach a box on a high shelf, you cannot grow yourself taller (your height is fixed and uncontrollable). You could try and jump, but unlike the Red Squirrel, human beings cannot leap ten times their body length. If the box is too high to jump up to, the exercise is beyond your physical limits. So what else can you do? You could use a ladder, or solid object to stand on. Or you could get something to reach up and grab the item with.

If you don't have a ladder, box or grabbing arm; and you don't have the time to go out and buy one, you are limited by that position. Those options have become uncontrollable factors. So think again. What else can you do? What isn't fixed? You could ask someone else to reach it for you. Alternatively, you could throw something to knock the item off, or more radically you could pull the shelves off the wall or you could even knock the whole wall down. All of these will get the item down from the shelf. They are all solutions are within your control. They all have different costs and risks. Which one is the best one for you? How desperately do you want to get the item down?

We should stop focusing on what we can't do;
and focus on what we can

Working out what cannot be controlled or changed is vital. We need to exclude those apparent options, as they aren't options at all. Assessing all the remaining (and therefore possible) solutions is where our time should be spent. Assessing which of them offer us the best chance of success allows us to be the most competitive we can. Once we have our priorities, we need to calculate the cost of each option as that helps to ensure that we chose the best option for an overall, rounded win.

Where competition and winning is concerned, I have discovered that eleven key controllables are consistently present. All eleven of them can be continuously honed, developed and improved.

If you, your team or your organisation master all of these eleven controllables you will be win ready. However, if one or more of these eleven controllables is ignored or undercooked, you won't be fully win ready.

GET WIN READY
HOW WINNING IS REALLY DONE

3.1   WINNING MISSION

The first winning controllable is mission. A clear and agreed mission dictates what success will be achieved. Every organisation needs a clear, agreed, central purpose for its existence. That purpose should be clear. Every member of every organisation should be able to easily recite their organisation's purpose. It's the answer to the question 'Why does our organisation exist?'

An organisation's central purpose should be its raison d'etre, its reason for being. That purpose could be supporting a vulnerable group in society, winning a sporting trophy, increasing bottom line profits, making great products, saving lives or something completely different. There are many possible reasons for an organisation to exist. By knowing what the purpose is, we can work out how to achieve it. If we can't tell what success looks like, we are very unlikely to find it. If we don't know why we're bothering, then we won't.

"A small body of determined spirits, fired by an unquenchable faith in their mission, can alter the course of history"[84]

Fulfilling that core purpose is an organisation's mission. Having a core mission, based on that central purpose, provides a focal point for action and decision-making. Without a clear mission, no one can be sure where to focus their efforts. You can't create Winning Standards or Winning Team Behaviours without a mission to base them on. Working without a core driving mission is a very inefficient way of operating. Where there is uncertainty about a team's purpose, you tend to get confusion, disengagement and losing behaviours.

In contrast, where there's a clear mission an organisation can focus all of its efforts on delivering it. All tribes and Super-tribes have a defining purpose[85]. Lesser groups do not. Operating without one creates a potentially fatal flaw.

"To organise the world's information and make it universally accessible and useful"[86]

---

[84] Mahatma Ghandi.
[85] I have explained how fundamental this is to tribe building, in 'Build Your Super-tribe' and also 'Lead Your Super-tribe'.
[86] Google's declared purpose.

The presence of a unifying mission will enormously increase the chances of success. Similarly, the lack of a unifying mission dramatically reduces the chances of winning. An organisation's central purpose should be its raison d'etre, its reason for being. That purpose could be winning a sporting trophy, increasing bottom line profits, saving lives or something completely different. There are many reasons for a team to exist. Each purpose demands an individual and tailored approach. By knowing what the purpose is, we can work out how to achieve it. If we can't tell what success looks like, we are very unlikely to find it. If we don't know why we're bothering, we won't.

Designer Wayne Hemingway MBE of 'Red or Dead' and 'HemingwayDesign' fame[87] is certain that we have to find our motivation for getting involved in any project. I asked him for a single word, phrase or sentence to summarise the most important reason behind success. Wayne's response was the single word 'Purpose'. That's where winning begins. Without a shared purpose, any mission will falter. It's the word that matters most.

~~~~~

In November 2020, 'Deadpool' Actor Ryan Reynolds and US television sitcom actor Rob McElhenney[88] bought Wrexham football club. If there had been a list of unlikely acquisitions of 2020, this deal would have been right up there. Why was it so unlikely? Because there was absolutely no link or no family connection between the two American actors and Wrexham. The only link is a tenuous twitter exchange in 2012, about the chances of Ryan visiting Wrexham. Eight years later this happened and Ryan tweeted "I've waited 8 years to respond to this tweet".

Buying the local football club seems a bit excessive, but the pair's Mission Statement indicated a genuine commitment to the club's name and heritage, as well as the prospect of much needed investment. Within it, the mission is clearly set out. "Our goal is to grow the team, return it to the EFL[89] in front of increased attendances at an improved stadium while making a positive difference to the wider community in Wrexham."

---

[87] Wayne runs HemingwayDesign. He is also a member of the Design Council Trustee Board and an advisor to House of Commons Select Committees on coastal regeneration.
[88] Rob McElhenney stars in the hit sitcom 'It's Always Sunny in Philadelphia',
[89] At the time of writing, Wrexham A.F.C. play in the Vanarama National League, one division below the start of the English Football League.

There are then four 'Guiding Principles' and thirteen 'Hard Promises.' The second Guiding Principle is 'To reinforce the values, traditions and legacy of this community. We understand and respect the intense loyalty and love for this club and how it's woven into the fabric of the town and its supporters.' This a pledge full of respect and an indication of good faith. One of the hard promises, 'Always beat Chester' is repeated three times, which will have gone down well with Wrexham supporters.

The club's stakeholders were told in advance what the new owners were promising. The previous owner, The Wrexham Supporters' Trust was convinced that the club would remain in safe hands. Ryan and Rob were trusted to deliver on their Mission Statement. The club's stakeholders (supporters, staff, coaches, players, sponsors, suppliers, local authority and community leaders) have to support Ryan and Rob in their ongoing efforts to improve the club. If all the club's stakeholders stay behind the mission, it has far more chance of success. Whilst at the same time, those same stakeholders need to hold Ryan and Rob to their promises. This isn't mission impossible, it's a very achievable goal, that you'd expect them to score.

~~~~

Mission statements are everywhere. Understanding why they exist is revealing. That can explain how likely one is to be delivered. Some are very personal. In the 2017 film Wonder Woman, Diana Prince leaves the safety of Amazon life on Themyscira to face life during the Second World War. After spending time amid the politicians, she travels to the front and witnesses the chaos, suffering and death. Her fictional bravery helps to turn the war in favour of the Allies. At the end of the film, Diana reflects on what's happened and her purpose in life.

"I used to want to save the world. To end war and bring peace to mankind. But then, I glimpsed the darkness that lives within their light. I learned that inside every one of them, there will always be both. The choice each must make for themselves - something no hero will ever defeat. I've touched the darkness that lives in between the light. Seen the worst of this world, and the best. Seen the terrible things men do to each other in the name of hatred, and the lengths they'll go to for love. Now I know. Only love can save this world. So I stay. I fight, and I give... for the world I know can be. This is my mission, now. Forever"

This is of course deliberately grandiose for movie purposes. Despite that, there's an important underlying point. It's our experiences that shape us. If we can use those experiences to shape our mission, then we will come at it from a position of knowledge, strength and passion. Powered by an inner purpose, we are far more likely to achieve our mission goals.

~~~~~

Every organisational mission has to inspire and motivate the whole organisation to make it happen. There has to be 'mission appeal'. The first element of an appealing mission is that it has to enhance and improve the organisation, not weaken it. Secondly, a successful mission should maintain, if not increase, the rewards it offers to every stakeholder and their loved ones. That's not just about money, it's about health, happiness and wellbeing too.

"We are a global organisation that is socially and environmentally responsible, *that embraces creativity and diversity and is* financially rewarding *for our employees and shareholders"*[90]

The third element of mission appeal is the future protection and sustainability of all the organisation's stakeholders (including its employees, customers, funders and suppliers), its infrastructure, its environment and its community. Any mission that jeopardises the organisation's ability to operate, may be the wrong mission. Fourthly, an appealing mission has to achieve something worthwhile, something that's worth the sacrifice.

~~~~~

If anyone asks "Have we achieved our mission yet?" every team member should know the answer. And if that answer is "No" then everyone should know exactly what remains to be done. That is only possible when an organisation lays out its mission statement at the outset and keeps its stakeholders regularly updated on progress. No one should have to ask the frustrating question "Are we nearly there yet?" Every stakeholder should already know the answer.

Where an organisation has several things it wants to achieve, that can create confusion around the central mission. Don't ever let confusion reign. There

---

[90] Adidas mission statement.

should always be one central, driving mission. There can be secondary goals, but they should always play second fiddle to the core mission.

A mission is a clear, unambiguous, inclusive and inspirational quest. If yours isn't, then it needs to be. Your mission literally has to be fit for purpose. It has to fulfil your organisation's core purpose. To generate tribal power, it has to appeal to every stakeholder in it. A mission also has to be aspirational but achievable. It has to be easily distilled into a few words or phrases. It needs to be easily measurable, so that clear updates can be provided. Do every stakeholder know what's been achieved? Does everyone stakeholder know exactly what needs to be done to complete the mission?

Not understanding what's going on is irritating and demotivating. Our organisations owe us the opportunity to be part of something collective and inclusive. They should include us in a joint enterprise, rather than making us an insignificant cog, in an unknown wheel. A shared and compelling purpose is what lifts us all higher. Every team can build engagement around a central mission, simply by letting every stakeholder in. If your current organisation is successful, then it probably has a mission that you can get behind. You may have to dig for it, but there should be one at its heart. The declared mission may be to make high-quality products, improve lives, reduce pollution, create customer satisfaction or anything else. Whatever it is, it should be easily said and easily understood.

Starbucks understands the difference between purpose and mission and the link between the two. Starbucks defines its core purpose as "To establish Starbucks as the premier purveyor of the finest coffee in the world while maintaining our uncompromising principles while we grow." And it goes on to define its related mission as being "To inspire and nurture the human spirit — one person, one cup and one neighborhood at a time." That mission is aspirational, but every stakeholder in the business can help it to be realised, by approaching it one person, one cup and one neigbourhood[91] at a time.

~~~~~

Once the purpose and the mission have been established, you need to test the connection between them. There needs to be direct and genuine link between the core purpose and its mission in order to build engagement and persuade every stakeholder to drive the mission outcomes.

---

[91] The English spelling.

Try asking, "Does the mission deliver the essence of our purpose? Then try the reverse "What's the real purpose behind this mission?" Is it really to [saves lives or make customers satisfied etc.], or is it something else?

Remember that every stakeholder will be subconsciously testing their organisation's decisions against its stated purpose and mission. Are they consistent and genuine? Or are they serving a secret and controlling purpose, which is only focused on making profits?

"You've got to find a place of your own
Before they carve your name on a stone
You've got to lift yourself up from the ground"[92]

If the true driving purpose is simply about making money for the organisation's owners; and you're an owner, then that will motivate you. But it won't motivate anyone who can't be an owner. It's deluded to think otherwise. Will stakeholders just accept whatever job they're given and get on with it? The answer is that some may, but many workers want to know what their organisation stands for, what it is really trying to do.

To get everyone's buy-in, the purpose needs to be inclusive, engaging and authentic and the mission needs to reflect all that. Everyone can see straight through a fake mission that has nothing in it for them.

~~~~~

As human beings we owe it to ourselves to be involved in a compelling mission. Becoming part of a tribe (or Super-tribe) is good for us. Collaboration is good for social belonging and mental health. The opposite, antagonistic working, is bad for us. That could stem from the wrong purpose, the wrong mission or the wrong team for us.

We need to find a cause that fires us up, one that makes us willingly sacrifice ourselves to it. In his highly successful book "The 7 Habits of Highly Successful People," Stephen Covey recommends that we should write a personal mission statement. We should look to achieve a mission of our own. This is based on his second 'habit' which is "Begin with the end in mind." That's the whole point of a

---

[92] 'Please Please, Please' by Sleeper.

107

mission. It is outcome focused. With a specific mission in mind, success can be measured and achieved.

"Outstanding people have one thing in common: an absolute sense of mission"[93]

Having a set of personal goals can get the best out of your time and performance. Successful people tend to set themselves clear goals as a form of personal mission statement. By setting out your personal goals you can see whether they match your organisation's goals. If they do, it can help you to explain the merits of them to others, to build their engagement. They help us to choose which tribes we should be part of.[94] If your goals and beliefs don't match up, that might explain why you're not doing your very best work there. You can ask yourself:

1. What goals do I want to achieve and by when? - Can I achieve them here in my organisation?

2. Do I want to achieve personal successes or team ones? - Can I achieve my team ones here?

3. What impact do I want to make on other people? - Can I make that impact here?

4. What impact do I want to make on the World? - Can I make this impact in my organisation?

5. What's my legacy going to be? - Can I achieve it in my organisation?

If you have a personal mission statement, it will keep you focused on what you're trying to achieve. Check it against your organisation's published purpose and mission, as well as any secret purpose or mission it has. Hopefully there is consistency across them all. Having a personal philosophy helps to keep us focused on what we need; and keeps us asking why we are doing what we do.

The same questions apply to every stakeholder in a team or organisation. Hopefully every stakeholder can find a personal match with their organisation's purpose and mission. If so, all of those people will be motivated to deliver the mission together. Collaborative working makes emotional, economic and social sense when the mission matches every stakeholder's needs. When the match is strong it can create a

---

[93] American author and motivational speaker Hilary Hinton "Zig" Ziglar.
[94] For more, see 'Build Your Super-tribe'.

tribal wave of support. When the match is widespread beyond your organisation, it can create a Super-tribal wave of support.

However, when there's a mismatch it can be disastrous, especially when that happens at a leadership level. The mission has to be shared and every stakeholder has to be aligned to it. When it's not clear what the mission is, you haven't got a chance.

"So. The food was SHOCKING, below par, disgusting, dated shit... What do you mean you don't have a Head Chef?!! ...What you're employing is a ship with no captain at the helm and the team desperate for guidance. No guidance is no standards. No standards is no consistency"[95]

The World doesn't fit together like a jigsaw puzzle. Being realistic, there will always be a degree of conflict, inconsistency and disengagement with your organisation's stakeholders. A double question analysis is needed. Firstly 'What is conflicting with the mission?' Secondly 'What change is needed?'

You might find that your organisation's purpose doesn't match your own, or its mission doesn't motivate you to positive action. If you have little or no investment in your organisation's mission, you either need to change that mission from the inside, or you need to leave. Having people on board who are not committed to delivering the mission will always reduce the chances of success. If those people are in key roles that effect is amplified. If it's you that feels like that, then do something about it.

~~~~~

Nigella Lawson is a household name cook and television presenter. Nigella doesn't just cook for commercial purposes, her motivations are much wider.

"Even if you love cooking as I do, it cannot always calm, but it does much else that is so very necessary: it imposes order; gives us purpose; unleashes creativity; sustains us bodily and emotionally. So often in the past it has been written about as a hobby, when it is the thing that underpins life."[96]

---

[95] Gordon Ramsey OBE on 'Ramsay's Kitchen Nightmares USA.
[96] The Sunday Times Style Magazine, from 2020.

That is a very powerful philosophy and a persuasive commendation for learning to cook, to cook more or to start a career in cooking. In fact it's a mission statement for cooks and chefs the World over.

~~~~~

In 1838, Grace Darling looked out of her bedroom window and saw a ship had crashed into Big Harcar Rock. As the daughter of the Longstone Lighthouse keeper Grace immediately told her father and together they rowed out to help.

The SS Forfarshire had crashed and was wrecked on the rocks. There were passengers who needed to be rescued. Some missions are simple to explain. Carrying them out is often something different. Sometimes extreme bravery is needed. To save a life, you sometimes have to risk your own. That is an incredible ask of anyone and yet some people bravely step up without thought for themselves. For that you need a higher purpose than your own interests or self-preservation. Finding a sense of higher purpose can be incredibly motivating. We need to feel the heat of passion in order to feel brave. We need to find the sweet-spot where what we feel and what we do dovetail neatly together.

"Explore this next great frontier where the boundaries between work and higher purpose are merging into one, where doing good is really good for business"[97]

The mile journey to the rocks was fraught with danger. They only had a small rowing boat (called a coble) and there were ferocious waves and powerful winds. Despite the immense struggle, Grace and her father managed to reach the rocks and rescue four people. Then, as she and her mother tended the injured, her father and two crew men went back for the others. Between them they rescued a total of nine people off the rocks.

The mission to save lives was accomplished and their reward was saving nine of them. Grace's efforts were also rewarded with a medal for bravery and gifts from admirers[98]. Grace Darling didn't row out into danger for glory or medals, she rowed out to save lives. It gave her the physical and mental strength to face all her fears and carry on regardless. Sadly Grace died of tuberculosis four years later,

---

[97] Sir Richard Branson.
[98] Amongst the gifts, Queen Victoria sent her £50.

110

but her memory lives on in the RNLI Grace Darling Museum in Bamburgh, Northumberland.

~~~~~

Missions come in all shapes and sizes. One of the most ambitious ones is to climb Mount Everest. At 8,844.43 metres tall, Mount Everest is the World's tallest mountain. Since Tenzing Norgay Sherpa of Nepal and Sir. Edmund Hillary first scaled it in 1953, 5,780 different people have managed to reach its summit[99]. With a current World population of over 8 billion people, those climbers have been a miniscule proportion of society. And some of those climbers have managed to get safely up and down more than once. Kami Rita Sherpa of Nepal has reached the summit the most. How many times is that? It's an astonishing twenty-four.

Setting 'Climbing Everest' as your mission is clear and unambiguous. It allows every effort to be focused on achieving that single goal. As it has been done before, there is a process to copy and apply Winning Standards to. You need to take time to plan for this kind of mission. You need a licence, a guide and a rescue team (three of the absolute necessities) as well as all the equipment. Training and preparation take many months. The cost of an attempt totals somewhere in between £60,000 and £100,000. Then there's the climb itself.

Most expeditions to Everest take around two months to complete. Climbers start arriving at the mountain's base camps in late March. They need to acclimatise before they can hope to make the climb. Then the ascent has to be attempted within the narrow climbing season of 'mid-May' (an uncontrollable reality) because the temperatures in May are briefly warmer and the winds are not so strong. The first challenge is to make it safely to base camp, which is 5,300 metres up and sits at the foot of an icefall (which is the first major climbing obstacle). Then there is the progressive climbing process, up and back and up and back until on Summit day, the final climb begins at around midnight. Climbers aim to be on the summit in the morning, with plenty of daylight left to get down again before nightfall. All told it is an extraordinary endeavour that fewer than 5,780 people can feel extraordinarily proud of.

---

[99] As of June 2020.

"It's not the mountains that we conquer but ourselves"[100]

In 1953, the equipment was fundamentally different to today. Science and technology have dramatically increased safety through improved climbing gear, sleeping equipment, nutrition and rescue helicopters, as well as the invention of weather predictors and satellite communication systems. The climbing experience itself has also improved. Unlike Tenzing Norgay and Edmund Hillary's time, climbers can now go up on high-end luxury packages to Everest. They can include five Sherpas per climber to carry comfortable tents, bedding, shower equipment and spare bottles of oxygen[101]. But however much the Everest experience might be easier than it was, it is still an incredible undertaking. The combination of too many inexperienced climbers and unpredictable weather leads to multiple deaths every year. Many people don't complete the climb and over 300 people are believed to have died on Everest. Personal preparation is a controllable that all climbers have to get right, perhaps in this endeavour above all others.

Age appears to be no boundary to this kind of mission. Japanese alpine skier, Yuichiro Miura, was 70 years old when he climbed Everest in 2003. Then he had two heart surgeries in 2006 and 2007, before climbing Everest again in 2008. Later, after his age record of 75 was beaten by an older Nepali climber, Miura reclaimed his title in 2013, by reaching the summit at the age of 80.[102] Miura has described his diet as healthy eating that included organic food. He set himself high winning standards and reportedly trained by walking with 5kg on each leg and 30kg on his back. Whatever prepares you best for your mission.

Most missions are far easier than 'Climbing Everest' but the same focus and preparation should apply to them all. Setting off ill-prepared on any mission heavily reduces your chances of success. Understanding what inputs your mission requires is absolutely essential. What aspects of the mission are within your control?

The mission of Climbing Everest involves a mixture of controllables and uncontrollables. The uncontrollables include the mountain's height and shape, the terrain, the narrow time window for climbing, the need for a licence to climb and the unpredictable weather. The controllables include your fitness and training,

---

[100] Sir Edmund Percival Hillary KG ONZ KBE.
[101] Information from an article by Pradeep Bashya on the BBC website.
[102] Some people dispute this climb because he had to be airlifted off the mountain before descending, but this is still remarkable.

your climbing experience, your knowledge of the mountain and likely weather conditions, your choice of guide and your selection of equipment.

When others have carried out the same mission before you, tap into their knowledge and experience. You can learn from those have succeeded and those that haven't. Where your mission is new, learn what you can from those who have attempted similar endeavours. Don't be afraid to ask. It's much easier to ask for help before you start, than during the course of your mission.

~~~~~

Arguably the most famous "successful failure" is the 1970 Apollo 13 mission to the moon. With a mission motto of "Ex luna, scientia" (meaning From the Moon, knowledge) the Apollo space shuttle was focused on carrying out a series of scientific experiments on the Moon. The level of financial investment in the expedition was absolutely colossal. The pressure on the space and ground crews to deliver new scientific discoveries was just as big.

However, the Apollo 13 never got to land on the moon and there were no new scientific discoveries. An oxygen tank 'failed' two days into the mission. Suddenly those important science experiments were secondary. Three crew were in mortal jeopardy. Three lives had to be saved. The Apollo 13's mission had to be switched from a scientific lunar landing, to a deep space rescue. That was a fundamental shift of mission, with no advance notice. Everyone involved must have panicked. This was never part of the plan.

The new mission was simple "Get the crew home safely". But it was fiendishly difficult to achieve, with such limited resources and time. The need to re-focus and re-engage was critical to saving those three lives. Adapting quickly to the new mission could make all the difference between success and disaster. The struggle to get these astronauts home was the subject of the 1995 film 'Apollo 13' starting Tom Hanks. How would everyone respond to the extreme stress and uncertainty?

Robb Stark "When I gathered my Lords together, we had a purpose, a mission. Now we're like a band of bickering children"

Talisa Stark "Give them a new purpose"

The cause of the incident was the harmless stirring of an oxygen tank. That innocent action had accidentally ignited a damaged piece of wire insulation inside the tank. The resulting fire caused an explosion. That vented the contents of the service module's oxygen tanks straight out into space and rendered them useless. That oxygen was critical for both breathing and for generating electric power. Without it the service module's propulsion and life support systems couldn't operate. Tough decisions had to be taken urgently and wisely.

Without a clear focus on getting the crew home, valuable time and resources could be lost. They included the decision to shut down the command module's systems, to conserve its remaining resources for re-entry. This forced the three crew members inside the lunar module. Both oxygen and time were running out. The lunar module was cramped, cold and damp. The oxygen supply for the lunar module was designed to support two men on the Moon for two days. There were three men and time was not on their side. The mission control team on Earth worked endlessly around the clock, to find a workable solution to bring the crew back home alive.

Improvising with only what the crew had on the shuttle, the mission control team on Earth created a brand new process for the oxygen supply. As a result, the lunar module could now support three men for four days. But the danger was far from over there. There was also the need to remove the carbon dioxide that was building up around them. Once again, mission control improvised, by adapting the equivalent equipment on the ground and then talking the crew through how to adapt the cartridges on board.

The crew had to make these unscheduled adaptations in dark, cramped conditions, without the help of gravity. The pressure to make the correct changes to the equipment was enormous. Every step had to be taken through a remote collaboration, across thousands of miles of space. Without creating and sharing ideas, the mission was doomed to failure.

"Spread ideas" [103]

A sense of fear must have impacted on everyone concerned. To add to this, there was the shortage of oxygen and safe drinking water. One crew member managed to fill some drinking bags with water from the command module before the crew decamped into the lunar module, but that wasn't enough on its own. Their survival needed multiple wins. Firstly, maximising the air and water available, as they were finite and dropping fast. Survival also meant directing Apollo 13

---

[103] TED's declared purpose.

around the moon (like a slingshot) and re-positioning it for re-entry into the Earth's atmosphere. This required extraordinary calculations and extraordinary judgement on board the shuttle. All of these processes had to be done successfully. At every stage, the quality of decision-making on the ground and inside the cramped shuttle had to be incredibly high. If the crew came back alive it would be something close to a miracle.

Despite all the extensive preparations before launch, Apollo 13 had not been win ready. The investigation board later found fault with the pre-flight testing and the presence of Teflon inside the oxygen tank. The mission was in jeopardy from the moment of take-off. But despite the technical flaws, the shuttle crew on board was ready to adapt and fight for its survival. The recruitment process had assembled the highest calibre of people. The mission commander on board, Jim Lovell, was on his fourth spaceflight and his calming experience proved critical. The training of the crew had been extensive, at over 1,000 hours. And over 400 of those hours had involved flight simulations and scenario planning in various problem situations. Critically, those practice sessions included using the lunar module as a 'lifeboat' if needed.

The crew's dress rehearsals for danger continually put the crew outside its comfort zone and practiced many eventualities. The crew's ability to problem-solve and adapt to change was substantially enhanced. Scenario planning was a great way to train the crew for difficult scenarios. After long hours of training, the crew developed a resilience that supported them in their efforts to return home. The mission training programme proved itself to be win ready.

Once the lunar module had landed safely in the South Pacific Ocean, an investigation began immediately. The review board considered all the lessons from the Apollo 13 mission. The board recommended a series of changes which were implemented for the Apollo 14 mission. Those changes made Apollo 14 a safe and successful mission. Learning the lessons from every failed mission makes winning the next one far more likely.

~~~~~

For some organisations their mission isn't about glory and medals, it's about their own sustainability and survival. No organisation is guaranteed success of any kind, whatever its past history. Every type of organisation needs to be sustainable, month on month, year on year. Every organisation has the daily challenge of generating sufficient revenue to 'balance the books'.

That's more difficult when an organisation has different teams, departments or divisions. In a sporting context, a club has a playing side and a commercial side. They involved different people, different skills and different priorities. On the one hand, the playing side needs to win enough games to fill the club's stadium on match days. That's because the club needs enough success to make fans proud to buy match tickets and merchandise. In turn, the commercial side of the club needs to make the merchandise relevant, attractive and affordable.

The two halves of the club have a symbiotic relationship. Each side could be too 'tribal' and forget the other side's needs. Each half should think 'club first' and work closely with the other to achieve the club's mission. That mission needs to be inclusive enough to appeal to both halves.

"Remember upon the conduct of each, depend the fate of all"[104]

Turning a mission statement into a diagram can help everyone see all its elements. Below is an example of a sporting club mission diagram. It takes all the elements of sustainable success required by a theoretical sporting club, with two distinct 'divisions' (playing and non-playing), to achieve what are joint goals. Most organisations contain different teams, departments and divisions, so the principle is transferable.

Both sides of the club have a role to play in every element. The non-playing commercial side has to provide a major input into every element, with the possible exception of the very bottom one. That's the domain of the playing side at the club. It is the role of the playing-side to achieve on-field success, which supports and drives all the other elements. Supporters buy more tickets and merchandise when the team is winning. And in turn, the playing side needs all the other elements in place to be able to produce that on-field success. The relationship between the playing and non-playing departments is symbiotic. The club cannot be successful without both halves coming together to become one whole.

Once you've created a mission diagram for your organisation, you could also colour-code each element to indicate who has responsibility for delivering it. Some responsibilities will be individual, but very many will be shared. That offers everyone a repeated reminder about the need for continuous collaboration.

---

[104] Alexander the Great.

Copyright © Simon James Rhodes

3.2   WINNING PHILOSOPHY

The second controllable is a winning philosophy. A clear and agreed philosophy dictates how success will be achieved. A controlling philosophy provides a method of approaching every action and event. Having the right controlling philosophy for your competition gets you much closer to winning. Every organisation needs an overarching approach and style to operate by.

Picking the right philosophy for the challenge ahead is crucial. Going in all guns blazing, when a diplomatic solution is quicker and easier, points to the wrong approach. Appealing to people's heads, while leaving their hearts unmoved, won't create the social movement you want to inspire. Playing a highly defensive game when you're already 2 v 0 down, might remove any chance of winning. Choose wisely 'how' to go about your mission. Having the right controlling philosophy gets you much closer to winning. Employing the wrong one gets you much closer to losing. That's true in sport, business and every other kind of organisation.

"We decided that sports, lifestyle and fashion were three elements that could be mixed together to a very unique formula. That's what we did: make Puma a very sports-fashion brand when, at the time, everybody talked about sports and sports performance and functionality. We said, 'Well, it's about more'."[105]

~~~~

---

[105] Jochen Zeitz at Puma.

118

When a team is faced with competition, it needs to find a competitive advantage in order to be successful. Deciding which approach to employ is a strategic question, but it's also one of philosophy. In business, if you want to get ahead of the competition, you need to offer something that your competitors don't. That means offering at least one of the following:

higher quality, lower cost, more choice, greater comfort or convenience, more personalisation, faster delivery, extra features; and/or products or services that are rare or niche (if not unique).

Every organisation has to decide which of these differentiators it wants to back. This is a choice about which competitive edge will work best; but it's also a choice about what kind of organisation you want to be. Your philosophy should match the competitive edge you're trying to create. Your philosophical approach will underpin all your decision-making.

Your choice of philosophy will heavily influence your choice of business strategy and vice versa

A commercial approach would ask "Which of these will give us the greatest competitive advantage?"
An ambitious approach would ask "Which allows us to grow the fastest?"
A mercenary approach would ask "Which option will make us the most money?"
A moral approach would ask "Which option does the most good and the least damage?"
A tribal approach would ask "Which option is best for all of our stakeholders?"
A Super-tribal approach would ask "Which option is the best for everyone?"
A flexible approach would ask "Which option are we trying out first?"
A philosophical approach asks "What type of organisation do we really want to be?"

Your chosen philosophy can be a single approach or a blend of approaches. That's up to you and your organisation's stakeholders to decide. Remember to align your competitive and philosophical approaches to your organisation's mission? Your philosophy shouldn't stand alone, it should always be mission focused. Will it make us more likely to win? Will it suit all our stakeholders? Will they all get behind it? Think widely and choose wisely.

~~~~~

Sometimes a philosophy comes from a belief in the way things should be done. Sometimes a winning philosophy comes from choosing a way to operate and making it so successful that results persuade you to adopt it permanently. Sometimes the belief and the results feeds each other.

In football, a team's balance of attack and defence is key to its success. When Pep Guardiola joined Manchester City as its Manager, he immediately altered the club's playing philosophy. Shifting from a more conservative and restricted approach (which had achieved some success) Pep sought to find a higher level of performance and inspire the club's supporters. So he set about constructing a more attacking team; and introduced what he calls 'Total Football.' In practice it means driving up skill levels across the squad and developing players who can play in more than one position. According to Pep a defender can't just tackle and head the ball away, he she or they has to be able to pass really well too. This sounds obvious, but that was a big ask in the English game at the time. The passing skills of goalkeepers and defenders was very limited and prone to error.

"It's about winning. If you're challenging for the championship, the people above and the supporters will stick with you. If you are not, then they look at the football. If that's not right, then you're under pressure. But in the end, it's about winning"[106]

Total Football required higher skill levels than Manchester City (or anyone else in English football) had been able to achieve previously. It risked more mistakes, including giving the ball away close to the team's own goal. But with greater risk can come greater reward. Pep's philosophy was to drive a higher level of performance above his competitors. The Manchester City players started to work the ball forward from defence more. The team attacked whenever possible. Not every player was good enough, but everyone had to try. About his philosophy, Pep wryly said "We concede a lot but we score a lot (more)." In his first season (2016-2017) there were too many costly mistakes. The players weren't good enough or ready enough to make the system work. Manchester City finished in third, fifteen points behind Chelsea. The philosophy had worked in Spain and Germany, but not in England. The big question was should Pep stick with his philosophy?

---

[106] Joe Jordan, formerly of Leeds United.

"We believe it's about much more than winning. The message isn't "win, win, win". Winning is the result of how you play. The philosophy is the most important thing"[107]

Although Pep's belief in his system must have been sorely tested during that first English season, there was no change of heart. Pep just had to be realistic. Not every Manchester City player was good enough could play Total Football. So he signed some new players who were. They would go on to prove that his system worked. In Pep's second season (2017-2018), Manchester City controlled the ball much better. They dominated possession. Manchester City won the Premier league at a canter, with 100 points (the first time it had ever been done) nineteen points ahead of their biggest rivals Manchester United in second place. They also scored 106 goals compared to only 27 conceded. Total Football totally dominated.

In his third season, Manchester City won the Premier league by a single point from Liverpool. This wasn't because Manchester City had hugely dropped their form, it was because Liverpool had observed and taken on the challenge of playing a more attacking brand of football. Liverpool had adapted their own philosophy and style of play. Both teams had a clear philosophy and had heavily invested in the players to deliver it. Both teams were exceptionally good. Chelsea, who finished in third, were twenty-five points behind Liverpool. It was a two-horse race. Total Football had won again. In fact, Liverpool's own version of Total Football was so good that the club won the 2019 Champions League. The two big winners of 2018-2019 played an attack-first brand of football, passing their opponents to a standstill.

Pep's Manchester City won the Premier league, but they lost in the semi-final of the Champions League to Tottenham (who went on to lose to Liverpool in the final). Pep must have been devastated. However when he was interviewed, he returned to his philosophy. "Of course we have to improve but the way we play we've scored 154 goals, the way we play with a good game for everyone here and around the World we're not going to change." The loss hurt deeply, but it didn't challenge Pep's philosophy. Sticking to your principles is brave, unless you're right, in which cases it's the best option. When success doesn't come, make sure you re-think your philosophy. Is it the right one? Review and stress-test it regularly.

---

[107] Xavi, former Barcelona player under Pep Guardiola from "Take the ball, Pass the ball: The Making of the Greatest Team".

Every Manchester City player and supporter wants to win the Champions League, but they also absolutely love Pep Guardiola and his 'Total Football'. If and when Pep wins the Champions League playing total football, they will love him like no other manager in the club's history. Cruelly for Pep, the club was banned from the competition for two years, for an alleged breach of the FIA Fair Play rules. But that decision was overturned. Now we will get to see whether Pep proves that Total Football can win the Champions League for Manchester City. Only time will tell, but I wouldn't bet against it, if they stick to total football.

In the 2019/20 Champions League, Manchester City inexplicably chose to play a more conservative brand of football against Lyon in the quarter-final. The sudden switch of tactics saw them beaten 3 v 1 at home and knocked out of the competition. Manchester City have lots of fantastic attacking players, but against Lyon, most of them were left out of the starting team. Total Football is a winning philosophy, but only if you buy into it totally.

The 2019-2020 Premier League season had to be paused because of the Coronavirus Pandemic. With twenty-nine of thirty eight games played, Liverpool led the table by twenty-five points from Manchester City (having played one more game). Liverpool's brand of total football was dominating and they went on to win the Premier League at a canter, having own the Champions League the previous season. Both Manchester City and Liverpool have now proven that introducing a more demanding philosophy can produce higher-performance levels. Total Football wins. So does a multi-skilled approach to work generally.

Pushing up expectations and skills can benefit every organisation. But that process of adapting has a lead-in time. During the transition period, more mistakes might happen and doubt can creep in. A high-skill philosophy requires people who are capable of raising their games to the meet those new standards. If the people you have aren't able to perform at the higher-level, mistakes will happen too regularly to win anything. If the teaching, support and training isn't good enough, too many mistakes will happen. Monitoring and assessing why mistakes are happening is critically important. Working on how to reduce them is vital. Having an agreed philosophy is only the start.

Ultimately, driving up skills will lead to greater performance levels and greater success. Introducing a demanding philosophy requires faith, time and adjustment. Backing it wholeheartedly is the only way to ensure it works. If anyone stops believing along the way, they might become the very reason that prevents it from working (ironically proving their own doubts were correct).

Nothing is guaranteed or 'meant to be,' But having a philosophy for success can provide a reason to believe. It brings a rationale to kick-off a mission. If it proves successful then it builds a conviction. "We are better than everyone else because of our philosophy. That's why we're winning. Trust in the system". Believing that a philosophy will bring success makes that success more likely. A strong collective belief in your team's philosophy will give you positive momentum towards success. It's a virtuous circle. Belief in what you're doing makes you happy.

"Success is not the key to happiness. Happiness is the key to success. If you love what you are doing, you will be successful"[108]

Pep Guardiola's introduction of 'Total Football' was a form of slipstreaming. It took his Barcelona, Bayern Munich and Manchester City teams to the top of the sport. Jürgen Klopp's Liverpool then performed it in 2019/20 but added a greater energy and tempo with and without the ball. In defence they used a system of 'gegenpressing' (counter-pressing) which was more slipstreaming. Jürgen Klopp had introduced gegenpressing at Borussia Dortmund and his Liverpool team adopted it too.

When Marcelo Bielsa's Leeds United re-joined the Premier League in 2020/21, after sixteen years out of the top flight, they brought more slipstreaming to the Premier League. They didn't copy Liverpool's high tempo attacking version of 'Total Football' and they didn't copy the high energy, high pressing game first introduced by Rinus Michel's with Holland in the 1974 World Cup (and adapted by Jürgen Klopp). They copied both. This new form of high energy football might be named 'relentless football'. There is no sitting back and counter-attacking, or selective counter-pressing. The philosophy is full on attack with the ball and full on pressing without it. It is the most energetic form of football ever played in the top-flight.

In their first game back Leeds played the 2019/20 Premier League Champions and 2018/19 Champions League winners, Jürgen Klopp's Liverpool. Leeds managed to gain 52% of the possession at Anfield, but lost 4 v 3 after giving away an avoidable penalty late on in the game. In all other respects it was a match worthy of a draw. At no point did Leeds United sit back or take a breath. At the end of the

---

[108] Albert Schweitzer a theologian, organist, writer, humanitarian, philosopher, and physician. Winner of the Nobel Peace Prize.

game Jürgen Klopp saw a television camera and looking towards it just said "Wow!!" If your team can slipstream (like Manchester City, Liverpool and Leeds United), rather than mainstream, it can get itself much closer to winning.

~~~~~

Music artists have to decide which songs to write and perform. For some of them, fame and making millions is more important than the messages within their music. But for many others, music is their opportunity to tell the World what they feel passionately about. There is therefore a balance to find between writing throwaway lyrics that sell ('Love me do, Whoa, love me do'[109]) and lyrics that explain a personal perspective on the World ('And in the End, the love you take is equal to the love you make[110]').

Having a core philosophy helps singers to differentiate themselves from the millions of other artists across the World. It centres them around a set of values and influences. It comes from an inner passion and values set. The biggest question for any music artist is "Why are you singing?" They just need to find the place their desire comes from and start from there.

Grammy and BRIT Award winner Dua Lipa has a clear philosophy about her music. The song 'Break my Heart' from 2020's Future Nostalgia is a good case in point. The track is about the "shoulda, woulda, coulda's" of Lipa's relationship choices and about being unable to resist the temptation to pursue love. So what is Dua's philosophy?

"Everything that I do is very autobiographical.
I'm trying to be as much of an open book as possible and give the
audience every single piece of me."[111]

Offering every single piece of yourself is as brave and invested as it gets. That's authenticity at maximum. No wonder Dua Lipa has had so much success. No everyone is as open.

Within a song, the music creates the melody, pace and tone; and the lyrics express the sentiments the writer wants to get across. The vocals and instruments deliver

---

[109] From the Beatles' first single 'Love me do' (recorded in 1962).
[110] From 'The End' the last song recorded by the Beatles and the last track on Abbey Road (the last album they recorded in 1969).
[111] Dua Lipa.

the power and impact of the song. With so many variables amongst them, the choice of music and lyrics for a new song is absolutely vast. Despite the millions of songs that already exist, new combinations of music and lyrics can always be created. So how do you choose? Knowing what your guiding philosophy is, gives you a framework to work within. If you want to inspire and motivate other people, then you can take yourself off to your own places of inspiration (in real life or in your imagination) to produce great songs.

Songwriters who want to express their hurt and disappointment can take themselves to their darker places and memories. We can tap into our feelings to stir ourselves and others. Personal emotions produce personal songs. And personal songs tend to have a more powerful impact.

Only songwriters know how a song feels when they sing it. Adele Adkins knows when she has a good song. Having sold over 60 million albums, she uses a method of selection that's worked incredibly well for her. If a song doesn't pass this test it doesn't make the cut. What is the 'Adele' test?

"In order for me to feel confident with one of my songs it has to really move me. That's how I know that I've written a good song for myself. It's when I start crying. It's when I break out in fucking tears in the vocal booth or in the studio, and I'll need a moment to myself."[112]

~~~~~

There are endless potential philosophies to choose from. Only a few are likely work well for your organisation, in your competition. Many others will be lead to failure. So how do you choose? Matching your philosophy to your mission is what's critical to success. There has to be a compelling reason to pick this one over the rest. Questions should always focus back on delivering the mission.

This raises a 'Chicken or Egg' question. Should our circumstances dictate our philosophy? Or should we choose a philosophy first and use it to change our circumstances? Pep Guardiola seems to have selected his philosophy and stuck to it. Many leaders will choose a more flexible approach. Their philosophy might be 'We change our strategy and tactics to suit each project'. Which one is right?

---

[112] Adele in a 2015 article in Hello Magazine.

We always need to have a primary philosophy, a system that we believe in and one we can always turn to. But we also need to be adaptable, to have a Philosophy B ready, just in case. We might need a Philosophy C too; and any number of other options, depending on the circumstances. We therefore need a blend of theory and pragmatism, giving us a primary philosophy, as well as other available options. Choosing a philosophy is a continuous loop of a process. What's good enough to win today, might not be tomorrow. We need to make a decision, apply our philosophy, review it, adapt it, change it (if necessary) and go again. A decision shouldn't be made in a kind of theoretical vacuum. When we're unsure, we need to re-focus on what the mission requires.

In practice, which philosophy you choose should depend on how successful your organisation's existing philosophy is, how successful an alternate philosophy is likely to be; and what best fits the challenges and circumstances your organisation is facing at the time. In business, there are a number of influencing factors, including the mission in hand, the available budgets, the strength of competition, together with the team members and resources available to you. In sport, the influencing factors will include the team's form, its position in the league, the players available to play, the opposition and even the score in the game.

When you've got a primary philosophy, you can spend time building everyone's understanding, familiarity and confidence in it. Communication and training are easier, because you can create organisational routines, patterns, terms and standard operating procedures to support that primary philosophy. New arrivals can get up to speed quicker when there's an established system. You can also scenario plan more easily when you have a preferred approach. The downside of a fixed philosophy is that your competitors will get to know what you'll do and when you'll do it. That's why you need to swap it for Philosophy B or adapt it to as better Philosophy A from time to time. That will keep the competition guessing.

Without a primary philosophy, great communication and training is even more vital. When we operate in an extremely adaptable way, we have to ensure that everyone is crystal clear on what the current plan means. With frequent changes and less time to embed an approach, any team will struggle to operate as 'one'. Total certainty is impossible, but complete understanding is essential. Misunderstanding usually results in confusion, disengagement and mistakes. In order to sing from the same hymn sheet, you need to agree what's on the hymn sheet. Without a primary philosophy to lean on, we are likely to fall down.

If you cannot agree a philosophy in time, then adopt one of simplicity and delegation. Keep the structure and direction from the top short and simple. Then delegate authority and decision-making down to the lowest operational level you can (mission control). You can't be sure what decisions you'll get, but at least you'll get quick local decisions based on first-hand local knowledge.

~~~~~

Dr. Sabrina Cohen-Hatton is the Chief Fire Officer of the West Sussex Fire and Rescue Service. In her book 'The Heat of the Moment' Sabrina explains how she's helped to ensure that Fire Service Commanders have more 'operational discretion' on scene at major incidents. The changes to the National Guidelines followed criticism of the service's standard operating procedures, following the Kings Cross bombings in 2005.

On that very sad occasion the first fire crew waited half an hour for a second crew to arrive, before taking action. This was due to a procedure that said that no crew could deploy with breathing apparatus into Underground tunnels without another crew present. The decision to wait followed the standard operating procedure. The first crew to arrive did exactly what the Guidelines said, wait for a second crew. But the resultant delay may have cost lives. The frustration for that crew must have been immense.

The goals of Fire and Rescue include saving lives and saving livelihoods. They are essential missions. But how should they be implemented? In any major incident, there are always difficult balancing acts to carry out. There are many judgement calls to be made. They are volatile, uncertain, complex and ambiguous (VUCA) events. Which begs the question "Who is best placed to make the big decisions at a major incident?" Should it be a set of National Guidelines or very senior officers away from the scene? The rigidity of the standard operating procedures caused Sabrina sufficient concern to try and change them. Sabrina saw the need for a different approach. Sabrina's worry was that too many avoidable errors were being made. Her logic was simple. Any changes to the National Guidelines, that reduce human error, will help to achieve better outcomes.

Those Fire and Rescue National Guidelines were re-written, with Sabrina's help, to allow more Commander control at the scene (which I would call mission control). This flexibility has allowed more Commander discretion in whether or not to follow the standard operating procedure. This shift in emphasis has reduced the number of occasions where the standard procedures are applied too rigidly.

That is the right approach. The 'boots on the ground' should always have the authority to override the standard operating procedures whenever following them would be counter-productive. In her book, Sabrina summarised the philosophy behind these national improvements very succinctly.

"The procedures should provide handrails not handcuffs"

As long as the Commander focuses on the right 'operational goal' (mission) then his or her decision-making should always support that goal. What's needed to support that independent thought, is accurate information on scene; and intensive training off it. Commanders need to be able to take incredibly complex decisions quickly, under extreme pressure. They need a philosophy that gives clear guidance and flexibility to adapt it where necessary.

That's exactly what Sabrina is helping to do in other aspects of the Fire and Rescue Service, by introducing greater clarity, support and flexibility. Her philosophy has a dual focus, based on improving the outcomes for those in need of rescue and supporting the firefighters trying to save them. By a combination of clear and established guidelines, more training under pressure, better supervision and human support; and more flexibility on the ground, operational effectiveness has improved.

Sabrina has helped to establish 'The Joint Emergency Services Interoperability Principles' to help the emergency services make better group decisions in emergency situations. She has also helped to establish THINCS (The Incidental Command Skills Behavioural Markers) to help train Commanders to function better in highly-pressurised situations. The headline areas covered are leadership, decision-making, communication, personal resilience, situational awareness and teamwork. Sabrina has also assisted in establishing more real-life fire and rescue training, to increase practical experience. There has been a positive impact on fire and rescue outcomes. Sabrina's philosophy is now having a far reaching impact on the country's fire and rescue operations.

Sabrina's approach has Super-tribe thinking behind it. Instead of just helping to improve her own Sussex Fire and Rescue Service, she has sought to effect change at National level. That has benefitted every Fire and Rescue service across the country. In addition, Sabrina has gone a Super-tribe level higher, to help improve the interoperability of all the emergency services whenever they work together. Collaboration requires a common understanding as well as a common mission. It's clear that Sabrina completely gets that.

"It's imperative that firefighters train alongside other blue-light responders. Knowing how we operate on our own simply isn't enough"[113]

If I may quote a brief passage from Sabrina's book, because it explains the practical benefits so well. "When the fire and rescue service trains with the other emergency services, we learn how the other agencies think, the roles they play and how they respond. We then know not only our song sheet but theirs too, which helps us to better predict what might happen in certain situations and the effect our decisions may have on other parts of the jigsaw. Most importantly, training together builds personal relationships so that, should there be a major incident, we're working alongside people and services that we know and trust."

This is Super-tribe thinking and it is incredibly valuable that someone is fighting so hard for it. Conceptually it is not rocket science, but it needs to be said, because there is so little Super-tribe thinking in joint-operations across all sectors. The more trust, respect and mutual understanding there is in any collaboration, the more effectively it operates. Hopefully Sabrina's philosophy will help our emergency services collaborate even better, producing even more positive outcomes. We can all take note of what's written on Sabrina's song sheet.

~~~~~

A new or adapted philosophy can emerge from a gut instinct, observation or a statistical analysis. The key question is "Will it make us more successful?" If not, then why would be adopt it? How can we tell, if it'll be better? Quire often there's data to show you the way.

In 1999, inside the world of baseball, Billy Beane and Paul DePodesta studied vast amounts of data to find the statistical secret to winning baseball games. Ignoring traditional baseball wisdom, which valued the eyes and personal hunches of team scouts, the Oakland Athletics cut out the humans and went straight to the statistics. They knew that the scouts couldn't watch every at bat, of every batter, in every game. So a one-time scouting mission could give a very false impression of a player's abilities. Whereas the statistics covered every single at bat, of every

---

[113] Chief Fire Officer of the West Sussex Fire and Rescue Service and author of 'The Heat of the Moment'.

single player, in every single game. The statistical version of the 'truth' was also imperfect, but it was much more reliable.

"The idea that I trust my eyes more than the stats - I don't buy that, because I've seen magicians pull rabbits out of hats and I know that the rabbit's not in there" [114]

Building on the writing of Bill James, they discovered that there was a single statistic that made the biggest difference to winning. Their theory started with how to win baseball matches, or in fact how not to lose them. They started with the fundamentals (back to basics). A team stays in and can score runs until three of its batters are out. When they are out, your innings ends and you can score no more runs. With only three 'outs' in each innings and only nine innings, those twenty-seven outs are incredibly precious. Billy and Paul knew that the longer their hitters stayed 'in' the more chance their team would score runs and the more chance it would win matches. Staying in (and not getting out) was the secret to success. Those twenty-seven 'outs' were deserving of more value than all other teams were giving them.

According to the rules of baseball, batters can be out in perhaps twenty-four different ways. There are in fact so many that there isn't unanimous agreement on exactly how many ways there really are. With twenty-four different ways to get out, getting out is easy. Staying in is much harder. The pivotal question, that the Oakland Athletics' asked themselves, was whether all those 'outs' were as likely as each other? Should they ask the scouts for their views and hunches? No. The answer was to look at the data. Statistically most of the ways to get out, take place before a batter makes it to first base. And, to back that up, statistically most batters are out before they make it to first base. That initial part of every batter's innings sees the most outs. So that was where the biggest gains could be made.

Once Paul realised that, he and Billy developed a laser-focus. There was only one question to ask. 'What was a player's chances of making it safely to first base?' Billy and Paul also knew that this was being measured already. The data was in the public domain. On Base Percentage (OBP) is the historical percentage that a hitter makes it safely to first base. Like many baseball statistics it is measured in thousandths. So if a hitter made it to first base every single time, the player's OBP would be a perfect 1.000. Alternatively, if a hitter made it to first base once in

---

[114] Billy Beane.

every two at bats, the OBP would be half that, namely 0.500 and so on. Whilst the Oakland A's were switching their focus to On Base Percentage, all the other teams were focusing their philosophies and budgets on the glamourous statistics of home runs (where the hit leaves the playing area, like a six in cricket) and stolen bases (where a hitter can sneakily run to the next base in play). In trying to excite the crowd, teams were throwing away their outs too cheaply by trying to hit more home runs and steal more bases.

To illustrate this data driven philosophy, with modern data, we can briefly look at the 2019 Major League baseball season, Mike Trout of the Los Angeles Angels was the player who finished with the highest on base percentage (OBP). His figure was 0.438. That means making he made first base just under 44% of the time. That shows how hard an act it is. The player in twenty-fifth place, Justin Turner of the Los Angeles Dodgers, had an OBP of 0.372, making first base only 37% of the time. Over the course of baseball season, with its 162 regular season games and nine innings a game, Mike Trout could potentially bat at least 1,458 times in the regular season[115]. With an on base percentage of 0.438, he could make it to first base 638 times. Justin Turner (with 37%) would make first base 542 times. That's nearly one hundred more first bases for Mike Trout. Under the Oakland philosophy, if both players had been available and cost the same wages, Mike Trout would have offered Oakland much better value for money.

The average on base percentage for the whole of Major League baseball in 2019 was 0.323 (reaching first base less than a third of the time). Compared to that average, Mike Trout gets on first base up to 167 times more in a regular season. The chances are that Mike Trout's additional first bases helped him and the other members of his team get round all the bases, making more runs and generating more wins. Interestingly, even though that will have been true, Mike Trout's team, the Los Angeles Angels, finished fourth in the American League West. That's fourth out of five. Whilst Mike was the voted the Most Valuable Player in the American League, there simply weren't enough other Angels players who could get themselves onto first base. They would have pushed Mike Trout and the others round to score more runs. One player doesn't make a team.

For many years before them, the other teams didn't value OBP as highly as the Oakland A's came to. They favoured an offensive attitude to score runs, rather than a defensive one to avoid 'outs'. This fundamental difference in philosophy

---

[115] Sometimes players can bat more than once in a innings if the other team is struggling to get the 3 outs it needs.

meant that the players with the best OBP weren't always the best paid players back then. Sometimes they were hugely underpaid. In those cases, the poorer Oakland Athletics could afford to recruit them. By buying the players with the best OBP that they could afford, the Oakland Athletics were able to outperform teams with far bigger playing budgets.

"In disciplines as disparate as baseball, financial services, trucking and retail, people are realising the power of data to help make better decisions"[116]

The science went further. The Oakland Athletics also valued the Slugging Percentage (the average number of bases reached for each player's at bat). If a player reach first base more often and created a higher percentage of bases for the team then that player was even more valuable. Added together these statistics produce a combined OPS figure. But the Oakland A's didn't think they were both equal. Adding them together undervalued the on base percentage element. So they calculated a ratio for themselves (which wasn't made public). OPS was an important statistic, but to Billy and Paul it was the on base percentage that mattered the most.

As Oakland applied its new philosophy, the higher the team's total average on base percentage, the better the team's results became. The team's players got out less and the team won more. This logic gave them a major advantage over other teams and made them competitive. That was until everyone else found out what they were doing, when Michael Lewis published his best-selling book 'Moneyball'[117].

You would have thought that everyone adopted this philosophy. But based on 2019 data above, the Los Angeles Angels weren't playing Moneyball.

~~~~~

Joe Gilgun plays Vincent 'Vinnie' O'Neill in the television series Brassic[118]. The idea for the programme came from Joe himself. Brassic is a humourous take on criminality in Northern England. It's been a hit for Sky One and has been commissioned for a third series as I write this. It's edgy, inappropriate and rude.

---

[116] Paul DePodesta.
[117] It was also made into a film called 'Moneyball' starring Brad Pitt and Jonah Hill.
[118] Brassic is cockney rhyming slang for 'boracic lint' and means skint.

But it's warm, charming and funny too. That is a very difficult balance to achieve. From the start, Joe Gilgun had a clear concept of how he wanted to make the series. That was a philosophy he inherited.

Joe's career started with Coronation Street at ten years old. He has also stared in Emmerdale. But his big break came with the BAFTA award winning film 'This is England' directed by Shane Meadows. Joe credits Shane with providing him with his philosophy for making films and television programmes.

"Just be honest and truthful in everything you do."

When you know that your material is funny and getting laughs, there must be a temptation to ham it up and push the humour. However, that's not the way Joe sees it. "Don't play it for laughs, play it as it is and tonally everything should fall together."[119]

The show's warmth and humour come from everyone playing their part and trusting in the process. Joe Gilgun is not the only person who is searching for truthfulness in their acting. Comedy actress Rebecca Front[120] was asked how she chooses a script in a BBC interview. Rebecca's answer was "If the characters seem believable, I'm drawn to it."

Joe reportedly has dyslexia, bi-polar and ADHD. By his own admission he has been a "criminal" and suffered from anxiety and depression. But despite all his personal challenges, Joe has managed to cling onto the rails through his acting ability. As his career has developed, there is much more to Joe Gilgun than just his acting. His story-telling and production skills have taken his career to another level with Brassic. His guiding philosophy has brought him and his project success.

Joe is quick to credit others for their work. They include Brassic's fellow Executive Producer Danny Brocklehurst, the founder of Calamity Films David Livingstone and his co-star who introduced them, Dominic West. Despite the show being his brainchild, Joe is not looking for total control. He is convinced that the production process has to be a collaborative one.

---

[119] Quotes from an online interview for "Joe" in May 2020.
[120] Rebecca has starred in 'The Thick of It', 'The Other One', the underrated 'Up the Women', 'Knowing Me, Knowing You with Alan Partridge', Poldark, War & Peace etc. The interview was on the BBC's Saturday Kitchen Live.

"Listen to everyone. Don't be a dictator.
Let people know they're trusted"

Danny Brocklehurst agrees "Joe clearly put a lot of thought into what the show could be. Joe would be the first to admit it was rough around the edges, but we soon discovered we could collaborate and work well together, and knock it into something that could be a really entertaining comedy drama."

Joe's philosophy of honesty, truth and high level of trust allows everyone to play things honest and true. Playing it straight has created a very popular television series.

~~~~~

Journalism provides a vital truth. Good story-tellers can flourish if they can find a compelling approach that grips their readers and viewers. Fiona Bruce's career at the BBC began as a researcher on the Panorama programme; and she quickly progressed to assistant producer, Fiona then made the change to reporting on Breakfast News. After that, Fiona was a reporter for the hard-hitting journalistic programmes Panorama and Newsnight where she learned how compelling story-telling worked.

In 1999, the BBC's relaunched its news output and Fiona was named a presenter of the BBC's Six O'Clock News. Since then Fiona has gone on to become a highly successful and well-known British journalist, newsreader and television presenter. As well as being a leading newsreader on the BBC's News at Ten, Fiona presents a number of flagship BBC programmes including Question Time, Antiques Roadshow and Fake or Fortune. She is also a former presenter of Crimewatch. Throughout Fiona's career, she has based all her work on a core philosophy.

"I'm all about the story. And the stories I remember tend to be the
ones of sorrow, or family history, or revelation of the self." [121]

Fiona Bruce is 'all about the story' and it shows in everything she does. Fiona has become highly adept at story-telling in many forms. Sticking to this core premise has earned her respect and given her a varied and high-profile career. That's because if you tell a story first and you tell it with passion and compassion, the storyteller is as memorable as the story.

---

[121] Fiona Bruce, from an interview in the BBC Radio Times.

In the UK, the military has to be trained and equipped for all kinds of eventualities. These can include full warfighting, peacekeeping and humanitarian operations, taking over during a fuel or a firemen's strike, or carrying out mammoth logistical tasks in support of the Government (such as during the Coronavirus crisis).

The military is a hugely flexible and valuable asset to the UK. But a political and economic compromise is always required. To be ready to meet all of these potential tasks at once would be extortionately expensive, at a price the public would not be prepared to pay. So the military has to train and develop its people mentally and physically to cope with the breath of its all potential tasks.

Royal Engineers Motto: 'Everywhere'

There are three differences between a good and an excellent military. They are adaptability, endurance and resilience under pressure. To consistently provide these key facets, the British Military has adopted ten principles of operation. Together they amount to a military philosophy. Whilst not all military concepts can be applied to non-military organisations, many of these ten can be adapted and adopted.

The selection and maintenance of the aim is the starting point for any kind of action. The selected aim provides an unambiguous focus for coordinated effects and a clear point of reference against which to measure progress. This aim (aka purpose or mission) must be realistic and achievable. Having a focused aim helps to conserve valuable energy and resources. All plans and action must be checked regularly against your aim (and any subordinate objectives) in order to maintain that focus. Choosing the correct aim is absolutely vital. Its importance cannot be overstated, as it influences the direction of the entire organisation. A mistake at this stage will adversely impact on every single facet of the operation.

The maintenance of morale underpins any successful aim. Morale is the combination of confidence, belief, resolve, hope and the will to prevail in the face of adversity. Morale is a fragile thing and every opportunity must be taken to invest in it. Leaders cannot assume it's 'ever-present' because morale will be quickly lost, unless substantial effort is put into building and maintaining it. Many non-military organisations fail to appreciate this. 'Morale' consists of three elements, which are spiritual, intellectual and material. In practice, an operation's participants must be completely convinced of several things if morale is stay high:

the worthiness of the aim, that their contribution is essential, that they are valued and supported by the organisation, that they are led well, that they are getting the best tools for the job; and that they are getting a fair deal for their efforts. Where any of these are missing, good morale is vulnerable.

Offensive action is a commitment to take a decisive action, rather than just to respond to your opponent's actions. Offensive action is built on the ability and freedom to strike. It often follows a form of defensive action to create the right conditions for the offensive action. This is derived from the core trait of offensive spirit. According to Sun Tzu, "You can prevent your opponent from defeating you through defence, but you cannot defeat him without taking the offensive". A sporting example of taking offensive action was Tyson Fury's second fight against Deontay Wilder in February 2020. Deontay Wilder, a previously undefeated World Champion, was decisively out-boxed by an offensive onslaught from Tyson Fury that Deontay was totally unprepared for.

Special Air Service Motto: 'Who Dares Wins'

Commanders must use the element of surprise to limit their opponent's ability to make timely decisions, to restrict their opponent's decision-making; and to prevent it acting as it intended. Likewise, commanders must also anticipate and protect their own forces against the enemy's own attempts to create the element of surprise. Otherwise, they will struggle to safeguard their own freedom of action. Surprise can be achieved through mind-games, deception and generating false expectations.

"Roger's idea was to get back at the enemy the hardest way he could, to mess up the works. From what we've heard here, I think he did exactly that"[122]

Surprise has the ability to affect physical cohesion and morale. Surprise can seize the tactical, operational or even strategic initiative. It is worth stressing that surprise is transient (it quickly evaporates) and it must be rapidly exploited through swift offensive action.

The principle of security is about balancing the benefits of risk and reward. In practice it means assessing the likely losses against the probability of a successful

---

[122] Group Captain Ramsey about Squadron Leader Roger "Big X" Bartlett, in the 1963 film 'The Great Escape'.

operation. Security involves maximising the best opportunities and best timing for operational success. That means being bold when the situation dictates, whilst always protecting the organisation. It also means exercising patience and retaining your combat power when the situation dictates restraint. If the security principle is applied too offensively, it could lead to over-committing too many resources to attack, leaving the force vulnerable to a decisive counter-attack. That could jeopardise the success of the whole operation.

"We'll burn that bridge when we get to it"[123]

Equally if the security principle is applied too defensively, it could lead to over-committing resources to guard against every possible perception of threat. That would diminish the force's fighting power and the success of the whole operation. Security involves a careful balancing act. It's about taking your opportunities with the maximum resources that you can justify.

Concentration of force is not about massing an entire force or the bulk of it in a particular location at a particular time. It is about amassing sufficient combat power to overwhelm the enemy at critical points in time during the operation. Ideally the application of combat power should have a disproportionate impact on the enemy, as it involves strategic and tactical risk. Commanders have to accept that concentrating their forces in one place means that their forces will be thinner elsewhere. This is where surprise plays its part. Where possible, commanders should appear weak where they are actually strong and, more importantly in this case, strong where they are weak. Otherwise your opponent will strike where your force is most vulnerable. Concentration of force is also about choosing the right location and terrain to give strength to your forces, or weaken your enemy. Finding the right balance is critical. In that regard, it's always an advantage to know your enemy.

Special Boat Service Motto: 'By Strength and Guile'

The principle of economy of effort is central to conserving fighting power. Commanders must continually prioritise their available resources between four operational actions: engaging the enemy, moving between locations, taking other necessary actions and rest. This decision-making has to fit within the sustainability demands of the operation as a whole. In essence it is about creating

---

[123] From Mission Impossible.

the right effect, in the right place, at the right time, with the most appropriate resources to achieve the mission. Applying an economy of effort means applying enough effort to get the job done, ideally no more and no less. In sport, too much training and not enough rest can unbalance a team's ability to perform.

Flexibility is vital to enable forces to act rapidly, with confidence, in a complex and ever-changing environment. For an organisation to be flexible it must have the right mix of structural, procedural and cultural elements in place. Its structure and processes can't be allowed to stifle it. As Charles Darwin reportedly said "the species that survives is the one that is able best to adapt and adjust to the changing environment in which it finds itself". An organisation has to be adaptable.

"What we anticipate seldom occurs.
What we least expect generally happens"[124]

An organisation's structural, procedural and cultural elements should all encourage people to think creatively, be resourceful and use their imagination. This is vital when the pressure is really intense, especially during time-sensitive situations, in order to gain or regain the initiative. A supportive and encouraging culture must be developed and maintained by the commanders at the top. The focus on the aim must never be lost. The structures, processes and mindsets must not be too fixed. The ones that apply in peacetime are not necessarily the ones required for war.

The principle of cooperation is built on four pillars: mutual trust and goodwill, a unity of purpose for a common cause, a clear delineation of responsibilities (who is responsible for doing what); and an understanding of the capability and limitations of your partners. Cooperation reaches beyond 'tribal' boundaries to create Super-tribes. In doing so, it maximises the effect of each pillar, to help strengthen the bonds of co-operation. The principle of cooperation involves pulling together the breadth of talent available into a coherent force with a common mission. For the UK military this process is required for our units and battle groups, as well as third party allies and other international partners. This is an extremely complex process.

Parachute Regiment Motto: 'Ready for anything'

---

[124] Former British Prime Minister Benjamin Disraeli.

Where this is successful it takes multiple tribes and builds a Super-tribe from them. The key is to create joined up training that is demanding and imaginative. This similar to the approach taken by the Fire and Rescue Service. Meeting this challenge creates cohesion in the joint-team and engenders trust. The process of developing cooperation makes or breaks mutual-understanding and it exposes strengths and weaknesses. Super-tribes are founded or individual teams flounder under the pressure of cooperation.

On the face of it, sustainability of fighting power is perhaps not the most interesting principle on the list but in many respects it is the most important. Logistics is a critical enabler of fighting power, covering the deployment and return of the force and also its ability to continue the fight. The ability of an organisation to sustain its force in 'theatre' dictates how feasible an operation is and what time period can be given to that operation. Substantial resources are required to sustain the military in its operations. The role of operational sustainability is encapsulated in a military adage "Amateurs think tactics, professionals thinks logistics".

~~~~~

Giles White is the Director of Cricket at Hampshire County Cricket Club. Since 2008, under Giles' time as Head Coach and Director of Cricket, Hampshire has won five major trophies[125]. In 2019, Hampshire finished third in the First Division of the County Championship and made the final of the Royal London One-day Cup. The club looks set to challenge for more honours in the coming years.

Why has Hampshire been able to achieve this success? Giles' philosophy is about "creating a pathway to self-improvement." That ticks two major boxes. It is inclusive (as it benefits everyone at the club) and it offers the club a sustainable future (as self-improvement is a continuous and enduring process). The club has approached the difficult challenge of squad building by the dual-approach of "developing our young players and signing really good players from outside the club." Most organisations claim to provide this support, but many don't deliver it. Having dual-philosophies can work well, as long as they don't conflict. These two are complementary.

---

[125] The five are: 2009 Friends Provident Trophy, the 2010 Friends Provident t20, the 2012 Friends Life t20, the 2012 Clydesdale Bank 40 and the 2018 Royal London One-day Cup.

"Success isn't about how much money you make, it's about the difference you make in people's lives"[126]

The more money your organisation has, the more attractive it might 'appear' to buy-in new talent. That's generally perceived to be a much faster route to success. The logic goes, if we buy good players from other teams, they will be good for us too? But that ignores why are they successful where they are. What are the reasons for that success? Can we replicate them here? Can we afford to? Do we want to? Will a competitor's star player thrive in your environment? Maybe, maybe not.

Where the dominant focus is on buying-in talent, it indicates either an impatience for success, a poor environment or an inability to develop and improve players. If you don't invest in developing your own players, you're unlikely to get the best out of any new ones. 'Growing your own' applies to old and young, to existing and new. Everyone needs a pathway to self-improvement. Hampshire Cricket's blended mix of homegrown and signed talent is ably supported by the club's self-improvement culture. Without this supportive, development-focused environment, the club wouldn't have won any trophies.

In terms of winning cricket matches, Hampshire has created "a clear game plan, role clarity within the game plan; and a good combination of skill, personality and chemistry." That's what's made the team competitive and made it ready to win. Without those foundation stones in place, Giles believes winning trophies would have been "incredibly difficult".

But winning isn't just about trophies. It's about "bringing through new coaches and players, developing county players into international ones and building a winning environment around them". This circles back to a pathway to self-improvement. Every time a young player develops into a regular county player the club wins. Every time a county player progresses to an international one, the club wins again. Every player who makes it, persuades other players to come to the club and try to emulate their success.

All the long hours spent planning, studying, learning and observing are teaching Hampshire's coaches how to develop themselves and their players. If every coach develops faster than their counter-parts at other counties, Hampshire will perform

---

[126] Michelle Obama.

at a higher level. Then the club will win more trophies. Learning A career of learning is not for the impatient or lazy. A career of learning is for anyone who wants to be successful.

Each practice session offers the opportunity to learn and develop skills. Every game offers the opportunity to put them into practice. As part of the club's development philosophy, the mantra of "Prepare, perform, reflect, refine, repeat" has served it well. Continuous evaluation and improvement have seen development at all levels. Giles' willingness to follow his own pathway to improvement has helped to ensure that self-development is happening at all levels. By investing in the philosophy himself, Giles White is leading by example.

Every kind of organisation has a difficult balance to achieve. There are pressures to win now and win later. Developing a team to win this year's competitions and ones five years down the line is "very hard to balance". Giles' philosophy to address that challenge is one of "constant regeneration." It's an endless task of building for now and for later at the same time. It's a process that simultaneously grows what it has and replenishes what is being lost. It's a process of passing on time, expertise and encouragement. Everyone learns from the experiences of everyone who's come before. The principle of constant regeneration is helping to make Hampshire win ready.

"None of us is as smart as all of us"[127]

Giles believes that "cricket is a game of relationships." That's because of the enormous amount of time that the coaches and players spend together, playing long cricket matches and travelling the length and breadth of the country. In Giles' words "We are like a family." Within the Hampshire family, Giles see the senior leaders and senior players as having a key role in embedding the club's "values, behaviours and standards." Many Hampshire players have done that very well over the years. One of them is Adrian Dimitri Mascharenhas, known as Dimi. Giles was quick to praise him as a role model for others. "Dimi came to the club from Australia, but he quickly became ingrained in the club. His 'never say die' attitude on the pitch and his support and helpfulness to others off it made him a great player and a great role model." Every organisation needs people like Dimi, who lead by example.

---

[127] US Author, Ken Blanchard.

Australian legend Shane Warne spent the 2005-2007 seasons playing at Hampshire. According to Giles, "Warney brought an attitude to winning" that hadn't previously been at the club. "He strived to win every game. He was a hard-nosed competitor on the field. But he was very empathetic and he could be great fun off it." Giles credits Shane with leaving a very important legacy behind him. "His impact at the club was the foundation stone for our white-ball trophy success in 2009 to 2012."

Giles also held out other former players like Mark Nicholas, Robin Smith, Neil McKenzie, Jimmy Adams, Nick Pothas and George Bailey amongst others for their positive influence at the club. Hampshire seems like a club where the player and coaching relationships have made the biggest difference between getting close and going on to win trophies. Skill is only one aspect of getting in the team. Cricketing ability and good character have to go hand in hand, if you want to get picked. Everything at the club comes back to the central philosophy of creating a pathway to self-improvement.

~~~~~

'Undefeated' is a documentary about the Manassas High School American Football team[128]. Based in North Memphis, Tennessee, the team plays in a deprived socio-economic area. The kinds of challenges that brings are dramatically summarised in the opening words from Coach Bill Courtney.

"Let's see here. Starting right guard shot, no longer in school. Starting middle line-backer shot, no longer in school. Two players fighting right in front of the coach when he's trying to make things work out. Starting centre arrested for shooting someone in the face with a BB gun...For most coaches that would be a career's worth of crap to deal with. I think that sums up the last two weeks for me."

Coach Courtney doesn't dwell on the negativity though. He speaks passionately about his commitment to the team and about having a football season that they can be proud of, telling them "I will kill myself to make sure that happens." Finally, after he has finished his pep talk, he ends with the words "This is our season. I don't care what happens."

---

[128] 'Undefeated' is a documentary film by Dan Lindsay and TJ Martin and I wholeheartedly recommend it.

"Players win games, and coaches win players"[129]

Bill Courtney's abiding philosophy is revealed early on in the film; and it's insightful. "The foundation has got to be a solid platform that you stand on and can speak to these kids and say this is the way you build yourself. If you build yourself this way and handle yourself this way and have character, you get to play football. And winning will take care of itself, because young men of character and discipline and commitment end up winning in life and they end up winning in football. But when you flip it and the foundation of what you're doing is football and then you hope all that other stuff follows, well then you think football builds character, which it does not. Football reveals character."

By focusing on character development first and American Football skills second, Bill Courtney sought to first develop a group of strong individuals. Then he layered a team mantra and team ethics on top, giving them a joint mission and a reason to collaborate. Finally he and the other coaches taught the team how to be better American football players. This 'build the person' approach could apply to any kind of team. Bill's philosophy works in every walk of life. Whatever your business, character is more important than any other skill or attribute you might possess.

"We should feel grateful instead of entitled. We have a moral obligation to give back"[130]

Bill Courtney's levels of understanding, commitment and belief are very admirable. When I tell you that Bill was an unpaid volunteer, that becomes more impressive still. Then when I explain that before Bill arrived, Manassas High School hadn't won an American Football game for somewhere between ten and fourteen years (the records are incomplete) you'll understand why his philosophy changed so many lives for the better.

~~~~~

Castleford Tigers is a rugby league team in Superleague (the top division of the domestic game). Between 2014 and 2019 the club finished the season in 4th, 5th, 6th, 1st, 3rd and 5th. The 2020 season was heavily affected by the COVID-19 pandemic. Pre-lockdown Castleford were challenging for 1st. Afterwards the

---

[129] Bill Courtney.
[130] Bill Courtney.

season fell away. 2020 aside, the hallmark of the Daryl Powell coaching era has been consistently challenging for trophies. Winning the 2017 League Leaders' Shield[131] is the highpoint so far. Finishing top after the regular season was an absolute success for any Superleague club. Castleford have also come very close to winning three other trophies under Daryl Powell. The lost finals in 2014 (Challenge Cup) and 2017 (Grand Final) and the last game loss to Catalans Dragons in 2014 (League Leaders' Shield) were all only one win away. For a club with the resources of Castleford this record is at least qualified success, if not an absolute success.

Success depends on your vantage point. Success is relative, contingent on each club's history, relative wealth, supporter numbers and Expected Minimum. For the biggest teams in the sport, namely Wigan, Leeds and St. Helens, this record might be described as a qualified failure. Only one trophy in six years would be seen as underachieving for those clubs. The expectation at those clubs is to win everything, every year. The next tier of teams contains big clubs too, but they have less recent history to put pressure on their present. They include Warrington and Hull. For those big clubs, Castleford's recent record might be seen as a qualified success. Then there are other traditionally big clubs which have fallen far from their dizzy heights and now play in the Championship. They include Bradford Bulls and Widnes Vikings. Historically this record would be a qualified failure for them; but now in their current state, this record would be a huge overachievement and well beyond their current Expected Minimums.

Daryl Powell is former Great Britain international and understands the game from a player's point of view. In sport and business, key management roles tend to be given to people with experience of the industry. That's understandable and advantageous, as long as there is a place for new thinking. Daryl is widely regarded for his work in helping Castleford to punch above its weight. Without the stadium, facilities, supporter numbers and financial backing of the bigger clubs to assist, Castleford is expected to battle in the bottom four, not the top four. Castleford has to overachieve year on year to finish in the top four, let alone win a trophy. So how is this being done?

"Winning doesn't always mean being first. Winning means you're doing better than you've ever done before"[132]

---

[131] For finishing the season in first place.
[132] Five times Olympic Gold Medal speed skater, Bonnie Blair.

Daryl is clear about his philosophy. Winning is his starting point. "I've always wanted to win everything I've been involved in." But winning isn't Daryl's only focus. "I want to win but there has to be a style about it. We have a history and a culture to protect at Castleford and we have fans to entertain. My philosophy is about "meshing together a winning focus and our 'Classy Cas' playing style." This approach meshes together two philosophies which don't conflict.

Over recent years two questions have been asked about the club "Why do so many players improve after they move to Castleford?" and "Why do so few players improve after they leave Castleford?" The questions are different but the answers are the same. Playing for Castleford Tigers offers a special mix of three ingredients: driving and supporting coaching, the opportunity to become the best player you can be; and a tight and enjoyable culture. Nothing is allowed to settle or stand still. When standards are achieved, they become standards to be beaten. Even the most stubborn attitudes and ingrained habits can be broken down and reassembled. There is always room for new ideas. "Change gets us closer to being Champions."

The club's growth mindset starts at the top. Daryl Powell wants "to be the very, very best coach" that he can be. Daryl works endlessly to find improvements in his own knowledge and understanding; and even in his own character. No stone is left unturned. Not only does he want to find a higher level of performance, Daryl wants everyone else at his club to be "the very, very best that they can be" too. He will help anyone to develop any aspect of their role or character.

Daryl sets high standards and he believes in everyone's ability to reach them. He believes that his team can become the champions and he regularly tells them that. Setting high standards has raised the bar on everything, from timekeeping to technical skills, from conditioning to collaboration. Believing in the ability of people to grow and develop had led to phenomenal growth and development.

As well as having a developmental outlook, Daryl is highly driven, highly determined and highly ambitious. "I want us to be the best ever Cas team and the best ever rugby league team. I want every player to play at the peak of their ability and to enjoy doing it." Continually setting the bar ever higher, has raised the team's performance levels ever higher.

"Winning is not a sometime thing. It's an all the time thing. You don't win once in a while. You don't do the right thing once in a while. You do them right all the time"[133]

Daryl is very ably supported by the whole coaching group in his quest. The vastly experienced Ryan Sheridan, Danny Orr and Matt Crowther have provided top level expertise and bags of character. There are no egos. Daryl himself supported the team growing up so "it's in my blood." The whole coaching group clicks. It brims with enthusiasm and determination. At Castleford, winning isn't a one person game, at Castleford it's all about mutual growth.

When recruiting, the club doesn't just look at playing ability, it also looks at getting the right 'fit' for the 'Classy Cas' playing style, the right character and cultural ethos, a good injury record and physical robustness; and most of all, there needs to be room for improvement. If a player can't grow as a player and a person then Castleford might not be right club for them. But if there's a willingness to develop yourself, then it seems to be the perfect environment to develop in.

Daryl requires everyone to be honest, hard-working and committed to becoming the very, very best they can be. He will not accept anything less. Daryl will drive and support anyone to achieve that. He tells any potential player "You can achieve everything you want at this club. We have numerous examples of improvement that we could tell you about."

Seasonal sport requires all year round planning and activity. Within a season, the focus is naturally on winning trophies that same season. During 2016, the squad was according to Daryl "annihilated by injuries" and the chances of winning trophies slipped further and further away as the weeks rolled by. 2020 was the same. As Daryl Powell absolutely hates losing that was extremely hard to take. "I've never been good at losing. In the past I've taken it hard and seen it as a personal slight. But I've learned that how you respond to losing is what matters. How quickly can you turn things around and win again? Since I've been Head Coach at Castleford we've been in a really bad place maybe two or three times. I'd handle those times differently now. But we got through them. It's all about growing and we have. Our consistency started to come when we started handling losing better."

---

[133] American Football coach Vince Lombardi.

"For me, as far as winning rugby football games is concerned, I think it's about the team that has the best discipline for the 80 minutes and does the basics and fundamentals well, for longer periods than the opposition. That's what's crucial in winning rugby games" [134]

Winning has a huge mental element. Bad losers don't make good winners. Winning comes from handling losing well, by moving from being a temporary loser to become a winners. But don't be too good a loser, or you won't become any kind of winner. Winning is about having a positive attitude. Don't look back in anger. Learn and understand the reasons for each loss. Makes sure you improve after each loss. Don't repeat the same mistakes. Don't lose for the same reasons you've done before. The more ways of losing you can learn to avoid, the more chance you have of winning.

During the frustrations of 2016, Daryl and the whole team started adapting their approach in preparation for 2017. The learnings from 2016 were instrumental. The new approach was re-established in the 2017 pre-season and applied right across the season. Castleford finished top that year. "Our 2016 adaptations led to our 2017 success." 2020 could well lead to a very good 2021.

~~~~~

Global fast-food chain, McDonalds, has 36,000 restaurants across one hundred countries of the World. How did it become so successful? One word 'uniformity'. Design, make, repeat. Don't alter, just repeat. Then repeat again, in every restaurant, in every country, every second, of every day.

A Big Mac is probably the most well-known item on the McDonalds' menu. When was the Big Mac first added to the McDonalds' menu? Have a guess. Did you say 1968? That's over fifty years ago. What about the move to French fries instead of potato chips? Have another guess. Did you say 1949? That's over seventy years ago. Chicken McNuggets are a more recent addition from 1983, but that's still over 35 years ago.

---

[134] Ellery Hanley, former Wigan and Great Britain international rugby league player.

McDonalds' winning philosophy has been to invent and relentlessly repeat. Its philosophy of uniformity and familiarity has been phenomenally successful on a global basis.

~~~~

Tesco plc is one of the ten largest retailers in the World and its story is one of changing philosophies. To begin with, Jack Cohen set up a single market stall in Hackney, selling war-surplus groceries. As his ambition grew, his philosophy grew with it. Jack Cohen moved away from a single stall and gradually built up a group of profitable London market stalls. In 1924, Jack created the iconic brand name we recognise today, by merging his own name with that of Thomas Edward Stockwell (from whom he bought tea) combining TES and Cohen to produce TESCO.

In the 1930's, the TESCO philosophy changed again, with the bold decision to move from stalls into grocery shops. Initially, what we now know as supermarkets really were just 'super' market stalls. The first TESCO supermarket opened in Barnet in 1931. The concept was instantly popular. As sales grew, so did the number of these supermarkets. The TESCO philosophy had to be adapted again. It became one of rapid expansion. By 1939, TESCO had amassed one hundred supermarkets in the UK. As progress was made, the level of ambition changed again.

"Red Bull is still a young team. We have a cabinet full of trophies, but we'd like to make some more cabinets"[135]

From the 1950's onwards, TESCO pursued a joint-philosophy of building its own stores and acquiring sites from other providers. From the 1960's onwards, TESCO also adopted a philosophy of diversification, growing its business beyond groceries. TESCO now sells food from all over the World, as well as books, clothes, electronic goods, furniture, toys, petrol, software, financial services, internet contracts and mobile phones.

In the 1990's TESCO expanded its philosophy and went out to target the whole consumer market, from top to bottom. As well as its regular products, there were new low-cost "TESCO Value" items and a "TESCO Finest" range on offer as

---

[135] Red Bull Racing Team Principal, Christian Horner OBE in Business Leader magazine, January-February 2020.

well. This gave customers more choice about how to spend their money. During the same period, TESCO's competitors tried ever harder to lure its customers away, forcing TESCO adopt a protective philosophy. The TESCO Clubcard was launched in 1995 to help the business retain its customers' loyalty[136].

Not every change in philosophy has been successful. A foray into the US with a store called 'Fresh and Easy' was deemed to be a failure and led to a complete withdrawal from the US market. TESCO has also invested into a number of non-core business areas, which it has since extracted itself from. The current philosophy has changed from massive sector diversification, back into its core supermarket market. Learning from failure is vital preparation for success.

"If you find it difficult to accept failure then you simply won't get any innovation because employees will be too frightened[137]"

Despite its less successful ventures, TESCO's supermarket business has been an astonishing success. Trying new things has brought it success and has taught it where to draw the diversification line. TESCO is now a £2billion international supermarket business, which is a World away from Jack Cohen's first market stall.

Like Tesco, every organisation needs to find a successful operating philosophy. What works best to give your organisation the resources, adaptability, resilience and endurance it needs? Adapting a version of these principles might bring your organisation greater and more sustained firepower whenever it needs it.

~~~~~

With routine daily Worldwide travel for business and holidays, we are interconnected with every other country across the globe. The UK Government could not have prevented the arrival of Coronavirus Disease 19, during 2020. That was an uncontrollable. The challenge of COVID-19 was always going to be double barrelled. How could we limit it's spread and how could we find a cure? If scientists could work out what the winning controllables were, we could master them. At first, the mission was to work out the nature of the virus; and what threat it posed. Then the mission naturally morphed into reducing infections, restricting the virus from spreading and to save lives.

---

[136] Bizarrely this led to a five month letter bomb campaign from someone calling himself "Sally" protesting to make the Clubcard capable of withdrawing money from cash machines.
[137] Terry Leahy, former CEO of Tesco plc.

The Government's philosophy, for dealing with COVID-19, had to balance twin threats of disaster, the risk to lives and the risk to livelihoods. That philosophy was essential. Selecting and balancing the two winning outcomes required has been the key to the Government's response.

A combination of controllables has been used simultaneously to achieve the mission. One factor alone was never going to be enough. Those controllables have included social controls, such as regular hand washing, two metre social distancing, tiered restrictions and wearing face masks. They have also included medical controls, such as hospital care and the creation of vaccines. In addition there have been economic controls, including a £multi-billion financial investment in finding a vaccine and the Coronavirus Job Retention Scheme. It's the combination of all these winning controllables that has tackled the disease.

Takeaway thoughts:

- Match your philosophy to the mission and higher purpose
- Which philosophy works best for all your stakeholders?
- Are you mainstreaming or slipstreaming?
- Use data science to help decide what's best
- Having dual philosophies can work, if they are not in conflict
- Repeating a winning formula can be a winning philosophy
- Adapt your philosophy to fit a changing mission

3.3   WINNING CULTURE AND VALUES

The third controllable is winning culture and values. Every organisation needs a sense of what it stands for and what it stands against. Without an inspiring, empowering and inclusive culture to support you, no one will be able to give their very best. Having deep-rooted values that encourage mutual support, will empower your organisation towards winning.

Winning teams tend to collaborate and cooperate well amongst themselves. They have managed to undertake the difficult transition from being a group of disparate individuals to becoming a tribal force. Collaboration means working together to achieve the mission, not acting alone or blaming other people for the lack of progress. Cooperation and collaboration are tribal traits. They come from a joint sense of mission and a common set of values. They come from a mutual investment in the mission.

Without effective collaboration, winning is incredibly hard. The more elements there are to any mission, the more collaboration is needed to bind them together. With a culture of voluntary collaboration, a team can harness all its stakeholders to work as one. Sharing a mission, values and rewards are the keys to peak performance. When helping every colleague becomes ingrained and automatic, it is a powerful driver for success. True collaboration takes lots of hard work. But when it works well, everyone wins.

> *"Coming together is a beginning, staying together is progress, and working together is success"*[138]

The complete opposite is also true. Division and disharmony, in an organisation, create under-performance. If the whole group hasn't bought into a mission, that group cannot possibly reach its peak performance. We are naturally social animals. So we react to the words and actions of other people. We want a good trade for our own words and actions. Who wants to give their free time to selfish, badly behaved people? Who wants to help someone who won't ever help you back? Who wants to commit to a shared mission with people who won't commit the same effort? What kind of team does that make?

The reality is that people don't just form organised teams (let alone tribes) automatically, overnight, without thought. A group of individuals will always behave like independent individuals unless and until there is a shared mission and a set of shared values linking them together. When a new group begins working on a task together, there will always be uncertainty, suspicion and anxiety. Some group members will wait to see what others do, before deciding how much of themselves to commit. But any hesitation will delay, if not destroy, the chances of a genuine group collaboration. That negative kind of outcome is by no means evitable. Good culture can be grown quickly if the seeds are all firmly planted in (everyone fully commits), the soil is nutritious (all the necessary resources are quickly available) and there is regular watering (and all necessary training and support is provided within the group and externally).

Good culture comes from one person's winning behaviours setting a good example, thereby persuading other people to adopt them too. The process of culture-building begins with the introduction of agreed mission values and winning behaviours. Culture-building continues its progression with the practical application of those values and behaviours, on a day to day basis. Finally, a good

---

[138] Henry Ford.

culture is established through the 'domino-effect' of other group members imitating, mirroring and copying those winning behaviours, until the whole group routinely behaves in a similar way. Someone has to step forward and lead the movement to establish good culture. That person may be a member of the Captain Class[139]. Once someone commits, others can follow.

"The men have found their Captain. They will follow you into battle, even to death. You have given us hope"[140]

Without a shared commitment, the chances of success are very limited. Someone has to 'go first' and make a humble act of self-sacrifice. Then other people need to follow that person's lead. This bond is what makes or breaks a winning opportunity. That's because if everyone acts selflessly, each act of selflessness benefits someone else, creating multiple virtuous circles. In contrast, a team that permits individualistic or destructive values will create multiple vicious circles.

~~~~

Rugby Coach Mike Ford believes there are three key values in any team "Trust, honesty and respect." He also has a clear view on how those values impact on the way his teams play the game. "We play by the laws of the game. We don't play to break the rules. We want to be better than anyone else at playing by the rules. If the rules can be ignored, there would be no genuine competition to win. That why we have referees, to apply the rules. If we had to cheat to win a game, it would be a hollow, empty win."

"It's important that athletes can compete on a level playing field. And youngsters coming into the sport can know that if they are working hard and training hard, they'll see a true reflection of where they stand and what they can achieve worldwide and not be swayed by people who are cheating"[141]

Mike Ford has coached at club level (at Saracens, Bath, Toulon and Leicester) and international level (England and Ireland) in rugby union. But as a player Mike played the other code of rugby for Wigan, Castleford and Warrington. Mike

---

[139] A reference to Sam Walker's excellent book "The Captain Class", which I also refer to in 'Lead Your Super-tribe'.
[140] Eowen to Aragorn in the final part of the Lord of the Rings trilogy, 'The Return of the King'.
[141] Marathon World Champion Paula Radcliffe.

remembers playing at Castleford under Australian Coach Darryl Van Der Velde during the 1990's. In an early training session, Darryl Van der Velde asked the players to do "Do a lap" of the training pitch at the club's Wheldon Road ground. Mike remembers several players cutting the corners as they ran round. Instead of turning a blind eye, Darryl called the offending players out. Instead of telling them off, he told them that they were cheating themselves and cheating their team mates. If they didn't do that 'extra' they were letting their teammates down. Some of the players got the point immediately. But the next time Darryl said "Do a lap" a few of the players still cut the corners.

There are always 'characters' in every team of people who think it's funny or tough to ignore authority. Some people struggle with authority because of bad experiences in the past. Other people are chancers and will break the rules whenever they can get away with it. For that reason, all rules need to be fair. The rules need to be in place for a good reason (so that everyone wins). But when they exist, rules have to have teeth. Rules need to be enforced.

Mike can remember which teammates weren't complying, but he didn't want to say. When they cut the corners again, Darryl called them out again. He made them run another lap. But some show-offs don't mind a bit of public embarrassment. It gives them the attention they crave. So one or two of the players continued to push their luck. Each time Darryl explained to them why it was important that they all did the same as each other. Darryl Van Der Velde was absolutely right. Personal self-discipline in each player provides all the individual bricks you need to build a wall of team discipline and resilience. You don't have a tribe until everyone commits to each other. You can't have a Super-tribe without tribes. Some players were not fully committing to themselves, or each other.

After it was clear that Darryl never missed a cut corner and always called it out, the players began to police themselves. Some quickly became frustrated with the ones who weren't complying. The players who'd laughed along initially began to join in the chorus of criticism. Darryl was "a very good coach and a good bloke". The more professional players got annoyed. A tiny minority was disrespecting the coach and all their teammates by breaking the rules.

Peer pressure can be powerful. Used for good, it can help to change a team from the inside. So the players took it on themselves to stick to the rules. The first player to reach a corner stood there until everyone had run around him. No one was allowed to cut a corner. One or two players tried it, but they were immediately called out on it by the others. As Mike explained "No one likes to be criticised by your own teammates do you?" Pretty soon no one cut the corners. After that, all the standards were lifted too and the team began to win more matches. Darryl Van Der Velde wanted the players to find another level and they did.

"Leaders fix the environment not people" [142]

Mike has taken on that approach in his own coaching career. Mike remembers the control that a player group can have over itself. He is a big fan of empowering the players as much as possible. "Passing the decision-making to the players, with challenge and guidance from the coaches, is the highest form of coaching. If you can reach the point where the players are truly empowered, that's the peak."

Empowerment requires high quality interactions between the players and the coaches and players. To work well, it requires high-quality feedback from the players. Mike likes to test for understanding and empowerment by getting "instant feedback after sessions and games before the players have seen clips or spoken to friends and family". Coaches shouldn't have to spoon-feed the players. "The more they 'get it' themselves, the better empowered they are."

~~~~~

Culture isn't just an internal dynamic, it stretches far outside your organisation until it reaches every stakeholder. Culture doesn't have boundaries, it reaches far and wide. A good indication of a businesses' real values is therefore its track record with all its stakeholders. Those stakeholders include the organisation's employees and customers in particular. Amongst all the many positive stories, there are some useful examples of how not to treat your stakeholders.

In 2020, high-street fashion retailer H&M was fined €32.3 million by an information commissioner in Germany for recording confidential employment discussions at its service centre in Nuremberg. The information was used to build up employee profiles that included private health and family issues, religious beliefs and what they'd done on holiday. The personal details were accessible by up to fifty managers throughout the company. It appears that H&M's activities only came to light when an IT error led to those employee records becoming accessible to the whole company for a few hours in October 2019. H&M has since apologised "H&M takes full responsibility and wishes to make an

---

[142] L. David Marquet, former US Nuclear Submarine Commander and author of "Turn the Ship Around".

unreserved apology to the employees at the service centre in Nuremberg."[143] Despite it only being for a few hours, the damage to H&M company culture is likely to be longer lasting.

In 2019, the French data regulator fined Google €50 million for a "lack of transparency, inadequate information and lack of valid consent regarding ads personalisation." The regulator said it judged that people were "not sufficiently informed" about how Google collected data to personalise advertising. There is immense power and influence within datagopolies like Google. How they use that power and influence really matters. Internet users won't stay loyal if they lose trust in the likes of Google. That's because we are all subject to the 'network effect'. We go where our friends and business connections are. If they leave Google, so will we. Google and the other datagopolies need to behave ethically to retain our trust and loyalty, especially as China's equivalents will soon be vying with Google for global supremacy.

In 2006, a consumer group called Scamsdirect reported NatWest to the UK's Information Commissioner's Office for failing to dispose of customer information securely, after it found customer details dumped in bin bags outside an RBS/NatWest branch in Fareham, Hampshire[144]. If your financial data isn't secure with a bank, is your money?

"Good customer service costs less than bad customer service"[145]

As well as employees and customers, there are other stakeholders in every business. They include local residents and the environment. In 2015, Volkswagen was forced to admit that it had used software in many of its cars to cheat emissions tests. It was discovered that its engines emitted nitrogen oxide pollutants up to 40 times above what is allowed in the US.

In 2017, Thames Water was fined £20.3m by the Environment Agency after it was deemed responsible for pumping up to 1.4 billion litres of untreated sewage into the River Thames. The prolonged leaks led to serious impacts on local residents, farmers and wildlife. Accidents do happen, but what controllables weren't mastered? The true cost of poor values is always high.

---

[143] Information from Personneltoday.com article on 6 October 2020.
[144] Reported by Finextra on 30 October 2006.
[145] Sally Gronow, customer service expert in the utilities sector.

To be fair, many businesses apply good values and treat all their stakeholders well. Their reputations continue to increase positively. That's because, if you trust and respect a business brand, you are far more likely to work for it or buy from it. The more stakeholders you value, the greater your relationships and reputational gains will be. The more valued your brand becomes, the bigger your business can grow. Businesses shouldn't just value profits and shareholder dividends. They shouldn't just pay lip-service to company values. Businesses should value good values.

"The key is to set realistic customer expectations, and then not to just meet them, but to exceed them, preferably in unexpected and helpful ways"[146]

Any organisation will be valuing its stakeholders if it provides: excellent value for money for their customers, fair prices and prompt payments for their suppliers, upper-quartile rewards and good working conditions for their staff, high-quality jobs for their local residents; and a lack of pollution for the environment.

~~~~~

Our values are shaped by many people, circumstances and events. Our most fundamental values are often shaped by our purpose in life. With billions of people on our planet, there are billions of purposes driving billions of thoughts, actions and omissions every day. The only thing that makes us all the same is our individuality. Every human life combines individual DNA, relationships, environments and happenings. Every human life is lived in the dark. When we are born, we aren't told what we'll become, or when we'll die. Our lives could be anything or next to nothing and they could be taken from us at any point. As a result we live with the uncertainty of life hanging over our heads, like the Sword of Damocles. So how do we react to that knowledge?

Some people try to maximise the length of their lives by adopting a fitness regime or healthy lifestyle. Their values align with that purpose. Their motto might be "Stay fit and eat healthily". Their values might include moderation and abstinence. Other people decide to live for the here and now. They aim to enjoy every moment they have alive on Earth. Those short-termists might have the motto "Live each day as if it were your last." Their values might include enjoyment and trying new things. This approach could potentially be more

---

[146] Sir. Richard Branson.

rewarding but it could also result in greater risk-taking and perhaps an earlier death.

The Ancient Egyptians viewed their earthly existence as a means to an end. Enjoying their short human life was not the goal, that was the earning themselves an eternal life after death. All their values on Earth were therefore influenced by this personal mission. The Book of Ani is on display in the British Museum. It was written in hieroglyphics more than 3,000 years ago, on seventy-eight feet of papyrus. Discovered near ancient Thebes, now known as Luxor, the Book of Ani is what's known as a Book of the Dead. According to Ancient Egyptian beliefs, a Book of the Dead contained a personal series of hymns, declarations and spells to protect the dead person on their travels and challenges until they reached the Land of Two Fields.

On their journey through the afterlife, the deceased person had to pass several tests along the way. All those tests were a reflection on the way the person had lived their life on Earth. The journey to the afterlife was a judgement process, in many stages. According to the Ancient Egyptians, one of these tests required the deceased to face up to forty-two separate Gods, in front of forty-two different doors, in the Hall of Truths. Each of the forty-two Gods required a different, truthful 'negative confession', such as "I have not killed anyone" or "I have not committed adultery".

If you passed safely through the Hall of Truths, the penultimate test took place in the Hall of Judgement. That involved a weighing of their heart against a feather of truth. The person's heart had to balance the weight of the feather. A 'heavy heart' would not pass the test. Without passing every test, a person could not pass through to the afterlife, in the Land of Two Fields.

With an eternal life to win or lose, the Egyptians were prepared to endure a relatively short human life of penance. Many decided that their eternal purpose was worth all the forfeits required on Earth. To achieve anything much in life, our values have to be aligned to our purpose. With the prize of an eternal life at stake, the Egyptian values were set as the limits and compromises they had to accept in order to reach the afterlife. Their Earthly values were driven by their eternal purpose. Living with good values was therefore a sacrifice worth making. That worked for the Ancient Egyptians, but it doesn't work for everyone. To an agnostic individual, earthly sacrifices need to offer a more immediate pay-off, that delivers during their lifetime. The sacrifices we make for a mission need to be worth making.

~~~~~

In the modern World, we are open to outside influences and susceptible to external pressures, but our actions are within our control. We are free to decide how we treat other people. We get to choose how we live our own lives. That's a privilege of modern life. What's much harder is the responsibility that comes with it. How do we make all the daily choices that we're faced with? How do we decide what's right for us and what isn't?

Whatever purpose we're part of, it cannot conflict with our personal values too much, or that purpose will lose its power and influence over us. No mission will be accomplished unless the sacrifices it requires are worth making. What is your mission? Are the values required to achieve it worth the sacrifices it costs you?

For many people, the long hours we spend at work have to produce a quick benefit while we're alive, not one after we die. For most people, our sacrifices need to be rewarding enough for us to give up our time to that purpose. We want to work for employers who have values of fairness, inclusivity and openness. If our pay, benefits or treatment are illegal, we won't want to stay in that job. That only happens if our employer doesn't value us enough and doesn't prioritise fairness as an organisational value.

Where we have strong principles (values), they influence our life choices. They can prevent us from doing certain jobs or make us behave in certain ways. There needs to be a close alignment between our personal values and our organisation's values. Without a match, a person may be the wrong fit for your organisation or its mission. Where there's a tight fit, there's the potential for a strong and lengthy relationship. Hiring someone whose values align with your purpose is far more likely to see your mission through to its end. Try not to recruit people with conflicting values.

Every mission has to be worth what we're asked to give up for it. If your values are family-based, then you might put your life at risk to defend your loved ones. But you might not do that for many other missions. In times of war, volunteering to fight means you could die. It's a level of commitment that might include making the ultimate sacrifice. Defending your country might be enough motivation to put your life on the line. But it wouldn't, if you didn't value your country. The decision to willingly risk your life requires a values-based motivation. Most missions are not life-threatening, but they will involve time, trouble and effort. The decision to take on a difficult mission also requires a values-based motivation.

"I just know that every man I kill the farther
away from home I feel"[147]

Some peoples' values are only loosely held and can be 'bought'. For them it's just a matter of what's on offer? How much are you paying? Their services are available to the highest bidder. When the road ahead is long and arduous, they are not dependable enough. They won't stay the course or help you achieve your purpose. Try not to recruit the valueless.

~~~~~

There is a paradox within winning. The more desperately we crave success, the less likely we are to actually achieve it.. Craving some things, means giving up others. By focusing our waking thoughts on a desire for success, we reduce our mission focus and our mission capability. We have to be truly 'present' in order to deliver success. We have to give ourselves over to the mission. Being desperate for success, may mean having to compromise our values to get it. The more that we surrender our values, the more we remove the motivations that make us winners.

The third Noble Truth of Buddhism is that suffering can be overcome and happiness can be attained if we give up our cravings. Wanting to win is a necessary part of achieving success, but putting that 'want' above everything we value reduces our ability to deliver it. If we crave something, we lose focus on what else we're doing, we make selfish decisions and we sell ourselves short. We are far more likely to win by sticking to our collective values as a group. By focusing on our role and our agreed ways of operating we can deliver on our commitments. If everyone does that we win. We win by lifting up our colleagues, not by dreaming of lifting ourselves up. We win by concentrating on the controllables.

Craving creates a deep-seated need, with the accompanying shadow of fear in case we miss out. We need to take away our fears to be able to perform now in the present. If we need to catch a ball that's thrown towards us, we need to focus on the ball, not on the consequences of dropping it. Similarly, if we need to negotiate a sale, we need to focus on the customer's needs, not on the consequences of losing our sales commission.

---

[147] Captain Miller (Tom Hank's character) in 'Saving Private Ryan'.

"I'm always fearful. ... Fear generates in you a huge energy.
You can use it. When I feel that mounting fear, I think,
'Oh, yes, there it is!' It's like petrol"[148]

We have to focus on the controllable inputs, rather than the possible output of failing and missing out. We need to reduce our fixation on winning and be more attentive to our own actions in the present. Craving something else can cost us focus on what we have. So can fear. Winning comes from mindfulness and concentration on the job in hand. The less our minds are burdened by what's at stake, the better they perform.

By learning to live one day at a time, we create more focus for the job in hand. By trusting in the programme we're part of, we can accomplish more of it. The more present we are, the more likely we'll be at our best. By sticking to our winning behaviours, we can win more often. Our values are at the very heart of our success.

~~~~~

Every employer has to establish clear working practices in order to operate consistently. Employers do this through a mixture of contractual obligations and statutory provisions, supplemented by company policies and procedures. All of which have to be applied and followed. On top of these compulsory 'rules' there may be a set of organisational values written up on a wall somewhere. Unlike the rules and policies, which are designed to offer specific direction and guidance, these values have a more ephemeral nature.

Values are often supposed to be "understood" (without any specific explanation), pervade everywhere (without you being told how), influence every decision (except when it comes to defining the rules) and control staff behaviour at work (except where office politics gets in the way). In practice, workplace rules are largely followed; and workplace values are largely ignored.

An obvious point is that a good set of values can be hugely valuable to any organisation. That shouldn't need to be said, but it does. The solution is equally obvious. Weave your organisational values into all of your contracts, rules, policies and procedures. Apply them so that you end up with a practical set of

---

[148] Oscar winner, Dame Judith "Judi" Olivia Dench.

'do's and don'ts'. That way all the positive (winning) behaviours are crystal clear, without the risk of conflict and confusion. What should those rules be? Other than the compulsory requirements laid down by Government, an employing organisation has choices to make. What's right and what's wrong? The single question to ask is 'Which behaviours will help us achieve our mission?'

~~~~~

By scenario planning all kinds of incidents and issues, you can provide specific guidance on a large number of predictable situations for your people. Providing practical guidance on what to do and what not to do, based on your values, you can shape everyone's behaviours at work. A set of written values alone doesn't offer enough. If there was a fire at work, would you look for practical guidance about how to put a fire out, or would you go and stare at your organisational values poster for inspiration? Every employee needs to know what to do in any predictable situation. Once you've modelled the key scenarios and the behaviours that you want, you should end up with a set of winning behaviours. When you've also agreed the losing behaviours that you don't want to happen, you'll have a preferred way of operating that supports your mission.

The Department of Transport has used a safety campaign called 'THINK!' which aimed to get vehicle users and pedestrians 'Road Ready'. The mission was to make Britain's roads safer. By using a form of scenario planning, the Department for Transport helpfully educated road users on a range of potential risks, helping us all to think ahead. What form did that scenario planning take?

With a strapline of 'Expect the Unexpected' the Department used videos and adverts on buses to flag up lots of possible scenarios to be mindful of. They included crossing in front of a bus, looking out for someone with a walking stick and how to carry a football safely by the road.

By helping us to plan ahead better, the campaign has kept Britain's roads safer than they otherwise would have been. The winning outcomes being sought were fewer accidents, fewer injuries and fewer fatalities. This method of scenario planning helped us to prepare for different eventualities and achieve those winning outcomes.

~~~~~

Wickes is a national chain of DIY stores, which was founded by two brothers in Michigan, USA in 1854. The first UK store was opened in Manchester in 1972.

The Company's mission is "to be the strongest brand in the market while offering outstanding value for money."With over 250 stores and 7,000 employees, the Company's values are a very important element of its operation. According to the Wickes website, its values are its 'winning behaviours'. This has the potential to be a good way of driving employee engagement and performance. The five 'winning behaviours' are: Can do spirit, Humility, Winning, Be your best and Authentic. These terms don't actually describe winning behaviours, but they do describe values around good mental attitude and collaborative working. These values support great customer service, which is turn supports the Company's mission. So far, not bad.

What's not clear is whether Wickes has anything more specific than these unattached values. Are they ingrained in its rules? The Company says so. "At Wickes we live by our Winning Behaviours. These are the behaviours that we want all of our colleagues to understand and display, to support us in achieving our future plans. Everyone has a part to play in making sure that they are embedded into everything you do at Wickes." But are these five values woven into all of its rules, policies and procedures? Are they taken into account in all its decision-making? Are they rewarded when they're done well? Do they make a real difference to the mission? If not, what would? Everything has to support the mission or it is wasted and misdirected energy.

"I don't like empty steps, steps that have got no purpose and no meaning"[149]

The Wickes' value of "winning" is broken down into five sub-values. These are more practical and therefore more like winning behaviours. They are: Strive for our targets and do everything possible to reach them, Celebrate and share success, Achieve with pride, Take your colleagues with you; and Accept that things will go wrong and move on positively. But that are still not directional enough to be winning behaviours.

Wickes appears to be very customer-centric and its values could be winning ones, but to be genuinely 'winning' they need to provide repeated wins for all the Company's stakeholders, including its employees, directors, shareholders, customers and suppliers amongst others. If there is genuine integration into Wickes' business operations, every stakeholder should be able to give examples

---

[149] Dance Choreographer Kate Prince MBE. The quote is taken from the BBC programme 'Imagine'.

of where colleagues have exhibited those five 'winning behaviours'. In practice, what winning is done? How is it recorded? How is it rewarded? And if there is any winning, who benefits from it? These are fundamental questions for every employer to ask itself. Values are only valuable when they're valued. Are they valued?

If its customers are well looked after, that prompts the supplementary question 'How well are the Wickes staff looked after?' With a Learn and Earn Apprenticeship Programme (LEAP) and Leadership Effectiveness and Development Programmes (LEAD), there seems to be a commitment to training and development. The Wickes' benefits reportedly include performance related bonuses, a contributory pension scheme, 'generous' staff discounts to group products, access to over 1,000 retailer discounts and financial education tool called 'Neyberhood'. The wider Travis Perkins Group has signed up to the Armed Forces Covenant and has earned a Defence Employer Recognition Scheme Silver Award. On paper this looks good.

The reality is difficult to assess from the outside. Without getting inside Wickes and seeing for ourselves, we can't be sure how well Wickes has embedded its values. According to online reviewer Glassdoor, Wickes gets a 3.1 rating out of 5 for Working at Wickes[150] based on 204 reviews. That's nether great, nor terrible. It is quite possible than the current staff are very happy and haven't felt the need to post. Most former and existing staff won't bother posting on Glassdoor, so this is a limited form of feedback. According to another site called Indeed, Wickes gets a 3.4 out of 5 approval rating based on 553 reviews[151]. That's better than 3.1, but again it doesn't strike me as being a winning environment for staff. Neither Wickes nor Travis Perkins feature in The Sunday Times Best Companies to Work for 2020, but most companies don't enter for it. In short, it's not possible to really find out unless you go and work there.

Having 'winning behaviours' in place should mean that the organisation as whole is a winning one. If more needs to be done, then the common behaviours at Wickes aren't all winning ones. Wickes includes 'winning' as one of its winning behaviours, which is circular and tautologous. But putting that to one side, it's a bold claim. Companies who claim to win have to ensure that all of their stakeholders end up winners, not just the owning shareholders. That would be done by applying the organisation's values to all of its 'rules' and operational

---

[150] On 01/05/20.
[151] On 01/05/20.

scenarios, to create a series of winning and losing behaviours that everyone benefits from.

~~~~~

The organisers of any competition have to offer participants a clear set of rules and a level playing field. Otherwise, winning that competition becomes devalued. Competitive events also need a culture and environment that protects fair play. Cheating and foul play have to be caught out and called out. And whenever the rules are broken, the guilty party has to be fairly punished.

The International Olympic Committee is responsible for ensuring that the Olympic Games are staged every four years and that they run smoothly. When an Olympic athlete enters an event, he she or they needs to know that no one is cheating.

Sharron Davies was the first child star of British sport. Pushed by her father Terry, from an early age, Sharron swam in the 1976 Montreal Olympics aged just thirteen. Her coach was Ray Bickley at the Port of Plymouth swimming squad. Ray encouraged Sharron to develop all four swimming strokes, rather than just concentrating on one. That meant even more hours in the pool. As a result of her demanding schedule, Sharron didn't have a typical childhood. She was totally focused on her swimming. School work was a distant second. Swimming was full-time, six hours a day, seven days a week.

In 2012, I got the chance to speak to Sharron about her swimming career and to hear her speak to an audience of business people. Sharron is as smart and engaging out of the pool as she was brilliant in it. I particularly remember one story she told. When Sharron was eleven years old, she fell out of a tree and broke both of her arms. Rather than having time off from swimming, she was urged to continue her training. So Sharron swam with plastic bags strapped over her plaster casts. As a parent, I find that approach difficult to justify, but all of Sharron's endeavour made her excellent.

In 1978, aged fifteen, Sharron won two Commonwealth Games Gold medals in Edmonton, Canada. They were in the 200 metres and 400 metres Individual Medley (using all four of the strokes that Ray Bickley had trained her in). Two years later, at the 1980 Moscow Olympics, Sharron won a Silver medal in the 400 metres Individual Medley. Sharron's Silver medal at the Moscow Olympics was a fantastic achievement, especially for a seventeen year old. However, for years afterwards, Sharron was angry about her Silver medal. Not because she hadn't swum well, but because everyone strongly suspected that Petra Schneider and the other East Germans were taking performance enhancing drugs.

Sharron beat two East Germans to take the Silver. However, Petra Schneider's ten second winning margin (and new World Record time) was too big a task for any clean swimmer to match. The size of that winning margin was the big giveaway as to what, rather than who, had really 'won' the Gold.

"It's all gone wrong Olympian, framed by God"[152]

Petra Schneider has since confessed to taking performance enhancing drugs before the 1980 Olympics. Indeed many of the East German athletes of the time have made a similar admission. After German reunification, on 26 August 1993, the East Berlin Sports Institute records were investigated. Reports say that there was clear evidence that the state secret police (Stasi) had supervised the systematic doping of East German athletes from 1971 until German reunification in 1990. The drugs in question were later tested and estimated to have improved a swimmer's performance by a massive 19%. If there had been a clean race in 1980, Sharron Davies may well have won Gold.

It wasn't just Sharron Davies who was adversely affected. East German women dominated the swimming events at the Moscow Olympic Games, winning nine of the eleven individual titles and both of the relay events. They set six new World Records between them. They also won all three of the available medals in six different races. In total, they won 26 of the available 35 medals. No single country can muster that sort of success without cheating. How did nobody notice? According to Sharron, the East German women swimmers had "very deep voices' and "five o'clock shadows." Despite all the visual and statistical evidence, the International Olympic Committee did nothing. That 'blind eye' still rankles with Sharron.

To her great credit, Sharron made her own peace with Petra Schneider years ago, after meeting with her and seeing how much her health was suffering because of the drug-taking. Sharron has since said "I don't feel any anger towards Petra, in fact I feel really sorry for her." Despite Sharron's olive branch it's not clear whether Petra Schneider has ever publicly apologised for her role in denying Sharron that Gold medal. Offered the opportunity to return her medal in the past,

---

[152] A lyric from 'Olympian' by Gene.

Petra reportedly didn't do so. It's not clear if she has now surrendered it. Maybe it is all she has left to cling to.

To be fair to her, Swimming World Magazine has since reported that Petra Schneider says she doesn't want to be honoured for her performances, stating "I'd like the current list to be reset at zero." That shows a belated honesty and sense of fair play. But it doesn't give Sharron Davies her Gold medal. Petra Schneider finished first and yet she didn't win. She was a victim as well as a participant, but she cannot be acknowledged to be a winner. Cheating isn't winning.

Speaking about the 1978 Commonwealth Games, Sharron explained that she "loved" those games because it was the only opportunity she had to swim "without sharing the pool with the East Germans." Her swimming career was relatively brief. After Moscow, Sharron had had enough and she retired[153]. Her father's demanding training regime was a key reason for that decision. Years later Sharron got to appreciate that his level of sacrifice had been similar to her own. In a deeply ironic event, Sharron had to undergo a drugs test after her swimming final in Moscow. She was the last person to be tested and when she'd finished there were only her and a GB team manager left. Well that is except for her father, who had waited to give her a hug, even though he'd missed the last bus back into the city centre. Terry Davies had to walk the long miles back on foot. Sharron said "That was the moment I knew half the medal was his." That half a medal should be a golden half.

The state policy of the former East Germany forced its athletes and swimmers to take performance enhancing drugs. The medal and medical repercussions of this have extracted a heavy cost, which will never be fully repaid. The reputational damage of drug-taking for the Olympics continues. Despite the testing programmes, some competitors are caught at every Olympic Games; and some supposedly winning medalists are caught years afterwards. For several periods in the history of the Olympic Games, the reputation of fair competition has been seriously challenged and undermined. That has led to public scepticism and mistrust. It is vital that cheating never wins, or the Olympics will lose its place in our hearts. Fair play is a critical component in any competition. Perhaps one day Sharron Davies will be awarded her Gold medal.

~~~~~

---

[153] After time away, Sharron found her love of swimming again and went back to competitive swimming in her thirties winning more medals.

Trust is a fundamental part of a winning culture. Trust is an essential ingredient in establishing employee loyalty and maximising employee performance. Without trust no one can operate at their best or fulfil their maximum potential. Mutual trust is vital inside every social grouping, including society as whole.

Trust isn't always instant. It grows and builds as our relationships strengthen. That process takes effort and time. Every member of the team has to make the same effort to build trust. Each member has to be prepared to commit first. We like other people to prove themselves, before we fully commit to them. A group of strangers may share the same mission, but each one will be thinking 'Can I rely on everyone else?' When we share experiences together, we find out who we can trust.

Trust is a feeling, a matter of perception. We have to work hard to maintain the reality and other peoples' perceptions. Putting different employees together on joint projects is a great way to build their mutual trust. Working closely together can create the right perception of trust and build it in reality. Doing anything to undermine that trust can have a negative effect on the group.

Manchester Evening News heading: "Manchester United players backing Paul Pogba amid Real Madrid transfer interest"[154]

Manchester Evening News sub-heading: "Paul Pogba was abysmal in Man United's 6-1 thrashing by Tottenham and days later fluttered his eyelashes at Real Madrid again"[155]

Another key part of trust-building is learning to expect failure along the way. We should accept failure for what it is, namely invaluable experience. We need to trust each other to provide support rather than judgement. As human beings we learn far more from our mistakes than we do our successes. And learn we must. Providing a safe and nurturing environment to practice and learn in is vital. Families rightly offer that security for their young children. Expectations need to be reasonable. We don't expect a new-born baby to be able to unload a dishwasher. We don't expect puppies to come to heel without training them. So why would we expect a new team member be able to everything that the most experienced member can?

---

[154] Manchester Evening News online article 13/10/20.
[155] Manchester Evening News online article 13/10/20.

Sadly, in too many working organisations there is a lack of skills training, a lack of true support and a divisive blame culture. None of these are indications of trust or positive values. Businesses have to allocate time and space for teaching and learning, or their development will be stifled. The issue to balance is this. How can you create more opportunities for personal development, whilst maintaining a safety net to protect your organisation?" Controlled failures produce controlled successes. Experiencing mutual failures together brings mutual learning and they build mutual trust.

How an organisation treats its people will either build trust, or destroy it. With ever more homeworking, organisations are having to be even more trusting. Although some are less trusting than others. Those less trusting employers are using cameras and keystroke software to monitor activity. A 2020 poll carried out by Prospect, revealed that 80% of polled workers would be uncomfortable with any camera monitoring and 66% would be uncomfortable with any keystroke monitoring. The same poll revealed that 48% of workers felt that the introduction of monitoring software would damage their relationship with their manager. That figure rose to 62% among younger workers. Trust is a vital part of engagement. Winning performances come from mutual trust. No organisation can afford to undermine it.

In society in general, good values built mutual trust and lead to mutual gains. In Australia, the concept of 'mateship' stretches beyond liking your close friends, to helping anyone in need. Mateship is a social obligation, a form of civic duty. The concept is even enshrined in the Australian citizenship test. Having a deeply held feeling of connection will power any group of people, even strangers. Society can teach business a lesson on this. How much mateship is there in business? How much better would business be for it?

By controlling the risks that come from developing people, we can build trust in our processes and grow our organisation's skills and experience. By training people to avoid making mistakes, we can build their confidence in themselves; and we increase the likelihood of them giving something back. Give and you shall receive.

By saving people from harm, we build their trust. In the military, mistakes can have fatal consequences. Military mistakes have to be avoided as far as absolutely possible. But if no one trains with a real gun, those mistakes will happen when it really matters, in battle. The inevitable mistakes from soldiering need to be made safely, during peacetime training, in order to avoid them happening in war. The military invests in its people and develops relationships across the chain of command like no other business. It has to if it is to be effective. It has the perceived luxury of time in its preparation, but it can have far shorter timescales in operation. The quality and depth of trust is perhaps the biggest single difference between military teams and teams in business, sport and other sectors. Why is the military trust so much stronger? It's because civilian organisations don't invest in enough training, to build enough trust.

~~~~~

Sir. Stirling Moss competed in seven years of the Formula One Championship from 1955 to 1962. He was the runner-up four times and finished third the other three times. Widely regarded as a brilliant racing driver in his day, the reason Sir. Stirling didn't win a Formula One Championship wasn't down to his driving ability. It was his decision to drive mostly British made cars, which were less technologically advanced. Sir. Stirling could certainly have chosen a more competitive team to drive for, but he didn't. As a British driver, he wanted to drive a British car. This principled decision cost him at least one Formula One World Championship.

In 1958, Stirling Moss won four of the ten Formula One races and finished second in one more. He should have done enough to win the Championship. However, Sir. Stirling had to retire in all of the other five races due to car trouble. His car's technical specification couldn't match his ability to drive it.

There was another reason why he finished second in the 1958 Championship. At that year's Portuguese Grand Prix, Stirling chose to defend Mike Hawthorn from unfairly incurring a racing penalty. The points that Stirling saved Mike Hawthorn, resulted in Mike Hawthorn winning the Championship himself.

The 1958 Championship was also lost because of an error in communication between Sterling and his pit crew. A point was given for the fastest lap in each race, and the crew signalled "HAWT REC" meaning Hawthorn had set a record lap. Travelling at high speed, Stirling read this as "HAWT REG" and thought Hawthorn was making regular laps, so he did not try to set the fastest lap. The error came because the lettering on the sign wasn't clear enough. In fact, the crew was supposed to write-up the time of the lap. That would have told Stirling what time he had to beat. Without two-way radios, there was no way that the driver and pit crew could speak to each other. The pit crew didn't know Stirling had misread their message. The point was lost and so was the Championship.

Despite not winning a World Championship, Sir. Stirling Moss was content with his lot. That's because his decisions felt right and everyone had tried their best. Stirling's love, respect and loyalty to Motor Racing, Formula One, British manufacturing and his fellow drivers meant that he fought their corners before he fought his own. By promoting the best interests of his sport, colleagues and country, Sir. Stirling Moss stuck to his values. He didn't sell out or lose his sense of identity. He put his Super-tribes before himself.

> *"You've got to stand right up for something*
> *Or you're gonna fall for anything"* [156]

At least one Championship would have been won if Stirling had been more ruthless and selfish. But, if that's what it had to take, the cost of winning a Championship was too high a price for him to pay. Sir. Stirling Moss may not have won a World Championship, but because of his values he was a winner in life.

~~~~~

Culture is a combination of all of the multiple human dynamics between all the people in an organisation. Culture has to be built from within. When someone changes their behaviours, it can have a domino effect. When a team member steps up their level of commitment, that step-change is noticeable and influential. It can inspire greater commitment across the team. That's because when one team member ups their game, someone else always notices and feels a need to copy the same behaviours. When that person steps up their own levels in response, a third person will notice and choose to give more to the cause. A group can subconsciously spread a behaviour in a way that feels natural.

The same is true in reverse. A drop off in commitment, sacrifice or performance from a team member can result in others easing off their own efforts as a direct response. According to former American Football coach Bill Walsh "Bonding within the organisation takes place as one individual and then another steps up and raises his or her level of commitment, sacrifice and performance." Each person is responsible for maintaining their own levels.

> *"I attribute my success to this. I never gave or took an excuse"* [157]

---

[156] From 'You've got to stand for something' by John Cougar Mellencamp.
[157] Florence Nightingale.

Leaders can't make their teams gel, but they can create the kind of environment that inspires mateship. That comes from create the right mission, providing the best environment, offering the right rewards and motivating factors, as well as recruiting the right characters into the team. These steps are within a leader's control. They will help to facilitate the natural bonding process. Then the human processes can take place between the team members. A collaborative organisation is made not born.

Clarify everyone's responsibilities; and sell the collective rewards

Where a team is full of employed workers, it's often tough to sell a corporate mission and vision of the future. That task is much easier where there is an obvious joint benefit (e.g. winning a championship or cup in sport). Making the both the outcome and the process to achieve it inclusive is absolutely critical. Winning teams have to find their way together. Giving the team its 'head' to make decisions for itself will help it naturally help to pull that team together. Mutual discovery builds mutual trust.

The term 'organisational culture' is a misnomer. Cultures are made by the way people behave in relation to other people. Positive cultures will work for every stakeholder, not just a few of them. Negative, exclusive cultures will dramatically reduce the chances of winning.

Leaders must promote and apply the organisation's values and they must make the biggest sacrifices for the cause. In short, leaders have to lead by example and by facilitation. That means working harder and taking more pain than anyone else. In corporate terms that typically means working longer hours, but it should also mean more focused and smarter working. Leaders shouldn't demand ever longer hours from their team. Longer hours doesn't guarantee any greater output. They lead to lower quality and more errors. Teams need leaders who can lead them to a better place, not an ever harder one. Leaders play a pivotal role in embedding the values that really apply. They get to choose what kind of environment they create. The best ones unite through the mission and facilitation, they defend through their words and actions; and they sell everyone the dream. Bad leaders bark orders, demand ridiculous working hours, set unrealistic goals and keep pay and benefits lower than they should be. Bad values get a bad reaction and result in a bad performance.

~~~~~

As we've seen, success can be qualified as well as absolute. Success is a relative concept. Every competitor starts a challenge with different odds of finishing first. Some teams have more of a head start than others. If those teams win, it's likely to be less impressive, than if another team wins without the same head start. If your organisation has the greatest resources and the most talented people it should win every competition it faces. Shouldn't it? Is your team winning the proportion of competitions that it should be?

Why doesn't the 'best' team always win? Why doesn't the richest team always finish first? That's because there are many other factors involved in winning beyond money, resources and people. Every form of competition has different controllables to master. Working out what to do with who and what you've got is as important as having the greatest pool of people or the biggest pile of things.

The team with the best resources and people should win more often, but a team can still beat the odds by mastering the controllables that really matter, like Leicester City winning the Premier League in 2016. With initial odds of 5,000/1 against their win, in a league of only 20 teams, no one gave Leicester City a prayer. But the team's excellent value for money spent in recruitment (attracting both character and skill), its tight playing group (using the fewest players of any team that season), genuinely playing for each other (due to mutual trust and friendship), dealing with the pressure the best (because of their togetherness and their relaxed environment); and their attitude of battling to the end of every game (winning several key games very late on) gave them the consistency that they needed to finish first.

Armies can similarly defy the odds and secure victories against superior opponents, like Henry V and his 8,500 men, when they defeated 30,000 French soldiers at the Battle of Agincourt. The principle reason for this success wasn't down to troop numbers, it was the mismatch of weapons and armour. The English forces included 7,500 longbowmen. The French troops wore heavy armour which limited their movement in the mud and which couldn't stop the longbow arrows.

Whilst there are exceptions to the 'bigger is better' rule of thumb, having better resources often leads to a win. So, if your team is somewhere down the resources, people and strategy league tables, winning is a much bigger challenge. If you're in the bottom quartile for resources then finishing in the third quartile is relative success, a form of win. Winning doesn't have to mean finishing first; and when an unfancied team manages to win the whole competition, against the odds, it should be lauded more highly. The fact that the richest organisations don't always win everything gives every team a chance. That gives hope to every competitor. Less wealthy organisations can win if they the controllables better than the wealthy teams.

Castleford Tigers is one of the smallest Superleague clubs. That starts with its geography. Castleford is a town of only 35,000 people. Nearby rivals Wakefield Trinity has a city of 330,000 people to call on for support. Close by Leeds Rhinos has a city of over 750,000, over twenty times its size. Financial clout is similarly small. Castleford's annual turnover is approximately £5million, which is less than half that of the Leeds Rhinos. As a result of its limited resources, Castleford Tigers cannot offer a big modern stadium to play in, marquee salaries, or her best facilities to train and operate in. Based on the measures of financial clout, stadium size, training facilities and supporter numbers, Castleford should always lose to Leeds Rhinos, Wigan Warriors, St. Helens, Warrington Wolves and Hull FC, but they don't. They produce performances that repeatedly surprise the pundits. How is that possible?

There seem to be two reasons. Firstly, although Castleford is financially poor, it is one of the richest clubs in culture. And that makes an enormous difference. The culture at the club is one of battling against the odds. Perpetually short of the resources available to the other clubs, the coaches and players could whinge, give in or get on with it. By accepting less, they can put up with more. When disruptions occur they are less of a shock and less of an inconvenience. This has created a resilience amongst the people at the club. There is a dark humour in laughing when the wooden cupboards in the kitchen are empty or the doors are falling off. There is no soft-underbelly. There are no wasted resources. The players that don't settle there, don't have the same mettle. They leave. United against the odds, just being at the club builds character. And then, when the people are tough, the coaches teach them what you need to know.

Secondly, Castleford Tigers develops its players better than most other clubs. Every sporting club can punch above its weight if it gets these two critical elements right. One clear sign of strong player development is that Castleford players have won four Men of Steel Awards between 2010 and 2020. The Man of Steel Award is presented to the best player in the top English league of the sport each year. Castleford has produced the best player in Superleague more than any other club during that time, despite its limited resources. None of the four winning players had won it before arriving at the club. The 2020 Man of Steel winner Paul McShane said on receiving the award "There's something about Cas that makes you want to be your best". These four recent winners, Rangi Chase, Daryl Clark, Luke Gale and Paul McShane were all born elsewhere, but they were made in Castleford.

Luke Gale plays for Leeds Rhinos. He is England's first choice scrum-half and a leading player in the game. Before he joined Leeds, he was at Castleford for five seasons[158]. Before he joined Castleford, Luke Gale hadn't played for England. He hadn't won the Man of Steel Award and he hadn't won the Albert Goldthorpe Medal for consistently high performances. Castleford Head Coach Daryl Powell watched him played for Bradford Bulls. He didn't see a great player, what he saw was a player with lots of room for improvement.

Castleford has been blessed with coaching riches. Daryl Powell, Ryan Sheridan, Danny Orr and Tony Smith have all played for England[159] at the controlling position of half-back. So when Luke Gale was persuaded to join the club, he had four of the very best coaches to learn from. However, it wasn't just skills coaching that changed his fortunes. It was the decision to switch Luke from playing on the right edge (passing mostly left to right) to the left edge (passing mostly right to left) and teaming him up with Michael Shenton (left centre) and Luke Dorn (fullback). From that point onwards, Luke Gale immediately started to find a higher level. How long did that take? Hardly any time at all, inside the Castleford environment.

"I used to have nothing. Then I got this, this job, this family and I was better because of it"[160]

In the three years Luke Gale played a full-season at Castleford (2015-2017) he won the Albert Goldthorpe Medal for the most consistent player in all three seasons (having never done it before), played for England (making his debut) and was awarded Man of Steel in 2017 (having never won it before). In his first season with Leeds Rhinos, after leaving Castleford, Luke Gale brought his playing level and helped Leeds to win the 2020 Challenge Cup.
Daryl Clark was Man of Steel in 2014 with Castleford and was sold to Warrington the year afterwards, because the club was close to administration at the time. Daryl Clark has gone on to help Warrington win the Challenge Cup.

---

[158] Luke was injured for most of the last two.
[159] Sometimes the national team plays as England, sometimes as Great Britain. In rugby league they are essentially synonymous.
[160] Natasha Romanov in 'The Avengers: Endgame'.

Of the current crop of players, Michael Shenton, Mike McMeeken and Liam Watts have also gone on to play for England at Castleford. In addition Jake Trueman, Paul McShane and Danny Richardson have also been called up to the England squad (and will almost certainly make their debuts).

A culture of development, where the person is put first, will always provide the foundations on which to build something special. If you create the best culture, values and environment you will grow the best people. That's because culture, values and environment are all mortar within in any team's walls.

Takeaway thoughts:

- Every organisation needs to know what it stands for and what it stands against
- Division and disharmony in an organisation, create under-performance
- Trust, honesty and respect create good culture
- Organisational values have to support the mission
- Peer pressure can be a positive force to drive standards up
- Cultures are made by people not organisations
- Culture reaches beyond the boundaries of every organisation
- Weave your organisational values into your contracts, rules and procedures
- Fairness is vital
- Don't sell your culture out

3.4 WINNING PEOPLE AND ALIGNMENT

The fourth controllable is winning people and alignment. Every organisation needs the most naturally talented, best qualified, best trained and happiest people that it can recruit and retain. That is far easier said than done. Recruitment and retention is a never ending challenge. The best people always have other options. You have to persuade them to repeatedly choose to be at your organisation. Recruiting good people is hard and 'growing your own' is equally tough. But both are vital. If you can truly control your recruitment and retention process, you will move past your competitors.

Convincing good people to join and remain with you is only part of the challenge. High-performing teams are full of high-performing people. Some of them will come as high-performing individuals at other organisations. That's a useful head start but they need to be aligned with your organisation's mission, philosophy, culture and values or they won't perform as well with you. The whole organisation needs to think and act as one. Super-tribe thinking delivers superb results.

"Marching on together. We're gonna see you win"[161]

Others will become high-performing individuals because of their time within your system. Blending and aligning them comes out of empowering and motivational leadership. Every person in the team has to be aligned with the organisation's mission, philosophy, culture and values. Every person has to be aligned with each other. Controlling who is in your organisation and how integrated they are will get you much nearer to winning. If you fail to offer a sense of togetherness and social belonging, your people will not be able to perform well.

~~~~~

At the time of writing, Little Mix is the biggest girl group in the World. The four original group members, Jesy Nelson[162], Leigh-Anne Pinnock, Perrie Edwards and Jade Thirlwall weren't just four solo singers who occupied the same stage. They operated as one unit. By becoming an integrated into Little Mix, all four women have created a musical and personal harmony that transcends them as individuals. So much so, that the BBC asked them to front a new television

---

[161] A lyric from a popular Leeds United song.
[162] Jesy has since left. Whether the band can continue to be as successful will be interesting to see.

programme called 'Little Mix The Search'. The band members were tasked with putting together five brand new groups from scratch; and then picking one to go on tour with them. The show's opening remarks from the four band members gives a clear insight into why they've been so successful.

They draw strength from their relationship with their fans, especially when playing live. When you consistently provide exactly what your customers want, you can have a very successful business. People buy things and experiences but they buy them from people and they are delivered to them by people.

Jesy "We've sold 50 million records and our music had been streamed billions of times, but nothing beats the roar of a live crowd"

They have a musical and personal alignment that binds the four of them together as one whole. When every team member focuses on the common mission, something special happens.

Perrie "When we're together we're a force. None of us could have achieved any of this without each other.

They have an emotional connectivity that gives them strength and 'Girl Power'. Their fans can feel it too.

Leigh-Anne "When I'm on the stage with the girls, we feel each other's energy. That's the beauty of being in a group"

They have developed a togetherness that seems natural. They also have a likeability that comes from seeing their complete commitment to their mission, their fans and each other.

Jade "It's so much more special that we get to share this experience as a group and as friends. When the four of us come together it's just magic"

The four of them must have worked exceedingly hard to build their success. There are no passengers in the band. Together, they are stronger than they could ever have been alone. Little Mix can definitely shout out to their X Factor.

~~~~~

Inexperienced people can grow into high-performers, if you can uncover their potential and give them the best environment to learn in. They also need to be similarly aligned with your organisation's mission, philosophy, culture and values. Whether a team member is bought in or homemade, every one of them has got to contribute to the harmony of the whole.

Every stakeholder takes actions. Every action creates a ripple effect. Alignment comes when all your stakeholder ripples conflate, rather than crash together and disperse. Alignment is where all your stakeholders create one powerful wave in support of the mission rather than lots of smaller, competing waves. Having an agreed mission and common culture help to produce one well-directed wave, rather than a series of wild, turbulent ones. What wave pattern is your team producing?

Alignment is the art of controlling the winning controllables. Alignment isn't just icing on the organisational cake, it's the critical creation process involved in baking the cake. Alignment is the art of choosing the right chef, kitchen, oven, baking tray, greaseproof paper, recipe and ingredients. Alignment is getting the all of the timings and techniques spot on. Alignment is the whole baking process.

"So with flour on my hands, I'll show them all how Goddamn happy I am. Sugar, butter, flour don't let me down. Let's see the next amazing thing baking does now"[163]

Alignment is the key process involved in winning. It's about discovering and managing the controllables needed to win. Alignment is the way that you pull together all of elements required. What are those elements? Well they vary from competition to competition, but there are three types: strategic, framework and people. The more aligned these are, the easier winning becomes.

Strategic: Mission, Philosophy, Positioning, Deployment and Firepower.

Framework: Culture, Environment, Standards and Winning Behaviours.

People: Character, Skills, Mindset and X-Factor.

---

[163] From 'What Baking can do" in the musical Waitress.

This book includes references all of these elements. They are set out together in the diagram below.

ALIGNMENT OF THE WINNING CONTROLLABLES

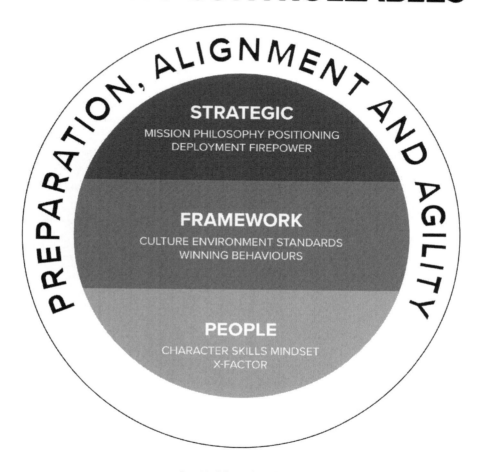

PREPARATION, ALIGNMENT AND AGILITY

STRATEGIC
MISSION PHILOSOPHY POSITIONING
DEPLOYMENT FIREPOWER

FRAMEWORK
CULTURE ENVIRONMENT STANDARDS
WINNING BEHAVIOURS

PEOPLE
CHARACTER SKILLS MINDSET
X-FACTOR

Each element forms part of the whole. Being able to align them all is the difference between winning and losing. Doing it once is hard enough. Then as our situations and challenges change around us, we have to be able to reposition ourselves and realign all these elements once again. We need to be able to do this repeatedly if necessary. Alignment is a never-ending process of preparing, adapting and holding it all together.

~~~~~

A team's official decision-makers have the formal responsibility for keeping every element aligned. But every single stakeholder shares the responsibility for a team's alignment. It's entirely co-incidental that the word 'alignment' contains the letters to spell the word 'team' but it's a good way to remember that alignment is a shared responsibility. As every single person counts in a group dynamic, it's critical to recruit and retain the right people for your team. Everyone has to play their part. Who is pulling things together and who is pulling things apart?

Before that process of recruitment can happen, you need to recruit your recruitment team. Who are the right people to put on this kind of project? The answer is simple. Your best people. The most engaged, most approachable and most charismatic people will sell your organisation in its best light. Equally, the wrong leaders and influencers will be lucky to recruit the people you need. The best forgers of team alignment will produce the performing team. Who do you need on point? Your best people. Who are they? They are the people who put your organisation and its mission first, before their own agendas.

"Side before self. Everytime"[164]

Alignment comes from all the daily interactions amongst the team's stakeholders and its contacts in wider society. Every interaction should help deliver your mission objectives. Alignment is a process of consistent directing, nudging and influencing. It's a continual and relentless re-shaping of every element, to keep it in place, or push it back there. This process is much easier said than done. Alignment has a human dynamic that is difficult to shape and control. On top of that, the VUCA World around us knocks us repeatedly out of whack. As a result, it's virtually impossible to be fully synchronised 100% of the time. But if we don't fight back, we lose synchronisation and fall into misalignment. Every

---

[164] A club banner on show at Leeds United matches.

stakeholder has to be observant (to look for misalignment) and diligent (about restoring any lost alignment). These two duties fall on everyone's shoulders. A complete focus and total buy-in are essential to maintain the alignment necessary for success.

"Now is the hour! Oaths you have taken.
Now fulfil them all, for Lord and land"[165]

Money alone doesn't earn a person's focus and buy-in to anything. Nor does fear or force. A team member's energy and engagement have to be willingly given. The act of surrendering to the team and its mission creates the biggest form of buy-in. But no one does that without the promise of something compelling in return. To earn that level of loyalty, a team has to offer something that its individuals will voluntarily choose to bind themselves to. To produce full power, a team needs to secure full commitment from its people. There has to be an emotional attachment to the mission, based on achieving an inspiring, common purpose. Great teams achieve this and go on to become tribes[166]. They can reach a higher level of performance than solo performers or enforced teams could ever muster.

Individuals can drive themselves to success by treating the people around them as being part of the same team, someone else on a shared mission. That way every individual can create the force needed for a team dynamic. Finding a common purpose with your co-workers will always improve your interactions and your outcomes. To win more, join in more.

In a winning team, all the medals and trophies are jointly earned and jointly shared. Winning as a team is much more satisfying. The pieces of gold, silver or bronze are nothing without the emotions they conjure. The feeling of being part of a team is of greater worth to us than the feeling of being independent. It taps into our need for social belonging. That's a good hook to draw new team members in with. If our team is aligned to deliver our mission, we can all enjoy winning together.

The memories from being part of a winning team will always have an extra level to ones from solo wins. They are shared forever. Ironically Niki Lauda, the two-

---

[165] Eomer to members of the Rohirrim in the final part of the Lord of the Rings trilogy, 'The Return of the King'.
[166] This is the subject of 'Build Your Super-tribe'.

time Formula 1 Champion and solo driver, is able to appreciate the memories more than the trophies.

"What's it worth a trophy? You can look at it and then...
it's not worth to me anything, because the memory of
something is much more than a trophy"

~~~~~

People make and break businesses of all kinds. Differences in thinking, approach, responsibilities and rewards can divide a team, but they can also make it. Division within a team is not inevitable. Alignment can be forged from the fiercest of fires.

Society is full of difference, based on many characteristics including gender, sexuality, marital status, nationality, race, religion, political and philosophical beliefs, socio-economic background, accent, earnings, career etc.. The daily interactions between all the different cultures and characteristics provide society with a healthy dynamic tension that brings shared understanding, respect and common ground. Finding unity through difference is a strength of winning teams. However, society's demographic diversity is often under-represented inside business and sport. That's a weakness. The links between a Company and its customers, clients, suppliers, advisers and local community have to be strong and vital. Every stakeholder matters. Every team has to be reflective of society, in order to appeal to it.

Internally and externally, diversity matters the same. A business needs to build a positive relationship with each of its workers, customers and other stakeholders. It needs their engagement with the mission, as it's their combined alignment that powers the organisation's performance. A mission has to speak passionately and inclusively to each stakeholder as an individual with their particular combination of personal characteristics. If an organisation respects, embraces and reflects the traditions and beliefs of all of its stakeholders, its engagement building exercise will be far more successful. The more demographic diversity there is inside any organisation, the greater it will understand its people and its markets. The more experiences it can call on, the greater its reach and power of delivery. Too much of a demographic imbalance creates a mis-alignment between a team and the wider World. Winning teams embrace difference and find good people who challenge your way of thinking. Duplicated ideas aren't twice as correct, there's twice the stagnation.

Different operating styles can be complimentary and successful.
Take Ben & Jerry,[167] Steve Jobs and Steve Wozniak,[168]
Clough and Taylor - the list is long and distinguished

All of the examples above are pairs of white men, with a similar age. They had different approaches to each other, but how differently could they think? How much of a challenge did they put up to each other? Did the rest of their support team share similar characteristics and thinking? Would that work as well now? It's commercially wise to go much further than this narrow degree of difference[169]. Every customer has independent wants and needs. To understand, empathise and meet those needs, your organisation needs a broad understanding of society. One of the many commercial advantages of demographic diversity is that it often brings cognitive diversity with it. The more ideas there are available, the more potential there is for growth and development. The greater the differences in thinking and approach, the more ideas can be created; and the more opportunities will be generated.

"In order to be irreplaceable one must always be different"[170]

We like people like us. We like people who agree with us, all the time. Homogeneity feels comfortable because there's far less disagreement and tension. But we actually need people who are different t us. We need their alternative inputs and understanding. The friction from our interactions with different concepts, traditions and behaviours is what produces the sparks of invention. It's not uniformity or similarity that generates change, its heterogeneity. That diversity of thinking isn't anti-commercial, having it is a huge commercial advantage.

When all the senior leaders of an organisation are the same and think the same, they produce very similar group thinking. That homogeneity might seem positive, due to the lack of conflict, but when decision-making is too easy it's too limiting. The same people and processes just produce more of the same. Don't get out the glasses and celebrate when your team quickly agrees on a solution. Think broader and invite some different people to join your discussion group.

---

[167] According to Ben, Jerry is the "warm, caring" people person and according to Ben, Jerry is the "never satisfied, risk-taking, driving force". Without them both we wouldn't have got to try Phish Food or Cookie Dough.
[168] Steve Wozniak was the technical computer builder. Steve Jobs had the business skills and foresight to sell what "Woz" could build. Together they created Apple.
[169] Every stakeholder's interests need to be reflected.
[170] Gabrielle Bonheur "Coco" Chanel, the founder of the Chanel brand.

"Someone once told me growth and comfort do not co-exist. And I think it's a really good thing to remember"[171]

Great music isn't formed by a single repeated note. Great music is more diverse and multi-layered than that, with different notes being played by different instruments. Yet it still manages to be tuneful. That's because it blends instruments and notes harmoniously to produce a combined melody. Dissonance is where there's a clash between different flows. In music, dissonance is where there's a clash of notes. Great music comes from consonance, by finding the right notes and frequencies that work together. Beethoven's 5th Piano Concerto (known as the Emperor Concerto) was written for a piano, two flutes, two oboes, two clarinets, two bassoons, two horns, two trumpets, timpani and strings. With so more than fifteen parts to be written and inter-connected, the eventual noise could have been a cacophony. Instead, due to Beethoven's skill in linking all the instruments and notes together, his Emperor Concerto is a masterpiece.

All tunes are a series of individual notes connected into harmonious patterns. Good organisations interconnect in the same way. Great organisations welcome in cognitive differences and happily accept the challenge of inter-connecting them together. Heterogeneity adds great value in an environment where it's respected, embraced and reflected. More diversity of thinking is a huge opportunity that we need to tune into. In this regard, it's interesting that the Washington American Football Team has dropped its "Redskins" moniker due to pressure from its sponsors and wider society. The Black Lives Matter and other equality movements are leading the drive to respect each other more as human beings. That's very wise and very welcome. It is Super-tribe thinking, rather than narrow 'tribal' thinking[172].

~~~~~

Online trading and investments provider IG produced a 2020 analysis of "Women CEOS in the FTSE 100." Of those top 100 businesses only five had female CEOs. That's an increase of just one since 2012. The same IG analysis showed that only two of the FTSE 100 had an executive committee made up of more women than men. They were[173] Burberry Group (61.3%) and Next (53.9%). The other 98

---

[171] Virginia "Ginny" Rometty, Executive Chair at IBM.
[172] The irony is deliberate.
[173] And possibly still are.

companies had a male imbalance of at least 56.1% on their executive committees. That's 'at least' 56.1%. For some of them the 'imbalance' is 100% male.

According to a joint Cranfield School of Management and EY Report, one in seven executive director roles (13.2%) were held by women in June 2020. The figure for the larger FTSE 250 was less, at 11.3%.

Why does this matter? The moral and social arguments are surely so obvious they don't need to be rehearsed here. Unsurprisingly, the commercial argument for diversity is just as strong. The Pipeline's "Women Count 2020 Report" found that London-listed companies with no women on their executive committees have an average net profit of 1.5%, whereas those with a proportion of more than 1 in 3 women reach a 15.2% net profit margin. According to the report and the Foreward from the Rt. Hon Theresa May MP, there are six female CEO's in the FTSE 100 (which differs by 1 from the IG report). Either way, this is reportedly less than number of CEO's called 'Peter'. The narrowness of thinking in some of these respective companies could explain the difference in their net profit margins.

Also according to the IG review, female FTSE 100 CEOs earn an average of 16.66% less total remuneration on average than their male counterparts. In October 2020, research by the Fawcett Society and the Global Institute for Women's Leadership at King's College London found that the UK lags behind other countries which have "much more robust systems" for tackling the gender pay gap. This all begs the question, 'Is a business better served by a CEO who feels well rewarded or one who feels undervalued?' It's a social, moral and economic no brainer. People make and break businesses. How engaged and aligned are your key stakeholders?

The percentage of BAME[174] executives in the FTSE 250 was 5.3% in 2019, according to the Sir John Parker Review. 69% of FTSE 250 companies had no BAME directors. The same moral and social arguments apply here too. I would expect the commercial argument to stack up equally well.

Influential institutions are pushing the diversity agenda ever harder. There is an unstoppable momentum towards equality of opportunity. In 2020 the UK's biggest fund manager, Legal & General Investment Management, warned every FTSE 100 listed company of "voting and investment consequences" if they fail to diversify their senior leadership team by 2022. Legal & General wants all FTSE 100 boards

---

[174] Black, Asian and Minority Ethnic.

to include at least one BAME member by January 2022. If FTSE 100 companies fail to meet that target, Legal & General has reportedly said that it will vote against the re-election of their company's chairperson or the head of their nomination committee.

Also in 2020, the Confederation of British Industry launched a campaign called 'Change the Race Ratio' designed to increase racial and ethnic participation in British businesses. The campaign has targeted the FTSE companies, demanding that the FTSE 100 have at least one BAME board member by the end of 2021 and FTSE 250 companies do so before 2024. And other stated commitments include the need for companies to disclose ethnicity pay gaps by 2022 and the need for an inclusive culture and the support processes necessary to bring more BAME candidates through.

I'm not aware of any survey or initiative that includes trans or gender fluid employees, perhaps because the data isn't measured yet. Every additional type of background and personal characteristic adds understanding and experience. This position begs the rhetorical question, 'Is a business better served by an executive group that reflects its customers, suppliers and local community, or one that is narrower than that?' There are plenty of roles to allocate in any executive team, so there are no reasons not to. How much diversity of thinking does your organisation have? The narrower our inclusiveness, the less we know and understand.

Professor Dame Wendy Hall is at the forefront of the UK's development of artificial intelligence and the semantic web[175]. Wendy is very clear about the need for diversity in the field of A.I. because an algorithm mimics and retains the opinions and biases of the person who created it. That's not always obvious, as it often comes from a subtle and subconscious permeation. But whether its accidental or deliberate, all of the data that follows from a bias is tarnished by it. In Wendy's opinion "A.I. needs a socio-technical solution. We have to incorporate diversity at every stage of every A.I. process. That doesn't mean 'rebalancing' through positive discrimination, it means removing all the biases". That's exactly how every organisation should operate for maximum success.

~~~~~

However broad an organisation's decision-making process, its alignment comes from getting everyone behind all of the decisions it makes. Firstly, there has to be

---

[175] The semantic web aims to build on the World Wide Web, to make internet data machine-readable. Dame Wendy is working on this project with Tim Berners-Lee, the founder of the World Wide Web.

total commitment from all the senior decision-makers. Unanimous decisions are hard to get to, unless the thinking behind them is restricted and narrow. Majority decisions are much more likely. They only work when everyone agrees to follow them. So getting everyone to agree that they will back the mission completely, is step one.

Then you need to get the buy-in of every other stakeholder. That's much easier if all of those stakeholders have been involved in choosing that mission, as well as the organisational philosophy and its values. Another clinching factor is the need for every decision to produce a benefit for every stakeholder. Unless a mission speaks to someone personally, it won't motivate them enough to make it a reality.

"Go beyond merely communicating to 'connecting' with people"[176]

There is a collective need to check that your organisation's decision-making supports its mission. Every decision should get you closer to achieving your mission outcomes, whilst maintaining your philosophy and values. If you need to adapt one element or another, that needs to be agreed first.

~~~~~

Castleford Tigers Head Coach, Daryl Powell suggests that sporting coaches want a job that's "intriguing and challenging" but they also want to be somewhere where everyone believes that success is "achievable". So, when it comes to contract negotiations, Daryl rotates the decision-making process 180 degrees and poses his own question "Do you believe in me and my philosophy?" Without top level support, no coach has much of a chance. However, if there is a meeting of minds at the top, the club has the chance of pulling together and winning a trophy. Winning in any organisation won't happen without the full commitment of the most senior executives and every other stakeholder.

In sport, the whole coaching team has to be in agreement about the philosophy, or it will be gradually undermined. Daryl works with coaches who are aligned on how to play and control a game. It probably isn't a surprise that Ryan Sheridan and Danny Orr were also halfbacks like Daryl. In their playing days, all three had to take responsibility for the team out on the field. Relevant experience is so valuable when it comes to planning to win. And isn't just the three of them. For Daryl the whole coaching team is very strong. That includes the rugby coaches,

---

[176] Author, Jerry Bruckner.

physios, strength and conditioning team, video and data analysts as well as everyone supporting them. "We're a small team but we're very tight. We all understand each other and we're all very determined to win trophies."

No manager or head coach can do it alone, whatever the sport. Alignment on the playing philosophy is crucially important. But like every other leader, Daryl needs to make sure that there is enough challenge and diversity in the coaching team's decision-making.

> *"We have an exceptional staff. We are all together a pretty good Premier League Manager. In all departments we brought really good people in. So it's not a coincidence that we are successful, but it's still massive that we are that successful"* [177]

Once the coaching team and its philosophy has got that board level buy-in, the club's recruitment needs to focus on bringing in the best players to fit that philosophy and moving on those that don't. Sport and business both involve human beings and their livelihoods. Changes in personnel will often be needed, to adapt a team to win its competition. But that doesn't excuse the ill-treatment of anyone, however badly they might fit into the new playing structure. How change is made is fundamental and goes right back to the club's values. People should be treated well, at all times, especially as they are leaving. Alignment comes experiencing and witnessing fair and equal treatment. How you treat a leaver is the mark of how much the organisation really cared about them. If a team of players see a popular colleague mistreated it will make them feel less engaged and less loyal. That's the same in any kind of team. In turn, every team member has to personally commit to the mission, the values and the philosophy. That's a minimum standard. No one should ever have to be asked 'Are you really with us?'

Players arriving from other countries need time to adapt to the social group. Any changes in language, accent, housing, routine, weather and food will all affect a player's performance. In sport, new players need a full pre-season to fully understand how the club's playing philosophy works in practice. They need experience of playing in the UK to understand the domestic game. They also need to find their best position in their new team. Castleford Tigers Head Coach, Daryl

---

[177] Liverpool Manager, Jürgen Klopp, in a BBC Sport Interview after winning the 2019/20 Premier League.

Powell says "However much due diligence you do, you never get a full picture of a player before you sign them. You never know what they'll be like at your club and in your team." You have to get them into your environment and get to know them. You need to give them time to adapt to your systems."

People time is a big investment. Time is in short-supply, especially when a team is on a losing run or a business is losing money. There doesn't tend to be much patience from company shareholders or owners and fans of major sports teams. But patience is a key ingredient in winning. People time is the best form of investment. If your people are at their best, then so will your performance be. There are three areas to support through investment. They are in a good working environment (for workers at home and in the office), personal career development (for every worker, at every level) and people interaction (by providing time and space for the social sparks of creativity to fire).

~~~~~

Putting the organisation's mission ahead of your own personal agenda is a winning behaviour. That kind of selflessness isn't just required of an organisation's leaders. Everyone has to put the 'team' first. But it's true that all leaders have to lead by example. You cannot expect a team to perform for you if you care less about that team than you do about yourself. Leaders have to make them same sacrifice and then have to make it first. The mission, not the leader, comes first. If the team isn't convinced, then its manager is vulnerable.

In 1973, President Nixon was impeached by Congress for the "obstruction of justice, abuse of power, and contempt of Congress" over the Watergate scandal. Nixon had thought he was above the law and democratic process. Congress felt that it couldn't trust or control him, so he had to go. There was no alignment.

"I don't think tension makes for great records.
That's a load of bollocks"[178]

In 1974, Brian Clough lasted forty-four days as the Manager of Leeds United. His blunt, outspoken management style made him appear arrogant. He came across as if he thought he was bigger than the club. The tight-knit Leeds team, which had

---

[178] Singer, Liam Gallagher.

been used to the positivity of Don Revie, rebelled against 'Cloughie' and quickly had him ousted.

In 1993, Kay Whitmore was the CEO of Eastman Kodak, the camera film production company. He famously fell asleep in a meeting with Bill Gates, which discussed integrating Kodak's products within Windows. A colossal opportunity to transfer into the digital market was missed. As a result, Eastman Kodak lost its place in the market. Kay Whitmore oversaw its rapid decline until he was sacked three years later. If you can't even muster enough energy to stay awake for that kind of kind of meeting, you're the wrong person for the job.

~~~~

The higher the levels of performance you can produce consistently, the more successful you'll be. Consistent excellence is the goal. Alignment brings that consistency. To achieve that you'll need enormous amounts of hard work and complete alignment, from every stakeholder. When any organisation manages to produce consistent excellence it is winning.

On 9 December 1960, the streets of Weatherfield came alive for the first time. Made by Granada Television[179], the fictional borough of Salford quickly became a hotbed of gossip and drama. By 2010, those streets had become the subject of the World's longest-running television soap opera[180]. With over 10,000 episodes under its belt, Coronation Street is over sixty years old[181]. How has this Northern English 'soap' known as 'Corrie' and 'The Street' outlasted them all?

"I've got this wonderful idea for a television series. I can see a little back street in Salford, with a pub at one end and a shop at the other, and all the lives of the people there, just ordinary things"[182]

From the beginning, Coronation Street wasn't ordinary. It was dramatic, realistic and funny. Once Southern viewers got to grips with the accent and dialect, they liked it too. On several times a week, events moved quickly, almost in real time. It became easy to 'share' what happened to the characters and invest in them. With

---

[179] Now ITV Granada.
[180] The Archers, first broadcast in 1950 is the World's longest radio soap opera. The term 'soap opera' comes from the fact that radio situation dramas were originally sponsored by soap manufacturers, who saw them as a great marketing opportunity.
[181] Very nearly, at the time of writing.
[182] Tony Warren, creator of 'Coronation Street'.

no weeks off or seasons like other programmes, 'Corrie' kept developing its storylines and carried on all year round. With plot developments in every episode, if you didn't watch for a few days, you lost the threads. You had to tune in, or you got tuned out.

Good television invites you to go inside other Worlds, to dwell there a while and forget your own. Great television doesn't just invite you in, it pulls you in headfirst. When a storyline's gripping enough, you feel you can't miss an episode. But even if you take time out, or want to join in late, you can pick things up in a few weeks of watching. You can join a 'soap' at any point and if it's good, you'll get hooked.

"When I got my first television set, I stopped caring so much about having close relationships"[183]

Just like a family's dedication to a sports team, loyalty to 'the Street' has been passed down through the generations. Once a mum and dad became viewers, so did their children and then their children after them. Millions of people have grown up with the characters, as if they were close friends and neighbours. Depending on the viewer's age, the show's viewers have got to know different generations of the characters, just like a real family. Sticking steadfastly to its DNA of drama, realism and humour, Coronation Street has ensured that there has always been a good a mix of characters and storylines.

Three dimensional characters like Elsie Tanner, Vera Duckworth, Deidre Rachid, Sally Webster, Steve McDonald, and Carla Connor have added plenty of drama. Gritty storylines covering drugs, cancer, gender reassignment, babies swapped at birth, murder and rape have added the realism. Characters like Hilda Ogden, Bet Lynch, Reg Holdsworth and Fred Elliott have added plenty of good humour. This combination of drama, realism and humour is a winning formula. Consistently maintaining all three, for over sixty years, is what's made the programme so successful for so long.

The show's viewing figures hit their peak in March 1989, when Coronation Street attracted 26.93 million viewers. That was getting on for half the country. Since then, the popularity of soap operas like Coronation Street has waned. In 2020, the regular viewing figure was down to roughly 7 million an episode. In the 2020's

---

[183] Andy Warhol.

there are several challenges faced by the programme; and its status as a successful show is under serious threat.

Firstly, society has changed a great deal since 1960. There are many alternatives to a family evening in front of the television. Even when family members want to watch something, they tend to be divided into different rooms, on different devices, watching different platforms and different channels.

Secondly, viewers are looking for more instant gratification these days and viewing behaviours have changed as a result. Channel hopping, binging on box sets, watching online vloggers, gaming and chattering over social media are all proving greater pulls than organising your life around the timings of a television programme.

Thirdly, Coronation Street has expanded its number of episodes to six times a week and its cast of regulars to over sixty people. The show now feels too big and impersonal. Following all of the storylines is harder than ever. Writing endless compelling storylines is proving too hard a task. The programme's consistency has fallen a level. The Street just isn't compelling enough. We need to invest and care about the characters we spend time with. But caring about the characters is much harder when there are so many.

On top of that, there's a fourth trend impacting on the show. That's our need for greater realism. Soap operas run storylines which mirror real events, but that format doesn't offer enough realism nowadays. Reality television shows are proving almost as popular, like Love Island with nearly 6 million viewers. Every programme has to adapt to stay aligned to its mission.

"Times and conditions change so rapidly that we must keep our aim constantly focused on the future"[184]

The changes within society are stacking up against the programme. This might be controversial with some, but the show may no longer be a winning show. The show's producers need to adapt Coronation Street for it to thrive again. Some dramatic action is needed.

Reducing the programme to two or three times a week might help to increase viewing figures. It's unrealistic to expect anyone to invest more fixed time than

---

[184] Walt Disney.

that. Watching six episodes a week is too big an imposition on modern life. Allowing people to binge watch the programme whenever they want (without having to wait for set times) would definitely help too. Giving viewers access to all of the past episodes online, on demand, might persuade people to re-watch old episodes and get back into the show.

Adding even more drama, even more realism and even more humour would help too. The formula is sound, it's a modern version of it that's needed. Securing one or more big name actors and actresses to join would help to boost the programme's popularity. Adding an established dramatic lead and a household named comedian could create more interest too. Ironically, hiring one or more reality stars could add a new audience. Corrie has been a winning show for too long, to let it become a losing one.

~~~~~

In 1992 Mike Ford helped to get his club Castleford to the Challenge Cup Final. At Wembley they faced up to his old team Wigan. Castleford had a team including international players Lee Crooks, Graham Steadman, Tawera Nikau, Tony Smith[185] and Mike himself, but it was only the team's first season together as a group. Wigan had many more internationals in their ranks and greater stability amongst the playing group. As a club, Wigan were far more used to winning big games. Their squad included several legends of the game: Shaun Edwards, Martin Offiah, Dean Bell, Gene Miles, Andy Gregory, Joe Lydon and Phil Clarke. Wigan had strong leaders right across the pitch. Both teams had some X Factor players, but Wigan had more big match experience. Wigan were great finishers. They didn't just play in finals, they won them. Their mental strength was what got them through the close games.

Wigan had won the Challenge Cup for the four previous years. Wembley was becoming their 'second home.' On the day, Wigan controlled the occasion and started the better team. They went on to beat Castleford and win the match 28 v 12. Wigan then went on to win the Challenge Cup for three more years afterwards, meaning that they won it an incredible eight years in succession from 1988 to 1995. That feat has never been equalled before or since. As well as being the cup holders, Wigan were also the reigning League Champions (1990/91 season) and they won the title again that same year (1991/2). Wigan were the

---

[185] Tony Smith (Casper) wouldn't forgive me if I left him out.

League Champions from 1989/90 to 1995/6 inclusive. So in 1992, Castleford came up against a winning machine. But what made Wigan so good, for so long?

"In the sports arena I would say there is nothing like training and preparation. You have to train your mind as much as your body"[186]

There are a number of reasons for Wigan's success, which were all aligned. They had excellent players. They had great confidence in themselves and each other. They had trust, honesty and respect for each other. They had strong leadership on the field. They set higher standards of training, winning, behaviour and self-discipline than anyone else. They were incredibly dedicated and professional. They played at a higher intensity and with higher skill than anyone else. They never gave in. The more they won, the more they wanted to win. They loved winning. Their success made other players want to join them, creating a conveyer belt of excellent players on standby. Wigan had created a virtuous circle.

All these were important factors, but which of them was the most important? Mike Ford believes "You only have a chance of winning trophies if you have good players." Recruiting and retaining the best people is almost always number one in the list of what matters. Then secondly you can build a winning culture with them. Without a winning culture, the best players will stop being the best players.

I asked Mike how you create a winning culture? "A winning culture takes a while to build. It starts with honesty, trust and respect. Those values build the strongest kind of relationships. Together they create a mutual belief and confidence between the players and the coaches. In that environment, relationships can develop faster and grow stronger. When that kind of environment exists, the players start to put their trust in each other. They feel part of something. That makes them work incredibly hard so they don't let each other down. That pushes the standards up. Then if the highest standards aren't met, the players call each other out."

Before you can start winning regularly, the process of creating success begins with recruiting the very best people you can. After that, creating the best culture is a close second. In that environment, good coaching can have its best effect.

---

[186] Venus Williams, winner of seven Grand Slam tennis titles.

According to Mike "Some people say that a winning team will always have a good culture and that a losing team must have bad culture, but that's not always true. Some teams have good cultures, but they don't have enough good players to win trophies. What's true is that winning definitely helps to create a positive culture and environment. Winning games makes you more likely to win more games. In my playing days, Wigan developed that winning culture very successfully." Wigan set incredibly high standards and then they topped them. They signed excellent players, improved them and then they signed more. The Wigan side of 1992 had extraordinary skill, confidence, leadership and experience. Overall, that 1992 Wigan team was too good for Castleford.

Two years later in 1994, Castleford and Wigan played each other in another competition final. This time it was the Regal Trophy. The core of the teams was essentially the same, although this time Wigan included legends Jason Robinson and Andy Farrell, to go with Shaun Edwards, Martin Offiah and Phil Clarke. At the time Wigan were still winning Challenge Cups and League titles. They were still in their pomp. However, Castleford started the game much better than the 1992 final and against the odds they went on to win the match 33 v 2. Wigan were never in the game. To say the result was a 'shock' in the sport is an extreme understatement. It's arguably the biggest upset in a rugby league final. What had changed so much at Castleford?

According to Mike Ford there had been a cultural change at the club. "Our leadership group had grown much stronger by then. We were more trusting in each other. The combination of Lee Crooks, Graham Steadman, Tawera Nikau and myself were better able to work together and control things at training and during matches. The more leaders you have, the stronger you are as a team. They don't accept any lowering of the standards."

Some of the senior players at Castleford had begun to set higher standards. Crucially the heavy-drinking culture was starting to reverse, with teetotal players like Mike and Tawera Nikau rejecting calls to go out on the infamous 'Mad Monday' binge after the weekend's matches. The destructive peer pressure began to reduce and a new breed of role-models emerged. Young players could now compete to become better professionals, rather than compete to become better drinkers. An ethic of hoping for some luck on the day, gave way to one of hard work and preparing to win.

"Luck has nothing to do with it. I have spent many, many hours, countless hours, on the court working for my one moment in time, not knowing when it would come"[187]

Mike is full of praise for former loose forward Tawera Nikau. "Tawera was much more dedicated than the other players to start with. He even had his own personal trainer in the early 1990's, when it was pretty much unheard of. He set really high standards and others followed." Winning standards can create alignment; and alignment creates consistency.

The improving fortunes of the club started to attract more good players. By 1994, Castleford had added the likes of Tony Kemp[188] at half-back and Simon Middleton[189] on the wing. The new players added more skill and more character. According to Mike "We also had X Factor players like Graham Steadman[190], Richie Blackmore[191] and St. John Ellis[192]." Castleford had created its own virtuous circle. And whilst the club never got close to emulating Wigan's long-term success, it proves that any team can create its own winning momentum.

Recruiting the very best people is of fundamental importance. Mike Ford has two key rules about recruitment. The first is "Never sign bad character." Mike is honest about not always getting that right. "The recruitment mistakes I've made have been mainly when I didn't look hard enough into the player's character before we signed him." Good character protects and preserves the team's values and culture. Bad character undermines them. Often, it's the other players that call this out before the coaches do.

"To be in the service of others, with men I respect, like you all, I shouldn't have to ask for more than that"[193]

Mike's second rule is "Aim to sign players who can add an X Factor or point of difference." Each new recruit should be better than the people you've already got.

---

[187] Serena Williams, winner of twenty-three Grand Slam tennis titles.
[188] A New Zealand International.
[189] Now England's Women's Rugby Union Head Coach.
[190] Who went on to coach rugby union with Ireland, Scotland, Newcastle, Cardiff and London Scottish.
[191] A New Zealand International.
[192] 'Singe' scored a club record 40 tries in the 1993-94 season; and went on to coach Doncaster Rugby League to some success, before he tragically died whilst coaching at the age of 41.
[193] The character Jack Horne in the 2016 version of 'The Magnificent Seven'.

And each player must be of good character. Ideally each new person brings a skill set you don't already have.

As for alignment, Mike has a clear piece of advice "When everyone's working together to find solutions to problems, the culture is probably positive. When everyone's looking to find problems to solve it probably isn't." The quality and quantity of communication is a good test of culture. Mike believes that "Talking to each other respectfully is vital. A group that trusts each other can find those solutions. A group that doesn't have that trust and respect, can't find the solutions it needs".

~~~~~

How a team of people gets on together will always make a big difference to that team's performance. The foundation stone is mutual respect, which is absolutely essential in any successful team. It's the first layer of bricks. Without it there won't be anything like a winning team performance. If one team member doesn't respect another team member, that has to be resolved. It's a point of misalignment. Don't allow a dispute to fester and don't allow one team member to be treated better than another. Otherwise, you can cause a fatal rift.

Resolutions of personal conflicts come in many forms, but the challenging question "Why don't you respect that person?" is a good place to start. If there is no respect there is not team. If, after steps have been taken, any team member cannot respect another colleague, then one of them has to leave the team. Which one of them that is may depend on who is more at fault. If both of them have broken the team's values or committed losing behaviours then both may have to go. When there is mutual respect, there can be a team. That doesn't guarantee any winning though.

Beyond respect comes liking. That's because we tend to work harder for people we like and care about. Liking our colleagues raises the level of mutual support we offer each other and our collective performance. Beyond liking comes higher state, that of caring. If every team member cares for every other team member, you get a richer, deeper, more powerful dynamic. Where there is genuine empathy between team members, you have the kind of teamworking that enables you to create a winning team. Finally, above all these, there is mutual devotion. If you can reach that level of self-sacrifice, then your actions move beyond conscious choice and into subconscious reaction. We becomes human automatons, directed solely on our joint mission. Devoted teams are the easiest to coach into winning teams. We need to nurture a state of devotion.

BUILD A WINNING RELATIONSHIPS' WALL

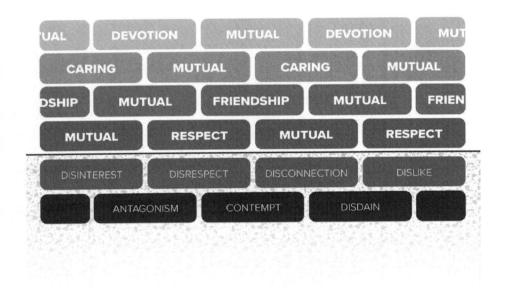

In addition to the people relationships, a mutual commitment to the team's mission is also essential. If any team member has higher priorities than the team's, it can create a schism in the team. Agreeing and publishing the team's mission, values and philosophy should allow team members to stick to each other and to their mission. Establishing the team's winning standards, winning behaviours and losing behaviours helps manage the controllables enormously. Agreeing these ways of operating helps every team member to call-out a colleague who isn't acting appropriately, or to praise one who is.

Mutual respect and mutual commitment are the key ingredients in creating a positive team dynamic. Winning is extremely difficult without either of these. If both already exist in a team, then that is a great start. If they don't exist, then immediate steps have to be taken to develop them.

Respect, commitment and bonding all come from the process of sharing. Having a genuinely shared mission fosters a mutual commitment. Having a shared philosophy also builds a mutual commitment and mutual caring. Having shared skills, abilities and roles brings mutual respect. Having shared values helps to create bonds of friendship and respect. Having positive shared experiences together creates respect, commitment and friendship. Aim to create a virtuous circle, a shared one.

~~~~~

In the real world, teams are usually made up of people who don't get on brilliantly outside work. The larger the team, the more of an issue this tends to be. Often, each team member dislikes at least one of their colleague. That tension can create feelings of frustration, irritation and disengagement. There has to be something more than other people to tie everyone in. If the mission is important enough, most people will function on a civil level. But unless it's truly compelling, they won't look out for each other or be pro-active. Team leaders therefore need to build up the importance of their mission's objectives, to a point where personal likes and dislikes become secondary. Once only the mission matters to all of us, we will see our team in a better light.

But what happens if an individual won't comply with the team's protocols? What should we do when a colleague puts self-interest first? How much selfishness and individualism should a team's management tolerate? Should an X factor player be picked regardless of their character, commitment and values? Or does that cause too much misalignment?

The names Kevin Pietersen (England, cricket), Roy Keane (Republic of Ireland, football) and Finn Russell (Scotland, rugby union) are famous for their prowess on the field. They are also rumoured to be allegedly 'difficult' off it. At what price does a person's ability come? Each one of these players was picked on their ability. But then each one had to leave their team after falling-out with their team's management. We don't know all the details, the background or the precise context, so I'm not going to offer a judgement on any of these people. But this does prompt an important question 'Should you ever tolerate losing behaviours from someone, because they have skills you need?'

When do you keep an X Factor team member? Under what circumstances do you let them go? There is always a tipping point to release anyone and everyone from a team. No one should have immunity. Ignoring employment law, so we can look more fundamentally, there is a sliding scale of possibilities. One option would be to say goodbye if the net result of someone's involvement is negative. At that point, a person's involvement reduces the team's chance of winning. Why would you keep anyone who reduces your chances of winning?

"In any group there will be some rascals and some villains. I would never keep a villain, even if he was the best player in the club. But I'd keep a rascal, as long as he could play"[194]

That first 'balancing' approach would give higher skilled people more behavioural latitude than others. The more able they are, the more they could misbehave and still be allowed to stay. Some people would see that as unfair. Shouldn't everyone in a team be treated equally? Many would say yes. Then why is everyone in a professional team paid differently? As Orwell famously wrote "All animals are equal, but some animals are more equal than others." How does that feeling sit?

Arguably a fairer and more appropriate tipping point is to judge everyone equally based on what it is they do? Applying the same behaviour rules for everyone is fair. For example, shouldn't every team member be treated the same if they deliberately break a clear and fundamental rule. That is very disrespectful. That kind of act removes the base layer for a sound working relationship. No respect means no relationship. When a team member no longer respects the team, they have to go, whatever their ability. Even if they are the most able person in the team, disrespecting your team mates should be an absolute non-starter.

For some people any breach of any rule is enough to pause or eject a team member. But that's only right when the rules are fit for purpose and the breach is a fundamental one (or repetition of other lesser breaches).

If a rule is fundamental to the mission and supports the agreed philosophy and values, then it's important and needs to be followed. Breaking a fundamental rule,

---

[194] As former Southampton FC Manager, Lawrie McMenemy, told an audience I was in.

in a way that undermines the mission, could mean facing expulsion. However, if a rule doesn't add value to the mission, or conflicts with the agreed philosophy or values, then changing it is vital. Ask what purpose each rule serves. Is it the mission or is it some other arbitrary tradition or demand? Challenge the rules, make sure they're fit for purpose. Change the rules when they're not fit for purpose. When they are fit for purpose, follow them and stick to them.

Change the rules, don't break them

A negative impact can come in many forms, including being a disruptive influence, repeatedly putting personal goals first, creating doubt and confusion as to what's 'right' by making unnecessary challenges of management, winding-up colleagues and arbitrators, getting penalised or disciplined, distracting another team member from the job in hand, causing additional pressure and tension in the squad, reducing effective communication between the team members; and causing a colleague to lose confidence in themselves or the team.

Looking at one example of a fall-out, it's important to remember that there are at least two sides to every story. In 2002, the Republic of Ireland Manager Mick McCarthy sent Roy Keane home from the team's World Cup camp. Mick is reported to have accused Roy of pretending to be injured in a game, in front of other players. Roy allegedly replied "Mick, you're a liar ... you're a f****** w*****. I didn't rate you as a player, I don't rate you as a manager, and I don't rate you as a person. You're a f****** w***** and you can stick your World Cup up your a***. The only reason I have any dealings with you is that somehow you are the manager of my country! You can stick it up your b*******."[195]

There was undoubtedly a history between the two men before this incident, which may explain the extent of the altercation. Roy was reportedly critical of the team's training facilities and travel arrangements before (and after) this conversation. That might well be fair compared to Manchester United, but were there much tighter budgets in place? We don't know all the details. Every player has to make the best of the situation and put the mission first. Equally, every player deserves treatment and facilities that are good enough. And if they aren't, it's fair enough to politely challenge that.

Roy Keane has been described as being aggressive and difficult, but his club managers repeatedly picked him for his tenacity. He might have been a difficult

---

[195] The Daily Mirror on 15 November 2018.

man to manage, but I'm sure that Roy, like most people, can be reasonable if he feels fairly treated. If Mick McCarthy did accuse him of feigning injury, in front of the other players, then Mick was wrong to do so. Whatever he thought, a private conversation around Roy's fitness was far more appropriate. Roy's reported reaction was completely over the top, but the accusation was such a fundamental one that any player would have reacted badly to it unless it were true. The problem for both men is that their relationship was irreparable after this incident. Roy Keane left the squad. The Republic of Ireland lost a key player's skills and the incident created a big distraction for the team's management; and the team's match preparations were knocked off course. The Republic of Ireland lost on penalties in the first round of the knockout phase. Had he been playing, Roy Keane was likely to have scored one. Everyone lost out.

Winning teams create the right environment for their members to flourish in. They provide support when their team members face challenges and difficulties. They deal with any complaints or grievances quickly and genuinely. They promote winning behaviours. But they also call-out losing behaviours and remove any team members who are not aligned to the mission.

~~~~~

When a team member has exceptional ability and skill, he she or they might be described as having the 'X factor'. When a single person can regularly make the difference between winning and losing, he she or they is a valuable asset to any team. That's why difficult characters with exceptional skills are often tolerated. Often the more someone is told they're brilliant, the more likely their character becomes challenging to deal with. Misalignment can come from something as simple as one person's pride and ego.

But that's not the only kind of X factor. The better kind is the team member with skill who motivates and influences others to perform well. It's the person who sets higher standards, performs to them and encourages others to do the same. The net gain isn't just one very able player, it's many. This kind of X factor is rarer and more valuable.

"I thought there was a lack of leadership at Leeds Rhinos and I suppose that's why they went and got me....I love pushing the lads.

I set the bar with the leadership and set the bar
on and off the field"[196]

Recruiting highly skilled and inspirational team members is a slipstreaming approach to winning. It's likely to be more successful that the mainstream approach of recruiting a team full of high-skilled individuals. Before David Silva arrived at Manchester City in 2010, the club hadn't won a major trophy since a League Cup in 1976. Manchester City's last league title was even further back in 1968.

When David Silva left, ten years later, in 2020, Manchester City had won 14 trophies (four Premier League titles, two FA Cups, five League Cups and three Community Shields). David Silva is an exceptional footballer, but that's not how the Manchester City Chairman, Khaldoon Al Mubarak, chose to describe him when he left. Instead, he spoke about him in a far more fundamental way. "David is a transformational player, a quiet leader who has inspired everyone around him."

Winning teams recruit transformational team members, rather than individuals. A good team will usually win more often than a team with some X factor individuals. That's because alignment is so important. So rather than hoping that a team full of egos will work things through between them, why not recruit a team full of humility and sacrifice? The influence of one or more transformational players can be the behind inspiration behind an X factor team. Rather than create a temporary home for 'difficult' mercenaries, organisations should look to character first. Best of the options is to build a team full of transformational players, who have all aligned themselves to each other and to their mission. With a compelling mission and the resources needed, that could produce a truly X factor team.

~~~~~

The same powers of inspiration and transformation apply to all kinds of leaders in all kinds of teams. Joe Klein of Time Magazine has offered a commentary on the essence of successful US Presidents. "Being a politician is a very visceral thing. Greatness of spirit is the most important quality that a President can have. The successful democrats Franklin Roosevelt, Harry Truman, John F. Kennedy, Bill Clinton and Barack Obama have all had it. To have greatness of spirit you have to be optimistic and you have to at least give the appearance of openness."

---

[196] Luke Gale, in a BBC Sport interview before the Challenge Cup Final 2020 (which he helped the club to win).

"Generations of Americans have responded with a simple creed, that sums up the spirit of a people. Yes we can! Yes we can!"[197]

Optimism is absolutely critical, as nobody wants a negative or defeatist leader. Openness is essential too. No one wants a known liar to tell them how it really is. But it's the third element, the greatness of spirit that makes the transformation. Just like football, transformation is not about personal skills, it's about the direct connections we build and our impact on others. President Obama had a way of reaching out to American society whenever he spoke. By doing so, he inspired others to do more, to be more. That kind of transformational impact will inevitably make more of a positive impact, than a single person could ever achieve alone.

~~~~

As we've already seen, the British Military has ten principles of operation, which collectively create its philosophy. And as we know, these principles establish an inbuilt flexibility, which is vital to operational success. To ensure that its operations are flexible enough, the British military operates an 'eleventh' principle of mission command (sometimes called mission control). This is designed to promote initiative, freedom of manoeuvre and responsive decision-making. The British military achieves this through decentralised command. It's a case of creating the necessary alignment of mission and actions, at a hands-on level.

Mission command is not just a question of the commanding officer issuing a mission and leaving everything else to the officers and troops on the ground. The overall commanding officer must ensure that every subordinate officer fully understands the intentions behind the operation (mission) and the effect that they are to achieve (the goals). Any other restrictions (such as when they might fire on the enemy) have to be agreed up front. The officers on the ground have to know what is set and what is flexible.

"Always have a plan" [198]

Mission command also requires the most commanding officer to allocate sufficient resources to complete the mission and to impose the fewest constraints as possible. This combination enables subordinate officers to use their initiative,

---

[197] Former US President Barack Obama.
[198] Ant Middleton, ex-SAS and the leader of the Staff on Channel 4's 'SAS; Who Dares Wins'.

imagination and flair to the full, whilst still delivering the desired effect. This mission command process is built on trust, through ever-decreasing supervision. In the case of the military, it's developed as an officer or soldier proves themselves in theatre.

Mission command has many advantages. But if the senior and subordinate officer don't communicate well enough there will be an operational misunderstanding. Any lack of alignment between them is a potential reason for failure. Mission command needs full operational alignment.

~~~~~

With time and patience, an organisation can pass on its skills and experience to develop its next generation. Without one there is no plan for the future. Bringing through a trainee or apprentice is usually cheaper, easier, more successful and more satisfying than recruiting someone from another organisation. The rewards you get from developing others are mutual. However, the pressure to achieve winning results is so intense that money and resources tend to go into recruiting the 'finished article' from outside. How often does that approach work out better?

Grow your own

To get the best from your development programme, you need to provide a creative, learning environment, a great work culture and a career on the end of all the hard work (not just a job). But even that's not enough. You have to compel those people to stay. Your organisation therefore needs to offer fair pay for all, an ethical approach to business, support for its local community and carbon neutrality. Is all that enough? Probably yes. Making something sustainable and worthy will certainly add to your organisation's appeal. Without offering a package of compelling reasons to engage, the next generation simply won't buy in. Without having lush soil, plentiful nutrients and regular watering, the tree of opportunity will bear no fruit.

Without reasons to hope, what is the point? Why make the effort? Telling people to be grateful will prevent that gratitude from naturally appearing. Offering money alone isn't very motivating. Offer development and the hope of something better.

"Boss screamin' in my ear about who I'm supposed to be
'Getcha a 3-piece wall street smile and son you'll look just like me'
I said "Hi man, there's something that you oughta know
I'll tell ya Park Avenue leads to Skid Row"
I look and see it's not only me. We're standin' tall, ain't never a
doubt. We are the young, so shout it out"[199]

~~~~~

Everyone needs a team behind them in order to operate at their best. Even when
your role is the finisher, you still need help. No one should be left to face anything
alone. In the 2008 Champions League Final, Chelsea Captain John Terry
famously slipped and missed a penalty. Manchester United won the biggest
trophy in European club football. That shouldn't have happened.

To get one thing straight from the start, John Terry's miss didn't lose Chelsea the
match, it just made the score 4 v 4 (after both teams had taken their first five
penalties). Chelsea could have won the game with his penalty kick, but Chelsea
didn't lose the match because he missed. Chelsea could still have gone on to win
the match regardless. If his teammates had all scored their penalties, there would
have been a different result.

In the minute of time he took, John Terry was alone in his efforts to achieve a
team goal. That's not fair and it's not sensible. Even penalty-taking is a team task.
And still now, long after the event, John wrongly shoulders the burden of that
miss alone. John Terry needed more support and still does.

Great players can miss a penalty kick. Cristiano Ronaldo is arguably the greatest
player of all time. Earlier in the same match, he stopped partway through his run-
up to try and 'trick' the goalkeeper, but missed with his shot. If you take enough
penalties, it will happen to everyone. And later, with Manchester United 6 v 5 up
in the penalty shootout, it was Nicholas Anelka's miss for Chelsea that finally
meant Manchester United won the Champions League trophy.

With so many chances to win the game during the match, the loss was never
really going to come down to a single penalty. Chelsea should have won the
match in normal time, without the need for penalties. Everyone, on and off the

---

[199] 'Youth Gone Wild' by Skid Row.

pitch at Chelsea, could have done more. Teams win and lose as one. So what I'm about to say about John Terry's penalty is only part of the reason why Chelsea didn't win the 2008 Champions League.

In the action of taking his penalty, John slipped and his standing foot went from underneath him. As he slipped, the ball slid off his foot, hit the right hand post and missed the goal. It was an agonising miss. Why did he slip? It was raining and the grass on the pitch was wet. That could explain it, but none of the other thirteen penalty-takers slipped. The slip was the end result, but it probably wasn't the reason John Terry missed.

Standing on the half-way line, the Chelsea team stood silently apart from one another. They didn't reassure each other. They didn't offer each other their support. Each penalty-taker was left to deal with the task alone. How much more confidence would John have had if his teammates had offered him encouragement, before he walked up to the penalty spot? No football teams seem to help each other when it comes to penalties. A few well-chosen words could settle a player's nerves and help him or her to focus. At the precise time that the players' collective alignment of purpose is most needed, there was silence. There was little if any eye contact. I find that absolutely baffling.

"Light is the task where many share the toil"[200]

As he walked up to the penalty spot, John started adjusting his Captain's armband. It wasn't a confident form of adjustment, it was a nervous one. It was as if John was struggling with the responsibility of the captaincy, at this pivotal moment. The pressure on him must have been immense, but it was predictable. Any sensible scenario planning would have included every player taking a penalty kick. Feeling the pressure was understandable. John's penalty could have won the cup for his only team, the club he is devoted to. This was his dream moment. It was the greatest opportunity for both team and personal glory in his whole football career. When it mattered most, the history and power of his club should have been a strength. It should have bolstered him, but it appears that it was actually a burden. Who worked with him before the game, to help him manage his likely emotions?

---

[200] From Homer's 'The Iliad'.

Scoring from a penalty is manageable for a professional player on the training pitch. You won't score every time, but the percentage of successful shots should be high. That's a very different story compared to being in front of tens of thousands in the stadium; and tens of millions on television. It was a moment of extreme stress. How much support had been offered to John and his teammates before the game? How has that been replicated during practice? John had to walk up and take the penalty alone. Millions of eyes were on him. Absolutely anyone would have been nervous. Other than a World Cup Final, his penalty was as high-pressure a kick in football as it gets. It seems that John wasn't emotionally ready for it. More mental preparation could have done prior to the game. More support could have been offered to him before he began his walk. Collective preparation is a key part of alignment.

Emotion wasn't the only cause. From a technical point of view, John had been practicing penalty-taking for two weeks before the game. That was useful preparation. But footballers don't tend to practice penalty-taking enough. There isn't enough alignment between planning, practice and delivery. Chelsea's penalty practice wasn't part of a continuous daily programme developed over many years. It was only done "in the build-up to finals"[201]. Had penalty practice been routine, week on week, season by season, it would have given every player several confident penalty options. The pressure would have felt less intense. All the practice had been done outside the pressure of a big game. Instead of giving more players the chance to take penalties in Premier League or cup matches, teams tend to nominate one player who always takes them. But that doesn't produce the skills required to win a team's penalty shootout. If only one player gets to experience the pressure of performing with a crowd, how can you expect the whole team to rise to the occasion?

*"The target of anything in life should be to do it
so well that it becomes an art"*[202]

Despite the lack of preparation, John felt confident, because he knew what he was doing. He could rely on his own routine and repeat what he'd rehearsed. Strangely, it seems no advice had been given to John or any of the other players about the best and

---

[201] All the quotes are from a 'bein Sports' interview, a 'Keys and Gray Special' uploaded on 4 May 2020 on You Tube.
[202] Arsene Wenger, Manager of the 'Invincibles' who went unbeaten in the Premier League in 2003/4; and the winner of 2 other Premier League titles, 7 F.A Cups and 7 Charity Shields at Arsenal FC.

worst type of penalties, or which penalty type would suit their skills. There are technical and psychological aspects which both need coaching. Without it, a players hasn't been well supported.

John has since talked about penalty practice before that game "I'd been dinking them down the middle like the Panenka" for the two weeks before the match. That is a hugely confident kind of penalty. Antonin Panenka had cheekily won the 1976 European Championships with an audacious chip straight down the middle of the goal. The goalkeeper had dived full length off to the side, as all goalkeepers did at the time. The goalkeeper certainly hadn't expected a simple chip kick straight to where he'd been standing. It was a risky but clever penalty. In 2008, John Terry's penalty practice had gone so well that the Panenka was John Terry's penalty of choice.

When the time came to take his kick in the match, John had two weeks of preparation behind him. He had the confidence that comes from being capable of scoring the most audacious kind of penalty. His skills weren't in doubt. John could win the Champions League by doing a Panenka. He'd been doing it regularly in the previous two weeks' training. But somewhere during his lonely walk to the penalty spot, John changed his mind. Out went the Panenka and in came a much safer pass into the bottom right hand corner.

Why did he change his choice of penalty? As he walked towards thew spot, the pressure mounted. Rather than viewing his penalty as a chance to win the Champions League, John's focus switched. Instead of aiming to score a glorious winner, his aim became more restricted. The pressure changed his thinking. As Chelsea Captain, with the chance to make history, he suddenly felt the weight of history on his arm. Under that extreme pressure, he couldn't be the one to let his club down. A Panenka style of penalty suddenly seemed a very bold move indeed. Far too bold in fact. It was a cheeky penalty that required the maximum nerve. This high pressure situation needed something else. John could not afford to miss. As John's mindset changed from how to avoid missing, John decided to change his penalty. Choosing instead to pass the ball into the corner of the goal, he chose a more conservative option.

By restraining his pre-match thinking, John sacrificed his practiced routine and gave away his advantage. As the moment came, John desperately wanted to score. But he became even more desperate not to miss. By scaling back his penalty choice, John withdrew within himself and became less able to score. His high level of training ground confidence gave way to a 'safety first' approach. His

Panenka chip down the middle, gave way to a low passing shot to the right.

The technique John needed to pass the ball into the right corner, required him to run straight and then open up his body and twist it as he shot. If he lined up his angle too soon, he would have 'told' the goalkeeper which way to dive. So the twisting action needed had to come late in his run up. John had just made his job more difficult. The wet grass underfoot was a potential hazard. As he twisted his body and kicked the ball, John was out of physical alignment. As a result, he slipped and miss-kicked the ball. The decision to open his body up and use the inside of his foot gave him less strength in both legs. A confident Panenka style penalty would have avoided the twist and given him more stability in his standing leg. John probably wouldn't have slipped in the wet.

I am not a Chelsea fan, but I felt for him instantly. It was a desperately cruel way to miss, especially for someone who wanted to score so badly. The rain had of course made the playing surface more slippery underfoot. But it was the choice of shooting action that made John slip and fall. What help did John get to avoid that? Did Chelsea water the pitch during penalty practice? If not, why not? What advice did the coaches give about taking penalties in the wet? If there wasn't any, why not? Scenario planning for penalty kicks is easy. Everyone in the squad might be asked to take one, even the reserve goalkeeper. Everyone needs more than one confident choice. The distractions of rain, wind, sleet, hail and crowd noise need to be planned in. Then you need to find ways to ramp up the pressure so it's absolutely intense.

John Terry would probably have scored in training, outside the pressure cooker atmosphere. If he'd used a Panenka style kick, he would probably have scored, as goalkeepers don't expect a chip down the middle. If the pitch had been a dry surface, John Terry would probably have stayed on his feet and found the corner of the net. But that's not what happened. The combination of the extreme pressure, a lack of mental support and preparation, the change of penalty style, the twisting action required; and the dampness underfoot collectively prevented him from scoring. The intense atmosphere was an uncontrollable. However it was a predictable one. The rain was another uncontrollable, but John knew about it and could have adapted differently to it. The lack of team preparation was a controllable, that wasn't mastered.

Overall, John Terry has had a highly successful football career by anyone's standards. With multiple trophy wins and international caps, John Terry is a high-achiever. Fortunately for him, John's Chelsea squad got to win the Champions

League trophy in 2012. John was banned for the final, having received a red card in the semi-final, but he helped his teammates to get there and to prepare for the game mentally. His efforts to help get Chelsea to the final meant he earned that medal like they did. Passing on his experience from 2008 will have been a vital part of the team's preparation. Even though he didn't play, John made a major contribution to that 2012 win.

> *"I can die a happy man because that's all I wanted to see in my lifetime as a Chelsea player"*

The impact of stress cannot be underestimated. Pressure occurs in all jobs and walks of life. We need to anticipate it and prepare for it. Otherwise our mental and physical alignment goes. Organisations need to plan for it and support their people. We all need guidance and reassurance when we're under stress. Practicing under pressure can help to us to build the mental resilience we need when that pressure ramps up for real. Rehearsing and scenario planning can build skills and confidence, by developing routines and familiarly for likely situations. Then, when the pressure is on us, we can stick to our well-rehearsed routines.

John Terry is now making his way in football coaching and management. With so much success and experience to share, he is likely to be a successful manager. But because of that penalty miss, John Terry understands the psyche of a footballer under pressure far better than most. What he learned from this heart-wrenching experience makes John Terry even more likely to be a successful manager. I definitely wouldn't bet against it.

~~~~~

In 1981, ITV launched new programme called "Game for a Laugh" in which its presenters played practical jokes and pranks on members of the public. It was probably the first show in which "the people were the stars". The programme was a huge hit and ran until 1984. Game for Laugh made household names of its four presenters Jeremy Beadle (who went on to present his own show 'Beadle's About'), Matthew Kelly (who went on to present 'You Bet' and 'Stars in their Eyes'), Henry Kelly (who went on to present 'Going for Gold') and Sarah Kennedy (who went on to present 'Busman's Holiday').

After a year's absence, ITV decided to bring the show back with a new presenting team. That put a huge pressure on the new presenters to hit the same high viewing figures. Jeremy Beadle was the only original presenter to return. His three new co-presenters were Martin Daniels (already known as a magician and the son of Paul), Rusty Lee (already known as a television cook on TV-am) and Lee Peck (who was making his television debut). This team had to emulate the original presenters and try to make its own mark. Successful teams complement each other.

"All businesses need business partners to grow. Tycoons know the importance of filling the gaps and weaknesses in their own skill set or business idea, by finding the parts of the jigsaw puzzle to create the best chance of success"[203]

I know Lee Peck in his post-TV life. Lee runs a public relations company and he's a very smart, confident man. But Lee admits that walking onto the set for the first time was "really daunting" for him. It was his first television presenting job. "Jeremy Beadle was famous. Everyone knew who he was. Martin and Rusty had already done television too. Then there was me. I was a complete unknown."

I asked Lee whether it was difficult to work together in a team of television personalities. Lee explained "Jeremy Beadle was very much the leader. We had to defer to him. He wasn't easy to work with and so from time to time we'd fall out with him. But when the cameras rolled, we all had to be the best of friends. All four of us were different characters and we had to make it work as a group. There was a programme to make. That's showbusiness."

If all the people in a team naturally get on well together that makes co-working much easier. But that's not always the case. Where there are differences of personality and opinion, a professional respect has to kick in or things will go wrong and fail. What matters more than friendship is respect. A highly-professional team is a respectful one. It can deliver regardless of the personalities in it. Friendship isn't a must-have, it's a nice to have. Mutual respect is essential, otherwise there's no alignment. It is a winning behaviour that incorporates elements of Appreciation, Balance, Collaboration, Decision-making and Endurance. Where there's real professionalism, there's a good chance that there's also a winning team.

~~~~~

[203] Entrepreneur and Dragon's Den star, Peter Jones, taken from his website.

Choosing the right person for the job is important in all organisations. Aligning a person's skills and experience to the tasks that need to be done is a core part of management. No line manager gets to pick the same person for a job every single time, due to a number of uncontrollable factors. They include existing work commitments, time off for holiday, periods of sickness, resignation; and changes in roles and skillset. But no line manager should pick the same person for the same projects every time anyway. You can't keep a whole team of people happy, engaged and 'project ready' unless everyone gets to build up their work experience. You don't want to put all your skills eggs in one basket.

Appointment for a role or project should be based on the needs of the mission first and foremost. After that, selection should be based on the development needs of the team. Choosing who does what should take into account current suitability and potential development, rather than length of service, friendship or sentiment. Current performance level is another key factor in selection. Everyone at every level has to perform consistently well. The threat of someone else being given the next big project should be a strong motivation to perform.

"No seat is ever really safe"[204]

In business, a team can recruit a new person to join it at any time. Teams can be as large as a business wants them to be. What's affordable and what will make more money are two commercial considerations, but there are no arbitrary constraints imposed on a business. The sky's the limit. This is very different from salary capped sports, where there's a maximum limit on the size of a playing budget. That kind of uncontrollable obviously restricts a manager's choice. In addition, every sport has a maximum limit on the number of players that can play in any match. That's another uncontrollable. A professional football team can't choose to play thirteen players because it can afford two more than its opponents.

In Rugby Union, the substitutes' bench plays a crucial role. Rather than being just a group of reserves, who may or may not get to play, the "finishers" as Eddie Jones calls them always play their part in helping to secure a win. If substitutions are used well, the team's intensity and performance level will be maintained right to the end. If substitutions are misjudged or used wrongly, then some players can be left playing on when they are "out on their feet" in the last ten minutes.

---

[204] Sir. Matthew Pinsent CBE, four times Olympic Rowing Champion, ten times World Rowing Champion and BBC broadcaster.

Tiredness will always leave your team vulnerable. Mental or physical fatigue can really misalign a team, team thinking suffers and begins a downward performance spiral. Is your team under too much pressure, too often? How much rest do your people get? Do you have a team of 'finishers' to step in and help complete your projects? It is crucial to involve everyone in the team, so everyone has enough skill to help whenever you need them to. Don't keep giving all the best jobs to the same people. What happens if they leave or become ill? Don't always give the most challenging jobs to the best people either. Otherwise you'll wear them out. Fairly and evenly distribute what you need to get done. That way improves everyone's skills evenly, ready for when you need every team member to step up.

Manchester Thunder made the final of the 2019 Vitality Netball Superleague season. Their Grand Final opponents, Wasps Netball, had been in the previous two finals, winning both. That experience meant Wasps started more confidently and quickly built a four point lead, finishing the first quarter five points head. After the first three quarters, the Wasps' big game experience saw them winning by six points. Never behind and winning 45 v 39, there was every reason to suspect that Wasps would go on to win a third Grand Final in a row.

With nine minutes left on the clock, Wasps were still ahead, by 48 v 46. Manchester Thunder had narrowed the gap. They were staying in the game. The team's star goal shooter Joyce Mvula was helping to keep them close. Then as Joyce stretched out for the ball, a Wasps' player fell awkwardly on her leg. Play was stopped. Time was paused. Joyce Mvula was injured and couldn't continue. Manchester Thunder had just lost its best goal scorer, with an 89% shooting success rate for the season. Joyce wasn't just the best player at Manchester Thunder. She had just been voted the Vitality Netball Superleague fans' Player of the Year. She was acknowledged to be the best player in the league. Losing her at that critical point in the Grand Final was a cruel blow. Wasps could now see the game out.

Thunder substitute Eleanor Cardwell came on to take Joyce Mvula's place. It was Ellie's big chance, but it doesn't get much more pressurised for a netball player than coming on in the last quarter of the Superleague Grand Final. Ellie had to get to grips with the challenge instantly, if Manchester was to have a chance of winning. Ellie had to find the perfect balance of red heart and blue head, so she could take every chance that came her way. There was no time for her to get up to speed and acclimatise first. There was no time for a practice session to re-align Manchester's attack around her. The team had to re-adjust itself in match conditions.

As soon as Ellie ran onto the court, she was immediately tasked with taking a high-pressure shot. The injury to Joyce Mvula had resulted in a penalty to Manchester Thunder and Joyce Mvula wasn't on the court to take it. With tremendous focus, Ellie scored and then she kept on scoring. Dominating the Wasps' circle, Ellie scored with every shot she made, until the very final shot that didn't matter because time was up. As her impact on the match grew, the Sky match commentators reacted to her physical and mental strength, using the phrases "Cool as a cucumber" and "Talk about taking your chance when you get it!"

"Cool as a cucumber"

At a time of uncertainty, Ellie brought a calm, focused influence on her team. She gave her teammates the confidence to give her the ball, because they saw that if they did, she scored. The Wasps defenders tried to put her under pressure, but her movement was superb and she stayed physically strong. Ellie Cardwell endured and Manchester Thunder went on to win the match 57 v 52.

If Ellie Cardwell hadn't been match ready, Manchester Thunder would have lost. Losing their team's best player could have flattened the team's morale and misaligned its attacking structure. But, despite missing 51 minutes of the 60 minute game, Ellie Cardwell decisively imposed herself on the result. Afterwards, Thunder Head Coach Karen Greig explained it very simply "We've been working with Ellie all year." Karen and the rest of the Thunder coaching team had prepared the whole squad to play. The squad's practice sessions ensured that every member was at the level required. So when Joyce went off, Ellie Cardwell was a win ready-made replacement. Planning for predictable scenarios can produce continuous alignment in every eventuality.

~~~~

Responsible business is a phrase that's being used increasing often. It means finding a higher purpose for your organisation that produces a form of success beyond shareholder profits. It's a voluntary anchoring of your business to its local community and the World we live in. There are clear practical rewards, including environmental and social, many of which are shared. Producing success for all of your stakeholders and wider society brings a greater connectivity to your customers, more support from others; and more opportunities. It's a virtuous circle.

The words benevolence and business are not common bedfellows. Nor are fairness and business. Family businesses can sometimes have more of long-term perspective, but not all do. The pressure of generating profit for the current owners can be pervasive and controlling. Short-term thinking brings a short-term approach, which can bring a short-term demise. When a business looks beyond its current year's profit and loss account, it can build a network of commitments and responsibilities to see it through many years ahead.

When a business respects and values its staff, customers, suppliers, funders, environment, local communities, local authorities, as well as its owners, it can harness them all to support its mission. Where that mission is inclusive and benefits every stakeholder, a tribe can be formed around that wider purpose[205]. Allowing every stakeholder to benefit brings greater fairness and commitment. Sharing the pot more widely tends to create the opportunities to create a bigger pot. Business leaders need to align all their decisions and actions to achieve success this year, next year and every year afterwards. Continued sustainability is a form of success.

"We live in a cynical World. A cynical World"[206]

Just talking about being responsible is not enough. Action is required. We live in a cynical World, with a 'Why should I help?' attitude. Obviously, if no one helps, no one benefits. Instead of short-termism, an overlapping-years' approach, with rewards for all, will make a business more balanced, more considerate and more responsible. In turn that builds more trust, more loyalty and more positive PR.

Being a responsible business has practical benefits. Longer-term thinking now will produce ongoing income and protect capital value. Aligning your current actions to a legacy outcome builds sustainability, which naturally makes your decision-making more responsible. Fostering and enacting a legacy will help to bring a sense of greater responsibility. This concept can also be described as custodianship, stewardship, guardianship and wardenship. Planning for the present and the future should offer success now and later.

Being aligned to 'responsibility' means being aligned to your own success and to leaving a positive legacy. You, your organisation and all of its stakeholders can have the Kwan. That's a reference from the movie Jerry Maguire.

---

[205] I have written much more about this in Build Your Super-tribe.
[206] Said by Jerry Maguire in the film of the same name. The quote goes on to say "I love you. You...complete me."

Rod Tidwell: "You know some dudes might have the coin,
but they'll never have the Kwan."

Jerry Maguire: "What's that?"

Rod Tidwell: "Love, respect, community and the dollars too,
the entire package. The Kwan."

Takeaway thoughts:

- Align every team member with the mission, philosophy, culture and values
- There are alignments needed at Strategic, Framework and People levels
- Get your stakeholders to create one powerful wave in support of the mission
- Every stakeholder shares responsibility for alignment
- Cognitive diversity is crucial for success
- The mission comes before personal agendas
- Winning standards create alignment and alignment brings consistency
- Respect, friendship, caring and devotion indicate increasing alignment
- Apply the same behaviour rules for everyone
- Transformational people can create alignment
- Support each other

3.5   WINNING MINDSET
(including Red Heart, Blue Head)

The fifth controllable is a winning mindset. Every day, in all walks of life, people talk themselves out of winning. That might be because life experience has 'taught' you how hard winning can be. It might be because your team doesn't have a good track record. It might come from an inner self-doubt. Whatever the reason, it can be changed for the better. Unless the competition you're in lacks real competition, winning takes a strong mental belief. We need to be enduringly positive in order to win. We all have doubts and we all make mistakes, but preparing for more of the same is not the way to win. Too much negativity and self-doubt are losing behaviours.

> *"Your attitude, not your aptitude, will determine your altitude"*[207]

By and large, the British tend to be fairly mild-mannered and humble rather than aggressive and arrogant. Even when our team's got a great chance of winning, we tend to say we're 'quietly confident' rather than a 'sure thing'. The British are generally relaxed and good humoured until stirred. That process of stirring us to action isn't an instant one. A short speech about 'death or glory' and fighting for 'the flag' will leave many people unstirred. Developing a winning mindset for a group of people takes more than a few platitudes and a bit of tub-thumping.

This leaves us with a conundrum. In competition, winning is usually the preserve of one person, one team, or one organisation, but if everyone has doubts and lacks self-belief how does anyone manage to win anything? Someone has to step up and try their damnedest to win. Those that do, win more. Fortune does favour the bold. Self-belief is vital to success. If we lack it, we can grow it. Actively searching for reasons to believe in ourselves and our team can help us to build a winning self-confidence. Find them and build on them.

> *"You have to have ridiculous confidence in your own ability.*
> *You have to believe that it isn't going to happen to you*[208]*"*

Unless the opposition is very poor or the competition is very easy, a team doesn't usually win if only some of its members perform. Team performance comes from

---

[207] American author and motivational speaker Hilary Hinton "Zig" Ziglar.
[208] Sir. Stirling Moss talking about the risks of motor sport.

having the right people, values, skills, resources and alignment for the mission. Performance also comes from having the right training, coaching and support in place to develop the aptitude, skills and techniques needed. They are important building blocks to securing improvement. Will pulling those elements together lead to success? Probably not unless the belief is there. Where the team has an inner determination and a deep, passionate desire to win, the answer is probably yes. Until we wholeheartedly believe in our mission, we won't have that passionate desire to win. Does your team believe?

~~~~~

In his book 'Man's Search for Meaning' Viktor Frankl describes the Holocaust from his time inside four concentration camps, including Auschwitz. According to Viktor, the survivors of those camps had to mentally battle for the chance of freedom every day, to will their own survival and will themselves safe. Without a determination to live, a prisoner couldn't stay alive. Once hope had gone, the fight for life was over.

Amongst all the horror, oppression and barbarism, Viktor Frankl tried to find meaning from his life, to feed his desire to live. Without meaning, he felt that he would have had nothing to hope for and that he would stop fighting to live. Viktor managed to find his meaning in three places. They were work (doing something significant), love (caring for his loved ones and looking forward to seeing them again); and courage (in finding a way to bear his suffering well).

"When a man finds that it is his destiny to suffer, he will have to accept his suffering as his task; his single and unique task. No one can relieve him of his suffering or suffer in his place. His unique opportunity lies in the way that he bears his burden[209]"

Viktor bore his suffering well, by embracing the challenge of it. He saw his great test as being to endure those unbearable conditions. He felt that he had to "face up to the full amount of suffering" in order to survive it. Perhaps it was the act of battling his instincts of fight and flight; and finding strength in the face of horror that saved him. Without such an enduringly positive mindset, Viktor Frankl may not have survived.

---

[209] Viktor Frankl, in 'Man's Search for Meaning' which has now sold more than 12 million copies.

We need to find meaning in our mission. Without it, we won't have the passion and determination to see it through. If we can't find meaning in our current mission or our current organisation, we need to change the mission or change the organisation.

~~~~~

Winners don't believe that they are they 'perfect' or the finished article any more than anyone else. Winners just find a way to convince themselves that their prospects are good enough to win. People who aren't win ready see the missing 'gap' in their skills or experience as being blockers that prevent them from winning. Winners can talk themselves into winning even when the odds are against them. People who aren't win ready yet can talk themselves out of it, from a winning position.

> *"Victorious warriors win first and then go to war, while defeated warriors go to war first and then seek to win"*[210]

Winners also commit to increasing their chances of success, through career-long self-improvement, learning and development. That practical response to a lack of experience or missing skills continually closes the gap, giving them even more reason to believe in themselves. Rather than setting goals that are elusive and impossible, we should be realistic and accept relative success (at least initially). We all need to pursue a state of excellence, rather than one of unobtainable perfection.

Bill Walsh was the General Manager and Head Coach at American Football team the San Francisco 49ers from 1979-1989. Under Bill's guidance the 49ers won three Super Bowl trophies from three Super Bowl appearances and won another the year after he retired as well. Bill Walsh is even better known for the mantra behind his success, namely "Do all the right things to perfection and the score will take care of itself."

Bill Walsh's mantra was used to underpin his detailed blueprint for success, which he called his 'Standard of Performance.' Within his performance standards were a series of values that applied across the whole organisation. They included: exhibit a ferocious and intelligently applied work ethic directed at continual

---

[210] Sun Tzu from "The Art of War".

improvement, be deeply committed to learning and teaching, be fair; and make sacrifice and commitment the organisation's trademark.

In his forward to Bill's book[211] former San Francisco 49ers quarterback Joe Montana commented on his old coach's mantra. "He taught us to want to be perfect and instilled in the team a hunger for improvement, a drive to get better and better. We saw his own hunger for perfection and it was contagious." And yet the team wasn't perfect.

What is your team hungry for?

Like Bill Walsh, leaders and their teams have to strive for the highest standards achievable. What is good enough to win? That will be a level of performance that's better than every other team can muster, whether that's achieved through mainstreaming or slipstreaming. But is perfection the right standard to chase? It may seem like semantics, but perfection is illusory and unachievable. At its very best it is fleeting and impossible to recreate. Perfection is virtually impossible and, as a result, chasing it is utterly demotivating. It is far better to focus on achieving your very best level of performance. Chasing excellence revels in the journey to get better. Excellence praises hard work and self-development. Excellence accepts losses and failures are necessary episodes along the way. Excellence is a lifelong pursuit of self-improvement. Excellence is achievable.

As I've already highlighted, Reshma Saujani has a deep concern about the effects of trying to achieve perfection, especially for women. In her book 'Brave not Perfect" she addresses the issue head on. "The difference between excellence and perfection is like the difference between love and obsession. One is liberating and the other unhealthy. Perfection is an all-or-nothing game; you either succeed or fail, period. There are no small victories, no "A" for effort. If you're a perfection seeker and you fail at anything it can really take you out. When you are pursuing excellence, on the other hand, you don't let failure break you, because it's not a win or lose kind of game. Excellence is a way of being, not a target you hit or miss."

"Even I don't always come up to my own standards of perfection"[212]

---

[211] Called 'The Score Takes Care of Itself'.
[212] Perfectionist Paul Hollywood from 'The Great British Bake-off' admits that perfection doesn't exist.

The very process of seeking perfection can defeat you. In contrast, seeking excellence should lead to a gradual and healthy improvement in performance and self-belief. Any path that respects skill, commitment, hard-work and dedication is better than one that respects nothing but impossibility. Seeking perfection leads to developing unhealthy obsessions, setting unrealistic expectations; and experiencing continuing feelings of failure. The idea of perfection highlights and reflects our imperfections back at us; and that isn't healthy. So teams need to forget about perfection and try to become more and more excellent. Apple CEO Tim Cook is quoted as saying "Apple has a culture of excellence that is, I think, so unique and so special. I'm not going to witness or permit the change of it." Fighting to protect a good culture is vital in maintaining an organisation's success.

~~~~~

L. David Marquet is a former US Nuclear Submarine Commander and the author of the brilliant "Turn the Ship Around". As a result of experiencing personal success in two careers, I asked David what he thinks winning is. David responded "Winning is about the willingness to prepare to win. Everyone can try hard once the whistle blows and there are 80,000 fans in the stadium. That doesn't distinguish winners. Winners do the hard work, in an empty stadium, days and weeks before they even know they might have an event." The decision to completely commit to something is a mental one. Winning takes that willingness to prepare to win, a dedication to the task and an almost obsessional commitment to it. As David's words illustrate, winning isn't accidental or coincidental, it's intentional. Winners embrace the need for preparation and the dedication to commit to it.

~~~~~

The pressure to perform can be intense. When we're under moderate pressure, we can use it to power our performance and give our very best. However, the more pressure we're under, the more we feel and exhibit stress. Our patience and tolerance can run out. We can become frustrated and angry. We can freeze or flounder. By compelling and cajoling people to do ever more, employing organisations will eventually push every one of their employees past his or her tipping point. If we are to win, we cannot afford to break our people, or allow ourselves to be broken.

Team leaders are repeatedly put under the spotlight. Every decision is analysed to an infinite degree. Trust seems far easier to lose than it is to win. Shareholder patience seems more transitory than ever. Only positive outcomes win brownie points, or very positive outcomes win prizes. Inputs are only good if you win and they are always bad if you lose. When results are against you, the pressure ramps up, quarter by quarter or match by match. The joy of having a great sales quarter or a winning game provides only a temporary relief, which immediately passes. And that is all wrong.

By agreeing realistic expectations (the Expected Minimum) at the very start, the pressure is much more likely to be fair and tolerable. Whether that's the case or not, team leaders have to manage their own stress away; and simultaneously try very hard not to pass it on. If a team leader is under too much pressure, the whole organisation will feel the ill-effects. Stress bites hardest when it's from the teeth of unrealistic outcomes. Working hard to achieve a mission creates enough pressure, without the organisation adding to it unnecessarily. People break under too much pressure. Don't push them past their breaking points. Help them to build the resilience they need to perform well under pressure. Help them to expand their pressure comfort zone, but don't expose them for long beyond it.

"And yet as a coach, I know that being fixated on winning (or more likely, not losing) is counterproductive, especially when it causes you to lose control of your emotions. What's more, obsessing about winning is a loser's game. The most we can hope for is to create the best possible conditions for success, then let go of the outcome"[213]

When organisations give their leader the wrong mission, ask too much of them or choose the wrong leader in the first place, they cause stress. When leaders can't cope with their own stress, it flows downhill, like a torrent, to all their direct and indirect reports. If a Chief Executive is under pressure from shareholder expectations, so in turn is every manager and employee below them. Extreme pressure can flood an organisation until everything inside it is submerged; and nothing functions properly. That should never be allowed to happen.

Expectations have to be set at levels that don't break employment law and company rules. Then there's health and safety law. Don't forget about

---

[213] Phil Jackson in his book "Eleven Rings" which examined his success in winning 11 NBA titles as a Head Coach (having won two as a player).

discrimination too. Treating anyone less favourably because of one of the nine protected characteristics is discriminatory[214]. Breaking the bond of mutual trust is unfair. Denying a worker any of their statutory or contractual rights can create a legal claim against the organisation. But operating legally is the barest of minimum standards.

A business leader's responsibility goes well beyond not breaking the laws and rules that protect workers. Every member of an organisation deserves realistic responsibilities, expectations and rewards. Everyone has to be judged by the same standards and supported equally. Fair treatment and an even distribution of workload will give a team the mental headspace to prosper. Leaders have to embody the organisation's purpose and values and lead by example. It's only when a responsibility is taken personally that it can be fully discharged. This protective 'air-bag' allows a team's employees to think clearly and operate free from extreme stress. That mental freedom will always contribute to its chances of it winning.

Every team member needs to be fully briefed about the organisation's mission and their own role within it. Understanding both is critical to success. Having clarity in your role allows you to do your best without the need for guesswork or constantly checking. If you tested every team member, would they all be able to explain the mission and their personal role back to you?

Once that mission planning process is complete, everyone should be practicing for the challenges ahead. During training and rehearsals, the leadership group needs to prime the team for action. That means reassuring everyone why the plan will work and they should fully commit to it. For example, using phrases like "If we sell the benefits of our product, we will prove it's better that the rest." The act of priming includes talking about your competitors too. For example "If we put them under pressure, they will make mistakes that we can capitalise on." This priming process can build the mental positively we all need.

"We will be ready for this team.
You will know everything they do"[215]

---

[214] Under the Equality Act 2010.
[215] Steve McNamara, Head Coach at Catalans Dragons. From his 'Tip Sheet' on the Superleague website.

Then when things go well, confirm that it's because the plan is working. Show the team how following the plan was what led to the success. Linking the process to the success will develop confidence in the process. That way the logic seems sound and everyone will stick to your process religiously when the pressure's on.

When things go wrong (and they will) calmly explain how the process wasn't followed and what should have been done instead. Then repeat the practice session, but following the process correctly. If it then starts to go well, confirm that it's because of the plan. That will build confidence in it. However, if the results aren't good when the process is followed, review the process and adapt it. If you need to change the process, 'improve' it and put it back to the team as an improvement that will make success even more likely. Then practice and train using that adapted and re-aligned process. The more every stakeholder is involved the review process the more it will deliver.

When things go well, don't just settle for that. Keep challenging, keep adapting where you can. Things can be continually improved. If you only get one shot at anything, then your preparation for it is absolutely critical. Don't do it 'live' for the first and only time. Scenario plan for it. Practice it beforehand. When we get to practice something, our understanding of it improves and so does our performance. Safe forms of practice will inevitably improve performance levels. In television and film making, an actor[216] gets several takes of a scene, and the production team can choose the very best of them. We only get to see the one they picked. When we get time to come back to something and reimagine it, our extra experience normally finds room for improvement. Given the time to repeat and retry anything, we should improve our technique and delivery.

"In the theatre you can change things ever so slightly; it's an organic thing. Whereas in film you only have that chance on the day, and you have no control over it at all"[217]

Test and adapt a game-plan until it's proven. At the same time, talk up the game-plan until there's complete commitment to it. Belief in any plan is vital. Proving that a plan works in practice and training will build increasing belief in it.

~~~~~

---

[216] I have used actor as a generic term and it includes all genders.
[217] Oscar winner, Dame Judith "Judi" Olivia Dench.

As a stakeholder in any organisation, we need to play our part in helping it to achieve success. If we were opening a new restaurant, we would need the company's leadership to involve everyone in creating a clear and inspiring mission, philosophy and values. We'd need our landlord to give us a lease with fair and acceptable terms. We'd need all our employee to work as hard and smart as they can. If we are an employee ourselves, we need to perform our work duties as excellently as we can. If we are a supplier, we need to provide a resilient supply chain. If we are a funder, we need to have sufficient funds, instantly available, to achieve the purpose involved. If we're the local authority, we need to provide a swift and robust process for issuing the food and alcohol licences we need. If we're a customer then we need to always pay our way, provide good feedback and show loyalty. Every stakeholder needs to play its part in an organisation's success.

That said, unless every stakeholder feels strongly enough about the mission, they won't all commit any more than they have to. Without full commitment, the mission is at risk. What is it that gets that level of commitment from us? We need to care about the cause and we need to feel invited in, included and important. We all want to be treated as part of our 'tribe'.

If every stakeholder fully contributes to their organisation, the collective fusion of those contributions generates a winning power

We need to feel emotionally invested before we fully commit. That's a key mental state in winning. As a result, organisations need to create an environment that nurtures these feelings. Without that, winning is much less likely. We want our opinions and views to be taken into account and respected. We can't expect to dominate the collective thinking, but we should not be ignored. Once we feel we belong, we can start to contribute to the mutual good being created.

~~~~~

'Will' is the mental function that we use to decide what we say and what we do. By extension, our 'will to win' is our mental desire to succeed, whether as an individual or at a team level. We can choose whether or not to use our 'will' to make something happen. That decision is up to us as an individual. When it comes to a team environment, one person can't do it all. A collective 'will to win' lies at the heart of any fully functioning organisation's capability. Without that collective spirit across the team, the ability to succeed will always be severely blunted. Appealing to every single stakeholder simultaneously is difficult, with all of their different wants and needs. But unless an organisation does provide a collective appeal, it won't be able to harness all the efforts and influence of its people.

The extent to which someone is prepared to make personal sacrifices is the defining measure of their commitment. This could be in terms of pushing through a physical pain barrier when training and competing, enduring starvation or economic hardship, or suffering a withdrawal from their closest relationships. A collective acceptance of sacrifice is the hallmark of a tribe[218] and it is an incredibly powerful collective mindset.

In a military context, there is an additional cost, which is measured in casualties. The sacrifice of battle acts as a handbrake on military life for many people. The 'will to fight' is a specific martial term, which operates first at an individual and then collective level. Each soldier has to possess sufficient engagement with the cause, sufficient physical courage to be able to fight (with all of its potential consequences) and sufficient skill (to be able to fight).

"The war is always inside your head"[219]

Everyone has an innate will to win but not everyone is prepared to make the personal commitments and sacrifices to ensure it happens. For some people, the desire to help others, wanting to win a trophy, or longing for material wealth drives them on with a burning passion, putting a fire in their belly. Without any flames there is far less chance of glory. However, this initial mental preparedness may not be sufficient to win. Success usually requires a longer burst of performance than that. Sustaining an unwavering focus and belief in a goal is a feat of significant endurance. Everyone can achieve some focus in short bursts, but that is rarely enough. Unwanted distractions, unexpected complexities, physical injuries and mental exhaustion can all prevent you from chasing your dreams. Not everyone has the right temperament, motivations or values to go the distance.

"For as every good warrior knows, the deadliest weapons a man[220] *carries into battle are not his hands. Rather, the boldness in the heart and the willingness of the mind are always the difference between winning and losing"*[221]

---

[218] What makes a modern tribe is discussed in my book 'Build Your Super-tribe'.
[219] Ant Middleton, ex-SAS and the leader of the Staff on Channel 4's 'SAS; Who Dares Wins'.
[220] Taking this gender restriction to mean person.
[221] Sun Tzu from 'The Art of War'.

The most successful teams are able to recruit and retain the best people. By choosing to protect and reward them, those people in return develop a loyalty and commitment to the cause. When your organisation feels your own, your will to win is far higher than when it does not. We all fight harder for what is ours, for the sake of our team. We are fundamentally tribal. When two or more tribes share the same desire to win, then partnerships, alliances and Super-tribes can be formed. A shared mindset applied to a shared task is more powerful than any individual skill. When everyone tries to win together, that winning becomes far more likely. Equality of effort is a feature of a winning team.

The military, and, to an increasing lesser extent, the police and the fire service are unique in the fact that there is no direct entry system. You cannot join as a Chief Constable or a Chief Fire Officer. Their organisational capability is grown from the bottom up, with rigorous selection and training along the way enabling the best people to promote within the system. The luxury afforded to these organisations is time. That's the time to assess, train, develop the individuals and the organisation. This 'grow your own' philosophy helps to reduce the mental distraction of potential conflict, but it can limit an organisation's diversity of thinking. A balance is needed to obtain clear, uncluttered thinking at all levels.

Keeping everyone on the same wavelength is critical to organisational success. Conflict is a disruptive state of mental distraction. Conflicts inside an organisation jeopardise the mission. No significant conflicts can be tolerated. If there is a conflict between different philosophies, or personal and team needs, then the team's mission is likely to suffer. No team member is bigger than the team. In sport, strong managers must be prepared to 'bench' a player who doesn't share the collective commitment to winning, as part of their education and moulding. In other sectors, a disciplinary warning, performance improvement plan or inter-department transfer might be needed. Misaligned interests are especially problematic when large sums of money have been invested, or the recruitment of the conflicted person was not the line manager's own choice.

~~~~~

'Quitting' as a single word sounds terrible, but it isn't always the sign of a defeatist mindset. Quitting drugs, cigarettes or alcohol undoubtedly takes a winning mindset. Quitting a highly dysfunctional team, or a bullying friendship group, can also be the sign of a winning mindset. Giving up what's bad for you, can accomplish as much as adopting what's good for you. It's the same within a team dynamic. When a team allows one of its members to behave selfishly, even tacit acceptance of that deems the behaviour acceptable. Tolerating poor behaviours and low performance standards tolerate losing.

"I just never give up. I fight to the end. You can't go out and say 'I want a bag of never-say-die spirit'. It's not for sale. It has to be innate"[222]

Holding on to your habits and relationships could be a strength, but if those habits are self-destructive and those relationships are damaging, they may be part of a losing mindset. Staying on board a sinking ship, to save other people is a winning mindset. But staying on board when there's no one left to save, indicates a losing one. No one should be 'loyal' to ways of losing. Find the ways to win instead. The ever changing circumstances around us force us to improvise and adapt. And that's good for us. Remember the old proverb "Necessity is the mother of invention."

In the 2016 US Presidential election, Hillary Clinton was blighted by allegations of alleged wrongdoing (no charges have ever been brought) and reminders of her husband's extra-marital activities. Remarkably Hillary seems to have been penalised because she stayed with her husband, the former President Bill Clinton. President Trump's aggressive campaign tactics made headway, but Hillary Clinton rallied when her own issues seemed to have gone away. But with a few weeks to go to polling day, the allegations against her resurfaced when the Director of the FBI suddenly re-opened the investigation into alleged wrongdoing. Ultimately no action was taken once again, but the late, public intervention of such a senior figure proved fatal to her campaign.

Hillary faced a nightmare scenario, a battle where she couldn't fight back. She was adamant that she had done no wrong, but how can you prove a negative? That's very difficult. You have to prove enough positives to disprove or outweigh the alleged negative. Under pressure, Hillary lost her focus and power. She couldn't adapt enough to find a way through. In her own words, Hillary has admitted "I didn't know how to win against the FBI Director until the whole things was resolved and they did not resolve it until the Sunday before the Election." Battered by the unfairness of the campaign, Hillary Clinton lost her 'fight'.

---

[222] Serena Williams, winner of twenty-three Grand Slam tennis titles.

Through a campaign of hopeful promises, Donald Trump found a way to win and become the 45th President of the United States in 2016. We will probably never know exactly what went on with the Russians and the FBI, but nothing deterred him. His team appeared to have adopted the view that anything which could help him to win was fair game. Remarkably, even his recorded admission of sexual misconduct didn't seem to knock him of course. Against such a force of personality, Hillary Clinton somehow seemed less than she should have. Hillary Clinton faded as Donald Trump became stronger. But Hillary could and should have found a way to win.

Attacking President Trump's character flaws had a very limited impact. President Trump suffered more self-inflicted wounds that the Democrats managed to inflict on him. Defending her own character didn't make much difference to Hillary's ratings either. Why not? Well both of these approaches dealt in negatives. They made Hillary look pernickety and defensive. Selling negatives doesn't help you to exude warmth and approachability. A positive case always inspires more people and sells hope better. Hillary Clinton needed to step out of the personal politics and appeal to the nation. There were millions more votes available if she had done. Only 55.7% of voters actually voted. That was the sure sign of an apathetic electorate that was hoping for something different.

Whilst Hillary's impact diminished, President Trump sounded ever more energetic and positive. Promising anything that helped, whether he could deliver it or not, his bandwagon rolled onwards. President Trump sounded terrifying at times, but he offered the promise of economic growth and an even greater America. Voters will always like the idea of becoming better off. And American voters will always like the promise of America becoming even greater. The response from Hillary seemed muted, shocked and out of her depth. When she appeared unwell late on, President Trump's team criticised her for lacking in stamina and labelled her unfit for office. It was a savage campaign that needed a different form of opposition. Following President Obama was always going to be tough. And more of the same is never a stirring message to push. President Trump's campaign for change had more momentum. Hillary should have presented her own positive campaign for change.

"The secret of change is to focus all of your energy not on fighting the old, but on building the new"[223]

---

[223] The Ancient Greek Philosopher Socrates.

By projecting messages of greater inclusion and greater economic growth Hillary could have fought a better end to her bid for the White House. By explaining that her love and loyalty to her husband were strengths that could be used for her country, she might have turned the critics around. By offering openness and actively welcoming the investigation she might have removed more doubt. By transcending personality and offering her service to the American people, she could have become a figure of American hope. Hillary needed to become a bigger force for good than her rival. Her election philosophy didn't work and Hillary couldn't adapt. As a result she lost her 'fight'. It could have been a very different story.

In the 2020, US Presidential election, the Democrat candidate was Joe Biden. He decided to fight his entire campaign on a single issue, which was President Trump's handling of the COVID-19 crisis. Rather than switching between topics or reacting to President Trump's outbursts, he repeatedly played out the same allegation of incompetence. During the periods of silence in between, Joe Biden sat back in silence to let President Trump dig himself a hole. He had a distinct advantage over Hillary Clinton in that he never faced the same level of personal attacks that Hillary Clinton had to put up with. That gave him a clearer run at the agenda he'd chosen. The end result of the election was President Trump gave way to President Biden. By dictating the key theme of the election and maintaining his resilience until the results were finally confirmed, President Biden prevailed. President Biden's campaign for change had more momentum that President Trump's 'more of the same' message. The promise of change wins votes. Now that President Biden has finally been allowed to take over, we will see what he actually does differently.

~~~~~

Confidence is a key element of a winning mindset. In every kind of work, decisions need to be made all day, every day. Those decisions need to be made with controlled enthusiasm and well-managed passion. There's also a need to be directing and to drive the mission forward with energy and verve. Every decision should at least indirectly contribute towards the mission. To produce that quality of decision-making, requires robust self-confidence and a strong confidence in the rightness of the mission.

A team member's lack of confidence in the organisation's mission, or its philosophy, will always undermine and under-power that person's performance. But this can be turned around. By reminding the doubter why the mission is so important, what benefits it will achieve and for whom, that doubter might lose their skepticism and re-align themselves to the mission. Or alternatively, the doubter might leave and allow you to find someone with greater conviction as their replacement.

Sometimes employees lack the self-confidence to bring all of their positive energy into play, limiting their ability to drive tasks and projects to a successful conclusion. Sometimes employees don't have the self-confidence to back their own judgements and decisions, clouding their own heads when they need to be clear. A person's lack of self-confidence can come from unfamiliarity or a lack of preparedness. Trying to be successful when you're not win ready is stressful and unlikely to happen. Preparing well can help you to build the self-confidence needed to perform at your best.

"Preparation fuels confidence, so the only way you can be sure in your actions is to prepare as much as you can"[224]

A person's lack of self-confidence will negatively affect their performance, restricting their decision-making and adversely impacting on the projects they're working on. But this mental state is temporary. It can be turned around.

Confidence ebbs and flows. Losing an important customer, or an important pitch, can really affect a person's confidence. But that doesn't mean the next attempt will produce the same result. We might catastrophise an event, assuming the worst case scenario for evermore. But, unsurprisingly, that's not the right approach. We all know that we have to learn and develop to reach our full potential. We also know that perfection doesn't exist. In our search for excellence, we should expect multiple losses and failures along the way. We should welcome them and face them head-on like Viktor Frankl.

"No matter where you're from, your dreams are valid"[225]

Losing shouldn't dent our confidence, it should increase it. What we learn each time we lose, is how we lost. Knowing what we did and what that produced gives us greater knowledge that we had. We can adapt what we do and try again, and again, and again until we find the ways of working that work for us. This doesn't mean we take all of our losses in our stride. Missing an open goal or failing to win

---

[224] Eddie Hearn in his book "Relentless".
[225] Actor (or actress if you prefer) Lupita Nyong'o, star of '12 Years a Slave,' as well as 'The Jungle Book' and 'Black Panther'.

a new account can flatten us for a while. However, instead of allowing ourselves to dwell on failure, catastophise, or wallow in failure as a personal weakness, we should focus on what learning each episode teaches us. What we can do better next time? If we aren't sure, then ask 'What can we do differently next time?' Might that be better? If we learn something, we are better off than we were. When we think about it, that should increase our confidence, not reduce it. Don't let your confidence slide. Don't stop believing in your ability to adapt and try again.

> *"If you can force your heart and nerve and sinew*
> *To serve your turn long after they are gone,*
> *And so hold on when there is nothing in you*
> *Except the Will which says to them: 'Hold on!"*[226]

Team leaders need to build up every team member's confidence and help to restore it if it's reducing. Everyone needs to believe they are good at their job, to be good at their job. Managers can help tremendously, by instill their faith and belief in their team. By working through all the processes and systems required with members of their team, managers can provide the techniques and methodologies needed to tackle every eventuality. With those skills stored in the armoury, every team member has something useful to fall back on, when acting under pressure.

By pointing out the things their people do well, managers can strengthen confidence with evidence, in the form of facts and figures. By offering praise, managers can build confidence in specific skills. By praising more and more skills over time, a manager can give a team members a general, overall feeling of self-confidence. Praise is under-used and under-estimated. Getting a public show of support from your boss can really help to build self-confidence. Leaders need to offer that backing for everyone in their team.

According to work done by Lord Mark Price's WorkL, employers haven't grasped the relationship between organisational performance and employee confidence. According to a recent study on the future of work, managers offer praise to employees on average once every four months. In contrast, criticism of an employee's performance is offered on average twice a week. If your manager praised you less than 3% of the time, how confident would you feel?

---

[226] 'If' by Rudyard Kipling.

A modern tribe is able to offer mutual, collaborative and shared support. There's no need to wait for the line manager to offer sparse praise. It's members can lean on each other at all times. An organisation without a sense of tribe won't offer the same reassurance and aid. Help needs to be available 24/7. There needs to be a strong feeling of psychological safety. The more sense of togetherness there is, the more stakeholders there are to provide that help. A dysfunctional team cannot, whereas a tribe offers automatic help and assistance 24/7, 365 to all its members. Where a tribe looks beyond itself for help, it can work with other external tribes to help itself and its members. When tribes come together to help each other, they can become a Super-tribe.

Confidence is contagious. We can pass it on. Doubt is contagious too. We have to try and prevent it gripping us, by building our self-confidence. When we have more self-doubt than self-confidence, we won't have the perfect balance of red heart and blue head. A penalty taker affected by too much doubt, can end up believing that their next penalty is going to miss. We've already seen the effects of doubt on penalty-taking. If we can't function through fear and doubt (even temporarily), we switch from being a net contributor (helping ourselves and others) to becoming a net taker (needing help from others). We need to try and help every team member to be a net contributor to the mission.

~~~~~

Sometimes pressure can prevent an employee from bringing their red heart into play, limiting their ability to compete. Equally too much pressure and stress can restrict a worker's judgement and decision-making, making them freeze when action is needed, or making them angry and emotional. A healthy amount of pressure can be good, but too much pressure will eat away at anyone's performance levels.

The good news is that work-related stress is not a permanent state. Internal factors such as resilience and self-confidence can help to manage the effects of stress. Offering better training and mentoring will help enormously. How much is needed? Put it this way, you can never offer too much training, guiding and mentoring. What else will help? Setting more realistic targets, timescales and expectations will reduce stress, so they will certainly help. Creating a clear mission, vision of the future (post mission) and framework to work within, will also help to reduce stress. Confirming roles, duties and expectations help to keep everyone on track and feeling important.

Providing more opportunities to get involved and safe places for team members to work creatively, can power an employee's inner motivations. We can build confidence through increasing knowledge and practice. We can learn to adjust to pressure through a mixture of safe practice and training outside our comfort zones.

Team members will feel more empowered when they're reminded of what's at stake and why the sacrifices are worth it. If the mission is worthy and worthwhile then it can stir a person's heart and engage them. If that messaging has been lost, then restate it. Pressure can be reduced and lost confidence can be found and restored.

Engaged project members bring focus and reliability

Tolerating unrealistic, or unmanageable, expectations will cause increased anxiety and reduced performance levels. The controlling effect of those factors can be alleviated, if project deadlines can be pushed back, targets and KPI's can be reduced; or additional resources are provided. By releasing the pressure value, leaders can give their team a purposeful but healthy working environment. Leaders will empower their team members by giving them the tools, support and environment where they can fill their hearts and clear their heads.

A higher level of pressure can come from performing your job or hobby live, in public. For some people, the presence of others observing them is absolutely terrifying. For others it's motivational, it fires their performances. Whatever our fears, we all need an audience of some kind to perform at our very best. Doing our job well is made even better, when someone who matters witnesses us doing that. Rather than getting stage fright, we need to find a way to use the added pressure of 'live' work to produce a higher level of performance. That comes from priming ourselves for a live environment, It comes from rehearsing without and then with an audience. It comes from developing a positive mental attitude based on our training, rehearsing and performing experiences. We can find we cope better by turning our fears into an excitement about what we're doing. We can tell ourselves that we are excited and looking forward to our performance, and that our nerves are actually thrills of excitement. That mental transfer process can really work, creating a positive energy that we can use to power our performance.

"There is something different about playing in front of a crowd, whether you are a singer of a footballer. It gives you this exhilarating energy that helps you perform - and you do things you don't even know you can do because you are filled with this adrenaline that comes from having an audience. It can take you to new heights"[227]

If we can stay in the moment, we can produce our best work. If, at any point, our mind wanders back to our fears, we need to switch our thoughts onto the mission and its higher importance than us. Our sense of commitment and duty can help to calm us down. Finding a way to 'centre' ourselves can bring us back to the matter in hand. Thinking of our family, our friends, our community, our country and our World can make us appreciate why our sacrifices are worth it. Then there's the enjoyment of being on the edge of our comfort zone. It's scary and thrilling in equal measure. Life is to be lived in the here and now, not in the shadows. Unless we're in the moment, we can't give our performance everything it needs. Performing live, is a bigger test. it demands a higher level from us. Performing live is our chance to live life.

~~~~~

As we've already seen, Dr. Sabrina Cohen-Hatton[228] has helped to improve the way the Fire and Rescue Service operates every day. The pressure on scene must be immense. The Commander at the incident has to weigh-up a series of potentially competing needs and interests. There are several groups of people and assets to take into account. They include the people inside the burning building, the firefighters on scene, other people living and working close by and relevant property owners. The members of the Fire and Rescue Service accept a level of risk in attending every single call-out, but that risk should never be too high. The lives of firefighters are as precious as any. Damage to property matters less than the risk to life, but the loss of a family home or business premises has detrimental consequences on people's lives and livelihoods. There are a tough series of decisions to be made.

Although some level of risk should be accepted at every fire, there needs to be a proper assessment and a well-judged balancing act. Each call-out requires an

---

[227] Soul singer Celeste.
[228] Chief Fire Officer of the West Sussex Fire and Rescue Service and author of 'The Heat of the Moment'.

individual assessment and a potentially different approach. No fixed set of rules or regulations can cover every combination of circumstances. If there are chemicals involved, a bomb threat or a school nearby then the approach will need to be adapted, to deal with that enhanced risk. The response to any uncontrollable element is controllable. That's why on scene decision-making is so vitally important. Every case demands a careful, risk-balancing act. Every decision-maker needs to have the clarity and mental strength to alter the plan quickly if the need arises. Working out where change is needed and how to adapt for it, takes calm and measured thinking.

"From the neck up is where you win or lose the battle. It's the art of war. You have to lock yourself in and strategise your mindset"[229]

Even with a full risk assessment and operational plan in place, the circumstances at a fire can quickly change, at any time (e.g. the impact of unseen flammable materials or a change in the wind direction). That means that the risks associated with a fire can suddenly and dramatically change too. If and when any risks change, an effective re-evaluation and re-balancing process is needed. Commanders need to constantly challenge their incident knowledge and thinking to stay focused on the mission.

To make this effective, every Commander on the ground needs to have enough skill, experience, confidence and support afterwards (when the post-incident questioning begins) to balance all the elements and make the big decisions well. We all need someone to be our sounding-board, to test our thinking. The chance to mentally offload can help us to re-balance ourselves. Everyone needs help to stay on track, whether that's a supportive re-boot or a verbal boot up the arse. Teams need to deliver that mental support for all their members, including their team leaders.

~~~~~

In sport, players arriving from other countries need time to adapt to their new social group. Any changes in language, accent, weather, humour and food will affect a player's mental state and therefore their performance. New players need a full pre-season to fully understand the club's playing philosophy. They need experience of playing, to understand the domestic game wherever they are. They

---

[229] Olympic Gold Medal winner and two-time unified World Heavyweight Champion Anthony Joshua OBE.

need to find their best position in the team. In all walks of life, there is a great deal for any newbie to learn.

The reverse learning process is also incredibly valuable, but it is incredibly under-valued. Each new arrival comes laden with different ideas and alternative ways to solve problems. That brings an opportunity for the whole organisation to learn and improve from every new joiner. Existing techniques and processes can be honed and improved (mainstreaming) by tapping into their knowledge and skill. And, as we all experience different events in different ways, every new person also brings the chance of doing things completely differently (slipstreaming). However, the window of opportunity to gain these benefits is brief. A stranger's ability to see their new organisation's flaws and areas for improvement is lost as soon as they start conforming to its routines and traditions. The more de-sensitised to what's 'new' that they get, the less diverse their thinking remains. For all the gains in flow and synergy you get with compliance, the less diverse your collective thinking is. Without regular questioning and challenge, your organisation will end up missing its chances to adapt and improve.

"When people tell me they've learned from experience, I tell them the trick is to learn from other people's experience"[230]

Instead of just assimilating a new person into your team, ask them for their views on everything including the mission, philosophy, values, positioning, training, action plans and team dynamics. Leaders of all kinds need to investigate and analyse every possible gain from each new team member. Business leaders can ask about organisational systems, and people processes, as well as operating skills and techniques. Sporting leaders can ask about matters such as tactics, team dynamics, diet, analysis, strength and conditioning. The timing of this deep-dive is critical. It has to be done instantly on arrival.[231] That's before that employee starts to absorb all your traditions and routines; and before he she or they forgets how to do anything differently. Welcome new-starters and their new ideas.

All organisations need to raise both the individual performance bar (signing a better skillset than you previously had) and the team collective performance bar (by taking on board new ideas and techniques) with every new appointment.

~~~~~

---

[230] Billionaire business tycoon Warren Buffett.
[231] Subject to legal restrictions.

Business operates 24/7, 365 days a year. There are no breaks between financial years or windows for regrouping, unless you make them. In sport, that reassessment and re-evaluation process comes in between seasons, in what's known as 'pre-season'. Every other type of organisation needs to find its own version of a pre-season. Otherwise the hamster wheel will spin round until it breaks. It's too easy to let things slide, whether that's through complacency, fatigue or indifference. Mentally we have to be on it. That means pressing the collective re-set button every now and again.

During a sporting pre-season, several things can happen. Firstly there can be reflection on the previous season's performance. That should produce ideas for improvements and developments. Secondly there can be planning for the next season and for the seasons after that. Thirdly there can be rest, both mental and physical recharging. Fourthly there can be a re-setting for the new season's mission, to instil a winning mentality.

It's important to have a strong sense of self-belief, but what's primarily needed is a strong belief in the club's playing philosophy and the squad's ability to deliver on it. Everyone at the club has to believe that their team can win the competition they're in. According to Castleford Tigers Coach Daryl Powell, "Pre-season establishes your philosophy. Pre-season builds togetherness and gets you going. But you never really know where you are until the season gets going. Then once you're off and running, it's the club's culture, drive for growth and development and will to win that keep you going."

If you've planned a pre-season that builds a winning mentality, that should pay off for you. As the season progresses, sports science and data analysis have key roles to play. Are we doing what we agreed? Are we adapting wisely? Has the team learned the lessons from previous matches? Do our strength and conditioning sessions and our technical skills training sessions complement each other? Do we all still share a winning mentality?

RED HEART, BLUE HEAD

Unleashing our emotions can really fire us up. To win competitions, teams need to operate with the maximum energy and passion that they can possibly generate. At those times every team member needs a big, red heart pumping full of desire and determination. Without it we are under-powered.

"The beating heart will never die"[232]

However if our unbridled passion is left unchecked, it will spill over into irritability, aggression, rage and even violence. Acting on our red heart alone, we can lose control of our values and our mission. What we want, is to be able to fully fire up our heart and bring a fearsome intensity, without ever losing control. Having the passion to get things done is a matter of heart. We have to be able to tap into our emotions at will.

"Risin' up, straight to the top
Had the guts, got the glory
Went the distance, now I'm not gonna stop
Just a man and his will to survive"[233]

To get things done, we also need to operate in the calmest manner possible, allowing us to make the best quality decisions we can under pressure. We need a cool head to make sure that we bring our logic, clarity and experience to bear. However, having a calm, blue head doesn't necessarily mean that anything gets done. Acting on your blue head alone can stifle activity, by talking you out of the action that you're proposing. We can end up over-thinking all the risks of action, leading to analysis paralysis.

Too much red heart (e.g. anger) or too much blue head (e.g. indecision) will miss the mark. But the opposite of too much blue heart (e.g. fear) and too much red head (e.g. frustration) will miss the mark too. We need our head under the control. We need our heart under control. We need both in balance together. That place of balance is what might be described as the Goldilocks sweet spot.

Peak performance comes where a person generates the maximum passion, determination and will to win that person can calmly control. Not enough desire

---

[232] From the song "Fields of Fire" by Big Country.
[233] 'Eye of the Tiger' by Survivor.

reduces the available performance, just as insufficient self-control reduces the effectiveness of the performance. Neither of our head or heart should dominate. Neither should hold sway over the other. The sweet-spot where our Red Heart and our Blue Head find balance is the point where we are generating our peak level of performance. Our blue head must always have ultimate control so that we make good inclusive decisions. But it must be pushed to its limits by our red heart, so that we can use our passion and desire to get things done.

Where that balance of head and heart is off, the wrong things get done or absolutely nothing does. Where the balance between them works well, our positive judgements and decisions are backed up by the determination and energy to follow them through. The balance between our head and heart governs the way that we live our lives.

~~~~~

Having enough fire to get yourself going (self-starting) and enough ice to put out your hot-headed reactions (self-stopping) are signs of personal knowledge and inner-strength. People with mastery of their Red Heart and Blue Head are 'self-controllers'. Finding that state of personal balance is not easy. It is worth striving for and reaching that point is a personal achievement. It's a matter of mental self-control. Self-controllers can be valuable team players and tribe members. Find them and recruit them.

There is a tribal level, above and beyond having command of your Red Heart and Blue Head. That higher level is having enough emotional control to pass on your feelings to your team mates and colleagues. It's having the ability and will to help your whole team, or tribe, not just yourself. We are talking about 'transformational' people like David Silva. Those people can create waves of emotion and calm that galvanises or subdues their teammates as needed. Not everyone can reach that higher level. 'Tribe-controllers' can positively influence a whole group for the better. They are relatively rare and they are absolutely invaluable. Find them, recruit them and promote them.

Search for the Self-controllers and Tribe-controllers

How many of your people are self-controllers? How many of your leaders are tribe-controllers? Without enough of them you'll have too much emotion or too little motion in your organisation. The wrong actions will hold back your mission and so will too much inaction. Your people's red hearts and blue heads need to be operating in inner-harmony.

~~~~~

In sport, every elite player needs to be a self-controller. That means practicing and embedding emotional control mechanisms. Too much red heart will damage a player's and the team's performance through violence and recklessness. Too much Blue Head weakens the individual and the whole team through passivity and over-thinking.

Tapping into your intrinsic motivations and recalling linked memories can act as useful triggers. The ability to flex between fire-up and ice-cool allows players to unleash their red heart or to regain their blue head at will. Best of all, is the ability to bring your fire with a controlling ring of ice. Self-controllers don't let themselves down. Self-controllers don't let their teammates and coaches down. The same mental toughness is needed in every other kind of work. Everyone who has control of themselves can be successful. That power of control can be utilised for a mission.

Self-restraint is a skill. It needs practice. Mediation can help. Forming and conjuring calming memories can help too. Each of us has a well of patience to draw on. Even the calmest and most self-controlled person can 'lose it' when their patience well runs dry. The good news is that through practice and self-development we can learn to deepen our well of patience.

In sport, particularly, there's a need to quickly fire up and quickly cool down. Having a trigger to help, can speed up the process. Colouring one boot (or training shoe) red and one blue can visually help players to re-focus during games. Using coloured laces would work for non-sporting situations too. Linking personal memories and feelings that inspire passion or calm can complement both of those colours. See Blue, think calm memories; and relax. See red, conjure memories and feelings that inspire passion; and fire-up. Outside of a sporting environment, we can use personal photographs, messages, gifts, special items and memories to trigger Blue and Red reactions. They can be there at our work station to help us when we need them.

~~~~~

We all need to find our own balance of red heart and blue head. I have an image I use to fire myself up. It quickly reminds me of a time and a purpose that fills my heart. It comes from a book. Miffy creator Dick Bruna wrote a children's book called Boris on the Mountain[234]. I used to read to my children. It didn't just make a nice story. It inspired me to do more with my career, to do more for my children. There are two pages in particular which instantly transport me back to how the book made me feel. I read the book to them so often that I can remember most of it by heart. I have a framed copy of it. Those two pages say.

"Boris Bear loved climbing, climbing up a hill.
The hill was steep but that is why it gave him such a thrill.

When he reached the hilltop he had a splendid view
and after all this climbing that suited Boris too."

It is a simple, universal message that still resonates with me. Looking at the illustrations or thinking about those words is enough to stir me to action. They speak to my intrinsic motivations, they link straight to my family. What words or images can instantly motivate you?

~~~~~

In every walk of life, we will come under threat or extreme provocation at some point. We will, from time to time, be left feeling frustrated and disappointed by the actions of others. We will be irritated when our opponents wind us up. We will be despairing of our bad luck, or our own failings. All of these situations, and many more, can make us feel emotional. Unfortunately, upset and anger are rarely helpful to us. Our aim is therefore to turn our emotions into controlled actions. The opposite, namely 'losing it' describes a loss of self-control that's most unhelpful. Uncontrolled anger or rage prevent us from focusing and acting as we'd like; and so does weeping uncontrollably. In contrast, retaining control of our emotions, allows us to use them as fuel. Feeling full of controlled aggression can be very useful. Being fired up, but mentally calm, is a great form of mental balance.

---

[234] Published by Egmont Books Ltd 1996.

243

"I have learned through bitter experience the one supreme lesson to conserve my anger, and as heat conserved is transmitted into energy, even so our anger controlled can be transmitted into a power that can move the world"[235]

In the heat of a hockey match, hacking your opponent down in front of goal will probably lead to a penalty for your opponents and to you being sent-off. In rugby, using a head-high tackle to stop a try, will do the same. Both forms of red mist have consequences. But the other extreme is no good either. Being so full of worry about the risk of a penalty or red card, that you don't even try to tackle the other player, will lead to the opposition scoring. Being clouded by blue mist is therefore equally destructive. Too much uncontrolled aggression and you'll be operating at high risk. Too much over-thinking and you'll be inactive and ineffective. Both offer too much imbalance between our head and heart. Both colour mists let down every stakeholder in your organisation.

Balancing our red hearts and blue heads takes skill, experience and judgement. We have to adapt to suit our mission and our circumstances. We need to understand our role in the team and the situation we are in. We need to develop emotional, social and situational awareness. These skills come from practice and experience. Being a cool, calm defender is generally better for the team than being a hot-headed one, but not if it makes us too hesitant and diffident. Leaders at all levels need to appreciate this. Too much criticism and our red heart stops pumping. Too little encouragement and our blue head slows us down. Our managers can help us to strike the right balance. If they have tasks beyond pure leadership, they need to perform their own individual tasks well too. On-field captains have to be both players and leaders. To become winners, we can't omit to do any part of our job.

Helping to get the balance right between your organisation's collective heads and hearts is crucial to generating tribal power. Does every stakeholder in our team or organisation know that? What is each stakeholder's role in that? Does everyone understand their role?

~~~~

---

[235] Mahatma Ghandi.

For many people, Roger Federer is the greatest tennis player of all time. He is known for being the epitome of calm, self-control on a tennis court. His supreme mental strength means that he is exceptionally difficult to wear down. You cannot break his spirit or his focus. On and off the court he is dedicated to his sport and his values. When you couple his extraordinary commitment with his immense talent, it is no surprise that he has become a winning machine.

John McEnroe is also one of the greatest tennis players of all time. As a left-hander with a deft touch, John could play sublime tennis. But John McEnroe's immense talent was sometimes blunted by emotional outbursts and a lack of self-control. Sometimes that fired him up to play even better. Sometimes it cost him the titles he was so passionate about winning. Controlled aggression is a winning behaviour. Emotional incontinence is a losing behaviour.

"When your time comes, you must lead with your head, not with your heart"[236]

Roger Federer and John McEnroe appear to be polar opposites. But somewhat surprisingly, Roger Federer had a major issue controlling his temper as a teenager. Just like John McEnroe, his behaviour involved giving back-chat to umpires, swearing and even throwing his racket into the net. His blue head couldn't gain control over his red heart. But after suffering from too many losses and too many broken rackets, Roger found a way to change. By his late teens Roger understood that he wouldn't win anything without better mental control. His deep desire to win began to exert control over his shallower and more immediate emotions. Through a process of self-analysis and learning, Roger found the balance between what he calls "fire and ice" (and what I call Red Heart and Blue Head).

Whilst his temper was largely under control by the time Roger reached his twenties, he still hadn't found his emotional balance or his maximum performance level. He did 't have enough controlled aggression. Roger found his balance when he met his wife. Roger is quick to credit the grounding and inspiring affect that his wife and children have had on his success. Roger hadn't won any titles before he met his wife. His family tribe gives him the strength and the desire he needs to push himself exceptionally hard. Roger Federer's family has given him the passion to want to win; and the self-control to let himself win.

---

[236] Ragnar Lothbrok from the History Channel's 'Vikings'.

Both Roger Federer and John McEnroe were immensely talented. Both of them won major tennis titles. Both of them come across as really likeable. But one of them has won far more titles than the other. That's because mental strength is at least as important as physical skill.

~~~~~

It is only when our head and heart are working together in harmony that we operate in a way that's best for us and for our tribes. Where that balance of head and heart is off, the wrong things get done or absolutely nothing does. Where the balance between them works well, positive judgements and decisions are backed up by the determination and energy to follow them through. By concentrating on our mission and values, we can motivate ourselves to positive action when crisis strikes. That helps us to overcome our concerns and bravely press on. We need to battle our fears to defeat them. Richie McCaw puts it more directly. "If you're shitting yourself, don't ever let that show because the team will pick up on it real quick."[237]

If we feel too hot-headed, we need to calmly refocus on the mission and our values. What is our role? What do we need to deliver for our team? Who will we let down if we use too much red heart? If on the other hand, we feel too relaxed and laid-back, we need to fire up our intrinsic motivations using the mission and values to drive us to action. What is our role? What do we need to deliver for our team? Who will we let down if we use too much blue head? Who is relying on our help?

As we get older, we can become more risk adverse. We need to avoid being a loose-cannon, or being too cautious and conservative. We need to find a way to maintain our lust for life, to release the shackles a bit more and try something new, rather than becoming middle-caged.

~~~~~

To achieve business success we need to bring huge ambition, energy and determination. We have to form a plan, call on our strongest motivations and drive the plan to completion. The more resolute and single-minded we are, the more likely we are to be successful. The more red passion we bring, the more

---

[237] The Real McCaw: Richie McCaw: The Autobiography" by Richie McCaw.

chance we have of lasting the distance. However if left unchecked, unbridled emotion and ambition can spill over into selfish actions, rampant egos and poor relationship building. Acting on pure ambition alone is likely to be counter-productive.

Business leaders need to operate in the calmest manner possible, allowing them to get the best out of their colleagues and make the best quality decisions under pressure. Aggression is a necessity in sport, but it has no place in business. Aggressive behaviour at work is usually an act of misconduct. Barking orders, banging desks and extreme rudeness all risk disciplinary action against the perpetrator; and constructive unfair dismissal claims against the company. We have to retain our cool at work in order to retain our place there.

We also need a state of inner calm to make sure that we bring our highest logic, clarity and experience to bear. Succeeding in business is about finding practical, cost-effective solutions to our organisation's challenges and problems. Calm, focused thought is essential, but it's not the whole story. Having a cool, blue head doesn't guarantee that anything much gets done. Leaders have to make difficult decisions and implement them. Too much thought in business leads to 'fudging' or delayed decision-making, which can have major commercial consequences.

Composure is a skill to be practiced like any other

A worker's peak business performance comes when there is a strong internal motivation to achieve success and a clear plan of how to deliver it. Our passion has to be engaged without affecting our judgement. Too much passion will jeopardise our working relationships, but so will not caring enough about our people.

The combination of high motivation and high engagement will generate the maximum performance when it's focused on the mission. Our peak level of usefulness is where our personal motivations and our team's needs coincide. That point is the performance bullseye. If instead our motivations clash with our organisation's values and goals, we will not perform well. There will always be some tension between our organisation's best interests and our own. However we are responsible for reducing that tension as much as possible, by put our organisation first when we are at work. The 'trade' for this is that our organisation shares that responsibility and should fairly provide for all its workers.

Putting the organisation first is not enough for leaders and managers. They must take on another layer of responsibility. They must put the organisation's interests first, the interests of their team second and themselves third. Controlling that dynamic increases the level of their contribution at work. Motivating yourself to put others ahead of you, takes selflessness not self-interest. It takes passion for the cause, rather than a passion for your own ego or pocket. The self-controllers can make worthy team members. Tribe-controllers can make worthy team leaders. They have the self-control to adapt and use their own state of emotion for the common good. They understand what's needed. They can read the room, adjust themselves and pass on their own state of emotion to the rest of the group. When it comes to difficult pitches, negotiations and staffing issues, sending a self-controller could get you a result. But sending a tribe-controller will have an even better chance of getting the result you want.

Takeaway thoughts:

- Winning takes a strong mental belief
- Find meaning in your mission
- Set realistic expectations for yourself and others
- Strive for excellence not perfection
- Winners embrace the need for preparation and have the dedication to commit to it
- Keep challenging and keep adapting where you can
- Minimise conflict, as it's a disruptive state of mental distraction
- Build confidence through increasing knowledge and practice
- Adjust to pressure through safe practice and training outside your comfort zone
- Stay in the moment to produce your best work
- A combination of Red Heart and Blue Head produces peak performance

3.6   WINNING PREPARATION AND POSITIONING

The sixth controllable is preparation and positioning. How we position ourselves for the challenge ahead will heavily influence our chances of success. We have to get ourselves into the best place and the best state of preparation before we begin. And then we have to keep ourselves in the best place and best state of preparedness throughout the task. That doesn't mean staying still. In business, sports and military operations, every competitor and opponent has to constantly re-position itself in order to be successful. That can involve hundreds or thousands of positional changes throughout a competition. Each relocation involves a new assessment and a new decision. One wrong turn and the campaign might be over. Good preparation and scenario planning are critical to success.

"Should I stay or should I go now?"[238]

Every mission is different, with its own controllables to master. One size doesn't fit all. We just have to assess what the relevant controllables are; and how best to take advantage of them. Whatever that entails, we need to ensure we're in the best state of preparation that we possibly can be. That's because the better prepared team usually starts the stronger. A good start can bring us a big advantage. It might keep us ahead all the way to the finish line.

Despite all the uncertainties of our VUCA world, we can still exert a great deal of control over where we start and where we finish. We can decide whether to maintain or adapt our plans, whether to advance or retreat and whether to stick or twist at any time. Before we start to make any individual decisions, we need to form a strategic plan based on our mission and philosophy. We need to write down what we're doing to complete our mission. That comes from a process of self-questioning. What are the mission outcomes that we need to deliver? What actions will get us there? What order do we need to complete those steps in? What timescales do we need to set for those actions? What people and resources do we need for the challenge? Where and when do we need them? What funding and logistics do we need to make this all possible? What scenario planning can we do to prepare? These preparatory steps are all part of the continuous process of alignment.

---

[238] From the song "Should I Stay or Should I Go?" from 'Combat Rock' by The Clash.

249

*"Our goals can only be reached through a vehicle of a plan,
in which we must fervently believe, and upon
which we must vigorously act.
There is no other route to success"*[239]

A strategic plan is all about positioning. Start with the mission outcomes you
need. Add the winning standards needed to achieve each of those outcomes. Then,
it's clear exactly what you need to achieve. Now work backwards from there to
where you are, to reveal the steps you need to take to produce those outcomes.
Ensure that you're sticking to your agreed philosophy and values at every point in
time. Through scenario planning, you can prepare for many scenarios along the
way, to help you become more win ready. Expect the unexpected. The approach
to different scenarios can be incorporated into your strategic plan. This will give
you a high-level strategic approach, an over-arching plan, with guidance for
dealing with likely scenarios along the way. After that, you can practice and adapt
repeatedly until your strategic plan is a living, breathing, way of operating.

~~~~~

Having a strategic plan, provides guidance and a reference point for all decision-
making. It's an essential part of becoming win ready. But, however much scenario
planning you do, a strategic plan can't tell you exactly what to do in every
possible situation. The more potential scenarios there are, the less you can plan
for them all. Meticulous planning can increase the correct responses, but long-
winded plans can stifle decision-making. The more you pack into your scenario
playbook, the more cross-checking you'll need to do and the slower you'll be able
to react. Don't be too prescriptive. Allowing for mission control is key. Keep your
scenario plans simple. Guidance is good. Pain-staking detail is bad. No one can
remember it all. You can't plan for absolutely everything. Unless you need to
adapt it, your philosophy should guide you on the approach to take. Prepare your
people so they can make good decisions under pressure.

*"The board is set. The pieces are moving.
We come to it at last, the great battle of our time"*[240]

---

[239] Artist Pablo Picasso.
[240] Gandalf the White in 'The Return of the King.'

Competition brings the need for consistent, winning reactions and adaptations. Within your strategic approach, tactical positioning can make the difference between victory and defeat. Tactics are the schemes, approaches, ploys, tricks, deceptions, ruses and routines that you deliberately perform in order to deliver your mission. Unlike following a strategy (which is pre-set, pro-active and predictable), applying tactics is situational and often reactive. There are a vast range of tactics that you can deploy. The circumstances that you're facing will shape what you tactics need, but remember that your tactics should always be part of your overall mission strategy. Your tactics should also fit within your philosophy and values. Every action, of every kind, needs to get you nearer to delivering your mission.

Examples of tactics include: moving locations to add logistical capacity or to gain an element of surprise, speeding up your actions when you lose the element of surprise, playing for time when you are waiting for resources or reinforcements, increasing your pricing when stocks are low, reducing your pricing for a period when you want to put pressure on a competitor, agreeing staged repayment terms to improve your cash-flow, pretending to commit one action whilst actually taking another, introducing a new product to plug a hole that's appeared in your product range (e.g. adding a vegan offering), guerrilla tactics such as a military ambush in favourable terrain, putting in more effort to shake off a competitor, promoting a tribal-controller to help pull a team together; and reducing waste and increasing recycling to add customer appeal.

~~~~~

Christopher Ahlberg is an expert in building cybersecurity businesses. His first company Spotfire sold for $100 million. In 2019, his company Recorded Future sold for $780 million[241]. How did he position that?

Christopher was one of the first to realise the potential damage caused by cyber-attacks. He could see that a product which successfully responded to cyber-threats would be a valuable business tool. One that organisations would pay for. But the defining moment was when Recorded Future created a product which can predict the nature of future cyber-attacks. This product doesn't just deal with them, it anticipates them. This was unquestionably a slipstreaming moment. By thinking one step ahead of everyone else, Christopher created an entirely new business opportunity.

---

[241] Information from Forbes online.

By planning for this market, Recorded Future is now helping businesses, of all kinds, plan for their cyber-safety. This information gathering product allows organisations to prepare for cyber-attacks well in advance. In risk management terms, that's a major step up from the uncertainty of 'firefighting' an unpredicted attack when it arrives. Predicting threats, through software, is a form of intelligence-based scenario planning. That new market is absolutely sure to grow.

~~~~~

Ideally we'd be able to travel in time and see what events are ahead of us. We could see how we win, or why we lose. Understanding which controllables we mastered or failed to master, would help us to focus on them now. We could come back to the present and prepare ourselves for that version of the future. Hopefully time-travel would give us the ability to change our future for the better. In theory, we could do that repeatedly, until we liked the version we got. But we can't travel in time. We don't get two goes at the future. Instead, we have to plan for all the possible eventualities and believe that's enough.

"I can't tell the future, I just work there"[242]

Scenario planning allows us to anticipate and role-play future situations that we might find ourselves in. The process allows us to plan for those situations and mitigate against them, preventing loss or all kinds. Every competing team can save itself later, by making contingency provisions now. Using scenario planning, you can practice tactical ploys that you might need to employ later. Scenario planning starts with questions beginning "What do we do if....?" By preparing tactical options; and then rehearsing, improving and adapting them in a safe environment, you can have them ready for deployment.

Mainstream tactics can be effective, but predictable. Slipstreaming tactics offer the added element of surprise. At the battle of Trafalgar, French Vice Admiral Villeneuve, concentrated all his French and Spanish ships in one place to try and break the British lines. This was a mainstream tactic and it was therefore predictable. Seeing this occurring, Admiral Lord Horatio Nelson broke with the traditions of naval warfare and sent two columns of ships straight into the French lines. As this tactical manoeuvre was unexpected, it threw the enemy into confusion. The tactic brought about close-fighting in a tight space, allowing the superior seamanship and gunnery of the British sailors to win a great victory. This

---

[242] Doctor Who.

act of innovative slipstreaming fixed the enemy's ships in a place where the British could defeat them. It prevented the French and Spanish ships from carrying out their own tactic of breaking through the British lines. Lord Nelson positioned this sea-battle as he wanted it fought. His tactical decision, was a calculated reaction that fitted within the mission (defeat the French) and successfully achieved a mission outcome (defeat the enemy fleet). The decision changed the course of the battle and gained decisive control of it.

Great leaders can perhaps deliver great tactical decision-making at the time it's needed. But we shouldn't leave our chances of victory to a rare moment of potential genius. Without all his sea-faring and battle experience, Admiral Lord Nelson would not have made the right decision in the circumstances. Practice and preparation are vitally important. They can help you develop a tactical playbook, of high-level scenario plans to secure you the victory you need. Extensive training and scenario planning experience are what allow a tactical advantage to develop. That's why the military battle plans its operations against super-computers. That's why chess computers now beat humans. We can anticipate most of the moves our competitors will make and plan for them.

Scenario planning helps us to predict and prepare for the future. We can plan and rehearse what we'd do in many eventualities, such as if your laptop freezes during a presentation, if one of your players is sent off during a game, if a key supplier suddenly increases its prices, if your CEO falls ill or gives notice to leave, or if a customer cancels a big order. All of these scenarios are easily predictable. They are all quite possible, if not probable at some point. Scenario planning needs to cover all these obvious possibilities (the known knowns) as well as testing and discovering what else might happen (the unknown unknowns) and plan for them too. The more scenarios you've planned for, the faster and better you'll react to them. We can't see the future, but we can predict it and plan for it.

A good example of scenario planning comes in fire prevention. Where you've got an area that's vulnerable to fire, it's wise to consider all the potential risks and hazards. The time to do that is when there isn't a fire, so you can plan how best to deal with one. By predicting what might happen, you can take steps to avoid the worst case scenarios and reduce the risk of damage and injury. One method of controlling fire is to add strategic firebreaks into high risk areas, which reduce the risk of a fire spreading. By opening up a big gap in any vegetation or other combustible material, you can establish a form of barrier that slows or stops the progress of a fire. Examples of firebreaks can be clearing a path, ploughing a field or building a road through a forest. Or they can be putting a flame-retardant material within the walls of buildings, to help contain a fire. This kind of planning and building work can't be done easily when a fire is already raging. Scenario planning allows preventative action to be taken and training to be done calmly in advance.

We can't provide for every eventuality, but by working through all the possible scenarios we can decide which ones we need to focus on. We should pinpoint the key risks, by multiplying how likely a risk is to happen, by how devastating that eventuality would be. If a particular scenario would permanently close our organisation and there is a reasonable likelihood of it happening, we need some form of contingency against it. If that Armageddon scenario is more likely still, we need an even more robust contingency provision.

From January to August 2019, a mixture of US National, State, local and private sector organisations carried out a joint exercise called 'Crimson Contagion'. The reason? To test the ability of Federal and State Governments to cope with a severe influenza pandemic emanating from China. Prophetic? Yes. Brilliant scenario planning? Yes.

The sixty-three page draft report highlighted how underfunded, underprepared and uncoordinated America would be in the event of a real pandemic. One basic, but fundamental, example gives us a clear indication of how little coordination there was. "Inconsistent use of terminology regarding vaccine types and stockpiles caused confusion amongst response partners at all levels of government." In short, different departments were naming and measuring the volume of vaccines differently. Another example spoke of the state of unpreparedness "The current medical countermeasure supply chain and production capacity cannot meet the demands imposed by nations during a global pandemic." This highlighted a massive shortage in vaccines, hospital equipment and personal protective equipment.

Was all this learning used to get America ready, for the real COVID-19 pandemic only six months later? It seems not. The New York Times' headline on 19 March 2020 was 'Before Virus Outbreak, a Cascade of Warnings Went Unheeded.' The lesson is stark. Scenario planning can save lives and livelihoods. But there is absolutely no point in scenario planning if you learn nothing and implement nothing from it.

~~~~~

After preparing and positioning ourselves well, we can make a good start. After that, we need to deliver a consistently good performance throughout a task, so that we finish in the best position too. Initially, we may have a good idea of where we need to be at each point in the mission, but that can quickly change. We are always limited by the uncontrollable we face, the fixed elements that are beyond our influence. But equally, we are always free to positively affect the controllable elements that apply to our challenge. The "goalposts" can move within any competition and that requires us to be flexible. We have to be ready to adjust our positioning, whenever it's advantageous to the mission for us to do so. Adaptability is a key part of success. Being adaptable allows us to re-position ourselves in a better location and re-adjust our state of preparedness in order to win.

We have to be agile, in order to stay strong. We have to stay strong, to avoid becoming fragile. Finding the best place to be is within our control. Separating the controllables from the uncontrollables brings us insight. Applying the best strategy and tactics to fit that combination of fixed and flexible elements is what brings us success.

> "You have brains in your head. You have feet in your shoes. You
> can steer yourself in any direction you choose. You're on your own
> and you know what you know. And you are the
> one who'll decide where you go"[243]

That said, we need to be realistic in our assessment of the controllables. We can't stop the 1st January following the 31st of December, or stop the sky from raining. Like King Canute we can't turn back the tides of the sea either[244]. Any energy we expend trying to do these impossible things is wasted. Our energy should instead be spent on managing the variables that we can control. Whilst a date in the year is fixed in its planetary rotation, but we can plan in advance what we'll do on that date. That's because we know how the calendar works and we can give ourselves time to prepare for it. The sky may rain but we can look at the weather forecast at least five days ahead. We can plan around bad weather days, or we can always bring a coat and umbrella with us. We can't change the calendar or the weather,

---

[243] From "Oh the Place You'll Go!" by Dr. Seuss.
[244] As King Canute (aka Cnut the Great) apocryphally proved on a beach on the South Coast of England (thereby showing that his secular power was subservient to the divine power of God). The story was first recorded over 100 years after his death, to illustrate his alleged piety. Sadly it is unlikely to be factually accurate. However it is worth quickly adding that Canute was an incredibly strong and successful leader; and in 1028, through multiple invasions, he was briefly King of Denmark, England, Scotland, Norway and part of Sweden.

but we can control the variables around them. Our preparations should focus on any slipstreaming that we can introduce, any mainstreaming that improves our chances; and maximising the controllables to help us win.

Under-preparation usually results in under-performance

By developing and stress testing scenario plans for our mission, we can prepare ourselves for the actions we might have to take. But if those plans are merely words on pieces of paper, we will not be win ready for those events. We have to actively prepare and position ourselves for all those scenarios. We need to have our people trained and our equipment ready. We need to have logistics and supply chains in place. Every organisation has to anticipate the unpredictable much better than it does. We need to plan for all the known knowns, known unknowns and unknown unknowns and train for them too. This will make the organisation win ready if the scenario ever arises. We need to get started on our future-proofing.

"The secret of getting ahead is getting started. The secret of getting started is breaking your complex overwhelming tasks into small manageable tasks, and then starting on the first one"[245]

The more we do in advance, the better we'll cope when the pressure comes. We are not going to be ready for anything, without planning and practising for it first.

~~~~~

Positioning your organisation to win doesn't mean copying the previous winners. We can use their data to help to set our winning standards, but everyone has that data too. Why do what has already been done? Why not try something better? If you can slipstream instead, you can go past all the mainstreamers. Thinking differently, produces different results.

"The waterfall is most important! It mixes the chocolate! It churns it up! It pounds it and beats it! It makes it light and frothy! No other factory in the World mixes its chocolate by waterfall! But that's the only way to do it properly. The only way!"[246]

---

[245] Mark Twain.
[246] From 'Charlie and the Chocolate Factory' by Roald Dahl.

During the 1970's and 1980's Gerald Ratner achieved enormous growth for his high-street jewellery brand Ratner's, He turned the original company into a multi-million pound, multi-brand retail group, that included the Ratner's, H. Samuel, Ernest Jones, Leslie Davis, Watches of Switzerland chains and over a thousand shops in the USA. It was an astonishing achievement. The success of the Ratner's Group was built on providing affordable jewellery to the mass market. Gerald Ratner created a whole new part of the market through slipstreaming. It's hard to believe now, but Ratner's' Group was the first jewellery business to offer low price discounts and promote those offers in its shop windows.

On 23 April 1991, with the business in its pomp, Gerald made a speech at an Institute of Directors conference at the Royal Albert Hall. During his speech, he made his most famous (or infamous) comments. They were about his Group's own jewellery. "We also do cut-glass sherry decanters complete with six glasses on a silver-plated tray that your butler can serve you drinks on, all for £4.95. People say "How can you sell this for such a low price?" I say "because it's total crap." Then he compounded his mistake with a comment that one pair of earrings was "cheaper than an M&S prawn sandwich but probably wouldn't last as long." The humour was misplaced. What happened afterwards? The Ratner Group reportedly lost £500 million off its share value; and ended up owing the bank a billion pounds. Gerald Ratner lost his job.

"Every failure is a lesson learned about your strategy"[247]

Many people will know that part of his story, about how Gerald Ratner lost it all. After a set-back of that magnitude, most of us would have never gone back into business. But Gerald bounced-back, opening a successful health club in Henley-on-Thames and selling it for a substantial profit, before opening an online jewellery business with its low overhead costs. Gerald Ratner bounced back, because he doesn't copy other people, he leads them. His 1991 comments were very ill-advised, but Gerald Ratner understands how to build a business.

In 2015, I booked him to speak at the Salisbury Big Business Event[248]. Gerald was very funny and very entertaining. So I booked him again for the 2016 Solent Business Growth Summit[249]. When I thought about business-people to contact for this book, I thought of Gerald. When I got in touch, he quickly responded with his

---

[247] Thomas Edison, the inventor of the first commercially usable light bulb.
[248] Which I created; and co-organised with Claire Burden, James Fry and others.
[249] Which I created; and co-organised through Trethowans LLP. I would highly recommend Gerald Ratner as an after-dinner speaker.

theory on winning and how it has worked for him during and since his Ratner's days. Not many people have built three different multi-million pound businesses.

"Winning in business is about being different. When I opened my health club people laughed at me for having an outdoor pool, as nearly every club's pool is indoors. It turned out to be our USP, everyone loved it. At Ratner's everyone displayed their most expensive products in the most prominent position. We've done the opposite with great effect. Don't follow the crowd. Regards. Gerald Ratner."

~~~~~

In professional sport, the matches have specific dates, kick-off times, time periods, rules, routines, patterns and method of adjudication (e.g. a referee supported by a television official). These are all fixed. They are uncontrollables. Despite that, there are many variables of preparation and positioning that a player or team can use to get ahead of the competition.

According to Castleford Tigers Head Coach Daryl Powell "In a game of rugby there are three basic phases: attack, defence and the transition periods in between them." There needs to be a plan for all three phases. Without a plan to deal with transition, the plan would have a fundamental hole in it. Without thinking about every element of the competition, in detail, a team will struggle to achieve success.

Sam Chisolm: "What's the plan?"
Josh Farraday: "I've always wanted to blow something up"
Sam Chisolm: "That's not a plan"[250]

The planning process for any form of competition involves a dual focus on "us and them." Planning has to include how to attack the particular opposition and how to defend against them. It also has to go into how the opposition will attack you and defend against you. There is a ying and yang to every aspect. The transition periods between the opposition's phases of attack and defence bring brief windows of opportunity. Plan for them.

---

[250] The Magnificent Seven, 2016.

With different opposition players and coaches to face every game, each week's preparation has to be tailored. With injuries, suspensions and changes in form within your own team, each week's team preparation will need to be different. There will be some core fundamentals and consistent themes that might not change much, but they should be under constant review. Change is good, as long as it's clear, necessary and agreed. Everyone should have a say in making change and everyone should know exactly where things are, at any given moment.

That said, too much change can knock a team off track. Pre-match routines tend to help with priming, so unless there's reason to change them, match day should have a familiar feel to it. Team talks "set the scene" and "provide important reminders" so they should be planned into events, but tailored to each match.

How much change can you impose? That depends on what's needed to win; and also on how adaptable the playing group is. According to Daryl "Flexible, confident groups in the flow can adapt more." Winning sides tend to adapt better to change. They can reposition themselves and have the confidence to take it in their stride. Winning teams carry on winning, after undergoing change, more often than losing teams do.

~~~~~

As we know, scenario planning for what's to come is a great way to remove or reduce the predictable risks. We all need to take steps to prepare ourselves for what might come next. But there are some more obvious things we can do without the need for too much speculation. Eating healthily is a key aspect of being win ready. Scenario planning should tell us exactly why and what we need for our mission, but we already know that healthy eating is a good idea. We should be doing it regardless. That's a given. What scenario planning offers us, is the chance to test out exactly what should be in that diet and the reasons why.

The macaws in Peru's Manú National Park eat clay. At face value that's very strange, because clay is not a foodstuff. So why would they do that? One theory is that the clay provides a sodium substitute for salt. That would mean their diet lacks salt and eating clay gives it to them. If that is true, how do they know? The other theory is that macaws can't eat certain foods because they contain toxic or caustic substances. But when food supplies get low, macaws need to eat a wider range of food to survive. By eating clay, they ingest a substance which absorbs and binds in the toxins, effectively neutralising them before excreting them. Eating clay allows them to eat other poisonous food in order to stay alive.

Whether it's a conscious or subconscious process, the Manú macaws are actively ingesting clay to protect themselves. That's great positioning.

~~~~~

In the late 1950s, actor Steve McQueen was the star of a hit television show called 'Wanted: Dead or Alive'. He'd had a few movie parts (including 'The Blob' and 'Never so Few' directed by John Sturges) but nothing to really stamp his mark on the film world. Despite having grown up in a boys' home and not finishing High School due to dyslexia, Steve McQueen had managed to become a star of the 'small screen'. But that wasn't enough for him. Steve McQueen wanted to be a big film star, on the big screen.

When Steve heard that Mirisch Company Alpha Productions was casting for a new film called 'The Magnificent Seven' he asked his agent to get him out of his television contract, so that he could be in the film. With it also being a Western, Steve felt he was perfect for the role. The director was John Sturgess, who already knew how he worked. The role was almost tailor-made for him.

Steve's agent asked for permission to release him, but the television show's producers refused. They needed to retain their star and they had him under contract. Steve made a personal plea to be released, but again the show's producers said no. The part was seemingly out of his reach. Steve was faced with an uncontrollable, a television contract that he had signed and committed himself to. Some uncontrollables will never change. They have to be accepted. However, sometimes an uncontrollable can change with time or with new events. When that's the case, we can adapt to those changing circumstances and quickly re-position ourselves, in order to take advantage of them. In life, some people accept their 'fate' but others continually seek to defy it. By nudging, we can sometimes instigate the events that can remove an uncontrollable.

According to his own agent, Steve McQueen was so determined to be in the film that he "took his rented Cadillac and ran it into the Bank of Boston and came out with whiplash." Steve returned to Los Angeles wearing a neck brace and telling the story of his shocking car accident. Once he'd used his injury to get himself out of his television contract, Steve McQueen was free to secure himself the supporting role of Vin Tanner in 'The Magnificent Seven'.

The Magnificent Seven's star lead was Yul Brynner, who had already had a string of hit films, including 'The King and I', 'The Ten Commandments and 'Anastasia' (which he won an Oscar for). The other six actors were effectively Yul Brynner's support cast. Eli Wallach, who played Calvera in The Magnificent Seven, is quoted as saying that Yul had a "magnetism"[251] about him. There is no doubt that Yul Brynner was an impressive actor at the peak of his career. Yul Brynner was exactly the kind of star that Steve McQueen aspired to be.

As soon as the script was out, Steve started to moan about the fact that Yul had far and away the best lines. As soon as they arrived on set, Steve bemoaned the fact that Yul had the biggest trailer and a luxury limousine. As soon as the props arrived, Steve bemoaned the fact that Yul had the biggest horse and the biggest gun. To Steve all of this was unacceptable. It all got in the way of his opportunity. Steve McQueen could have accepted the limitations of his role and waited for his turn to be the star in a later film. But that chance might not have come. Steve was impatient for success. So despite the limitations of his part, Steve decided to make the film his personal calling card.

In every scene he was in, Steve worked extremely hard to attract the audience's attention. Unlike the silent movies, where over-acting was necessary to get across meaning, the 'talkies' were looking for realism. Steve couldn't ham it up too much. He had to find another way of impressing in his scenes with Yul Brynner. With fewer lines, he had to create a spark through character development. So, instead of allowing the audience to focus on Yul Brynner, Steve used continued movement to pull the attention to himself. He took off his hat and he put it back on, he played with his gun, he checked his bullets, he touched his hat, he twisted his body in the saddle and he changed his body position. Steve McQueen made the very most of his screen time.

The scene where the Steve and Yul's characters ride a wagon up to the graveyard is full of these touches. Steve is sitting the far side of Yul Brynner and Yul has hold of the wagon reigns, not Steve. But you find yourself watching Steve McQueen. In the scene where the seven gunfighters cross a stream on horseback, Yul Brynner is up front, in the lead. To steal that scene, from behind, Steve swung out of his saddle, scooped water up in his cowboy hat and poured it over himself. In one of the gunfight scenes, Steve hurled himself over a wooden counter head-first to show off his physical prowess. He did not miss an opportunity to outshine his co-stars.

---

[251] Some of this information came from the documentary 'Discovering Steve McQueen' and thevintagenews.com

Yul Brynner was two inches shorter than Steve, so he reportedly arranged to have a mound of soil build to stand on, so that he seemed taller. Steve reportedly kicked away the mound before the cameras rolled. To be fair, that's a form of cheating and I don't condone that. Steve McQueen didn't need to do that. He was stealing most of the scenes already, without that kind of trick. According to their co-star Eli Wallach, Brynner was so concerned about Steve stealing scenes that he hired an assistant to count the number of times Steve touched his cowboy hat while Brynner was speaking.

Steve maximised every second of his time on screen. Although he had fewer lines and inferior proximity to the camera than Yul Brynner, it didn't matter. Steve made himself every part the star. Following The Magnificent Seven, director John Sturges picked Steve for his next film called 'The Great Escape.' After these back to back hits, Steve McQueen was the Hollywood star he always wanted to be. 'Bullitt', 'The Getaway' and 'Papillon' followed, by which time Steve McQueen had become the highest-paid actor in America.

It's said that, more than ten years after 'The Magnificent Seven' hit the cinema, Steve McQueen rang Yul Brynner to apologise for his actions during filming. By then Yul Brynner's career was in decline. Yul reportedly accepted the apology with good grace and humour saying "I am the King and you are the rebel Prince. Both are dangerous." Both of them worked out how and worked hard to become film stars.

~~~~~

As I write this, Liverpool F.C. are the Premier League Champions, Champions League Champions and World Club Champions. Liverpool's Manager Jürgen Klopp is a highly able and efficient planner, as well as being a great people person. He reportedly insists that everything operates like clockwork. Punctuality is vital. If a meeting is planned for 10am, then '10am exactly' is when it starts. The message is clear. We begin our day at 10am. Don't ever be late.

Jürgen believes the training ground is where the team's success emanates from. This is where all Liverpool's tactics and drills are tried and tested. First comes the mission of winning every possible trophy, then the philosophy of outplaying every opponent, then the analysis of attack and defence. The data is assembled and analysed. The drills and tactics are designed and then practiced over and over again, until they work to Jürgen's exacting standards. The coaching team plans each training session in fine detail. The planning process is tailored to suit

Liverpool's strengths and to beat the next opponent. Both elements are essential. There is very little that's played by ear.

> *"Give me six hours to chop down a tree and I will spend the first four sharpening the axe"* [252]

Communication is critical in live situations and in practice sessions too. It isn't just the Liverpool coaches who know what's going on. Every player does too. Before every session, Jürgen addresses his players to explain what the session is about and why they're doing it. During the session, the analysts give instant feedback, so tweaks and adjustments can be made. The repositioning process is relentless, until it is absolutely right. Afterwards, the analysis carries on. All the drills are reviewed and adjusted as necessary.

Liverpool play a very free-flowing natural style of football. As is often the case with things that look easy, the hard work behind it is deep and extensive. Hard work and extensive planning underpins Liverpool's success.

~~~~~

Piper Alpha was an oil and gas platform in the North Sea, located approximately 120 miles from Aberdeen. At 12:00 on 6 July 1988, routine maintenance began on one of its two condensate pumps. The pressure safety valve on Pump A was removed as part of this maintenance process. A temporary disk cover was put over the pipe, which was hand-tightened to seal it. At 18:00 the daytime shift ended. As the maintenance work wasn't finished, the temporary cover remained in place. The on-duty daytime engineer filled in a permit stating that Pump A must not be turned on in any circumstances. As the nightshift manager was busy, the daytime engineer left the permit in the Control Centre and went off to rest.

At 21:45, Pump B became blocked and couldn't be re-started. As a result, the night shift manager gave the instruction to turn on Pump A instead. The resulting oil and gas fires killed 165 of the men on board the rig, as well as 2 men on a standby vessel. Only 61 escaped with their lives and many of them have lived with post-traumatic stress disorder ever since. The fire took three weeks for Red Adair and his firefighting team to extinguish, due to the strong winds and high waves.

---

[252] President Abraham Lincoln.

Every disaster of this kind begs answers to many questions. How could that have happened? Why didn't the maintenance worked begin earlier? Why wasn't it completed before the end of the day shift? Why didn't the daytime engineer wait to give the nightshift manager a verbal update? Why were the permits for the valves kept in a separate box to those of the pumps? Why was the firefighting system switched to manual and not on automatic? Why were the rig's firewalls only resistant to fire and not to explosions?

The subsequent report from The Cullen Inquiry was absolutely scathing. It made 106 recommendations for changes to North Sea safety procedures. They covered changes to operating equipment, platform design and the involvement of the emergency services. The new protections eventually made it into law, in the form of the Offshore Installations (Safety Case) Regulations 1992. When you need 106 changes to your procedures, you probably haven't done much if any meaningful scenario planning.

"You can have it done fast, you can have it done cheap and you can have it done well. Pick any two"[253]

In truth, the Piper Alpha oil rig was not ready to operate safely, due to its design and operational flaws. The rig's systems were not set up to adequately protect the crew. Piper Alpha's mission was to get as much oil out of the North Sea as fast as possible. Safety was a stated priority, but in practice it wasn't the number one priority it should have been.

The rig was designed for pumping oil, not gas. When the job of pumping gas was later added to the rig's activities, the safety implications were not fully thought through or implemented. As a result, there was no safety planning for a gas explosion. Oil burns. It doesn't explode. But gas does. The rig's firewalls weren't capable of withstanding the blast of a gas explosion.

There is no justifiable excuse for providing unsafe working conditions. In this case, the insurance cost was reportedly close to $2 billion. The New York Times reported that payments to the survivors and the families of the victims totalled $180 million. The financial and public relations disasters alone confirm the false economy of scrimping on safety. When you add in the more important factors of

---

[253] Paul "Red" Adair.

lives lost and mental health trauma caused, it is abundantly clear that the failure to prepare for safety can bear a horrific cost.

In preparing to succeed, you have to plan how to avoid disaster. Sometimes there is an uncontrollable that causes effects beyond your control, but very often the risk was controllable and is self-induced. Outside the military, any mission that costs lives cannot be deemed a success. Health and safety are both vital components of successful operations, especially when you are dealing with flammable or explosive substances. You can have gas pumped out the North Sea 'fast'. You can have it done 'cheap'. But the Red Adair priority that matters most, is to have it done 'well.'

~~~~~

All your organisation's activities should be aligned to its mission. If there are too many non-core projects and other distractions, the core mission can unravel. Choose your mission projects wisely. What you take on, matters to all of your stakeholders. Is your mission purely self-serving and profit-making, or is it a more rounded than that? Do all your projects and activities benefit all of your stakeholders? What your organisation stands for matters to its customers, employees, suppliers, funders and every other stakeholder. Businesses doesn't just sell products and services, they sell values and feelings. Does your organisation pass each of their approval tests? Is there a match between your organisation's public imaging and the reality? How you publicly position your organisation's work matters to its sustainability. Corporate social responsibility initiatives can be complementary purposes and provide wider benefits for the organisation's stakeholders.

Some organisations have a thriving corporate social responsibility (CSR) programme, based on a genuine wish to do good, first and last. They set themselves up to deliver good, by allocating the funding, time, people and other resources needed. Then they do good. When a profit and loss analysis of their CSR work is carried out, they are always in the red. They are happy to be in the red. That's the whole point. They are net givers. They hope that someday, something good will come back to them. But that's not their reason for doing good. Good doesn't have to pay them back. Their other work will make them the money they need. Their stakeholders will feel pride in that and a sense of greater engagement.

"No one has ever become poor by giving"[254]

Some organisations want to do good work, but they want to be seen to do good even more. To those organisations a missed public relations (PR) opportunity is more galling than a missed opportunity to help. On a profit and loss approach they want to break even from their corporate social responsibility work. That might sound benign but it isn't. They want results from their giving. They want to be at least net balanced. If their philanthropy doesn't offer benefits, then what's the point of spending valuable time on it?

A third type of organisation wants to be seen to do good work, without having to do much at all. For those organisations it's all about their own PR. They are always looking to be in the black (or 'green' if they are attempting to greenwash their credentials, just think Volkswagen and fuel emissions). They want to make net profits from their philanthropy. They are net takers. Corporate Social Responsibility is just another business development tool.

Other organisations don't spend any time on corporate social responsibility. For them it's not any kind of priority. These organisations are focused on their own operational and commercial needs. They are missing a trick. They all bring positive benefits aside from profit. Doing good work in society brings a sense of inner satisfaction and pride which is beneficial to everyone who takes part. Giving your time and skills to others improves those skills and builds greater engagement with your organisation, your colleagues and your community. Despite any cash benefit from ignoring CSR, the rewards from being self-serving create an engagement deficit.

"No one is useless in his World who lightens the burdens of another"[255]

Claiming to be philanthropic is a risky position to occupy even if it's true. No one likes a smug donor. But it's so much worse if hidden underneath that apparent philanthropy is an inconvenient truth (that the good work is all smoke and mirrors). That sort of revelation that is likely to do terrible reputational damage to the organisation claiming it. For example, it's all very well claiming to be an equal opportunities employer, but how well do you know and control your supply

---

[254] Anne Frank.
[255] Charles Dickens.

chain? If your goods are being made in factories where human rights abuses are rife, it's a false claim and leaves you open to a different form of abuse. Several big names have had adverse publicity from allegations of underpaid and abused workers. They have included Nike in Asia during the 1990's, or more recently Amazon (in the USA) and Gap and H&M in Asia during the 2010's. Shoppers don't just look for value, they look for values too.

"The customer's perception is your reality"[256]

Promoting your own charitable giving is therefore taking a position of jeopardy. It almost requires a lack of authenticity ("I don't like to talk about it, but... [I'm going to anyway]...") to get the message across. That rarely comes across well. Alternatively, instead of self-promotion, why not promote the good work of others? If your organisation does something really good, then that's the win. Hopefully someone will say thank you or promote that work for you. But if not, don't seek publicity for it, just move on. A net red CSR policy doesn't grasp for murky praise. It willingly gives; and receives other rewards instead. Those non-monetary rewards include wider life experiences (which help with empathy), improving skills (which bring added confidence) and the warm feeling from genuinely helping (which makes us feel more human). When we benefit as people, our organisation always gets some of that benefit back.

"Don't judge each day by the harvest you reap,
but by the seeds you plant"[257]

So it's best not to position your organisation as a philanthropic hero. Let it be a real hero. Let it quietly do good work and promote the efforts of others. The net rewards of unconditional giving are wider and more laden with rewards.

~~~~

In 1847, Jacob Christian Jacobsen returned from Munich with two jars of Spaten yeast. Using his mother's copper wash basin, Jacob made his first batches of homemade lager. Taking the name of his five-year-old son (Carl) and the Danish word for hill (bjerg), J.C. Jacobsen created a new brewing company just outside Copenhagen. Carlsberg went on to become a global brand. In 1973, Carlsberg

---

[256] Kate Zabriskie, a US author and learning a development expert.
[257] Robert Louis Stephenson.

created its legendary corporate brand positioning. The new tagline was probably the best product tagline of all time.

'Carlsberg. Probably the best beer in the World'.

It was a bold decision, but by pitching itself as the World's leading beer, the public wanted to see if it were true. By consistently promoting a theme of market-leading excellence, people began to believe it. Forty years later, Carlsberg was in a different place. So the marketing went even bolder still. In 2017, Carlsberg introduced a temporary new tagline.

"Probably not the best beer in the World. So we've changed it."

Casting doubt on your own product isn't always wise, as Gerald Ratner will attest to. But Carlsberg managed to maintain its initial claim, whilst offering a compromise "Once true, but not today? Probably not." The press release went on "Somewhere along the line, we lost our way. We focused on brewing quantity, not quality. We became one of the cheapest, not the best." If that had been true, it was a huge statement of failure. However the statement didn't come across as capitulation. It came across as a humble statement of intent. Carlsberg had learned its lesson. It was ready to do better.

Carlsberg hadn't had a corporate meltdown, it just needed to launch a new beer. The thought-provoking campaign built on its long-standing branding. It invited customers to reappraise the beer and buy the new version. It was a brave move, but its new and improved Pilsner was ready to go. Was it a good move? Probably.

~~~~~

The Summer Olympics of 1968 were held in Mexico City in Mexico. Those Mexico Olympics are probably most famous for the black-gloved, black power salute of Tommie Smith (Gold medal winner) and John Carlos (Bronze medal winner) during the playing of the US national anthem for the men's 200 metres. Peter Norman won the silver medal.[258] The Mexico Olympic games are less well-

---

[258] Before the medal ceremony Peter suggested that Tommie and John wore one black glove each. During the ceremony Peter wore an Olympic Project for Human Rights badge, publicly showing his support. As a result, he was ostracised by the Australian media and reprimanded by his country's Olympic organisation. Worse still he was not sent to the 1972 Olympics despite running the qualifying time on several occasions. At Peter Norman's funeral in 2006, Tommie Smith and John Carlos were two of his pallbearers.

known for the fact that the Men's Triple Jump World Record was broken an incredible five times.

First, Italy's Giuseppe Gentile broke the Men's Triple Jump World Record by jumping 17.10 metres during qualifying. Then he improved his World Record to 17.22m with his first jump in the final on the following day. That record only stood until the third round, when Viktor Saneyev of Russia jumped slightly further with 17.23 metres. In the fifth round, Nelson Prudencio of Brazil jumped even longer with 17.27 metres. Finally, in the sixth round, Viktor Saneyev of Russia jumped 17.39 with his final jump to grab the World Record back again and secure Gold. To see one world record being broken is exceptional. To see three different people break the world record in the same event is truly extraordinary. That doesn't happen. So how did it happen?

"We have always to take into account that the ability to win any Olympic Medal demands truly Olympian application"[259]

One factor was the high quality of the competitors. It was a very strong field and the winner Viktor Saneyev, was a superstar in the making. This win was the first of his three consecutive Men's Triple-Jump Gold medals. Another factor was the effect of the early world record, which sparked the competition and drove each of the medal hopefuls on to longer and longer jumping. A third reason was the new all-weather track that was used for the first time. Creating less friction, greater speeds could be attained in the run-up. But the main reason was one of geography.

Mexico is positioned 2,240 metres (7,350 feet) above sea-level. No other Olympic Games has been held so far above sea-level. In fact only one other Olympic host city has been over 2,000 feet above sea-level. That was Rio de Janeiro in 2016, at less than 3,500 feet. At altitude the air is thinner. Mexico City is so high-up that visitors can suffer hyperventilation, a rapid heart rate, slower digestion, headaches, dizziness, difficulty breathing, difficulty sleeping, as well as swollen hands and feet. All of these effects come from 'oxygen debt' and the impact of that means performing far worse than normal. So how can that situation have contributed to five Men's Triple-Jump World Records?

The thin air at altitude is a huge problem for the ill-prepared, but its thinness offers less resistance as athletes move. So if runners and jumpers can acclimatise to the conditions, they can generate even faster speeds and jumping

---

[259] Sir. Steve Redgrave in his foreword to Katherine Grainger's autobiography.

distances. In scientific terms, if an athlete trains regularly at high altitude, they increase the production of red blood cells, carry oxygen more efficiently and perform better than normal. In the amateur days of 1968, athletes weren't allowed more than six weeks training; and only four weeks of it could be taken during the three months before the event. The athletes that didn't naturally live and train at altitude found themselves at a severe disadvantage, which some of them were totally unprepared for.

In Mexico, the long-distance runners who had trained at altitude, swept the medals. The others finished miles off the pace. The winning time for the Men's 10,000 metres was 1 minute 48 seconds slower than Australian Ron Clarke's world record. That was a very slow time and confirmed how gruelling the race had been. Based on that winning time, Ron Clarke should have found the race easy. However, the race toll was heavy on the athletes who hadn't trained sufficiently at altitude. World record holder Ron Clarke didn't just finish outside the medals, he suffered horribly and collapsed at the end of the race. He was reportedly unconscious for ten minutes before eventually coming round.

The altitude affected the sprint events very differently. With the advantage of less resistance (from the thinner air) and without the disadvantage of the longer-distances (which caused extreme fatigue) these shorter-distance events were much faster than usual.[260] As a result, the world records fell in the Men's 100, 200 and 400 metres races. The jumping events benefitted too. As well as the triple-jump, the world record for the Men's Long-Jump went too. Bob Beamon's twenty-nine and half foot long-jump shattered the world record and stood for almost twenty-three years afterwards, until Mike Powell eventually broke it in 1991. Bob Beamon's jump in Mexico is still the Men's Olympic Long-Jump Record more than fifty years later.

Sports science developed enormously after the Mexico Olympics. Preparing for the conditions as well as the type of event instantly became part of the routine process. Altitude training is now incorporated into most athletes' preparation. Mexico taught athletics a number of important lessons. The number one being that preparation is almost everything.

Knowing exactly what challenge you face is critical. What will the conditions be? Investigating what your event's controllables are, as your first step, helps you to understand and control them. Knowing what's up ahead will help you to work out

---

[260] The new all-weather track may have helped too.

how to position yourself for it. It's a lesson in making sure that you practice in competition conditions, or you'll be at a major disadvantage. In Mexico City, Ron Clark was not prepared. Luckily for Viktor Saneyev, being as a triple-jumper meant that he didn't need to be.

~~~~~

Which people and which organisations we associate with has a big impact on our success. We need to choose our projects, organisations, tribes and Super-tribes wisely. Deciding which people we shouldn't work with is a powerful as deciding which ones we should. We all need to try hard to make our relationships work for us. Every one of us has to take personal responsibility for our relationship choices. Even when we have no authority for decision-making ourselves, we can nudge and influence those that do. Sometimes, because of circumstances beyond our control, we are trapped and lacking in influence. That's when we have to be prepared to leave an organisation that conflicts with our values or becomes terminally dysfunctional. The other alternative to leaving, is to take control of your own projects.

In the film industry, actors and actresses[261] are typically paid a fee for each film. The industry has long had its 'Hollywood stars' as well as thousands of jobbing actors, extras and budding hopefuls. Just like any other industry, there have always been winners and losers. Some actors and actresses have no bargaining power and have to accept what they're offered. Some get to negotiate themselves a better deal, but within limits. Other actors are so in demand that they get to link their deal to the success of the film. Finally, some actors get to hold the reins on the whole film.

If an actor's performance excites the public and draws in paying customers, that should lead to better parts in bigger films, shows or plays. The more 'box office' a performer is, the more the production company will be prepared to pay them. Moving from a fixed fee to taking a percentage of the sales, can be a game-changer. But if the production 'bombs' you may get absolutely nothing. So the best acting deals involve a combination of up-front fee and a share of the back-end profits. Not many actors get that kind of win, win deal. What's clear is that with film contracts containing clauses about almost everything, from nudity to numbers of lines and scenes, it's difficult to for an actor to negotiate their way through it all without help. Otherwise actors might miss out on the best parts or be paid a fraction of what they're really worth.

---

[261] I'll use the gender neutral term of 'actor' if I may.

Leading actors bring their loyal fans with them to their next project. Actors with have 'star quality' can almost guarantee profits by simply being in a film. They are extremely valuable and they get to have a say in the production process. But in a tier above them are the actors who step up to produce their films as well as star in them. Producing and staring in your own films is the holy grail of creative control and can be a big money earner. It can also lead to recognition and awards.

"When I need to push myself, I think of all those nicely polished trophies waiting to be lifted up by the winner - and how that winner might be me" [262]

Unless it's their own production, an actor will generally have little or no direct control over the film-making process. That actor might get lucky and find they really like the Executive Producer, Director and fellow cast members. They might find their film becomes a commercial success, raising their star higher in the Hollywood sky. Perhaps slightly more often, an actor might get cast in a film that they're ambivalent about or dislike making, or one that's a commercial flop. Even if they're lucky enough to get paid something, that's still bad news. An actor's latest film will have a big impact on which projects are offered to them next (if anything). Being professional on set is a key controllable. That will enhance your reputation and make yourself more castable next time, even if it's the worst film ever made. That means exhibiting as many winning behaviours as you can and minimising any losing ones. However difficult the rest of the cast may be, the personal show must go on.

If an actor gets lucky and is hired into an already successful franchise, they become more sought after by association. Think Marvel, James Bond and Star Wars. If you're in a franchise from the very beginning and you become a key reason for its success, you get to be in even higher demand. You can't imagine Warner Bros. changing the actor playing Harry Potter for the final film[263] can you? Imagine what the audience reaction would have been. And Daniel Radcliffe hasn't struggled for work since then either. Picking your film projects is an art. Like every other art, you either need to learn how to master it yourself, or you need to work with someone else who has. That's where experienced agents and fellow professionals can come in very helpful. We need a good network to be our

---

[262] Maria Sharapova.
[263] Harry Potter and the Deathly Hallows - Part 2.

most successful. That certainly applies in acting. Building a support network is a key controllable.

Harrison Ford was plucked from obscurity to star as Han Solo in the Stars Wars saga. He was reportedly paid only $10,000 for Star Wars: A New Hope (the first film in the nine film franchise). But he had a negotiated a clause in his contract that gave him a very small percentage of the profits. That turned out to be worth several million dollars. With a film career that also includes the Indiana Jones franchise, Harrison Ford has reportedly earned over $250 million since Steven Spielberg discovered him doing some carpentry work. Negotiating the best deal you can is a key controllable.

Keanu Reeves is a Hollywood star, but he's isn't one that you'd necessarily expect to be a very top earner. With films like the cult 'Bill and Ted' franchise and the excellent Point Break[264] Keanu has had a good career in acting, but perhaps . His financial game-changer came from a three film franchise. Keanu Reeves reportedly earned over $250 million from the Matrix trilogy. He also reportedly earned the most money an actor's ever earned from a single film (at the time and for several years afterwards) being $126 million from the second film in the Matrix series 'The Matrix Reloaded'. Keanu is not the only Hollywood film star to become as big as a movie franchise.

Johnny Depp became a global superstar by playing Captain Jack Sparrow. The first of the Pirates of the Caribbean films[265] was a smash hit and reportedly took $654 million at the box office. Suddenly Johnny was able to negotiate a huge deal for the films to follow. Six films later, Johnny has reportedly earned over $300 million from playing Captain Jack. Now that's an act of piracy. Whether his alleged off-screen life will affect his acting and earnings going forward will have to be seen.

Tom Cruise has built a film career through major hit after major hit, through films like 'Top Gun', 'The Firm', 'Rain Man', 'A Few Good Men' and 'Jerry Maguire'. Tom worked himself into a position of bankability, wealth and influence that allowed him to acquire the rights to the Mission Impossible television series. Seven

---

[264] A high adrenaline film directed by Kathryn Bigelow (the only woman to win a Best Director Oscar, for the Hurt Locker) and based on a script Kathryn developed with her husband at the time James Cameron (The Terminator, Aliens, Titanic and Avatar).
[265] The Curse of the Black Pearl.

Mission Impossible films later Tom has created his own film franchise, which he controls. He reportedly earns himself around $75 million for each new film.

So far, so male. In 2018, the Center for the Study of Women in Television and Film at San Diego State University carried out a study of the lead roles in the top 100 grossing films of 2018. Thirty-one percent of them were women, the highest figure reported so far. This is partly due to commercial demand and partly due to the increasing number of women who are producing and directing films. Becoming a producer brings authority and choices. It's the biggest way to control your career, your film projects and your earnings. It allows you to help the careers of people you want to work with.

There are plenty of big female film stars. They include: Scarlett Johansson, Jennifer Lawrence, Anne Hathaway, Dame Judi Dench, Cameron Diaz, Elizabeth Banks, Natalie Portman, Evangeline Lilly, Lupita Nyong'o, Karen Gillan, Julia Roberts, Michelle Rodriguez, Helena Bonham Carter, Cate Blanchett and Zoe Saldana to name but some. Even if you don't recognise all their names, they've all been in big grossing successes. Female television stars are now joining the big earners too. According to the 2020 Forbes Rich List, Sofia Vergara earned $43 million for America's Got Talent and the final series of Modern Family. Grey's Anatomy lead, Ellen Pompeo, allegedly earned $19 million during the same period. All of these women are very successful actors[266]. However it's the women who are now producing and directing that are becoming the real game-changers.

"Women have brains and uteruses, and are able to use both"[267]

Creative success comes from taking control of the project. Directing a film gives a degree of creative control, but the overall control always sits with the producers. To make and shape the films they want to see made, an increasing number of female actresses have started their own production companies. They include Alicia Vikander, Charlize Theron and Drew Barrymore amongst others.

Elizabeth Banks has starred in films grossing over $5.5 billion, including the Hunger Games, Pitch Perfect and Lego Movie franchises. Elizabeth has also moved into producing and directing, with 'Pitch Perfect 2' and 'Charlie's Angels' being two examples. Angelina Jolie has starred in and produced 'Maleficent: Mistress of Evil'. Margot Robbie produced 'I, Tonya' as well as starring in it.

---

[266] Or 'actresses' if you prefer. I've used 'actor' as a gender neutral term.
[267] Baroness Karren Brady CBE.

Reece Witherspoon's company produced 'Gone Girl'. Sandra Bullock produced and starred in 'Miss Congeniality'. The list is ever expanding. In the film industry, it pays to produce and direct your own films. More and more big stars are doing just that.

In your competition, try to find the best position of control and influence that you can. It could be the Executive Producer's chair or it might be a seat around a board room table. The more you can shape events around you, the more likely you are to achieve your mission.

~~~~~

Preparation isn't all about what we do. We need to tap into our team around us. Despite the helpfulness of others, we tend to trust our own life-experience over that of the rest of the World. We don't challenge and dissect our experiences enough. We rely on gut instinct too often, rather than on our powers of listening and analysis. That's not to say our gut reaction isn't valuable, because it's our subconscious alerting us to what it thinks we need to know. But we shouldn't just rely on our individual instincts, we need more help than that.

By working with our team to select and managing the key controllables of our task, we can prepare for success. We need to analyse what's required to be successful (borrowing the experience of others), what the task's key controllables are (from analysing all the elements); and how we can master them (done as a group activity, to gain the benefit of cognitive diversity and avoid singular thinking). We can learn so much from other people if we let ourselves.

> *"There's no shame in stealing - any actor who says*
> *he doesn't is lying. You steal from everything"*[268]

Before we begin a project, we should look, listen and learn. We need to be humble and assume that everyone else has something that they can teach us, because they do. Acting solo, is a no no. We should properly test out all our feelings and hunches, rather than just acting on them. In truth, we don't use all the information that's readily available to us, even though it will help us position ourselves for winning. Adding the knowledge of others to our gut instinct, our personal experience and our powers of analysis, provides us with four vital tools

---

[268] Benedict Cumberbatch.

that check and balance each other. Don't exclude the forensic for the purely emotional.

We can learn from past successes and failures, if we can move through their emotional impact and understand why they happened. We can learn from our competitors too, by discovering why they win and lose. But without analysing and learning from our past actions and omissions, they just become memories rather than lessons. There is so much experience inside us and everyone else, but we don't mine for it enough. Everyone past and present knows things that we don't know. Many people will happily share it if you ask them. But do we ask? And more importantly, when other people do actually offer us their advice, do we listen properly and take it?

> *"Why is it that people who can't take advice always insist on giving it?"*[269]

We need to research and shape our mission before we begin it. We need to be methodical. So many questions can be answered by good preparation. We need to find and test the relevant data. There are many intelligence gathering disciplines that we can use. These include: research in open publications (OSINT), human source intelligence, by asking other people (HUMINT), aircraft and satellite photography (IMINT) and even codebreaking (COMINT). We can legally trace and decipher a great deal of useful information. Asking, researching, listening, watching, searching and analysing are all better than guesswork. Ask and you shall receive.

~~~~~

When you're outnumbered, power and strength comes from positioning yourself where it's easiest to defend your people and assets or easiest to strike against your enemy. In the film 'Skyfall', James Bond takes 'M' back to his ancestral home in rural Scotland, in order to protect her from the villain Raoul Silva. Using the tactic of feigned deception, Bond leads Silva away from London and deep into the Highlands.

> *"I want you to lay a trail of breadcrumbs that's impossible to follow except for Silva"*[270]

---

[269] James Bond to Vesper Lynd in Casino Royale.
[270] James Bond to Q in Skyfall.

Together with Skyfall's gamekeeper, Kincade, they rig up a series of traps throughout the old house that Bond and Kincade know well. These traps help them to protect M and kill the first wave of Silva's soldiers. But when Silva arrives with more soldiers and a helicopter gunship, they are eventually over-run. M and Kincade escape through a secret priest-hole. James Bond primes some propane tanks to explode, escapes down the same tunnel; and leaves just before the house and helicopter are destroyed. This mixture of defensive and attacking strategies, in familiar territory, allows them to kill virtually all the soldiers and even up the odds of victory.

~~~~~

Being fit enough to win, is a key element of success. That comes in part from eating a healthy and nutritious diet. Eating what you need for your mission, when you need it, can power you on. A diet of junk food or too much food won't help you. Nor will eating too little. Diet is a controllable that you can master. We can make food work for us by following a balanced diet that's tailored for our mission.

Being healthy also comes from physical exercise. We have to put ourselves in the best physical condition to achieve our mission. That comes from activities like walking, swimming, running, playing sport. A winning team is physically fit enough to win.

A third aspect of being mission fit is seeking medical help when it's available. We all need access to medical science to help keep us active and moving. We shouldn't hang back, through fear, if we have an issue that needs treatment. We need to help the medics to help us.

~~~~~

Another similar controllable that can help with success is relates to sleep. Good sleep is a key building block to achieving a great performance. When we are tired, we are under-powered and we under-perform. There isn't a single person or team that functions better when it's deprived of sleep. And yet, we all have bad nights' sleep that impact on our ability to function. Our need for sleep is an uncontrollable. However, our sleep pattern is very much a controllable.

Luke Gupta is a senior physiologist and sleep scientist for the English Institute of Sport. He produced a list of tips for the BBC's website[271]. I have paraphrased them as the first six tips below and added four others. The quotes are from Luke:

---

[271] 16 April 2020 – Five tips to sleep like an Olympian.

1. Calm down before you try and sleep. If we are in a heightened state of alertness, it's more difficult to get to sleep. Instead of just turning the light off and trying to sleep, it's better to do something relaxing, like watching television or reading a book first, rather than trying to go straight to sleep.

2. Only try to sleep when you feel sleepy. "Sleep is like an elastic band. It stretches while you are awake and the stretchier the band is when you go to bed, the quicker it's going to snap back - which represents falling asleep." Going to bed earlier won't make you sleepier. So the advice is not to go to bed until you feel sleepy. "You wouldn't go to a fridge unless you felt hungry... If you go to bed when you feel sleepy, you will fall asleep faster and will get better quality sleep."

3. Do some exercise and you will feel sleepier. Physical exertion can help make us naturally tired and ready to sleep. "By doing a certain level of activity in the daytime, it makes you sleepier at night." Doing no exercise during the day can disrupt your sleep pattern.

4. Try to sleep and wake up at the same times every day. Routines can be difficult to achieve in modern life and being too fixed about them lessens our ability to adapt. However, where sleep is concerned, a routine can be very helpful. "It's important to keep a structured bed and wake time. Once people have worked out what a suitable bedtime is for them, it's important to establish some regularity around that." It seems that deviating from your sleeping pattern too much will adversely affect your sleep quality. "You don't have to go to bed and wake up at the exact same time every day, but you create a sleep window and then there's a bit of a buffer of about an hour either end". That means we can adjust our bedtime or waking time by up to an hour, but no more. If you stick to a regular sleep window, you'll get a consistent benefit from having good sleep.

5. Try and sleep in a familiar and safe place, that's your place for sleeping. Having a safe, familiar and separate place to sleep can help us to fall asleep when we're in it. "It is great to keep the bedroom as a place of sleep where possible. If you can't do that, you have to try to avoid using your bed for anything other than sleep."

6. Organise yourself enough light during the day and darkness at night. As human beings, we are naturally awake during daylight; and asleep at night. Electricity has given us the ability to produce light whenever we want it. With so many sources of internal and external light, we can extend our working day and change our sleeping patterns as we need to. That can be very useful. The downside is that if don't match our exposure to darkness (at bedtime) and light (during our waking

hours) we upset our sleep pattern. "So if you get a constant level of light there is no real distinction between night and day. You have to be more creative, so if you are doing exercise try and do it in your garden. If you are going to sit down and work, try and do it next to a window."

7. Tackle the issues on your mind during the day. If you take thorny issues with you to bed, they will affect the quality of your sleep. So try to tackle or progress the issues on your 'to do' list every day. Then when you come to sleep, you'll know you've tried your best to resolve them. The peace from that feeling with help you sleep better.

"A well spent day brings happy sleep" [272]

8. Avoid too much screen time in the hour before you try and sleep. By turning off all your sources of blue light well before sleep, you can relax your mind and prepare it for sleep. That especially applies to mobile phones and computer screens of all kinds. This partially overlaps with the first tip, as we tend to have a heightened mental state when we're on our technology devices.

9. Try and avoid night-time disruptions. Sleeping through the night maximises our sleep time. Turn off your phone's sounds and notifications if you can. Use ear plugs or eye coverings if you need to. Where you sleep with a partner, try to time your sleep pattern with your partner's if you can.

10. Use your own bedding. It's easier to go to sleep on your own pillow, under your own duvet and on your own mattress. If you're staying away from home, you should take and use your own pillow for the best night's sleep.

Controlling our sleep pattern is vital to our success. Controlling our sleep pattern will help to make us consistently win ready.

~~~~

Organising and influencing our own lives and relationships is hard enough, let alone trying to support and motivate others. Despite that, some people choose to offer help, hope and inspiration. They can influence and positively impact on the lives of many others outside their own tribes. They can become Super-tribal-controllers.

---

[272] Leonardo da Vinci.

At age thirteen, Bethany Meilani Hamilton was surfing off Tunnels Beach, Kauai with her best friend. What Bethany didn't know what that swimming close-by was a 4.3 metre (14 ft) tiger shark.[273] When the shark attacked her, it bit Bethany's left arm clean-off below the shoulder. In an instant, her life was in the balance.

Rescuing his daughter from the water, Bethany's father made a tourniquet from a rash guard to try and stem the bleeding. But by the time Bethany arrived at hospital she was in hypovolemic shock, having lost over 60% of her blood. In an ironic quirk of fate, Bethany's father was due to have a knee operation that same morning and Bethany took his place in the operating theatre.

Thanks to her father's home-made tourniquet, Bethany survived the attack. But she was left with life-changing consequences. That shocking injury would have been physically and emotionally challenging for anyone, but Bethany was only thirteen with most of her life ahead of her. It would have been tragic for anyone to lose an arm and it was crushing for Bethany Hamilton, because she absolutely loved surfing. She had her family around her for support, but they couldn't help her to surf. Anyway, who would go back into the water after that kind of experience?

"Give me love, hope and strength to carry on"[274]

Despite all her fears, one month after the accident, Bethany returned to surfing. She had the mental strength to go back to what she loved doing. Initially Bethany had to surf differently, by using a custom-made board with a handle. Then she learned to kick more when paddling out into the waves. She adapted her positioning on the board and learned a new way of surfing. When she'd mastered that, Bethany set about teaching herself how to surf one-handed with a standard board.

Outside her surfing hobby, Bethany Hamilton was growing up, with exams to take and a career path to follow. Bethany had to choose a job that she could manage

---

[273] The tiger shark was killed a mile or so from the site of the attack and it was measured, which is why we know its length so precisely. Part of Bethany's surfboard was found in its mouth. The remains of that shark-bitten surfboard are on display at the California Surf Museum.

[274] From 'Strength' by the Alarm. The lyric also forms the name of Mike Peters' Love, Hope and Strength Foundation with its mission to save lives from cancer and leukemia.

with one arm. Bethany chose the thing she loved doing the most. She picked surfing. By taking up a mainstream challenge with only one arm, Bethany gave herself a much tougher challenge than her competitors. But that didn't stop her. She became a professional surfer, winning and placing high-up the leader board in surfing competitions right across the World.

Bethany's personal website focuses on wellbeing and uses the challenging strapline "Ready to be unstoppable?" And she is. In 2019, Bethany broke her "one precious elbow" which could have knocked her completely off her stride. Instead she wrote on her website "But it's just a speed bump right?!" Bethany has developed an incredible ability to adapt and reposition herself, physically and mentally. She could have developed a closed and defeatist mindset, but that's not Bethany Hamilton.

You'd expect that Bethany has enough to focus on and worry about, but she doesn't just focus on her own challenges. Bethany runs a foundation which helps amputees adjust to life, called Friends of Bethany. Bethany's ability to ride the speedbumps of life has given her the life that she wanted and inspired many others to do the same.

~~~~~

When we take a position of responsibility, we need to act responsibly in it. When we are given authority, we need to use it fairly, inclusively and wisely. When we don't have titles or authority, we need to nudge our way to success. Nudging is a process of influencing, through targeted actions designed to achieve a particular outcome. Those actions can be small or large, obvious or subtle, public or covert. As long as they have impact and push events towards the outcome you're targeting, they will be nudging it along for you.

Nudging can come in several forms. We can provide information and experience to our leaders that positively influences their decision-making. We can move from a self-controller to become a tribal-controller and help to support other team members. We can raise the standards around us by setting a better example ourselves. We can help our organisation to enforce its values and create a positive culture. All of these actions help to make us more influential and directing. All of these actions will help our organisation to become a winning one. That said, nudging can also have all the opposite effects if we do all the wrong things. Nudging can also undermine us, if it comes from our competitors and is designed to oppose us.

"We were once friends with the whites but you nudged us out of the way by your intrigues, and now when we are in council you keep nudging each other"[275]

Nudging is a controllable skill that's available in any competition. The more than your team masters it collectively, the closer to winning it will get. Don't under-estimate how effective it can be. Your competitors will certainly be trying their best to make it work for them.

~~~~~

I've been an employment lawyer for over twenty-five years, advising and representing clients in Employment Tribunal's across the country. I've lost count of the number of final hearings (trials) that I've been involved in. Through meticulous preparation, I have only lost two of them. One of those judgements was quickly overturned on appeal (for apparent judicial bias) and quashed from the record books. The other case was very different. It was going really well until a couple of my client's witnesses changed their evidence late on, without warning. In retrospect, the result was the right result for the truth. I just wish that I'd known what the real story was, several months earlier. I'd really rather not have found out during the hearing itself, because it was too late for me to do much to help. The Claimant's barrister had an open goal to shoot into; and he didn't miss[276]. That loss still rankles now, even though the underlying reason for it was outside my control. But there are always lessons to be learned. For example, that case changed the way I've taken witness statements ever since.

Courts and tribunals decide cases by applying judicial hindsight. We don't have the power of foresight and nor do judges. Hindsight is good in a courtroom, but it's useless in the moment that you need to act. That's why preparation is so important. Without preparation, our actions are just stabs in the dark. You just need to position yourself for the task in hand, learn what it takes to succeed and then action it.

Based on my experience I believe there are six key elements to winning legal cases; and they're all down to preparation and positioning. They are all controllables that you can master and apply to other forms of competition.

---

[275] Chief Black Kettle of the Cheyenne.
[276] He was made a QC a few years later.

1. Preparing to win. Unless it's a fluke, you can't win a legal case until you've thoroughly prepared for it. I have always worked incredibly hard before the hearing, so that I can calmly follow the events during it. I've seen too much panic in the faces of opposition lawyers and witnesses to ever want that for myself. Leaving your preparation until shortly before the hearing, is leaving it too late. You need time to visit (and revisit) every issue and every piece of evidence until it is all aligned and crystal clear. Prepare from the first moment, until the last.

Legal cases are decided by applying the relevant facts to the relevant law. Analysing who wins is an ongoing thought process, right up until the final judgement is given. Using a painting analogy, imagine that each lawyer paints a picture during the case. The legal issues dictate the size, shape and material for the frame, as well as the subject matter for the painting. The facts as each side sees them give us the subjects of the painting. The lawyer then gets to choose the style of their painting, how much detail to reveal, what colour palette to use; and where the light shines on the scene. At the end of the case, the Employment Tribunal[277] gets to interpret the two paintings and decide which one it prefers. In some cases, where neither lawyer has done a good enough job, an Employment Tribunal effectively paints its own picture and chooses that one.

"My momma always said, "Life was like a box of chocolates. You never know what you're gonna get"[278]

The first place to win a case is through influencing which decisions are going to be made. Early on in a case, the Employment Tribunal holds a 'Case Management Discussion Pre-hearing' to agree the way the case is going to be managed. As part of that process, a List of Issues is agreed. Which issues are included in the List, which are excluded and the exact wording for those issues can make a big difference between winning and losing. As a solicitor you can never mislead a Judge, but you can still try and nudge every issue in your client's favour.

The process of marrying the law and the facts together, is what reveals how good your case is. Gathering in all the relevant information and documents is sometimes painful. Ever since losing that case, I have never accepted that what I'm initially told or given is everything I need. There is often something else. Asking specific questions and requesting specific documents proves more

---

[277] Mostly made up of a qualified Employment Judge and two additional members (usually one with an employee and one with an employer background).
[278] Forrest Gump.

effective than a general question asking for information. Not every document helps but it's always best to know what each one says.

After the issues are finalised, there needs to be a deeper assessment of the legal strengths and weaknesses, based on what we need to prove (attack) and what we needed to disprove (defence). Both are vital to winning. Too many opponents concentrate on their 'positive attacking case' without adequately defending the weaker points that could lose them the case.

Surprises cause problems that you haven't prepared for

Written documents can help you work out what really happened, but I've learned not to take them at face value. You always need to investigate whether the event happened in the way described. I have come across many documents that were in some way misleading or only told part of the story. I've even been given document with a forged signature that had to go to the Police. Talking to all the possible witnesses is critically important to finding that out. As you now know, I've learned the hard way, that a witness might not tell you the truth until it's too late. So it's vital to investigate thoroughly early on, before the opposition gets to cross-examine your witnesses under oath.

To keep all of the key information in mind, I find it really helpful to prepare a spreadsheet with the whole case set out on it. That starts with a list of the legal issues, the relevant documents (and what they say), who witnessed the event (and what each witness says about the event) and then how that evidence affects the legal issues. That way, I can help to include everything in our witness statements and prepare the best cross-examination for the other side's witnesses.

2. Clarity and Fog. As a lawyer, you have to fit the relevant law to the relevant facts. However, there are usually alternative versions of the facts and often alternative interpretations of the law. Where there is doubt and debate, a lawyer can definitely make the difference between winning and losing. Whoever offers the most credibility and clarity, usually wins. Whoever's case is the foggiest, usually loses.

It's the lawyer's job to promote their client's version of the facts and the best interpretation of the law to go with them. But they cannot, as a matter of conscience or professional conduct, ever mislead an Employment Tribunal. Being open and honest makes it harder to win, but that's how things should be. That's an uncontrollable that lawyers have to accept. Non-lawyers have to play by the rules too. No one with a reasonable case needs to lie in order to win. And if you don't have a winnable case, you shouldn't be fighting it in an employment tribunal.

If you have the better arguments in any legal case, debate or negotiation, then explain precisely why they're the winning arguments. Never leave a Judge or other person to work that out for you. If your own analysis reveals that your case is weak, work hard to provide additional evidence or credible alternative explanations (defence). Also tie the opposition witnesses in knots and undermine their credibility (attack). If necessary, attack harder to compensate for any defensive weaknesses. Sow seeds of doubt around evidence and credibility, without ever acting unprofessionally, or misleading the tribunal.

"Above any commercial success one might enjoy, one's reputation for honesty is the most important thing"[279]

Each of the two lawyers needs to give the Judge an accurate and believable explanation that wins them the case. The easier it is to follow the better. Using the same painting analogy, those lawyers need to paint their own canvass in a realist or photorealist style. That means painting a picture that's simple, still and well-formed[280]. The more realistic your painting seems to be, the greater your chances of winning. At the same time, each lawyer will get opportunities to paint on their opponent's canvass, especially during cross-examination. When that happens, you need to try and make the opposition's painting appear unrealistic and overly-complicated[281]. The more confusing your opponent's painting appears to be, the greater your chances of winning.

3. Be passionate. If you don't care about the outcome of a case, why should a Judge bother to care? Lawyers have to be professional at all times, but that still allows room for genuine passion. The more determined you are to persuade a Judge, the more attention you draw to your own case. The more enthusiastic you are, the more persuasive your arguments will become.

4. Never be a smart arse. This particularly applies to cross-examination. Your aim is to ask questions that undermine the opposition's case (attack) and you put your client's case to the opposition's witnesses (defence). Be polite, calm and

---

[279] The late George Carmen Q.C.
[280] Think Manet's 'The Balcony' or 'Donut for Sale' by Goings.
[281] Think Cubism like Picasso's 'Guernica' or Surrealism like Dali's 'The Disintegration of the Persistence of Memory'.

patient. Wait for the witness to finish speaking. Never patronise them or try and make them look stupid. Make their evidence seem unrealistic and unreliable, but don't battle with them. Wait for the answer and then ask another question. You aren't allowed to repeat your questions to try and get a better answer. So instead you have to work around the issue with different or linked questions. Work hard to cast doubt on the opposition's version of the facts. Then once you've covered your ground, leave it and move on to the next issue. Often you've done enough, even if you haven't elicited a confession or a "You can't handle the truth[282]" moment. Knowing when to stop is very important.

Obviously, never, ever be smart with a Judge. Professional, polite and passionate are good behaviours. So are being respectful, reasonable and rational. Whereas irritation, impoliteness and interrupting are losing behaviours.

5. Finish with a short, sharp summary. Your closing remarks in a case are called legal submissions and they are your final opportunity to win a case. You have the chance to summarise your attack and defence (concentrating on the points you've won as the case developed). They are an opportunity to say what you want the decision to be and why (with your killer point or points only). This is the moment when you explain why your painting is so much more reliable and truthful that your opponent's. Finally, lay out your case as one simple proposition and ask the Judge to find in your client's favour. Ask nicely and it can be yours.

6. Tell the better story. Of all the controllables in legal cases, this is perhaps the most important. You have to execute all of the others well enough, but this is what really wins hearts and minds. When we are children we have stories read to us. When we grow up we watch television programmes, vlogs, videos, films and shows. We read messages, newspapers and novels. We tell and share stories with all our social groups, about our families, friends and the wider world. We read stories to our children and grandchildren. We all like good stories. We all groan when we hear a bad one. Most importantly, we know the difference between the two.

Good stories are easy to follow. The test is whether they can be quickly summarised and retold. Good stories have good characterisation, so we know who's who and what each person's role is. A good story persuades us to care what happens to each of those characters (good or bad). And above all, a good story is believable. If the ending you're suggesting is ridiculous or would come as an

---

[282] From the film 'A Few Good Men'.

unpleasant shock, your story hasn't worked. In exactly the same way, each legal case has to be told like a good story. What really happened? What is that fair or unfair? What should the ending be? Good stories fit all the elements together. Bad stories lose cases.

~~~~~

Becoming the UK's Prime Minister, means being chosen from amongst the 68 million people living in the UK. They are seemingly insurmountable odds. But, taking one particular step will dramatically reduce those odds. It is statistically the most important controllable. By being elected as a Member of Parliament, the odds on becoming the Prime Minister drop to 1 in only 650, as the Prime Minister has to be a sitting MP. The odds of any MP becoming Prime Minister may be even shorter than that. In reality, only the majority party gets to pick the Prime Minister. Since the World War II, the highest number of seats a winning party has ever held is Labour's 418 in 2007. The average number of seats held by the majority party, over the last ten General Elections, is in fact 361. So by taking the step of becoming an MP, you might reduce your chances of becoming Prime Minister from an impossible 1 in 68 million, to perhaps only 1 in 361.

After that, there are many more controllables to master. They include: performing your constituency duties extremely well (so that you are popular and repeatedly re-elected), speaking well in the House of Commons so you become noticed, pleasing the party whips when you vote, positively raising your profile and popularity outside Parliament, supporting the party at all times, doing a great job when you get ministerial and then cabinet roles; and building your relationships and networks with the most influential party members and media figures.

Boris Johnson was very successful at controlling his winning controllables, on his mission to become Prime Minister. Boris aimed to become a popular, likeable and trustworthy figure that was very electable. To these ends, Boris was prepared to send himself up, as he did on the BBC's 'Have I Got News for You' which helped him appear approachable and humourous. He has written books on Winston Churchill which have boosted his intellectual image and emphasised the link to his legendary, distant relative. Boris became London Mayor to grow his profile in the nation's capital and prove his leadership competence. He also built a relationship with US President Trump to show his diplomatic credentials, eliciting the highly unusual public support from U.S. President, with the comment "Boris would do a very good job."

Boris did not have a smooth path to becoming Prime Minister. He made a number of public gaffs and he unsuccessfully stood for the party leadership once before. Despite all his efforts, Boris clearly didn't fancy his own chances for quite some time.

"I have as much chance of becoming Prime Minister as of being decapitated by a frisbee or of finding Elvis"[283]

However, Boris successfully made himself appear a credible all-rounder to the voting public. At a time when optimism was in short supply, Boris played his strongest card, optimism. Some people don't trust him, believing him to be capable of saying anything that suits him. Others find him confusing and vague. Whether you love him or loathe him; and whether by luck or judgement, Boris controlled his winning controllables.

~~~~~

Rugby Coach Mike Ford believes that the pre-season period is crucial to a sporting team's chances of winning. "As a coach, pre-season is the time to set your vision, secure a good culture and build belief in the whole squad. Then when the wins come, there are clear foundations to point to and maintain."

Whether winning is the chicken or the egg, proving that your preparation works really helps everyone to buy into more of that preparation. When a team starts a season well, that preparation and planning is retrospectively 'proven' to have been correct. The particular pre-season may have been the main reason for a team's success or it may not, it may be the tablet or the placebo. Either way, 'proving' that the process is producing good results, raises everyone's belief in the preparation and in each other.

Over the course of a season luck should even itself out but when there are too many factors against you at once it's tough. Mike says "Confidence takes a while to build, but if things go wrong and the culture breaks down that confidence can be quickly lost." Culture is also crucial to handling losses, as Mike explains.

"A good culture can help a team to withstand adversity, bounce back after losing and deal with bad luck"[284]

---

[283] Prime Minister Boris Johnson.
[284] Mike Ford.

288

According to Mike, good leadership is about encouraging and allowing others to lead. "Let the winners talk." Not every player sets as good an example. Not every player can speak well to the others. But those that play well and set a good example through their actions will be good role models too. If they can show and tell their winning behaviours to everyone else, they will help to set high standards for the whole team. Some leaders are natural. Others can sometimes be coached to lead, but not everyone takes to leadership. "A player needs to be on the threshold of leadership already, through their behaviours and performances as a player and then as coaches we can help and guide them to become good leaders." Recruitment needs to include looking for people "on the threshold of leadership".

~~~~~

Positioning in crucial in every form of competition. Business decisions often involve a great deal of positioning. Which products and services are you selling? Which markets are you selling them to? How much are you charging? Who is selling them for you? What manufacturing and quality control processes do you have? What packaging delivery processes do you use? What branding have you adopted? These are all positioning questions. Are all the outcomes of those decisions aligned around the mission?

Growing a business involves more positioning questions. When your organisation is trying to win new business, should it focus on acquiring new customers, or look for more business from its existing customers? There is some debate, but the received wisdom is that focusing on your existing customers creates longer-lasting, more profitable relationships. That's because:

1. Securing repeat business usually takes less investment (in time and money) than securing new business.

2. Existing customers tend to trust you more, so they tend to buy more goods and more often.

3. Existing customers tend to buy more frequently, perhaps up to five times as often as a new customer.

4. Repeat customers recommend your business to others more often, acting as an unofficial sales team.

The easiest wins are likely to come from making your existing customers so happy that they renew, add new products and recommend you to others. That means giving every single customer a brilliant product, service and experience. Then every customer can become a three-source customer.

A business tends to make more money from having fewer, happier, repeat customers than it would from having a high-turnover, all-new business model. This confirms that working on your existing customers is commercially prudent. But does that mean giving up on new customers? Well no, otherwise a business is unlikely to sustain itself. There needs to be a flow of both new and repeat business. There needs to be a balanced approach to business development, because your organisation's next piece of business could come from any one of five different sources:

- a current customer renewing an order, or
- a current customer expanding their business with you and buying a new product or service, or
- a current customer recommending you to a new customer; or
- a former customer coming back again after time away, or
- a new customer placing an order.

As a result, at least some business development time needs to be spent pitching to former, existing and potential customers. But as three of them involve existing customers, then perhaps we should spend $3/5^{th}$ (60%) of our business development time with existing customers, $1/5^{th}$ (20%) with former customers and $1/5^{th}$ (20%) with potential new customers. This may be true for your business. However, rather than just estimating, you should calculate exactly what proportion of your business comes from each of the five sources? Are you under-selling to any of them? If you are, then you can adjust your business development accordingly. For example, if your existing customers never recommend you to any new potential customers, why not introduce an incentive scheme to kick-start that line of business.

Good positioning also means rewarding everyone in your organisation for securing new sales. Repeat customers, will repeat their business because they are happy with the products, services and experience they have received. Everyone in your organisation contributes to that. Rather than focusing all your commission and bonuses on your sales force, why not reward your research and development, production, logistics and service teams whenever existing customers make a new order? Then they will be even more engaged and committed to looking after those customers, thereby driving up even more sales.

Organisations, who are preparing to win, need to investing plenty of time in their retention and recruitment. Selecting your people is a huge factor in success. It's arguably the most influential controllable of all.

In a salary capped sport, playing budgets are limited. Clubs need to decide how best to use them. SKY Sports presenter and analyst Jon Wells is a former player and also the Director of Rugby at Castleford Tigers. Jon's job at Castleford includes playing a leading role on recruitment and managing the playing budget. Assembling the best squad for each season is not an easy job.

"In salary-capped sports, the general rule seems to be that the upward pressure on salaries outstrips the rate of increase in any centrally set salary cap. This leads to inevitable pressure on keeping the players you want to retain and signing the new players you want to augment your squad, whilst still keeping the squad size of a sufficient number so that, in contact-sports particularly, you can remain competitive without three or four front-line players.

As a result, you are constantly looking and challenging the youth department to identify and "fast track" the most promising talent in the positions you feel you will need cover for. In team contact sports, this will affect certain positions more than others. In rugby league this is most often back-rowers because of the highly-physical role they play in the game. A club that can bring through one or two youth players a year is doing well. They perhaps become 5 game a season players initially, subsequently becoming 10 and 15 game a season players as the seasons progress. Scouting and recruiting from outside the club is time-consuming and relatively expensive (particularly if players are coming from overseas). Home-grown young talent usually offers more bang for your buck and can help balance out a top level squad."

"Sir Alex has a special place in my life. In fact, he was the main man. I was not famous, I was not a star. I arrived at Old Trafford as just another young talent. He was the one who told me to do all the right things"[285]

---

[285] Cristiano Ronaldo, winner of 7 league titles, 5 UEFA Champions Leagues and 5 Ballons D'Or and scorer of over 700 goals.

With a maximum annual budget and variable contract lengths for existing players, planning several years ahead is the only way to operate successfully. That means simultaneously thinking of new players for the current year (if they become available and you have cap space left), next year and at least two years after that.

Any organisation should know its own people well. Deciding whose contracts to renew is a tough process, but at least there is plenty of inside information to base the decision on. What's more difficult is choosing which players to sign from other clubs. According to Jon there are four parts to the recruitment process: assessing playing ability, assessing character, assessing medical history and the contract negotiation. Even when you find a player you like, a potential deal can fall over for any of these four reasons. Making good choices with limited budgets is vital. It's even more essential in a salary capped sport. Saying no to the wrong player is as important as saying yes to the right one.

Jon outlined the recruitment approach for me. "Recruitment is generally done by playing position. Identifying a key player from another club and from watching him[286]play is only the entry level for recruitment. That watching process is done through a combination of attending live matches, viewing video footage, getting feedback from friends of the club and carrying out a statistical analysis against key performance indicators." The last of those elements is about each club's own version of Moneyball.

On the playing side it matters enormously "how fast, strong and skilful" a potential recruit is. But that invites a great deal of subjectivity when there's is limited data available. "These are the intangibles that you have to find a consensus on as a coaching group. Increasingly, we have used our on-field captain or specific members of our leadership group to add to the conversation on whether to move to the next stage of the recruitment process". Where there's limited data to analyse, then expanding the diversity of thinking will help to reduce the risk of error.

Beyond the playing skills is something more fundamental, character. In Jon's experience "When we spend time and effort looking into a player's background, taking independent testimonies, and talking with them about their motivations, goals and views on life in general we build up a much fuller picture of the individual and not just the athlete. In team sports this is massively important, as you have to assess how that personality and the values they hold will fit with the

---

[286] Or her when it's a women's or mixed team.

group you already have. Since I have been in my position with my club I would probably say we have passed over around half of our initially identified potential recruits because they wouldn't "fit" within the playing group." Every sports club does the same. A club's ability to find the best 'fit' with each new signing is a big factor in winning. That's a matter of good alignment.

The assessment of playing ability and character are therefore the first two steps in recruitment. They both have to be right in order for the club to proceed to the other two. As Jon explained "The actual contract and salary negotiation (done 90% via an agent these days) and medical history assessment probably only take up a tenth of the time that goes into the whole recruitment process".

~~~~~

Snooker is perhaps the sport that requires the most positional skill and sense. Most professional players take between twenty and thirty seconds per shot. That's lot of thinking to do in a short space of time. At the highest level, matches take place in front of crowds and are often televised. There must be immense pressure on players to perform their highly-skilled work 'live'. Every competitor has to be able to prepare and position themselves in the right place and mindset to be competitive. When that state is the no longer competitive enough, then form of re-positioning becomes crucial.

Sadly not everyone has the self-awareness and self-control needed to be able to adapt their game. Alex Higgins was a professional snooker player during the 1970's, 80's and 90's. Alex played a fast, skilful and entertaining brand of snooker that delighted the crowd and helped to popularise the sport. It brought him the nickname 'Hurricane Higgins'. Despite being highly-skilled, Alex only won two World Championship titles. Promoter Barry Hearn has since put this down to the fact that Alex "lacked consistency in his life off the table as well as consistency on it". The former undoubtedly had a very big impact on the latter.

Even when Alex was able to operate, in spite of gambling and binge drinking, he wasn't out of the woods. For whatever reason, Alex felt a strong driving pressure inside him to entertain. That drove him to take on riskier shots than other players did. The crowd loved him for it, but as a result he lost more close matches than he won. His eagerness to please other people and demonstrate his entertaining style cost him the chance to win several more World Championships. In the battle between his genius and his demons, Alex Higgins' genius won through often enough to leave an indelible mark on the sport. But, sadly over time, Alex's gambling and drinking exerted more control over him than he could cope with. Both his snooker and his behaviour suffered. In later years he barely practiced the game at all. During much of this period, the less entertaining, hard-working Ray Reardon won six World Championship titles.

"Sir. Alex Ferguson used to say that the hardest thing in life is to work hard every day. Forget all your ability, strip everything back: if you can work hard every day, in whatever job you do you'll be successful."[287]

Alex Higgins is amongst a number of sporting stars whose talent was labelled "genius" but whose attitude, off-field lifestyle or over-exuberance curtailed their impact and diminished their success. Footballers like George Best, Diego Maradona and Paul Gascoigne might also be members of that unofficial 'club'. Outside football, the likes of John McEnroe, golfer John Daly and cricketer Phil Tufnell might also be perceived in a similar way by some people. Flawed geniuses like Alex Higgins have been admired, idolised, written-off and pitied. All of them have probably been frustrating (if not impossible) to manage on occasions. But despite all that, they all brought performances that thrilled everyone who witnessed them. Their highs were superb, sporting moments. The ability to thrill an audience is a precious thing and it stays with us. We are still talking about them. The impact of greatness can't be underestimated, however brief or spoiled it seems to be.

Were they all winners? Yes they were. Could they have won more games and trophies? Popular opinion might say a resounding yes. Should they have behaved more professionally? The answer would seem to be yes. Should they have worked harder and prepared better? Probably yes. Could they have played for longer, if they'd taken better care of themselves? Probably yes. Were they their own worst enemies? Again, yes they probably were.

These were all controllables that weren't mastered. But no one chooses a difficult life for themselves. No one willingly surrenders to their inner-demons. So perhaps we should have even more respect and admiration for the likes of what Alex Higgins and the others did in their careers. Their "flawed" genius was hampered by a lack of self-control. So their genius came with a heavy cost to themselves and others. If winning is about creating a holistic whole and reaching the expected

---

[287] Wayne Rooney, England football's highest ever scorer with 49 goals.

minimum, then that would only make them qualified winners, but that's enough for us to be still hailing them as legends of their sports.

~~~~~

Alex Higgins isn't the only snooker player to face personal struggles. Jimmy 'The Whirlwind' White was a professional snooker player during the 1980's and 1990's. Immensely talented, he was a very popular player because he emulated Alex Higgins' attacking style of play. Jimmy played with a passion and a flair that made him very watchable, a crowd favourite. Unlike Alex Higgins, Jimmy never won the World Championship. Jimmy won one UK Championship, one Masters title and one Premier league title. He also won nine ranked events and nineteen non-ranking events in his career. But he lost many, many more, including six World Championship finals. Based on statistics alone, Jimmy should have won at least one of those six World titles. Based on ability alone, Jimmy should have won several of those World titles. So why didn't he win one?

Firstly, Jimmy didn't have a defensive game that was anywhere near as strong as his attacking game. Jimmy seemed to ignore the need for one for too long. Secondly, he didn't practice or develop his game enough to reach his full potential. Thirdly, Jimmy has admitted that taking cocaine probably cost him ten titles.

Steve Davis was a professional snooker player during the 1980's and 1990's. Steve played at the same time as Alex Higgins and Jimmy White. In contrast to Alex 'Hurricane' Higgins and Jimmy 'The Whirlwind' White, Steve Davis was given the ironic nickname Steve "Interesting" Davis by the television show Spitting Image. By comparison to Alex Higgins and Jimmy White, Steve appeared relatively boring. In fact, Steve is a funny speaker and a good raconteur, he's just not magnetic like Alex and Jimmy; and he played a very different style of snooker.

Steve was more of a student of the game. He developed a much better defensive ('safety') game and far better game management skills. He learned how to win snooker matches and he repeatedly put it into practice. Steve Davis created a higher level of snooker than everyone else could muster at the time. No one else developed their game like he did. No one else achieved the same all-round skill-set. Steve slipstreamed his way to success. He stifled other players and frustrated them until they made mistakes, then he punished them. It was snooker's equivalent of gegenpressing. In his pomp, Steve Davis was absolutely ruthless.

Steve Davis won six World Championships, in contrast to Alex 'Hurricane' Higgins' two and Jimmy 'Whirlwind' White's none. Steve Davis also won four UK Championships (compared to one for Alex and Jimmy), four Premier Leagues (Alex Higgins didn't play in any; Jimmy won one) and three Masters titles (compared to Alex's two, and Jimmy's one). Steve also won 18 other ranking events and 46 non-ranking events. His application set him apart. Steve was thoughtful, cool and calculating. He was dedicated to his craft. As a result, he won more World Championships than Alex and Jimmy combined. Steve Davis played winning snooker first and entertaining snooker a distant second.

"An error that beginners commonly make is to bring their Queen out early because they want to go on the attack with their most powerful piece. But experienced chess players know that it's better to wait and that you have to mobile all your forces before you're likely to able to execute a successful attack rather than going it alone with your Queen."[288]

When the next snooker legend came along, did he copy Alex Higgins and Jimmy White or did he copy Steve Davis? Which of them won more often? Stephen Hendry learned how to win by studying how Steve Davis won his titles, by building up his all-round game and finding a good balance of defence and attack. Stephen positioned himself in the best place to win. He was only interested In winning. With great dedication and a strong commitment to practice and self-development, Stephen won seven World Championships between 1990 and 1999. He also won UK Championships, six Masters titles, six Premier Leagues, 24 other ranking events and twenty-six other non-ranking events. His cool and methodical approach earned him the nickname 'The Ice Man' and made him arguably the most successful snooker player of all time.

After Stephen Hendry, there have been many players trying to become the next 'great' but none have been as good as Ronnie Sullivan. Ronnie plays the game like the Hurricane and the Whirlwind, but even better. 'Rocket Ronnie' is a hugely talented and admired player. He plays the game with a pace and tempo

---

[288] From 'How to Win at Chess' on BBC4.

that Steve Davis and Stephen Hendry couldn't have consistently managed. But unlike Alex and Jimmy, Ronnie O'Sullivan also prepares himself well. As well as practicing his shots much more than Alex and Jimmy ever did, Ronnie has developed a defensive game that's nearly as good as his attacking game. Ronnie has also brought another layer to preparation. He maximises his stamina through regular fitness training and eating really well. Having been "re-educated' about food by a Harley Street nutritionist, Ronnie O'Sullivan stopped "running out of steam." Instead of getting 85% out of himself Ronnie is "getting 100% now". Ronnie's physical preparation is another method of slipstreaming. Now that Ronnie is wise to nutrition, he isn't impressed by what's on offer out there.

"I think the UK's probably the worst place I've ever been for food. It really is. I see what some places serve up and I just think Wow. No wonder we're not producing great athletes"[289]

At the time of writing, Ronnie O'Sullivan has won six World Championships (only one less than Stephen Hendry), seven UK Championships (the most), seven Masters titles (the most), ten Premier Leagues (the most), as well as twenty-four other ranked events and thirteen other non-ranking titles. Ronnie has also won three Champion of Champions titles (which is a recent event and can't be compared to the others). Ronnie also has the record for the number of maximum 147 breaks at professional events (Ronnie has 15, compared to Stephen Hendry's 11). Ronnie has become a 'great' through a philosophy that favours attack over defence and has won multiple titles playing that way. But Ronnie also understands why he needs a strong safety (defensive) game and good physical conditioning too. We all need to choose the best philosophy and positioning for our competition and then use those advantages better than anyone else.

Eurosport presenter Colin Murray interviewed Ronnie after his 2020 Snooker World Championship semi-final win over Mark Selby. Ronnie had been struggling for consistency with his cueing action. Colin summarised his performance with the words "It was either genius or bad." Ronnie quickly replied "But genius and bad don't win you World titles. You need to be Steady Eddie man. You need to be Djokovic. I told you, you know all the flamboyant stuff doesn't win you World championships. You need to be in the middle of the fairway, chipping on the green, putt and thank you very much; and have a cigar walking down the 18th fairway." Ronnie knows that playing with passion alone

---

[289] From an article on betway insider by Tom Bowles.

isn't enough and that being an entertainer isn't the fight focus. You need to be the best prepared player too.

There is an ongoing debate about who is snooker's ever player. Joe Davis won the World Championship fifteen times (between 1927 and 1946). He is unquestionably a winner and a great of the sport. But is he the greatest ever? In the modern era with hundreds more professional players and much fiercer competition, there are three more deserving candidates for the title of Greatest of All Time (GOAT). Firstly, no one has won more professional events than Steve Davis. His ability to win snooker tournament after snooker tournament is as yet unparalled. He is snooker's most winning professional player. Secondly, Stephen Hendry who has won more World Championships than anyone else. The third candidate, Ronnie O'Sullivan, is thought to be the best player to have ever played snooker. But he is still behind Stephen Hendry in World Championship wins. Ronnie himself has dismissed the suggestion that he is the greatest player and believes that a player must equal Hendry's haul of seven world titles to be in the frame for the greatest ever snooker player. Unless Ronnie can equal Stephen Hendry's seven titles, the jury will remain out.

Three things are clear. The first is that Ronnie O'Sullivan, Ray Reardon, Steve Davis and Stephen Hendry are six or seven times World Championship winners and therefore snooker greats. Secondly, despite their ability and entertaining style, neither Alex Higgins nor Jimmy White can be the greatest snooker player of all time. Thirdly, if Ronnie manages to match seven World Championships, I think his attacking philosophy, mixed with the best form of preparation and will have produced the greatest snooker player of all time. How will the next generation follow him? They will need to choose the best philosophy and positioning they can; and then use them better than anyone else.

~~~~

Positioning is vital before a new project begins. Don't start first and think second. Plan first, act second. When beginning a new project, businesses and non-sporting teams should:

i.   Clarify the project's core purpose with the project sponsor(s). If it's your business then the sponsor is you and you need to help make that clear for everyone else. Assuming that the sponsor isn't you, then you need to ensure you're given clear instructions and all the authority and information you need. Exactly what do you need to do to complete the mission? Why?

By when? What benefit(s) will that bring and for whom? What's in it for every stakeholder? If it's an isolated project for one department or team, how does this project fit in with the overarching purpose of the whole organisation?

ii.   Clarify the version of the future that the project sponsor has in mind. Where exactly does the sponsor want to end up? What outcomes are needed for success? What does 'failure' look like (so it can be avoided)? How will you know when you've completed the project? What marker posts need to be hammered in and followed along the way?

iii.   Clarify the realities with the project sponsor. Whatever you're first told, what's the truth? What specifications are critical? What winning standards are expected? Do you have to provide absolute success or is good enough (qualified success) good enough? What deadlines are there? Which of them are hard deadlines? When do you really need final delivery?

Plan for success. Can your plan deliver the success you want? If not, adapt it.

iv.   Create a philosophy and a strategy which addresses the practicalities. What is the best way to deliver this project? What do we need? Who do we need? What level of training, supervision, mentoring should we provide? What winning behaviours do we expect? How hard do we expect everyone to work? Do our deadlines demand extra hours from the outset? How are we rewarding everyone involved? Which partners do we need to build working relationships with? What will we offer them to help us?

v.   Assess the likelihood of the project being delivered on time and to its specifications. How realistic are the project sponsor's expectations? Do any warnings need to be given now? Do any objections need to be raised now? Do you need to request more resources or more people now?

vi.   Create a set of project values that will make the vision a reality; and achieve the core purpose. Measure these against the project sponsor's values and your project team's. Are there are potential issues with 'how' the project will be delivered?

vii.   Recruit project members who suit the project plan and values and who are positively happy to work on it. Ambivalence is not good enough. Every project member needs to feel a strong, passionate connection with the project and project team values. Working in it needs to feel natural to them. Having a clear philosophy will make it easier to deal with recruitment agents and avoid hiring the wrong project members.

viii. Discuss and agree the purpose, vision and values with all the project members. Summarise all three for the wider project stakeholders. Is everyone happy for you to approach the project in this way? Will the project's activities and end-goals be in conflict with any stakeholder's interests? If so, how will you deal with that?

ix. Obtain adequate resources for the project in good time before they are needed. Secure future access to more resources in case they become needed.

x. Set up all the project systems and start specific project training in good time before the project starts.

In reality, projects often start without all of these steps in place. Retro-fitting the right structure to a project is important even after it's started. If there's an urgent deadline and pressure to get going it can be really hard to back-fill what's needed. Fight for the time, people and resources to make that possible. Most of all, get clarity from the project sponsor on what's expected. This is especially important if there's an urgent deadline, because there's so little time to re-adjust.

~~~~

Positioning is also vital before a new sporting season begins. Before the new season starts, sporting clubs should:

i. Clarify the mission and agree the winning standards and the expected minimum.

ii. Create a playing philosophy that is likely to be successful, that everyone can understand and that everyone is happy with. A philosophy needs to be good enough to achieve the qualified or absolute success that's expected. So it needs to be challenged and stress tested before it's adopted and implemented That doesn't mean that a team only ever play one style (as that's predictable), but there should be a primary playing style. Then you can add plans for B and C in case change is needed during a match. There doesn't have to be a single approach for every eventuality. Having different approaches, mindsets and coaches can work well. It's common to split attack and defence into two philosophical approaches. Transition phases may need a third approach. They can be distilled into two completed statements. "When we have the ball, we …" and "When we don't have the ball we…". They need to fit into the overall philosophy.

iii.   Creating a set of club values that complement that philosophy. Questions to ask include: Are we trying to be more aggressive than the opposition (accepting that sometimes we'll concede penalties and free kicks)? Or are we aiming to be calmer and more controlled (to avoid giving penalties and free kicks away)?

iv.   Discuss and agree the philosophy and values with the senior players. Is everyone happy to play that style in defence, attack and transition? Is everyone happy to apply the values and behave in the same way? Do they conflict with the club's historical style; and if so is that a problem? Will supporters to pay to watch us if we play the way we want to play?

v.   Recruit players who suit the club's playing philosophy and values and who are happy playing in it. Again, ambivalence is not good enough. The players need to feel a strong and passionate connection with the club's playing philosophy and values. It needs to feel natural to them. Having a clear playing philosophy and values will make it easier to explain the club's culture to sponsors, agents and potential new players. It can save the wasted time and costs of buying the wrong players.

vi.   Regarding players who can't adapt, or who aren't happy playing in that system, explain what they need to do to adapt. Offer training and guidance. Explain that unless they can adapt to what's needed, they will mostly be a substitute or not play at all. Or, explain that they will only play when the game plan switches to B or C (if that suits their skills and attributes). If necessary agree to transfer out a player who doesn't share the same philosophy and values, or the skills needed to perform at the level required.

vii.   Train and play using the club's philosophy at all age groups in the club (with sufficient practice for plans B and C in case they are needed).

viii.   Ask the first team coaches to spend time with all the age groups at the club, to improve the suitability and "fit" of the players coming through.

ix.   Liaise with every stakeholder to agree the playing philosophy, plan and values. Then plan and direct their contributions. Call on each stakeholder as and when you need them. But in return, ensure they share in the rewards when things go well. Those stakeholders will include: the sport's governing bodies, customers, the supporters' club, club sponsors, food and drink suppliers, professional advisers, the match day programme printers, fanzine and blog producers, local authorities, the Police; and local and national journalists amongst others.

Takeaway thoughts:

- Good preparation and positioning is critical to success
- Scenario planning will help you to predict and prepare for the future
- Being adaptable allows you to re-position yourself in order to win
- Winning is business is about being different (slipstreaming)
- In preparing to succeed, you have to plan how to avoid disaster
- Make sure you practice in competition conditions, or you'll be at a major disadvantage
- Find the best position of control and influence that you can
- Look after your health and sleep well
- Position yourself for the task in hand, learn what it takes and deliver it
- Simultaneously plan for the now and the future
- Choose the best philosophy and approach for your

3.7   WINNING SKILLS AND TECHNIQUES

The seventh controllable element is skills and techniques. Today, we have the skills, techniques and attributes that we have. If we have with a growth mindset today, we can be better tomorrow. Even though our physical abilities fade, our knowledge and experience grows. By honing our existing skills, adding to them and developing new techniques we can continually improve our performance levels. We can always learn from others, but we can teach ourselves too.

Every team member has a personal responsibility to continue their own learning and develop. Equally, teams should have a tailored, training and development plan for every single team member. Everyone matters to success. No one wins alone. Upskill everyone, continually. Every person you sideline is a lost or wasted resource. No one should ever be written off. Encourage everyone to push themselves on. It's easier to help five team members improve by 10%, than it is to help one of them improve by 50%.

Errors will always happen, but ones that come from poor skills and techniques can be reduced. The best production techniques tend to be focused on improving efficiencies, creating greater consistency and minimising errors. The ultimate objective is to create a 'zero error' production process from the outset, rather than hoping that mistakes can be picked up in quality control later. By the time a product gets to quality control it is probably too late to remedy any defect. All too often the product has to be scrapped. Getting this right at the beginning will save a great deal of time and money. What technical processes produce the best results?

"If you follow a good recipe, you will get success"[290]

'Lean Management' is a concept born out of Shigeo Shingo's work at Toyota in the 1960's. The Toyota approach was called 'Poka Yoke' means avoiding (yokeru) inadvertent errors (poka). It has been paraphrased to mean 'mistake-proofing'. A poka yoke process is one that prevents defects from occurring in the first place. Where that isn't possible (as we live in a VUCA World), poka yoke performs a detective function by eliminating the defects as early in the process as possible, rather than at the end or not at all.

Poka yoke isn't just useful for manufacturing processes, it can be applied to services industries too. By working towards winning standards, by sticking to standard operating procedures; and by providing routine training and guidance, a service provider can reduce its mistakes, improve its inefficiencies and create a consistent service offering.

~~~~~

Once your philosophy is clear, you can create techniques that impose your philosophy on the competition you're in, whatever that is. There are many skills, tricks and techniques for winning in all walks of life. Arguably the highest competitive skill is 'game management'. This skill goes beyond self-control, beyond tribal-control and into event-control. Game management is the ability to control a competitive encounter by tipping the scales in your organisation's favour.

---

[290] Mary Berry.

There are four scales to balance in your favour:

- Playing the game to your strengths (Attacking positioning)
- Preventing your opponent from playing to its strengths (Defensive positioning)
- Exploiting your opponent's weaknesses (Attacking positioning)
- Compensating for your own team's weaknesses (Defensive positioning)

Game management can involve a series of different techniques. Building pressure on your opponent is one. By making your opponent freeze its thinking, lose its cool, or rush its actions, you can increase its errors and help your team to win. The controllables of game management will vary, depending on your mission, but they will almost always include the management of time and space. By closing down your opponent's space to operate, or by speeding up or slowing down your opponent's movements you can tip all four scales in your favour. Similarly, by earning your own team the time and space to think and act, you can tip all four scales in your own team's favour.

~~~~~

New techniques have often revolutionised sport and taken the competition by surprise. The high jump is no exception to the art of slipstreaming. In the nineteenth century, the 'Scissors' jump was the technique of choice. That was until Michael Sweeney introduced the 'Eastern Cut-off' in the 1890s. That technique propelled Michael Sweeney and everyone who copied him (mainstreaming) to new heights. The 'Eastern Cut-off' prevailed for about fifty years, until it was replaced by the 'Western Roll'. In 1953, the 'Straddle' technique took over, powering Charles Dumas to produce the highest high-jump ever of 2.15 metres in 1956. This was the first official high jump over seven feet. The 'Eastern Cut-off' was ditched, just like the 'Scissors' had been before it. If you used an out of date technique, you couldn't win.

"I have a great respect for incremental improvement, and I've done that sort of thing in my life, but I've always been attracted to the more revolutionary changes. I don't know why. Because they're harder. They're much more stressful emotionally. And you usually go through a period where everybody tells you that you've completely failed"[291]

The Straddle jump lasted until 1967, until yet another technique was discovered. That opportunity came when the high-jump landing area was made safer. The changeover from sandpits or thin matting, to a form of deep foam matting meant that high-jumpers no longer needed to land on their feet to avoid injury. In the 1968 Mexico Olympic Games, Dick Fosbury won the Gold medal with his brand new technique, in which his head and shoulders went over the bar before his body. Landing on his back no longer risked certain injury. Landing on his back, onto deep foam matting, didn't hurt at all.

By adapting to the change in circumstances, Dick Fosbury repositioned himself and slipstreamed his way to success. His new curved run-in, leaning technique and "backwards" body position fundamentally re-wrote the high jump training book. 'The Fosbury Flop' soon became the only high-jumping technique. It is still in use today over fifty years later and has produced jumps of over eight feet high. At the time of writing, the current men's World Record is 2.45 metres (8 ft ¼ inch).

Mainstreaming will only help you to win whilst that is the best way to perform and you have truly mastered those skills. A mainstreaming approach to winning only lasts until someone else slipstreams and you have to start all over again. By slipstreaming, you can find a way to beat everyone who's mainstreaming. Why not be the team that slipstreams next?

~~~~~

Learning how to deal with criticism is a big part of making yourself a winner. Personal criticism can be difficult to take, especially if it's overly harsh, or if it comes at a time of high emotion or physical exhaustion. Developing a way of managing your 'bad press' is vital to retaining your confidence and readiness to win.

---

[291] Steve Jobs, co-founder of Apple with Steve Wozniak.

At some point in time, someone such as a manager, commander, coach, fan, journalist or friend will make a disapproving comment about you. That's likely to be whilst you're still learning and developing. No one should be judged against a perfect, flawless expectation, but that can happen. Receiving unfair criticism can feel like a rejection, which is hard to handle well. Sometimes criticism can feel barbed and deliberately designed to cause hurt. That's even harder to handle in a positive way. How do you deal with that criticism? Bite back, or rationalise it and move on? Will you get aggressive or retain a cool blue head? Having the mental power to take critical words on the chin, can be harder than taking a punch on it. Building the self-confidence to accept criticism, can take enormous self-control. Having the compassion to forgive the person dishing it out, takes another level of discipline and humility. The good news is that self-control is a skill that we can practice and improve. We can find strength from within, without the need for external approval.

> *"When the sharpest words wanna cut me down*
> *I'm gonna send a flood, gonna drown them out*
> *This is brave, this is bruised*
> *This is who I'm meant to be, this is me"*[292]

How should we deal with criticism? With sufficient self-control we can assess it, instead of dismissing it. However it's delivered, we have to concentrate on the content. We need to properly evaluate it before rejecting it out of hand. If there is a truth we needed to hear, then we should accept it and learn from it. If the opinion is unfair, we can ignore it and move on. By listening to our critics, we can learn what we need to know; and what we can safely ignore. The decision is ours. We should welcome it, if it helps us. Like Viktor Frankl we should face it head on. How else are we going to grow?

~~~~

Sir. Isambard Kingdom Brunel was a nineteenth century engineer and designer. Perhaps best known for his design for the Clifton Suspension Bridge,[293] Sir. Isambard also designed the Hungerford Bridge near Charing Cross Station, the Royal Albert Bridge near Saltash and the Windsor and Maidenhead Railway Bridges, amongst others. He was Chief Engineer on the Great Western Railway

---

[292] From the song "This is me" from the musical 'The Greatest Showman'.
[293] Which ironically wasn't completed until five years after his death, using a modified design.

and responsible for soaring viaducts like Ivybridge and tunnels such as the Box Tunnel (which, at the time, was the longest running railway tunnel in the World).

Isambard also designed the paddle-wheel SS Great Western steamship, which was the longest ship in the World at 72 metres (236ft). The SS Great Western successfully sailed across the Atlantic sixty-four times, carrying over 600 kilograms of coal in April 1838 to feed its steam engine. Then in 1843, Isambard's new six-bladed propeller design and steel hull was launched, as the SS Great Britain. This was the World's first modern ship. After that, he designed the SS Great Eastern, which was intended to carry 4,000 passengers as a cruise ship, but ended up being used to lay the first lasting transatlantic telegraph cable. The topmast of the Great Eastern is still in use today, as a flagpole at Liverpool's Anfield ground. These inventions required new construction and engineering techniques, developed by Isambard's passion and drive to find ever-improving processes.

There were other projects that weren't as commercially successful, such as the 'atmospheric railway' (which used a vacuum traction) and a 'broad gauge' railway (which was wider than the standard). But even where his designs were commercially unworkable, they expanded the scope of science and engineering.

> *"I am opposed to the laying down of rules or conditions to be observed in the construction of bridges, lest the progress of improvement tomorrow might be embarrassed or shackled by recording or registering as law the prejudices or errors of today"*[294]

But a lesser known invention came in 1855 when Britain was fighting the Crimea War. From her Scutari hospital, Florence Nightingale wrote a plea for help to the Times newspaper. Too many injured soldiers were contracting cholera, dysentery, typhoid and malaria as they tried to recover from their wounds. Reading this, Isambard volunteered to help and designed two fifty-patient prefabricated hospital huts that could be shipped to the Crimea and assembled there. The new Renkioi Hospital was cutting edge for the time. The huts incorporated access to sanitation, ventilation, drainage and basic temperature controls. The new designs had an extraordinary effect. Disease and mortality rates at Renkioi were reportedly only ten per cent of those at Scutari. Florence Nightingale described the new hospital buildings as

> *"those magnificent huts."*

---

[294] Isambard Kingdom Brunel.

And that wasn't all. According to some sources, Isambard's creation of a Mechanics Institute for recreation; and hospitals and clinics for his workers, inspired Aneurin Bevan to create the NHS that we appreciate so much today.

New thinking drove Sir. Isambard Kingdom Brunel to develop his designs. He was never satisfied by the existing design work and engineering principles. Isambard was a slipstreamer. He didn't approach a problem by studying the current techniques. He started again from scratch, with a blank sheet of paper. That allowed him to work through the issues without being burdened by the limitations of the past. Stretching what was possible, with every new design, Isambard made many improvements on what had gone before, in so many areas of engineering.

As with others who find themselves ahead of their time, Sir. Isambard had to contend with limited supplies, limited available materials and cynical potential investors. Despite all of the constraints he faced, Sir. Isambard Kingdom Brunel was never deterred. His creativity and passion for construction kept powering him on to develop new designs and methods of engineering. Without people to challenge the current techniques, we won't be able to improve them.

~~~~

Whatever size, power and influence your organisation has, it needs effective techniques and high-skill levels in order to be successful. That's equally true in the animal kingdom, where the predators at the top of food chain have all developed skills and techniques that help them to hunt their prey. Without some form of in-built advantage, they wouldn't be able to catch and eat the food they need to survive. Over the generations, each species develops its strengths and skills, to try and stay ahead of the competition. Every organisation needs to do the same.

Tiger sharks are fearsome predators, at twelve feet long and weighing over 1,300 lbs. But the sea is vast and every shark has to repeatedly find new prey. Swimming around, in the hope of finding something, wouldn't be enough. To help them, tiger sharks have developed an exceptional sense of smell, which can detect particles of blood in the water up to a mile away. To maximise this, they smell in stereo, using the technique of moving their heads from side to side to work out where the blood is most concentrated. In addition, their noses contain a series of electro-receptors which can detect even the smallest movements of water ahead. Tiger sharks use their natural gifts as hunting tools. These also include immensely strong teeth and jaws that can crack many forms of prey. All of this is very helpful, but the sea is still vast and prey can swim too. So tiger sharks apply a philosophy of focusing on dead and injured sea turtles, so that don't waste energy catching and eating what they need to eat. In sales terms, this might be called the 'low hanging fruit'. Sales teams need to work out what skills and techniques they need to find potential customers and to close out sales. What are the 'dead turtles' that can be pitched to most easily? What natural skills and what techniques can be used to assist that process?

Some animals live and hunt alone, so ambush is their most successful philosophy. The Peringuey's adder lives in the Namibian desert. It hunts by burying itself just beneath the surface of the sand, leaving only its eyes and the tip of its tail exposed. There it waits for prey to investigate its twitching tail. Then, when they do, it springs its trap and envenomates the unsuspecting prey, before eating it.

Crocodiles apply a similar technique. They hide under the surface at muddy watering holes, patiently waiting for Wildebeest and Impala to drink at the water's edge. With a bite of 5,000 lbs per square inch, there's no escape from a crocodile's vice-like jaws. After that comes the death roll under the water. Sometimes, a nervous Wildebeest or Impala jumps back far enough and fast enough to escape the lunging crocodile, using a potentially life-saving, defensive technique. Added to that risk, is the threat of losing the meal to a bigger crocodile. The more silently and secretly a crocodile takes its prey, the more chance that it will get to eat it all. The stealthiest crocodiles kill and eat more prey. Despite their size and powerful jaws, crocodiles need winning skills and techniques as much as any other animal.

Hunting is much easier as a group, using members of the pack to push the prey towards the best place for an ambush and towards the waiting hunters. Collaboration is a winning philosophy. Lions can hunt almost any animal in the daylight, but not buffalo. In the daylight, a buffalo herd stands firm as a group, with too many sharp horns and powerful hooves. In the dark, buffalo get frightened more easily, causing them to stampede and separate. So lions hunt buffalo at night. Having caused a stampede, a pride of lions can move in on a lone buffalo. Even lions need to be able to calculate when the odds are too great. Working out the most efficient way to be successful, with the least risk of harm, is a wise investment of time and energy. That's a winning technique in itself.

~~~~~

With a vast array of potential skills and techniques available, we need to work out which ones are mission critical. We should prioritise those, wherever we can. Starting with our mission, what are the successful outcomes we need to produce? When they're agreed, we can look to the winning standards that have to be attained to deliver them. Working backwards, which skills and techniques will best help us to meet those standards? Are our current techniques good enough? Which new techniques would help us achieve those standards more easily? Once we know the skills and techniques we need, we can start learning them.

In 1987, Jim White created a cross-country team at McFarland High School. That doesn't sound remarkable, but McFarland was one of the poorest towns in the USA with no cross-country team. Added to that, cross country was the preserve of the wealthy schools. McFarland had very different social and economic demographics.

Added to that, there was a lack of relevant skills and techniques. Jim White wasn't originally a cross-country coach. In the 2015 film 'McFarland, USA' Jim is portrayed as an American Football coach with a history of falling out with other people. Some of the reality is different from the Hollywood script, but the real story is very similar. Jim, played by Kevin Costner, had ended up in McFarland as a last ditch option, to be the assistant coach for American Football and athletics ('track'). He didn't want to be an assistant football coach, let alone a cross-country coach. But there were no other offers on his table.

During an American Football game, Jim intervened to stop an injured player returning to the field. He and the head coach fell out. The School Principal decided to permanently separate them. The head coach kept football and Jim was given track. With no athletics experience or coaching history in the sport, Jim decided to create a cross country team, because there was funding available to help pay for his coaching. That meant he had a paying job.

With no existing programme or athletes, Jim had to find pupils who would take up cross-country. He spotted two pupils who ran their way home and pulled them and some of their friends together as a team. Facing much more affluent schools across the state, the team was at huge disadvantage in terms of pupil numbers, coaching skills, running kit and competition experience. With no prior experience of athletics, Jim White had to start learning the skills and techniques from scratch.

At their first meeting, McFarland were well beaten. Why? The course included a very long, steep hill and all their training had been on the flat. As the race progressed, Jim could see why they were under-prepared. Once the race finished, he immediately took the blame for it himself. He also saw a great opportunity, which he expressed to his down-hearted team members. It came in a short and pithy phrase.

"Now we know what we didn't know"

Once the team understood which skills they lacked, their training could be developed and adapted. To be fast at cross-country, the team couldn't do all its running practice on the flat. That didn't build the muscle groups or practice the techniques required. So, Jim designed a training programme that involved running over huge piles of almond shells tied down under sheets. These man-made hills proved to be a good substitute for the real thing. As the coach and his team understood more, they developed faster. The muscle groups they needed, strengthened as they ran.

Benefitting from Jim's unusual recruitment and training techniques, McFarland started to win races. They beat far bigger schools, with far longer-standing athletics programmes. Jim and his team became highly-regarded. Turning down the opportunity of a full-time position at the more affluent Palo Alto School, Jim White set down firm roots in McFarland. From absolutely nowhere, McFarland won nine Californian State Championships in fourteen years. The lesson? Find out what you don't know yet.

~~~~~

Hundreds of thousands of musical artists never make it into the charts or achieve financial success. Most play for fun and for them their success is a good performance and an enjoyable time. Some of those artists find themselves on the cusp of commercial success, but it doesn't happen for them. A few lucky artists get to have success. For some of them it's fleeting, gone almost as soon as it arrives. One hit wonders (such as Los del Rio with 'The Macarena') get a brief burst of fame and fortune. Artists with one massive album, like the eponymously titled 'The Miseducation of Lauryn Hill' and 'The Stone Roses' get to enjoy success for a little bit longer. These are both wins.

To make the step up and become successful over several albums is a much rarer and special kind of success. The notoriously 'difficult' second album has shattered many dreams of longevity. If an artist can get past that, then it can bring a long tail of royalties. The most enduringly popular artists have created a unique sound (slipstreaming) that remains enduringly popular, such as Chuck Berry, Elvis Presley, The Beach Boys, The Sex Pistols and Bob Marley).

Bands like The Smiths, with four studio albums, are still popular now, over thirty years since their last album 'Strangeways, Here we Come'. The most commercially successful bands found that unique sound and then kept producing variations of it year after year, album after album, moving from slipstreamer to mainstreamer. Those artists include Status Quo, The Rolling Stones, and Bruce Springsteen (who have each released over fifty albums).

"I taught myself how to sing by listening to Ella Fitzgerald for acrobatics and scales, Etta James for passion and Roberta Flack for control."[295]

But perhaps most impressive artists of all are the multiple slipstreamers, the re-invention royalty who kept on finding another winning version of themselves. They include The Beatles (from clean cut rock and roll, to introspective, psychedelic and hippy), David Bowie (Ziggy Stardust, Aladdin Sane, Plastic Soul, The Thin White Duke, Commercial artist and Rocker) and Madonna (all the way from 'Virginal bride' through 'Marilyn' and Jean-Paul Gaultier mannequin to 'Mistress Dita', referencing Western and Eastern religions along the way).

Finding a popular point of difference can begin a winning formula. Turning an innovative concept into your own unique place in the market can give you repeated success. Whether you're slipstreaming or mainstreaming, you need to give it everything you've got.

~~~~~

Focusing on your own technique, session after session, takes single-mindedness. At the 2019 Athletics World Championships Dina Asher-Smith won a silver medal in the 100 metres sprint. She then followed that up with Gold in the 200 metres. That's truly exceptional. How did she manage it? Dina is very hard-working, very focused and a great technical runner.

After all the months of training, Dina excels at delivering on all her preparation. "When you arrive at the major championships it's all about just making sure that

---

[295] Adele, from an article on MyPlay.com

you do yourself justice and do your hard work justice and it's just making sure that when you're there nothing gets in the way of that and you're able to go and perform to the best of your ability." One part of that stands out as a useful mantra for self-development.

"...do your hard work justice..."[296]

Dina's single-minded focus means that she doesn't get distracted. Commenting on her Silver in the 100 metres she said "I wasn't entirely sure where I'd come because I wasn't looking at the other people, I was just focusing on myself." Blocking out distractions is a winning technique. As I know all too well, from distracting my daughter.

Dina is also great at applying the skills she's been taught and practiced endlessly. Reviewing her 200 metres Gold winning performance she said "I executed all my phases and I got all the boring technical stuff right." Winning at the highest level requires meticulous planning and exact execution. Dina Asher-Smith is constantly learning her trade and she applies herself extremely well. She follows her technical lessons. She follows her training regime. She follows her race plans. More medals seem destined to follow.

~~~~~

There are useful techniques for doing many things in life. Their purpose is to increase your chances of success. The better your techniques are, the more likely you are to win. That even applies to competitions where the odds are heavily stacked against you. For example, how can you become 'win ready' in relation to the winning the National Lottery? There are many theories and schemes. But it has to be said, if someone had worked out how to win every lottery, every week we'd already know about it. And we don't.

Perhaps the uncontrollables (such as the number of numbers and the utter randomness) are too big for any controllables to get the better of. If that's the case, we may not be able to ensure a win. However, we can still increase our odds of winning a lottery. These are some of the possible ways to be master the controllables and become more win ready. Before we start, no one should ever spend too much chasing a lottery win.

---

[296] Dina Asher-Smith.

1.	Play the lottery with the lowest jackpot odds. Or, if any win will do, play the lottery the highest odds of any kind of win. You can google what these odds are. According to the UK lottery website[297], the chances of winning the UK Lottery Jackpot is about 1 in 45 million. By contrast, the chance of winning the EuroMillions lottery is about 1 in 140 million.

2.	Buy all the possible combinations of numbers that you can reasonably afford to spend[298] and then stop. The more combinations you have, the greater your chance of winning. However, to win the UK jackpot, you would have to buy at least 45 million tickets. Even if you could do that financially and logistically (and both are an incredible challenge), there would be absolutely no guarantee of ending up net ahead. That's because, whilst you would win a share of the prizes, other people would share your prize money. In reality, you would almost certainly end up millions of pounds in debt. No one should ever spend too much chasing a lottery win.

3.	Join lottery syndicates. Syndicates share their tickets and their winnings. Linking to point 2, the more tickets you are in on, the more chance you'll be sharing a winning one.

4.	Ensure all your tickets are for different number combinations, to cover as many possibilities as you can.

5.	Bet every time your favourite lottery is drawn, but only if you can afford it. If you only bet once a year, your chances are obviously more remote than if you gamble every week. I am not promoting gambling or the lottery itself, I'm just pointing out this obvious statistical fact. Because of the high odds involved, not everyone thinks the lottery is a worthwhile form of investment.

"I despise the Lottery. There's less chance of you becoming a millionaire than there is of getting hit on the head by a passing asteroid"[299]

6.	Choose your numbers entirely at random, rather than copying obvious patterns. If you win, you are likely to have to share the prize with fewer people.

---

[297] Lottery.co.uk
[298] I am not advocating that anyone spends any money on lottery tickets, only that buying more different number combinations will increase the chances of winning.
[299] Attributed to Brian May on Brainyquote.

7. Choose the numbers that have come up the least. From November 1994 to October 2015 the UK Lotto had 49 numbers. The UK lottery added numbers 50 to 60 in October 2015. Which number came up the least from November 1994 to October 2015? In fact two were drawn the least, featuring in 215 draws. They were the numbers 13 and 20. So, number 13 really has been unlucky for some. Number 40 was top, featuring in 279 draws.

8. Many people tend to use the dates of family birthdays to pick their numbers. This will produce numbers from 1 to 31 only. Choosing numbers above 31 won't increase your chance of winning, but it should increase the probability of you not sharing a pay-out with anyone else if you do win.

9. Work out the overall total number that each week's numbers add up to, for say the last six months. For example, if your five main numbers were 1, 11, 21, 31 and 41 the total would be 114. You can do the same for your two bonus numbers. The last six months' worth of draws will give a total for each draw. Some will recur more than others. You could then pick numbers which, when added together, give a total that's higher-recurring than others.

10. One final point, after each draw always check and double-check your lottery tickets. Otherwise, you might get a winning ticket and never realise. There are millions of pounds worth of winning tickets sitting unclaimed.

I'm apologise for not providing a guaranteed winning formula. That's because there isn't one. The National Lottery's uncontrollables are designed to prevent that. If you follow the tips above, you would be more likely to win more money or more often than if you didn't. That's not anything like a guarantee of success. But maybe this is as 'win ready' as we can get in relation to a lottery. If it is, then that's all we can do.

Whatever the competition, we need to put ourselves in the best possible position to win. That's always worth doing. Being the most win ready person means you're in a better place to win than everyone else. It's true that being win ready doesn't guarantee you a win, but it gives you a better chance than everyone else who isn't. Sometimes that's the best you can get to. When it is, take it.

~~~~~

Initially a Native American bow was made by hanging a stave of ash wood high in a warrior's lodge beneath the smoke hole. It was not a quick process. To be strong, the stave had to be left in place to cure for up to five years. That meant it had to be taken down and put back up there every time the lodge was moved.

This process of making bows was used for many generations until it was discovered that a wooden stave could be fire-cured for use in a period of days, rather than years. Bow making suddenly became much faster and more efficient. Even bow-making can experience the effects of slipstreaming.

~~~~

Winning military battles can come down to an imbalance in the numbers of soldiers and weapons. But it can also come down to who has the better tactics and fighting techniques. In 490 BC, King Darius I of Persia and 25,000 soldiers invaded Greece, in an attempt to subjugate it to Persian rule. The Persian Army contained 20,000 infantry with additional cavalry and archers. Their forces included the 'Immortals', so called because when one fell another instantly took his place. The Athenians had less than half that number, with only 10,000 infantry and no cavalry. As the Persians journeyed towards them, the Athenians stood almost alone, with only limited soldiers from Plataea for help.
Faced with twice as many Persians, the Athenians sent a runner called Pheidippides to Sparta, to ask them for help. But the Spartans could not come immediately. They were delayed due to an important religious festival, requiring them to wait for the new moon before they could fight. With only half the soldiers of the Persians, it made sense for the Athenians to wait for the Spartans to join them. Why take on overwhelming military odds?

"You're gonna need a bigger boat"[300]

Miltiades was one of the ten Athenian Generals who formed the Strategoi[301]. Those ten generals rotated who had the overall leadership of the Strategoi. The initial delay, caused by asked for Spartan help, meant that the overall leadership passed to Miltiades' for his turn. Should they wait for the Spartans? After more debate, Miltiades convinced the other nine Generals to go into battle. The decision was not without challenge. Others wanted to wait for the Spartans, who arrived with 10,000 soldiers the day after the battle had ended.

---

[300] Brody in the 1977 film 'Jaws'.
[301] Giving us the modern term strategy.

Faced with superior enemy numbers, the Athenians had to outsmart their enemy or lose the battle. The terrain favoured the Persians as the plains of Marathon were largely flat, giving the Persian cavalry and Persian archers a significant advantage. If he was to set a trap, Miltiades had to find an area of rough ground to help his cause.

> *"The first Lords of the Vale didn't have much, but they had these mountains and they knew how to use them. And the fortress they built here has never been overcome. Not once in 1,000 years. Know your strengths, use them wisely, and one man can be worth 10,000"*[302]

Having done so, Miltiades chose to bulk his forces on the flanks and to hide over 1,000 soldiers amongst the brush. When the Persians attacked, the Greek centre began to lose ground and slowly withdrew. The Persians pushed on through the Greek lines, pressing ahead for victory. As they advanced, the Athenian flanks closed around the Persian forces crushing them in. The Persians wanted to turn and run, but the hidden 1,000 Athenian soldiers came out of hiding and attacked them from behind. The Persians were defeated.

The Persians had expected to win the battle of because of their superior numbers. They couldn't see the hidden soldiers until it was too late. The element of surprise can often create a sudden advantage for one competitor over another. When setting a trap you need to make sure that your opponent isn't wise to it. Once your strategy has been revealed, the chance of it proving successful lessens enormously. If that happens quickly review your plan.

> *"Building a better mousetrap merely results in smarter mice"*[303]

Despite their inferior numbers and firepower, the Athenians won a famous victory. Pheidippides then famously ran the twenty-six miles from Marathon to Athens to tell the city of their victory[304]. The Persians were routed and fled

---

[302] Lord Petyr Baelish (aka Littlefinger) in Game of Thrones.
[303] Charles Darwin.
[304] Running the first 'Marathon' and inspiring thousands of similar races ever since.

Greece. It wasn't until ten years later, when Darius's son Xerxes I invaded Greece[305], that the Athenians had to defend themselves against the Persians again.

Modern day military operations require winning techniques too. On 30 April 1980, the Iranian Embassy in London was invaded by six men with machine guns in the name of the Democratic Revolutionary Movement for the Liberation of Arabistan. Twenty-six people were taken hostage. Negotiations began and five hostages were released for relatively minor concessions. The terrorists' chief demand was the release of prisoners in Khuzestan, well beyond British control. There was an impasse until the sixth day.

After threats of executions were made and shots were fired, the dead body of a press officer hostage was thrown out onto the street in front of the Iranian Embassy. At that moment the British Government's tactics changed. COBRA decided to use force and the British Special Air Service was instructed to storm the Embassy.

To add the element of surprise and wrong-foot the occupiers, the SAS decided on a double-pointed attack. Firstly, special forces soldiers scaled down the front of the building in plain sight and burst in through the building's windows. At the same time, the SAS were also breaking through an adjoining ground floor wall, from a neigbouring property. This simultaneous, double-attack took the terrorists by surprise and allowed the SAS to successfully re-take the Embassy.

~~~~~

Dame Katherine Grainger competed for Great Britain in five Olympic Games, winning Silver medals in Sydney (2000), Athens (2004), Beijing (2008) and Rio de Janeiro (2016). Katherine also won a Gold medal in London (2012) to the sound of the "Dorney Roar". It would be easy to rush straight to the Gold Medal and laud that magnificent achievement, but it needs to be said that each one of those Olympic medals made Dame Katherine Grainger a winner. So did her six World Championship Golds; and her World Championship silver and bronze medals. There were many other competition medals besides all these. Dame Katherine Grainger is unquestionably one of Great Britain's most successful sporting figures.

---

[305] The second invasion under Xerses I led to the Battle of Thermopylae in 480 BC (where 300 Spartans and a few others stood against the whole Persian army) and then in 479 BC the Battles of Platea (fought between approximately 80,000 soldiers on both sides) and Mycale (fought at sea) where the Greeks united to form a Super-tribe and defeated the Persians on both land and sea.

To perform at Olympic podium level, for over sixteen years, shows exceptional ability and consistency. To accept all the sacrifices that 'life' required of her, shows Katherine's extraordinary dedication and resilience. To complete five Olympic cycles shows character and ability in equal abundance. The following are the opening words in Katherine's autobiography.

"Over the years a commitment to excellence in my sport has meant an incredible level of attention to detail: the preparation and the practice have been everything"

Olympic medals in rowing are only handed out after years of early mornings, extreme fitness sessions and thousands of miles of rowing. It takes an exceptional performance to win an exceptional medal. For Dame Katherine there were three different events to master (Double Sculls, Quadruple Sculls and Coxless Pair) in order to win the medals she won. And each medal had a different partner (or partners) to work in tandem with. To medal with one partner must be unbelievably hard, to medal with five different partnerships across three different events is truly astonishing.

The quadruple sculls involved a team of four. The Double Sculls and Coxless Pairs were all about developing a working partnership with one other person[306]. On her relationship with her Gold medal partner, Anna Bebington-Watkins, Katherine has said "Although we were different in many ways, we were also similar and so it was a healthy balanced and fresh relationship. The key thing for both of us from the beginning was to feel we had equal status in the boat." Equality is a key element of success. That's an equality of responsibility and an equality of effort.

Other than a feeling of equality, what made the difference in 2012? Why was that medal a gold one? Talking about the 2012 Olympic Final, Katherine has said "But most importantly we had come out in our rhythm. Our wonderful, solid, consistent, dependable rhythm. It was a rhythm that allowed us to apply huge amounts of force and acceleration but with an accurate timing so that the flow of the boat was uninterrupted."

---

[306] Being, in turn, Cath Bishop (Athens), Anna Bebington-Watkins (London) and Victoria Thornley (Rio).

It all came down to efficiency and technique. Applying their power smoothly and rhythmically meant they could turn the huge force they generated into the maximum form of momentum. No energy was lost or wasted. The boat was projected forward using all their power. The more efficiently we can operate, on a sustainable basis, the more chance of winning we have.

Katherine describes her own story as a "simple and strong narrative, a tale of never giving up, of following dreams in the face of sometimes huge doubts; and it has a wonderful happy ending." The whole time Katherine was aiming for Gold she was getting better and better. By pursuing excellence rather than perfection, Dame Katherine Grainger actually got to reach her own excellence. For most people that has been pretty close to perfection.

~~~~~

Just like Martin Johnson, we are all born with our own individual dimensions. We cannot grow ourselves taller or expand our bone structure. We cannot put in an advance order for bigger shoulders or smaller feet. Our natural physical attributes are uncontrollables. But we can improve on our natural strength by training. What kind of training and how much of it are controllables that we can master. Edward Stephen Hall remembers watching the World's Strongest Man on television as a child. "I was just obsessed with it. At sort of five, six years old. Just watching these huge guys lift planes, pulls trains, lift stones. I was just mesmerised by it." After being expelled from school at the age of 14, Eddie had some lift choices to make. "Whilst everyone else was studying for their GCSEs, I got a membership for the gym, and I just started lifting weights. So while everyone else was in school, I was in the gym sort of bulking up, and when I got to 17, I got a full time job." That job was as a mechanic.

Outside of work, Eddie began training as a bodybuilder and in 2010 he entered the strongman circuit. Making exceptional progress through the ranks, Eddie became England's Strongest Man later that same year. He went on to become the UK's Strongest Man, the year after; and held his UK's Strongest Man title until 2016. Eddie also became Britain's Strongest Man in 2014 and held that title until he retired in 2018. This is undoubted success.

Being an English, British and UK Champion meant a lot to him, but the highest level of strongman competition is the World Championships, known as the World's Strongest Man. Incredibly, Eddie managed to reach the finals in 2012, barely two years after starting to compete in the sport. Eddie didn't progress out of his qualifying group, but it was a major achievement. In 2013, he qualified but again finished outside the final. All the time, Eddie was learning from these 'failures'.

In 2014, Eddie managed to qualify from his group and made the World's Strongest Man final, finishing sixth out of eight. Eddie was becoming smarter and that was making him stronger. All the time, Eddie was learning and adapting his training regime. There was only one mission, to win the World's Strongest Man. To do so, Eddie had to acquire the skills and techniques for events that only lasted a few minutes each. To win the Giant Log Lift, Keg Toss and Atlas Stones, competitors have to generate enormous, explosive power in their legs, arms and body. Each Strongest Man event tests a different type of lifting, throwing, pushing or pulling power. Every muscle group is tested to the point of breaking. If that isn't enough, extreme endurance is needed to last the pace, event after energy sapping event.

Building core physical strength is a necessity, but raw power and effort won't work on their own. To be the World's Strongest Man requires the maximum delivery of that power. That, in turn, requires exceptional technique, to focus of all the available power into the lift. Wasted power is wasted energy. Eddie wasn't a great student at school, but he became a great student of strongman techniques. By studying hard and practicing them in every event, Eddie learned and developed the techniques he needed to maximise his body power.

"But Mr. Fox was too clever for them. He always approached a farm with the wind blowing in his face, and this meant that if any man were lurking in the shadows ahead, the wind would carry the smell of that man to Mr. Fox's nose from far away" [307]

The winner of the World's Strongest Man doesn't have a lithe athletic physique, he has a heavy, muscular one that can generate extreme brute force. Eddie Hall gradually built up his muscles through intensive training, until he weighed twenty-eight stones. As he said at the time "My workouts are based on very heavy, fast movements using weights, the science behind it being that the faster you move a weight, the more fast-twitch fibres you rip and then repair." This is an extreme technique that requires professional and medical support.

---

[307] From 'Fantastic Mr. Fox' by Roald Dahl.

In 2015, Eddie again made the World's Strongest Man final. This time he finished fourth, only just missing out on the podium. Year by year he was making progress. The competition at World level was incredibly fierce. Eddie trained ever harder and in 2016 he finished third and finally got to stand on the podium. For many people that would be enough of an achievement, but for Eddie it wasn't. The mission was winning the event.

Returning in 2017, Eddie Hall faced two four time winners, in Brian Shaw and Žydrūnas Savickas. He also faced the up and coming Hafþór "Thor" Júlíus Björnsson[308]. This was almost certainly the toughest final in the competition's history. All of the four big guns put themselves through daily pain and suffering to get ready for that 2017 final, but only one of them could be the World Champion. When the final scores had been counted, the winner had won by a single point. Eddie Hall had become the World's Strongest Man.

Eddie's extreme physical strength and power were essentials in his armoury. However, it was his clarity of focus, mental strength and mastery of technique that won him the title he dreamed of as a child. The moment must have been sweet, but immediately after winning, Eddie retired. He had always planned to retire as soon as he achieved his goal. Once he was the World's Strongest Man there was nothing else to prove. Eddie Hall now co-presents the television coverage of World's Strongest Man and has appeared in the food and travel series "Eddie Eats America". Having conquered the world of strongman, Eddie is now conquering the world of television.

~~~~~

Humanity has achieved innumerable feats of technological brilliance. People have worked out how to make a three hundred tonne aeroplane take off and fly. People have given us a combined telephone and personal computer that fits in our hand. People have sent space shuttles to other planets. How did human beings manage to do all this? The answer is creative inspiration and we all need it.

Everyone has to feel highly-motivated in order to do their best work. Employers need to make work challenging, fun and rewarding to get us thinking creatively. Work shouldn't feel like work. If should feel a natural extension of who we are. We need to feel passionately about what we do. So much so, that we feel an inner-compulsion to step outside our comfort zones. Work should feel like a mission to

---

[308] Who played Gregor "The Mountain" Cegane in five seasons of 'Game of Thrones'.

create something inspirational. Every job should feel part of something 'simply marvellous'[309].

Every person should feel included and inspired. Then we can all slipstream our way to produce something technically marvellous.

In 1998, Sir Antony Gormley's most famous sculpture was unveiled. "I wanted to make an object that would be a focus of hope at a painful time of transition for the people of the North East, abandoned in the gap between the industrial and the information ages." The work is made of Cor-ten weather resistant steel, weighs 200 tonnes and has 600 tonnes of concrete foundations. The site of the sculpture is the former Lower Tyne Colliery near the A1 motorway.

"The scale of the sculpture was essential given its site in a valley that is a mile and a half a mile wide, and with an audience that was travelling past on the motorway at an average speed of 60 miles an hour." As a result of its setting, the Angel of the North is a 20 metres (66ft) tall steel structure with wings measuring 54 metres (177ft) across. It is a technological and aesthetic marvel.

The plaque beside it reads "The hilltop site is important and has the feeling of being a megalithic mound. When you think of the mining that was done underneath the site, there is a poetic resonance. Men worked beneath the surface in the dark.... It is important to me that the Angel is rooted in the ground—the complete antithesis of what an angel is, floating about in the ether. It has an air of mystery. You make things because they cannot be said."

How was this 'thing' that "cannot be said" actually made? The answer involved a technical engineering solution, as Anthony has explained "We made a series of models to work out how this was going to work. The challenge was to transfer a rib structure that radiates from a central axis in the bodyform onto the wings". After modelling small scale versions "the solution was to have an increasing distance between the ribs, suggesting a broadcasting of energy." The final sculpture was made in three parts (one body and two wings), transported as three huge steel structures; and assembled on site. It took Anthony's incredible vision and enormous technical skill to create the Angel of the North. Both were vital components.

---

[309] A phrase often used by the late and cricket commentator Richie Benaud.

In the words of Sir Antony Gormley "The work stands, without a spotlight or a plinth, day and night, in wind, rain and shine and has many friends. It is a huge inspiration to me that the Angel is rarely alone in daylight hours, and as with much of my work, it is given a great deal through the presence of those that visit it." By being so passionate and inspired himself, Sir. Antony Gormley has produced a statue that inspires thirty-three million passes-by every year.

~~~~~

We probably all should have heard of Yovanka Houska, but most of us won't have done. Yovanka is an International Master and a Woman Grandmaster in Chess. Yovanka won her first British Championship in 2008. After that she successfully defended her title in 2009. Then she repeated her defence in 2010, 2011 and 2012. That's very impressive. Yovanka then won the British Championship again in 2016, 2017, 2018 and 2019 which is more remarkable still. It seems that the only reason that she didn't win it in 2013, 2014 and 2015 was that she didn't enter the competition. Her record is truly remarkable.

Yovanka has won many important chess matches, but she has lost plenty too. Instead of shirking difficult opponents, Yovanka likes them, because she knows that she can learn from them. Losing isn't something that worries her.

"Don't be afraid to fail! Even if you lose a game in the most painful way, try and learn to use it as inspiration"[310]

In competitions that require physical stillness and mental agility, you don't just need techniques for playing the game in question, you also need techniques for retaining your focus. Yovanka understands that and drives herself to become physically and mentally better. Yoga has been very helpful to her. "Yoga has taught me how to handle moments of unbearable tension by actively breathing deeply and calmly facing the fear"[311]. In addition to yoga and regular fitness work, Yovanka spends two to four hours studying chess every day that she's not competing. Learning new techniques and combinations of moves keeps her current. Continually developing her game keeps her win ready.

During competitions, Yovanka prefers to calm her mind by "meditating, listening to positive affirmations\binaural beats and going for brisk walks". In such a

---

[310] Yovanka Houska.
[311] From HonestMum.com

cerebral game, Yovanka has to have a blue head during competitions. Too much red heart would derail her focus and stop her from concentrating.

"To play well, you need to be cool, objective and logical and this is so much easier to do when you have a positive mindset – there is much less nervous energy"[312]

A positive mindset comes from being well-prepared. All the hours of study and competition have given Yovanka the confidence she needs to go into competitions feeling relaxed and ready to win. Yovanka's results have re-enforced her self-belief. The positivity that brings, allows her to be "cool, objective and logical" and it has been very successful for Yovanka Houska.

~~~~~

We love to know how things work. Many things operate using mainstream technology and techniques. So we can often work out how it's done. But when a mystery process results in something incredible, it peaks our interest. If after thought, we still can't work out the technique involved, we might describe the process as being like "magic".
Stephen Frayne spent his childhood growing up on the heavily deprived Delph Hill Estate in Wyke, near Bradford. Brought up by his mother, because his Dad left the family and then went to prison, Stephen Frayne had a tough start. He now views his start as being helpful. "It's often the case that places where there is extreme poverty are also places of incredible creativity."[313]

Luckily, for us and him, Stephen was introduced to magic by his great-grandfather, who taught him all the tricks he'd learned in the Navy during World War Two[314]. From there it was a process of self-development, a painstakingly slow journey spent in long hours of practice. Once Stephen acquired the skills he needed to perform a trick, he went out and tested it by performing it until it was faultless. Stephen built up his knowledge and slowly established his reputation as Stephen Frayne, the magician. That was until the Houdini centenary event in New York in 2001. Whilst performing his tricks a member of the crowd reportedly shouted "This kid's an effing dynamo" and the name stuck. 'Dynamo' was born

---

[312] Yovanka Houska.
[313] Dynamo's quotes are from 'Dynamo: Nothing is Impossible: The Real-Life Adventures of a Street Magician'.
[314] From the Sun online, on 16 April 2020.

and Stephen Frayne's career began to really take off. Dynamo is now a multi-award winning, globally recognised magician.

When Dynamo started out there were many doubters. "So many people told me I couldn't do it and they were wrong. You have to be stubborn but be smart with it. If you can prove others wrong, go for it." Dynamo is highly-determined and powered by an 'obsession' with magic.

Dynamo sees magic as his "way of bringing people together". He performs it for the reactions it produces in other people. "Magic only happens in the spectator's mind. I don't believe magic exists as a 'thing' at all. To me it's more a physical feeling and emotion that you get when you see something that you can't explain." Fired by his determination to bring people together and his obsessional commitment to practice and trick development, Dynamo has become a master of magic, one of the greatest ever magicians. To go with his wide range of tricks, Dynamo has a warm and engaging style, a phenomenal imagination and an exceptional level of performance. By suspending 'reality' and believing in magic you can be royally entertained.

Being a good magician is about performing well-honed techniques that create illusions of magic. If an observer is convinced that something magical has happened, then the trick has worked. Technique is everything. Walking on water (using a form of plexiglass under the water), walking down buildings (using ultra-thin, ultra-strong wire) and pushing a phone inside a bottle (using a second bottle with an identical phone inside it) are just a few of a master magician's well-executed illusions.

Understanding how magic tricks work is interesting, but once the magic's gone it's never the same. Roald Dahl is credited with a quote about magic that rings true. "Those who don't believe in magic will never find it." In the modern world we live in, everything we do to create success should be focused on producing something magical.

~~~~~

We can't all be inventors and we don't have to be. Some skills and techniques work by adding value to other people's work. Sometimes a technique can take something that's good and turn it into something exceptional.
John Barry Prendergast OBE was born in York in 1933. His father was a film projectionist and then a cinema chain owner, which meant John's childhood was

lived around and influenced by cinemas in the North of England. Growing up, John learned to play the piano and trumpet. Investing his spare time in developing his skills, John learned to read, play and write music, taking lessons from a jazz composer called Bill Russo. John used his time on National Service overseas to hone his musical skills by playing with several military ensembles.

Afterwards, John began playing in his own band (the John Barry Seven) building up a distinctive sound, having a few hit singles and making appearances on the television programme '6.5 special'. During this period John composed 'Hit and Miss' the title track for popular 1960's television programme 'Juke Box Jury'. Building a reputation for composing his own music created opportunities to arrange music for other acts. Most notably, John he wrote the arrangements to Number One singles 'What Do You want' and 'Poor Me' for Adam Faith.

Opportunities can create more opportunities, you just need to get started. Success bred succeeds for John Barry and in 1960, when Adam Faith made his first feature film 'Beat Girl', John Barry was asked to compose, arrange and conduct the score. His music for 'Beat Girl' was later released as the UK's first soundtrack album. Three film soundtracks later, John Barry was invited to help to arrange the music for a new feature film in 1962. It's title was 'Dr. No'.

Working on the Dr. No soundtrack, John Barry arranged a jazz version of Monty Norman's 'James Bond Theme', which catapulted him into the big league of film composers and arrangers. The credit and royalties for the James Bond Theme all went to Monty Norman, but the distinctive jazz arrangement is unmistakably John Barry's work. The Bond theme has become recognised the World over. The film was of course a hit, so John was asked to compose for the soundtrack of 'From Russia with Love.' As a result of his work on the first two films, John was given overall writing duties for the soundtrack to 'Goldfinger'.

"However varied you try to make your work, you still bump up against the end of you. You keep knocking into a wall, and the wall is your own skull. But when you adapt somebody's work, it's like a door into somewhere else. It feels like a holiday from myself"[315]

John went on to compose the soundtracks to the first eleven James Bond films, up to and including Timothy Dalton's 'The Living Daylights'. For each of those

---

[315] Nick Hornby, author of 'Fever Pitch', 'High Fidelity' and 'About a Boy'.

eleven films, John orchestrated a slightly different version of the James Bond theme. These are heard during what's known as the 'gun-barrel sequence' at the beginning of each Bond film.

The success of his work on James Bond led to many other projects. John Barry composed the soundtracks to many other hit films including Zulu (1964), The Ipcress File (1965), Born Free (1966) Midnight Cowboy (1969), Body Heat (1981), The Cotton Club (1984), Out of Africa (1985), Jagged Edge (1985), Dances with Wolves (1990) and Chaplin (1992). He also composed the theme music for the television show 'The Persuaders' (1971) staring Tony Curtis and Roger Moore (still in his pre-Bond days).

John Barry's work was recognised by the Academy Awards and BAFTA. John Barry won Oscars for Best Original Score and Best Original Song for Born Free (1966) and Best Original Score for The Lion In Winter (1968), Out of Africa and Dances with Wolves. He also won a Grammy for his part in writing the soundtrack to the Cotton Club (1986).

In 1991 Barbara Streisand reportedly commissioned him to write the music for her directorial debut, 'Prince of Tides'. When but John felt that Barbara was interfering with his work, he resigned, telling her: "You don't buy a dog and do the barking yourself." When Barbra Streisand protested that she adored all his scores, he allegedly replied "Yup. And I wrote them all without you."[316]

John Barry wrote many great scores, but his most notable work came from applying his jazz training to Monty Norman's 'James Bond Theme'. John's saw an opportunity to make someone else's work sound better and the rest is his history.

~~~~~

Michael Gough is an international, test cricket umpire. To do his job well, Michael has to make accurate, split-second decisions on the field. In test cricket the ball can be bowled at up to 95 miles per hour. At that speed, it is very difficult to see the ball, let alone exactly what it hits. With a series of uncontrollables including variable bowling speeds, variable wickets and variable light, an umpire's decision-making is very challenging. And that's before the batsman[317] starts moving.

---

[316] The Daily Telegraph John Barry Obituary.
[317] Of any gender.

In contrast, the television umpire, match commentators and viewers at home get to watch television replays of every incident in slow motion, as many times as they like. They have 'ultra-edge' technology to hear if the ball touched the bat (using a microphone in the wickets). They also have 'ball-tracker' technology to assess whether a ball would have hit the stumps if it hadn't hit the batsman's pads. Michael Gough doesn't have any of these technological aids. He gets one high-speed opportunity to see what happens and a few seconds to decide what that means.

During a match, both team Captains can refer an old-field decision to the television umpire to check. When that happens, the television umpire tests the on-field umpire's decision. With all the technology available to the television umpire, that person should make correct decisions 100% of the time. Whilst there are no published expectations, an on-field umpire will inevitably have a significantly lower percentage of accuracy. From a period between 2018 and 2020 Sri Lanka's Kumar Dharmasena had an approval percentage of 78.75%. When Michael Gough's decisions were referred to the television umpire, over the same period, his approval record was 92.54%. Michael is the most accurate cricket umpire in international cricket and Kumar is the second most accurate.

So why is Michael Gough so good? According to Michael, he does a lot of work to build his eye muscles and eye exercises throughout the match. Michael also keeps his ears meticulously clean, so he can hear every sound. He also does a lot of personal fitness work, to help him concentrate properly for a whole day's play. As a result, he feels relatively fresh at the end of play. That enables him to stay in the moment. His long attention span and growing experience allow him to "go with my gut feeling" when he makes his decisions.

"Success occurs when opportunity meets preparation"[318]

In addition to all the physical work, Michael takes his time to make decisions. He also reflects on his decision-making after matches, by carrying out a detailed analysis of what he got wrong and why. That helps him to continually develop his skills. That helps him to feel confident and "relaxed at the crease" which in turn helps his decision-making, creating a virtuous circle. Michael Gough is successful because he is fully committed to improving his skills with every new decision. He continually hones his techniques, in the same way that the software developers at

---

[318] American author and motivational speaker Hilary Hinton "Zig" Ziglar.

'ultra-edge' and 'ball-tracker' are continually trying to improve their products for television use.

Michael reflected on this success in an interview for 'Stumped' on BBC Sport[319]. "I never really got the best out of myself as a player. I didn't really work hard enough. I didn't really motivate myself or dedicate myself enough to my profession. When I was fortunate enough to get into umpiring and the world of officialdom, I just wanted to make sure that I gave myself the very, very best chance to succeed and do well at this level." Michael Gough's preparation before matches and his analysis afterwards make his techniques nearly as good as the best technology available. Michael has managed his umpiring controllables.

Like every other individual performer, Michael doesn't do his job alone. He has help off the field, which in turn helps him on the field. And it's help which Michael is quick to credit. Behind him there is a supportive Umpire Manager, a team of umpire coaches and umpire resources (to help him analyse how to make the best decisions). That is great tribal thinking. On top of all that, there is regular interaction with other umpires across the World to share best practice, which is a good example of Super-tribe thinking. No one ever performs at their best by acting alone.

---

[319] On 10 October 2020.

Takeaway thoughts:

- We have a personal responsibility for our learning and development
- Every team needs a tailored training plan for each member
- Skills and techniques should aim for a zero error rate
- Slipstream rather than mainstream
- Evaluate and learn from criticism
- Start again with a blank piece of paper
- Preparation and practice are key
- Work out the most efficient way to be successful
- Focus on what's mission critical
- Finding a popular point of difference can begin a winning formula
- Get all the 'boring technical stuff' right
- Get yourself win ready for your competition
- Find the best way to deliver maximum power
- Make things that cannot be said
- Obsession can power the learning process for technical excellence
- Adapting someone else's work or idea can improve it

3.8   WINNING SCIENCE AND TECHNOLOGY

The eighth controllable is science and technology. When we're looking to achieve improvements in our performance levels, we go back to our processes, techniques and ways of operating. What changes can we make? When we're considering this, we shouldn't forget all the opportunities available from science and technology. These can offer fantastic opportunities for slipstreaming. Any gains you make need to stay within the laws, rules and regulations of the competition you're operating in. But as long as they are, then anything goes.

"I'm gonna give you an engine low to the ground... extra thick oil pan to cut the wind from underneath you. It'll give you thirty or forty more horsepower. I'm gonna give you a fuel line that'll hold an extra gallon of gas. I'm gonna shave half an inch off you and shape you like a bullet. I'll get you primed, painted and weighed, and you'll be ready to go out on that racetrack. Hear me? You're gonna be perfect"[320]

~~~~~

Retail businesses are seeing extraordinary change brought on by technological advances. 'Click and Collect' and home delivery changed the nature of shopping and effectively killed the high street. The ability to do your week's grocery shopping and any other kind of retail therapy from your mobile phone, made it ludicrously easy to buy. Now you can ask Alexa, Siri or Echo to do it for you. Drone deliveries will soon begin do carry out deliveries. So will autonomous delivery vans.

Retail technology hasn't stopped there. Augmented reality allows customers to have a more interactive experience online and instore. The challenge of choosing the correct size online is being addressed. Customers can now try clothes on virtually. The same developments are affecting furniture sales online. IKEA and Anthropologie have ARKit apps which allow you to check out which products will fit in your house, so that you can confidently buy them from inside your home. These developments are the industry's response to customer demand. Retailers are placing greater emphasis on customer convenience than ever before.

Those same retailers are collecting individual data on all of us and pooling it all together to create big data. What we search for and what we order tells retailers about our shopping preferences. When the data from thousands of customers is collated together, retailers can predict shopping patterns, get all their supply chains in place; and reduce waste. Search tools can be used to automatically direct us to the best products for us. The same data can be fed into recommendation engines, which can be fine-tuned to generate relevant buying ideas and push up sales. Deals with celebrity vloggers promote products openly and subliminally, creating sales trends. Upselling has never been so automated.

---

[320] Harry Hogge (Robert Duvall) speaking to the stock car he was building, in the film 'Days of Thunder'.

Automation is having an effect in all parts of the retail process. Automated tills are allowing customers to check-out themselves inside shops. Autonomous mobile robots (AMRs) are working in warehouses 24/7, picking stock to satisfy customers orders. Sensor-embedded shelves are monitoring stock levels (so re-ordering can be automatic) and providing increased security. Walmart is using self-scanning robots to replace stock when it runs low. Online, customer Chat Bots can help us if we're not sure what we need. Some high-street shops are now using customer service robots to help serve us.

> *"My model for business is The Beatles. They were four guys who kept each other's kind of negative tendencies in check. They balanced each other and the total was greater than the sum of the parts. That's how I see business. Great things in business are never done by one person. They're done by a team of people"* [321]

The Internet of Things (IoT) will make in-person and online shopping increasingly tailored to our personal needs and enjoyment. Smart technology can link our technology products to the IoT so they can put themselves in for a service or order their own replacement. This experience can be at home or in-store. Guideshops and product Showrooms are replacing retail outlets, with the ability to try before you buy, but not to actually buy them. As a I write, Bonobos and Zalora are examples of this.

Is the high-street really dead? Yes but only as we know it. Once physical stores have developed a personalised 3D shopping experience then customers will return. One approach is the Nieman-Marcus 'Memory Mirror' which provides 360 degree videos to compare how different clothes look on you. ClothCap offers 66 cameras to record what you look like trying on clothes. Lowe's Kitchens can be planned using augmented reality in its "Holoroom'. Google Lens enables you to point at something and it will tell you what it is and where it's on sale, directing you to physical shops as well as online retailers.

Checkout-free stores are on the way too. They use technology to read what you're taking away with you, automatically billing you for the products you've taken. Shoplifters beware. In China, you can buy by simply looking into a face-reader, which knows it's you and activates your chosen account to pay with.

---

[321] Steve Jobs, co-founder of Apple with Steve Wozniak.

We have to stay vigilant against technological threats, as well as staying ready for any technological opportunities. The World is changing very fast. How we adapt is a controllable within our power. Civilian technology often comes from adapting military applications and military technology is always developing at great pace. The next great war is likely to be a cyber-war fought by computers against each other. That is already happening surreptitiously between the biggest powers. At some point military computers will be able to fight each other using autonomous tanks, planes and ships like a computerised war-game. At some point, there won't be any need for soldiers in national armies, just computer programmers. The applications from military technology will eventually become available to commercial businesses. Protecting our organisation's systems and preparing for an ever-looming cyber-threat are essential steps in today's commercial world.

Science and technology can increase your organisation's chances of success from the moment of installation. Working out which mission-critical controllables you need to manage, should be the starting point. Armed with that information, you can search for any technological solutions to your challenge. If one doesn't exist, someone can probably make it for you.

~~~~~

We have a better chance when we work within a tribe of people. A tribe will always have skills and understanding that a computer doesn't have. A Super-tribe collaboration between tribes will have even more. But, technology has developed to such a level that its speed of data analysis too fast for almost any group of humans. The team that wields the best machine power can potentially secure victory before the competition even starts.

Garry Kasparov is a Russian Chess Grand Master. From 1986 until his retirement in 2005, he was ranked world No. 1 for 225 out of 228 months. He is widely believed to be the greatest human chess player of all time. In 1997, he famously faced a $10 million IBM supercomputer called Deep Blue. Garry Kasparov has since written about the experience. "Instead of a computer that thought and played chess like a human, with human creativity and intuition, they got one that played like a machine, systematically evaluating up to 200 million possible moves per second and winning with brute-number-crunching force."[322]

---

[322] In his book 'Deep Thinking: Where Machine Intelligence Ends and Human Creativity Begins'.

The fight wasn't a fair one. Garry Kasparov felt that very keenly at the time. Garry wasn't a gracious loser and openly admits it "I believe that accepting losses too easily is incompatible with being a great champion – certainly this was the case with me. I do believe in fighting a fair fight, however, and this is where I felt IBM had short-changed me as well as the watching world." The IBM computer was simply too advanced. The best chess brain in the World couldn't beat it. Technology won and that result won't be reversed.

~~~~~

Technology can almost always help you to be more successful. If it's permissible under your competition rules, gives you an advantage and doesn't compromise on your values, then seriously consider adopting it. Imagine working in the modern world without a smartphone or computer of any kind. Unless outward appearance counts as part of the competition itself, functionality is far more important than how it looks. Technology has to help you to win, it doesn't have to be aesthetically pleasing.

"The most ugly car, if you win with it, is beautiful"[323]

Having the best technology is usually enough to give you a clear advantage. But it's only the hardware. You still need the best software, best programming, best development, best data capture, best analysis and best applications to take the best advantage. Just buying yourself a great laptop doesn't cut it.

"Before you become too entranced with gorgeous gadgets and mesmerising video displays, let me remind you that information is not knowledge, knowledge is not wisdom; and wisdom is not foresight. Each grows out of the other and we need them all"[324]

~~~~~

Every customer likes choice. So every business needs to offer it. There's choice and then there's personalisation. Aston Martin is a World leading luxury and sports car brand. Offering some choice to its high-end customers isn't enough to satisfy them. Personalisation is required. How many different interior

---

[323] Two-time Formula 1 World Champion Niki Lauda.
[324] Arthur C. Clarke.

combinations can a customer choose for an Aston Martin DBS? The answer is over three million[325]. Now that's personalisation. The chances of anyone having exactly the same car as you are very slim. This attention to detail is possible because of Aston's blend of mechanised processes and technical skill. The systems and tools are all cutting edge and the technicians are all highly-trained and highly-skilled. This winning combination of technology and technique is absolutely key on a high-end car like a DBS.

Take the leather interior. Two hundred individual pieces of leather are sewn together to make a DBS interior. Imagine the precision involved. It takes four years training at Aston Martin to be allowed to do leather work. Or, take the carbon fibre chassis. That's created from two hundred separate panels. The chassis is held together by a sophisticated form of adhesive and cured in an oven. Then it's checked by four robots, before any further work can take place. That checking process is quick, which is remarkable as it checks the car in 1,000 places.

It's not just the car's looks that matter. There also has to be an Aston Martin performance. Known as "The brute in a suit" the DBS has to be able to reach its stated maximum speed of 211mph. The downforce required to hold the car to the road is colossal. This is generated from multiple sources including vents and extended sills. Every element has to be assembled with incredible precision. Every part of the design has to be functional too. That's because every component has to contribute to the aero-dynamics. The car's technology and aesthetics work in harmony.

Built in 49 hours from thousands of parts, an Aston Martin DBS is a technical marvel. Although much of the process is 'by hand', state of the art technology is used for tooling, process control, the interlocks for the production track (which ensures all the critical processes are completed); and series number scanning for parts. Humans alone couldn't build this car on a commercial basis.

Each car goes through two hours of post-assembly simulation testing. No car makes it through the process without meeting Aston's exacting standards. Only then are the famous Aston Martin wings added to the car bonnet. How is possible to build such a complex car in the time? It's Aston's unique combination of technology and human techniques. That approach is underpinned by Aston's 'Right First Time' philosophy. The technical process are all on-screen at every

---

[325] From Channel 4's 'How to build an Aston Martin'.

work station, but with such well-trained technicians, the human inputs are almost automatic too. At Aston Martin, the mechanical processes and the humans operate seamlessly as one.

~~~~~

Ever since childhood, Maggie Aderin-Pocock MBE has loved science. Desperate to see the stars close up and to meet The Clangers[326] Maggie made her own working telescopes as a teenager. Powered by her love of science, Maggie has since defied the artificial boundaries of class, race, disability, gender and family break-up to become a leading British scientist.

> *"Dreams don't show up on government surveys or school league tables, but they are the fuel that makes us want to get up and get on"[327]*

Since adulthood, Maggie has been involved in major scientific developments, including hand-held instruments to help detect landmines, a high-resolution spectograph to analyses starlight; and satellite instruments to investigate the effects of climate change. Maggie's passion for her subject has given her a lifetime of joy and brought many practical benefits for wider society. In between her work and family, Maggie has spoken to over 25,000 children to help inspire them to become scientists and follow their dreams. Maggie also co-presents the television programme 'The Sky at Night[328]' which brings living science into our living rooms.

> *"You don't need a big brain the size of a planet, or mad hair. You need a passion to understand things"[329]*

Passion drives us to learn more, do more and be more. Without passion, tomorrow is just the same as today. Maggie Aderin-Pocock became a scientist because she is "inquisitive". In her words "Science is about asking why?" And therein lies a great truth. Successful people and successful organisations tend to share that same

---

[326] 'The Clangers' is about a fictional family of mouse-like creatures who inside a small moon-like planet. They can only speak by whistling. The programme was originally aired in 1969-1974 and was re-made in 2015.
[327] Maggie Aderin-Pocock MBE
[328] Made famous in the 1970's by former presenter Sir. Patrick Moore.
[329] Maggie Aderin-Pocock MBE

inquisitive nature. They question the status quo, they demand more. Successful people are bored by mainstreaming, that's just repeating yesterday's developments. Winners in all walks of life are always looking to slipstream. Science and technology is where many of those opportunities arise.

Our ambition is reflected in the scale and nature of the things we think about. How big does Maggie think? In her Brixton TEDx Talk Maggie provides the answer "Our galaxy is the Milky Way. It has approximately 200 billion stars. The Universe as a whole has approximately 100 billion galaxies." Maggie Aderin-Pocock thinks as big as there is. The idea of space flight remains as thrilling to the adult Maggie, as it did during childhood. Maggie still wants to travel into space. "I still want to go. It's my dream."

In 2020, an eighteen year old called Alyssa Carson graduated from the Advanced Space Academy in the USA. Alyssa is training to become the first person to walk on Mars in 2033. The scenario planning for that mission must be incredible. I bet Maggie would love to be in Alyssa's shoes.

~~~~~

On 18 March 2020, Marcus Rashford sent a tweet. It said "Guys, across the UK there are over 32,000 schools. Tomorrow all of these will close. Many of the children attending these schools rely on free meals, so I've spent the last few days talking to organisations to understand how this deficit is going to be filled". What followed was a series of tweets which received nearly one million likes. More importantly, what followed was Government support and three million meals for school children.

Marcus's fame as a Manchester United player helped spread the initiative, Twitter gave his voice wings; but it was his first-hand experience of going hungry that gave his campaign credibility. His message was heart-felt and really chimed with the British public. Children going hungry in modern Britain is unacceptable. Marcus called it out. Government Ministers listened. Then when Marcus came back and asked for free school meals in the holidays too, the Government relented and gave in again.

Social media has as much power as the speaker and message can generate. It's a controllable that needs a great deal of self-control. Respect, authenticity and passion (RAP) are key. As social media gradually replaces speaking as our chief method of communication, its prominence will only grow. Social media is a technology controllable that can increasingly create wins and losses on its own. We need to make each post contribute towards a win.

~~~~~

Combining two tribes of people behind one cause can create a Super-tribe. In the same way, combining two separate materials into one new one, can produce a composite that's better than both of the individual ones. The development of new composites can significantly enhance strength, flexibility and durability. Some of these composite materials can be used to increase sporting performance. In golf for example, polymers have been added to natural rubber compounds to create golf balls which can be hit harder whilst still holding their shape. So, propelled by an identical swing, this new type of golf ball travels further.

The same developments have been true in many other sports, including tennis. In 1947, traditional wood tennis rackets were instantly outmoded when Lacoste introduced its new 'Lacoste Laminated' racket, made from laminated wood[330]. The first steel racket followed in 1968 with the Wilson T2000 favoured by Jimmy Connors. In 1980, graphite rackets took over from wood and steel. John McEnroe and Steffi Graff promptly switched to the new graphite framed Dunlop Max200G.

The innovation didn't stop there. Wilson pushed things on in 1987 with its 'widebody' racket that used a larger beam width, which created more powerful shots. Then in 1990, Wilson introduced the Wilson Hammer which had a heavier head to produce more power. Innovation comes from rebelling against convention. As long as someone is always banging on the door of change it will keep on opening.

*"I've always been a rebel, always curious
about the world around me"[331]*

By 2003, the heavy rackets had been replaced by ultra-lightweight ones which still produced great power. Andy Roddick developed his incredible service game off the back of Babolat's Pure Drive. In 2005, manufacturer Prince produced its Prince 03 with larger string holes to gain more racket speed. The same year

---

[330] Information sourced from complex.com – the evolution of the tennis racket.
[331] Martina Navratilova, the winner of 18 Grand Slam singles titles, and one of only three women to win the 'Grand Slam Boxed Set' being the women's singles, doubles and mixed-doubles in all four Grand Slam events.

Babolat produced the aerodynamic and Rafa Nadal favourite AeroPro Drive. That racket was designed to require less effort and produce smoother strokes. In 2007 Roger Federer chose the Wilson K Factor, winning 17 major titles with it. Head's composite graphine 2012 YOUTEK became Novak Djokovic's racket of choice when it was introduced. In the past, a tennis player chose the best racket from the range offered by their brand. These days they design it with their partner brand.

Serena Williams plays with a Wilson Blade SW104. The 'SW' stands for Serena Williams. The 104 is the head size. It's larger than the average racket to fit Serena's specific requirements. The length has also been extended, to 28 inches. No leading professional player wants an off the shelf racket anymore. Serena doesn't just take a reactive interest in technology, she is pro-actively chasing it down.

"I am always asking Wilson is there new technology, something I can be doing? I love new technology. I am in that industry and business and I love the idea of never being left behind"[332]

Novak Djokovic reportedly now plays with a personally customised racket. Some believe it's based on the Head PT113B, others say that it's a mix of the Head Liquidmetal and the Head Microgel Radical. Novak reportedly strings his racquet with Babolat vs Natural Gut 17 in the 'mains' and ALU Power 16L in the 'crosses'. He also appears to use his own personalised lead tape around the frame. Other than the R&D people at Head, no one knows exactly what racket Novak is playing with.

Personalisation is where it's at. Tennis rackets have come a very long way in their development. Player performance has made similar leaps as a result. Imagine Serena or Novak taking the court with a traditional 1940's wooden racket. Despite their exceptional ability, that racket would make it impossible for them to win a single professional match. We need the very best tools to do our jobs with. No team can afford to be left behind. Winning comes from creating a technological advantage over your competitors. Outmoded teams will always struggle to be win ready.

~~~~~

---

[332] Serena Williams, winner of twenty-three Grand Slam tennis titles.

Maria Salomea Skłodowska was a passionate, inquisitive woman with a powerful, inner-drive for scientific discoveries. Maria wanted to study at the University of Warsaw, but it was illegal for women to attend higher education. So she had to study at the secretive Flying University, which regularly moved locations to avoid being detected. In 1891, Maria moved to Paris where she enrolled at the Sorbonne University. Maria Skłodowska is better known by the name she adopted when she moved to France.

Through her relentless commitment to scientific discovery, Marie Curie discovered the chemical element Polonium, which was named with her birth country in mind. Polonium can be used in machinery to eliminate static electricity, in brushes to remove dust from photographic films; and it can be combined with beryllium to form neutron sources. Marie also discovered the element radium. She invented a portable X-ray machine which was used to help injured soldiers in the First World War. Now, put to use in the form of radiotherapy, radium is helping to treat cancer, every day, right across the World. Both of these elements can be used for good or for bad, for society's benefit or for its harm. Marie Curie's mission was to use science for good.

"One never notices what has been done; one can only see what remains to be done"[333]

Scientific developments come from painstaking exploration and discovery. Marie and her husband had to do their work in poor conditions. Needing to break down ore into its component parts, they worked in what was described as "a cross between a stable and a potato shed". To put in the long days and years the work took, there was a driving passion to succeed. Behind that passion there was a mission that fired her progress. Her mission drove her to overcome all of her obstacles, doubts and worries.

"Nothing in life is to be feared, it is only to be understood. Now is the time to understand more, so that we may fear less"[334]

Marie Curie won the Nobel Prize for Physics in 1903 and the Nobel Prize for Chemistry in 1911. Marie remains the only person to win a Nobel Prize in two different areas of science. Her remarkable achievements have been an inspiration

---

[333] Marie Skłodowska Curie.
[334] Marie Skłodowska Curie.

to many, including her daughter who discovered "artificial" radioactivity and was awarded her own Nobel Prize for Chemistry in 1935.

In a tragic irony, Marie Curie died from aplastic anaemia, caused by too much exposure to radiation. Her notebooks remain highly radioactive and are still stored in lead-lined boxes over 100 years after she wrote in them. It seems that they will have to stay in there for over a 1,000 years to come. By the time, Maria Skłodowska died, she had completed her life's mission. Her personal sacrifice has saved many thousands of lives since then. And her scientific legacy lives on. The Marie Curie Centres, in France, continue to make medical breakthroughs in her name. Feeling inspired and passionate about a shared mission, can drive us and our organisation's to success. What is the inspiration behind your team's mission?

~~~~~

Over the centuries, explosive population growth and technical military advancements have forced change across the World. That has often come with a cost. In the nineteenth century, the Native American population in the West of the USA was overrun by white settlers. The nomadic plains hunter lifestyle was soon gone, having lasted for over 13,000 years.[335] After the tipping point had been reached, there was a momentous inevitability to it all.

Native American tribes lived an inclusive, supportive existence. They cared for each other, meaning they all had more chance of survival. Tribal life meant a happier life for all of them. Their reverence and respect for the land and their sources of food and water, meant that Native Americans lived sustainably for thousands of years. By comparison modern society is selfish and unsustainable. Nowadays there simply isn't enough land for us all to live like plains Americans. The planet's ever expanding population has made that impossible. Too much of England's green and pleasant land isn't green, having been concreted over for housing, shops and offices. Space is at a premium, as evidenced by high land and property prices. We certainly haven't improved on these aspects of Native American life.

"Look after the land and the land will look after you.
Destroy the land and it will destroy you"[336]

---

[335] The first evidence of plains hunters was found in New Mexico. Dating back approximately 13,500 years, these people have been termed 'Clovis' society.
[336] An Aboriginal proverb.

The takeover of Native America started hundreds of years earlier with the Spanish invasions in the 1490's. Some advancements worked well for the Native Americans. Ironically, the image we conjure of Apache or Sioux riders galloping on horseback was a result of the Spanish importing horses into America and teaching the Native Americans how to ride them. However, many other changes were unfavourable and enforced. The on-rushing white settlers and their shiny gun barrels created the modern American society we have today. Superior weapons, in the form of rifles and pistols, were mismatched against bows and knives; and ever increasing numbers of armed Europeans developed a foothold in each part of the country and pushed through into domination.

That is not a surprise, as throughout history, the most technologically advanced societies have tended to make better weapons and physically dominate their competition. The ever-increasing flood of people onto the Earth has forced the pace of those technological developments. Great engineering is to be admired, but housing people in a high-rise block of flats is a World away from them bedding down in a tipi under the stars.

Science and technology can provide us with a cutting edge over our competitors. So the temptation to have ever more of it is strong. Our ever-growing population has fierce demands, whilst our resources are finite and dwindling fast. Without the land and buffalo to live like a Native American, we have to be creative. Innovation can help us to cope with modern challenges. But we need to establish a healthy balance between our need to be competitive and our need to be human. We need to make science and technology work for us, rather than becoming a slave to them. We should limit our technology to what we need, otherwise we will be overrun by it. We use it to help our organisation become ever more sustainable.

~~~~~

Mike Ford appreciates the advantages that sports science can offer professional rugby "Data can help you plan training and it makes analysis easier, but it should never rule decision-making. Coaches can become too dependent on it." Mike values its benefits, but he is clear that having "drones, computers and data" is not a panacea. "Rugby is an awareness, heads-up, skills based game which shouldn't be over-complicated."

~~~~~

Technological advancements don't have to be hugely sophisticated or expensive. When I was growing up, I used to play snooker next door at my next door neighbour Jeremy's house.[337] The table was half-size and up in the loft. The attic roof sloped away on two sides. One of those sloping walls was really pronounced, leaving you with a very tight, awkward shot from that side of the room.

I remember our first match, because I struggled to play any sort of shot when the cue ball was up against the right hand side of the table. Jeremy kept putting the white cue ball back into the same awkward place. As the game progressed, I decided to do the same to him. I played a shot that left the white cue ball right up against the sloping wall. I thought I was being clever and I probably laughed as Jeremy was left with an impossible shot.

That's when he suddenly produced a sawn-off, half-size snooker cue from behind something in the corner of the room. As it turns out, he was fully prepared for this moment. He had no problem playing the shot with his extra short cue. I can still picture him laughing. Sometimes technology is as simple as having a tool that your opponent doesn't. Sometimes preparation is as simple as holding your advantage back, until you really need it.

Takeaway thoughts:

- Science and technology can help us to slipstream
- Technology can bring much greater personalisation
- Big data can help us to prepare better
- Be inquisitive
- Outmoded teams will always struggle to be win ready
- Feeling inspired will help us to find our best solutions
- Science and technology should work for us, rather than being a slave to them
- Having technology that your opponents don't, can be a big advantage

---

[337] Jeremy Atkinson, the friend I used to stand with at Castleford Tigers.

3.9 WINNING SUPER-TRIBE THINKING

The ninth controllable is Super-tribe thinking. Super-tribes[338] are created by bringing two or more tribes together on a joint mission, for mutual benefit. Examples include the United Kingdom, made up of England, Northern Ireland, Scotland, Wales and the islands around the UK. Another example is the NHS, made up of all the regional NHS bodies. The same applies to the Fire & Rescue Service, which is made up of regional fire and rescue services. In sport, an example is the British and Irish Lions, which is made up of players from England, Ireland, Scotland and Wales.

Super-tribes are built by bringing different tribes together to support a common cause. As individuals we operate as part of many collaborations, teams and groups. But are they all operating as tribes? The answer is 'rarely'. Do we try to get the best out of all of our social and working relationships? This answer is 'less often that we should'. That's very self-limiting.

It is extremely difficult to work alone, because we rely on so many people for so many things. Some people deny this. But try operating without a computer. Try building your own laptop from scratch with no ready-made components. Try living in a house you've had to build without any ready-made bricks, or tools. Try and feed yourself without any farms or supermarkets. It's incredibly difficult. Cooperation is absolutely essential. We should embrace it and maximise the benefits from it, as Dr. Sabrina Cohen-Hatton has done for the Fire & Rescue Service.

> *"We could have been anything that we wanted to be*
> *Yes, that decision was ours*
> *it's been decided we're weaker divided*
> *let friendship double up our powers"*[339]

When we work in informal groups and teams, do we really work together for mutual interest? Or do we just work for the things that we want? If so, that's a false economy. No one will help us if we never help them. By actively collaborating with other people, we can make bigger and faster progress towards

---

[338] I have written about my concept of Super-tribes in detail, with modern and historical examples, in the first two books in the Super-tribe series called 'Build Your Super-tribe' and 'Lead Your Super-tribe'.

[339] Lyrics from the song 'You give a little love" from the musical Bugsy Malone.

our vision of success; and so can every other team member. When we work out what we all want, we can form a tribe and give each other mutual help.

If we can build a tribe we can use the power of every tribe member to deliver the tribe's mission. Then we can find other tribes who share our missions and build a Super-tribe.[340] It's our choice whether to progress from individual to Super-tribe.

FROM INDIVIDUAL TO
SUPER-TRIBE

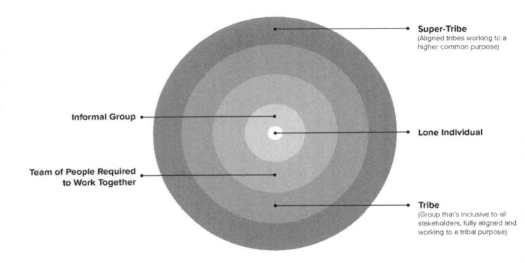

Copyright © Simon James Rhodes

The Sioux were made up of layers of Super-tribes. At the bottom were individual bands based around a family. There were usually between one and two hundred people in each band. Those bands were part of a larger tribe. There were several thousand tribe members in each tribe. In the case of Sitting Bull, his tribe was the Hunkpapa. For Crazy Horse it was the Hunkpatila[341].

---

[340] My concept of Super-tribes is covered extensively in the first two books in the Super-tribe series 'Build Your Super-tribe' and 'Lead Your Super-tribe'.
[341] The Hunkpatila were a sub-tribe of Red Cloud's Oglala.

Above the tribal layer were three Sioux nations based on geography and speech dialect. The three were the Lakota (which brought together Sitting Bull and Crazy Horse), the Dakota and Nakota. All of those nations were in turn part of the Great Sioux Nation.

Each Sioux band had its own strength, but it also had its tribal strength above it. Beyond band and tribe there was the strength of the relevant Lakota Nation and then the whole Great Sioux Nation. Using my modern definition of tribes and Super-tribes, the first level Sioux bands were 'tribes' and every level above them was a Super-tribe. Today, modern Super-tribes come in all shapes and sizes[342].

~~~~~

In 2019, HSBC ran a UK advertising campaign based on the strapline "We are not an island". The advertising said "We are not an island. We are a Colombian coffee drinking, American movie watching, Swedish flat-pack assembling, Korean tablet tapping, Belgian striker supporter, Dutch beer cheers-ing, tikka masala eating, wonderful little lump of land in the middle of the sea. We are part of something far, far bigger." HSBC was criticised by some for appearing to be anti-Brexit. In response, HSBC explained that it was only promoting the UK's connectivity with the rest of the World.

The UK is a small an island group with the degree of independence that gives us, but we are also inter-connected to everywhere else in the World through geography (we share this planet), society (through friendships and social media connections), demographics (many UK residents have family right across the globe) and economics (through international business groups and transactions). So we are an island and we are part of something bigger. HSBC got that spot on.

HSBC is a global bank, made up of it banks and branches across the World. Its advertising was promoting Super-tribe thinking. HSBC was reminding us that due to its own global connections, HSBC is a Super-tribe that we can join and benefit from. Brexit or no Brexit we were always going to need those connections. In that respect, HSBC got it absolutely right. We are all inter-connected. The more we play on that, the better.

~~~~~

---

[342] See 'Build Your Super-Tribe'.

During the period from 2004 to 2017 Leeds Rhinos were the dominant team in English rugby league, winning sixteen major honours. Former player, Rob Burrow played for Leeds throughout that golden period.

In 2019, Rob was diagnosed with Motor Neurone Disease (MND) at the age of 37. When he needed help, who rallied around him? All his old Leeds teammates. His "rugby family" stood strong. Players including Kevin Sinfield, Jamie Peacock, Barrie McDermott, Jamie Jones Buchanan and Danny McGuire came back together, to help their former teammate and lifelong mate. They have all supported him personally, as you would hope, but they've gone much further. They immediately went into fundraising mode and they have run and cycled many miles to raise money for MMD. They are a strong tribe, a brotherhood for life.

Instead of pressing on alone, or with just his Leeds tribe, Rob immediately sought out fellow sufferers in other sports. Working with Doddie Weir (Rugby Union) and Stephen Darby (football), Rob has raised the profile of MND to reach the national consciousness. By uniting their three sports behind the cause, they have created a Super-tribe to fight against MND.

In the BBC's documentary 'Rob Burrow: My year with MND' fellow sufferer Doddie Weir commented on their battle against MND. "It's a bit like a game in some sort of way. We're here trying to beat MND. And the only way we're going to win is by a collective effort with the boys here and the charities and fundraising. Let's work together and fund it. As we've been involved in teamwork, we understand that the bigger the team, the better the result." Battling MND requires a Super-tribe, cross-sport, society-wide effort. The 'Motor Neurone Disease Family' is doing just that.

~~~~~

The Bruderhof is an international Christian community organisation. Founded in Germany in 1920, by Eberhard Arnold, members lead a simple Christian way of life. The community provides every member with housing, food and clothing. Every adult works to sustain the community, but no one takes a salary.

The jobs on offer are ones that bring in income to keep everyone housed, fed and clothed (in Darvell, East Sussex it's a multi-million pound wooden toy factory), or they are the jobs needed to look after the community (in Darvell's case its community is 300 people) such as farming, teaching, cleaning and catering. There are traditionally male and female work roles, like the Sioux, which doesn't reflect the equality ideals of today's society. There have also been some complaints of poor treatment from former community members. But across twenty-three Bruderhof communities around the World, thousands of people are prepared to sacrifice their freedoms and control of their lives to God.

The community emphasises that there is a free choice whether to stay or go. Bruderhof members have stressed that they are not oppressed. The proof of this freedom to opt-out seems to be that at age 18 everyone spends a year away from the main community. Each person then decides whether or not to commit to the community for life. According to a BBC documentary about the Bruderhof, 25-30% of those 18 year old's decide not to return. Being a Bruderhof community member is intended to be a permanent lifelong commitment, but some adults have left and been allowed to return.

It's important to note that the Bruderhof is not a democratic society. It is a life dedicated to God and to each other. There are personal sacrifices to be made. In return all the essentials are provided and there appears to be a strong sense of social belonging. Each Super-tribe member gives up his or her personal ambitions and the chance of personal wealth. In turn that person gets social belonging and a higher purpose, quite literally a mission from God.

Whether you like the idea or not, the Bruderhof is a form of Super-tribe. First there are dozens of families (tribes) within each of the twenty three communities, like Darvell (Super-tribes). Those communities are themselves part of an international network of Bruderhof communities (a higher form of Super-tribe).

"I hope someday you will join us and the world will live as one"[343]

Are those Bruderhof communities thriving? Well they seem to be able to survive inside all the challenges of the modern World. Despite the numbers leaving, they seem to have enough members remaining to sustain themselves. They live a life dedicated to God and no one appears to go short of life's essentials. So the answer appears to be yes. Would everyone want that life? No. I'm sure that most people wouldn't. However, it has to be said that the Bruderhof use fewer resources than the average Western adult, cause less pollution and they live a peaceful and lawful existence. Therefore the Bruderhof seem to pose less harm than many other groups within society.

---

[343] From 'Imagine' by John Lennon.

Are the Bruderhof successful? Well as we've seen, that depends on how you define success. To their standards, their lifestyle might be an absolute success. To the rest of us, the Bruderhof communities might constitute a qualified failure due to the gender stereotyping and lack of democracy. As with success generally that all depends on your perspective.

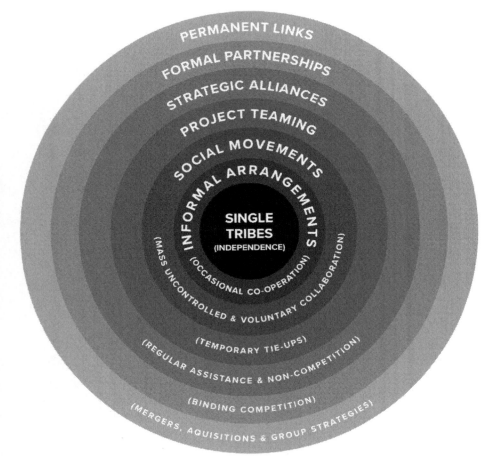

SUPER-TRIBES
(ALL SHAPES & SIZES)

PERMANENT LINKS

FORMAL PARTNERSHIPS

STRATEGIC ALLIANCES

PROJECT TEAMING

SOCIAL MOVEMENTS

INFORMAL ARRANGEMENTS

SINGLE TRIBES (INDEPENDENCE)

(MASS UNCONTROLLED & VOLUNTARY COLLABORATION)

(OCCASIONAL CO-OPERATION)

(TEMPORARY TIE-UPS)

(REGULAR ASSISTANCE & NON-COMPETITION)

(BINDING COMPETITION)

(MERGERS, AQUISITIONS & GROUP STRATEGIES)

Copyright © Simon James Rhodes

Super-tribe thinking is about joining forces. One way of slipstreaming is to analyse the techniques used in other processes and adapt them for your own purposes. Scouring the World for processes that you can adopt and adapt, should bring advantages. This is Super-tribe thinking, because it aims to bring together the strengths of two or more systems, to produce a new and improved model. We can take a technique from a totally different walk of life and see what it can offer us. Better still, we can combine our current techniques with borrowed ones to produce a brand new super-solution that enhances our existing process and increases our performance levels. Joining the best elements of one process with those of another, can create something that no one else is doing. At least not yet.

The Romans are famous for the number of their modern day legacies. But many of them were 'borrowed' from other civilisations and then enhanced. The Romans were a Super-tribe of peoples and cultures from all the countries they conquered. They copied and adapted many items from the Etruscans, Greeks, Spanish and Gauls amongst others.

The Romans are famous for their architecture. But they copied the Etruscan arch, which was a half-circle of wedge-shaped stones that rested on two pillars, with a keystone in the centre to hold the stones in place. They also copied the Etruscan cuniculus, which was a long underground water trench. The Romans used this technology with their invention of concrete, to build aqueducts, bridges and stadiums (like the Colosseum). The Romans also used Greek designs in their public and private buildings, such as for the Pantheon in Rome. Greek columns were a very popular design feature which could be added for extra effect.

The Gladius Hispaniensis was the definitive sword of the Roman army. It was double-edged and relatively short at about 25-27 inches long. This type of sword was originally developed by Iberian tribes (in modern day Spain) who the Romans encountered during the Punic Wars. The advantage of the Gladius Hispaniensis was that a soldier could thrust it forward without having to move his shield and leave his body exposed. So a Roman version was designed, crafted and issued to all Roman soldiers.

"Arthur: What could be greater than a king?"
Atlanna: "A hero. A king fights only for its nation,
but you fight for everyone" [344]

---

[344] From DC's 'Aquaman'.

The Galea was the archetypal Roman soldier's helmet. With side and rear pieces to protect their soldiers, it was a protective and well-designed helmet. Yet again, this wasn't a purely Roman invention. The name and basic design came from Gaul (modern day France), where the Romans discovered a better helmet design than their own. By creating a new amalgamated design, their soldiers ended up with a better version than both of the existing ones.

Roman art is World famous, but it was heavily influenced by the Greeks. Greek pottery was highly-valued by the Romans for its usefulness and beauty. The Greek influence on Roman painting and sculpture was so important that historians refer to it as "Greco-Roman art." It was Greek mythology that influenced the Romans; and they adopted many of the Greek gods, giving them Latin names. The Romans also adopted the Etruscan sport of chariot racing and built venues to watch it in, such as the Circus Maximus which seated more than 200,000 spectators. The famous 'Gladiator' fights also came from an Etruscan tradition, which the Romans took to a new level.

Without condoning the violent uses of these items, borrowing, copying, adopting and adapting[345] ideas from other walks of life can help to slipstream your organisation ahead of its competition. That point is sharp and well made.

~~~~~

'Fusion' cooking takes ingredients and techniques from different cooking styles and combines them together. Fusion cooking typically combines foods used in one culture and prepares them using techniques and flavours from another culture. It can also involve blending different techniques as well as mixed-up ingredients. Made well, a fusion cooking process can harness the best of two or more food cultures. Made badly, it can create something inedible. The testing and preparation processes for creating fusion food are vitally important. For every fusion offering that tastes good, there must be dozens of versions that taste terrible. We certainly don't want any of those on our menu.

Examples of popular fusion cooking include: Terimayo Japanese Hot Dogs (hot dogs with added seaweed), Gobi Manchurian (combining Chinese and Indian flavours to cauliflower), Greek Quesadillas (with mozzarella, feta, sun-dried tomatoes, spinach and dill), Sushi Burritos (sushi rice, guacamole, cajun chicken and vegetables wrapped in seaweed), (Falafel scotch eggs (scotch eggs made with Falafel), Mexican Ravioli (ravioli with chorizo, cilantro and

---

[345] Subject to legal rights, including copyright law.

Mexican cheese) and Taco Pizza (pizza made with cheddar and pepper jack cheese, salsa and refried beans).

These combinations are all counter-intuitive options, at least initially. We like to eat what's familiar to us. We have learned how to cook things the 'right way' and that is difficult to forget. Fusion processing requires us to start again from scratch and re-learn what's possible. This is slipstreaming in action. Which processes can you fuse with your own, to adapt and improve them?

Takeaway thoughts:

- We are all inter-connected and we need to play to this
- Partnering with other organisations can bring mutual success
- The bigger the team, the better the result
- Super-tribes can offer greater sustainability and chances of success
- We can improve on the best by adding to it or adapting it
- Fusing ideas can produce something better than either individually

3.10 WINNING STRENGTH AND FIREPOWER

The tenth controllable is strength and firepower. Every organisation needs to be strong enough to secure its own survival, otherwise it is lost. Who doesn't want the strength to thrive and be successful?

Strength comes in many forms. They include having the physical ability to compete, having the mental ability to hang in when the going's tough, having sufficiently robust people and systems to function under pressure; and having the strategic ability to gather all your firepower in one place, to concentrate your forces. Strength comes from having a clear, inclusive and motivating mission and the alignment of all your structures and resources to deliver it.

However successfully a team begins, it has to maintain its fighting strength in order to achieve success. Without a passionate desire to achieve the mission objectives and the stamina to last, there will be failure. Without an ongoing state of communal sacrifice, any organisation can be surpassed and defeated. Without an inclusive and motivating mission, there won't be sufficient reason for anyone to make the sacrifices that are needed.

~~~~~

The strengths that any team needs, are the strengths that it takes to win the competition you're in. Of them all, perhaps the ability to endure is the greatest. The survival of any organisation requires it to endure. Its sacred homeland, culture, people and resources have to be protected and defended. New followers and resources have to be gathered and bound in. Momentum has to be built and maintained. An organisation's powers of strength and influence have to continually grow and develop, or they will decline.

"Even the wolf fails more often than he wins, but he doesn't stop. He has great fangs, he can smell a trail two days old, and he can hear you over the next hill. But his real strength is endurance. He never quits."[346]

Endurance comes in three parts. Together these three elements provide the strength needed to succeed. No organisation can be successful without all three of these elements of endurance. They are the ability to stay competitive and not be out-manoeuvred (based on skill, positioning and experience). The stamina to last the journey, whatever the pace (resources, supply chain, physical and mental resilience). The will to win (a heart-powered, head-driven determination to succeed)

Organisations need a fully engaged and devoted group to fight for its past, present and future. Engagement comes having a vested interest in the organisation's success. Stakeholder engagement might be enough to secure its survival. But is that enough? Often it's the highest form of engagement that's need for an organisation to really thrive. Devotion is more powerful that engagement. Devotion comes from love. The greatest strength comes from love. Inside your organisation, where is there the love?

~~~~~

Rob Halford is the lead singer of the heavy metal band Judas Priest. Rob loves performing live. The band has released 18 studio albums and toured the World.

---

[346] From 'The Journey of Crazy Horse" by Charles Marshall III.

With sales of over 50 million albums and millions of concert tickets, Judas Priest is a very successful rock band. That success has been fuelled by its highly popular live shows, which give the fans what they expect and more.

In Rob Halford's words "Part of what heavy metal is about for most singers is the intensity of the performance. It's like when I've done a show and I go back to the hotel room and I'm lying in bed and I'm like "Was that me?" "Did I just do that?" You've got to be able to balance it out. I'm not on stage 24 hours a day. I need to be able to go down to Morrisons and do my shopping."[347] Rob needs to live a normal life outside of performing, so that he can bring a live intensity when he needs it.

"I see the crowd, I hear the roar!
I feel my body start to leave the ground and soar!"[348]

The band doesn't have to perform live 24/7, 365 days a year. The band only needs to find is power and strength when recording in the studio (to produce great albums) and during its live shows (to produce great live performances). A rock band peaks exactly when it needs to. Judas Priest wouldn't have sold so many albums and concert tickets with lacklustre studio or live performances. Saving itself for performance time has helped power its sales and longevity.

~~~~~

Having good people, facilities and resources is only part of a winning solution. How you use them all is equally important. The expression 'playing to your strengths' means making strategic and tactical choices to suit your own skills, techniques and resources. It's crucial for any team, to take advantage of the assets it possesses and not to mismanage or waste them. Matching what you have, to what you're facing, is a key skill in winning teams.

Choosing a deliverable mission (that supports your purpose), a suitable operating philosophy, appropriate values and recruiting and retaining the right people are all part of playing to your organisation's strengths. Strength comes from getting those big decisions right.

Strength also comes from getting the smaller decisions right too. If your mission

---

[347] This quote is from a television programme called 'Metal Britannia'.
[348] From 'Hot Rockin' by Judas Priest.

is 'to grow our business through excellent customer service' you need to build and play to customer service as a strength. If your team has someone with great front of house skills, don't put them in the kitchen or back office. Use them out front, where they can impress your customers. If you've got a team member who's great at strategy and seeing the big picture, don't give them a job that's all about fine details. Deploy them in a strategic oversight role.

The starting point for 'playing to your strengths' is discovering what you have. How well does any organisation really know its people and their strengths? There will be untold skills and experiences 'hiding' inside every team, because they didn't come up at interview and no one's ever asked about them since. The same goes for physical and digital assets. Do you really know what resources you have at your disposal? How good are your stock inventory and supply chain? Are your warehousing and logistics fit for purpose? If you don't know what's available to you, how can you use it to its maximum effect? A superficial knowledge isn't good enough. Know your own strengths.

~~~~~

There's an expression 'Don't judge a book by its cover'. And yet, we can still under-estimate people when we shouldn't. Maya Reis Gabeira is 5 ft 5" tall and suffers from asthma. She has undergone multiple surgeries on her back and nose. On paper, Maya is perhaps not everyone's most obvious candidate to hold the Women's World Record for the biggest wave ever surfed. However, in February 2020, Maya surfed a 73.5 ft (22.4 m) high wave in Nazaré, Portugal. This created a new World record, which broke her own existing record. Reportedly, Maya rode a bigger wave in 2018, off Nazaré, Portugal, which reportedly measured around 80 feet (24 metres) high. That's ten feet taller than the White House. Anyone who wrote her off was wrong to. Our size is only partly relevant to our strength.

Maya's physical strength comes from her core. Maya complements her technical and physical training with yoga and pilates. According to a report in the Latin Times online, Maya explains "I need to train my body and mind to be ready at all times. When I am competing during the season, it's all about surfing, I practice five hours a day. During the training months, I split my schedule between surfing and the fitness routines that I need to accomplish weekly. Aside from that, I also do yoga regularly".

"One killer exercise that's really great is pull-ups with your legs out level. That's my favourite. It's such functional core strength, and that's why I can climb up trees and down vines"[349]

Maya is physically strong, because of all the core work she has done. But it's her mental strength that repeatedly puts her back into the danger zone. Her mission is to surf ever larger waves, so she can be the most successful that she can possibly be. Maya clearly has the skill and ability to compete at the highest level, the stamina to compete at the highest level; and the will to win. Strength doesn't always depend on physical size, it also depends on desire and belief. Maya Gabiera has all the strength she needs and more.

~~~~~

Our chances of success are partly what we believe them to be. When we feel confident, we behave differently compared to when we feel lacking in confidence. How we relate to ourselves will always affect our chances of success. How we relate to other people will also affect our chances of success. If we perceive that there's an imbalance of power with someone else, that influences our behaviour towards that other person. For example, we behave differently at work depending on whether we are the manager or the person being managed. At home, our behaviours can depend on whether we are the parent or the child. The balance of power affects all relationships. We tend to be stronger when we are the one to exert power and influence over others. We tend to be weaker when we are under the power and influence of someone else.

The boss and the parent examples apply where there is a traditional form of hierarchy in place. What about where we start as equals? In most competitive situations we face our opponent on an equal footing. So the balance of power should be equal. What happens then? The competitor who gives the best pre-competition impression of power, starts with more of it. The competitor who wins the early skirmishes grows in power. The competitor who shows more determination and resilience in every encounter increases their balance of strength. Why? Because we tend to believe the evidence that see, hear and read, even if it's not true. If someone looks strong we believe they are strong, even if that's the only due to a well-honed technique. Perception can be more important than reality, because our perception can become our reality. Winning comes from

---

[349] Bear Grylls.

357

dominating the perception game, by using it to create strength in your own team and weakness in your competitors.

Historically, in Iceland, you had to lift a hálfdrættingur stone to qualify for work on a fishing boat. That was the minimum standard set to assess their strength to fish. The bigger the stone they could lift, the greater their share of the catch. The meaning of hálfdrættingur is 'weakling'. That stone weighted approximately 54 kg (8.5 stones) and it although it was heavy, it certainly wasn't the biggest stone being lifted. The stone called hálfsterkur ('half-strength') weighed approximately double that at 100 kg (15.75 stones). The biggest stone was called fullsterkur ('full strength') and weighed approximately 154 kg (24.25 stone). If you could lift fullsterkur then you were perceived to be very strong and you received a full share of each day's catch, as well as social prominence.

No Icelander should attempt to lift that kind of weight on their first ever lift, especially when their career and earnings depended on it. So it paid for them to practice lifting dead stone weights whilst growing up. As they grew, they lifted heavier and heavier weights until their reached their maximum upper limit. That built strength and improved their lifting technique at the same time. A lifetime of stone lifting could really pay off in adulthood. There are limits to human strength based on our genetics, but we can push those boundaries to their extreme through practice and development.

~~~~~

Winning stone lifting competitions was one historical way of demonstrating strength. In the modern World, there are many ways to demonstrate strength. One is by something very similar, lifting the Atlas stones in World's Strongest Man like Eddie Hall, but they certainly don't have to be that physical. Nowadays we appreciate that strength comes in many different forms. Olympic legend, Usain Bolt, was exceptionally fast. He wasn't a weightlifter or discus thrower, but we still perceived him to be strong. Winners seem strong. We credit them with the strength to win.

Showing off our strength can adjust other people's perceptions and alter the way that people treat us. That's especially true where that strength is hidden from sight. If we saw Maya Gabeira in the street, we might not appreciate her strength, but if we saw her surfing those monster waves, we'd rightly perceive her to be exceptionally strong. A change of context can really change our perceptions. If we saw Stephen Frayne in the street, we might not appreciate his power to impress, but when we watch 'Dynamo' perform we can all see his mental strength and skill. Practicing our skills and techniques in private can make us strong. A public showing of our skills and techniques can make us seem strong. We can use a change in context to push out the perceptions we want.

If you can make your opponents fearful of taking you on, they won't be at their best when you compete together. Why do some countries have military parades if not to say "Don't think you'll win, if you fight us, because you won't." Why do senior managers have more important titles if not to say "I have more authority to you." A Chief Executive is not just an ordinary executive. Putting on a 'show of strength' is a classic tactic to put off your opponent. If you fall for it yourself, it will weaken you. The external pressure you apply will affect your competitors internally. We need to fight the perception battle and win it.

> *"There is a lot of pressure put on me, but I don't put a lot of pressure on myself. I feel if I play my game, it will take care of itself"*[350]

Perception is a controllable which you can become a master of, or a servant to. Serving anything, other than your mission, only lessens your chances of achieving that mission. It's easier said than done, but don't get caught up in what your opponent is projecting. In your own defence, the secret is to do your own homework, set your own winning standards and plan to beat them. Don't let your opponent get the upper hand.

In attack, you can master the art of projecting a perception of strength to weaken your competitors. The aim should be to project a strong impression of strength, power, authority, determination, calm, resilience and endurance. By focusing on actually becoming those things, the more natural your projection process will become. As you strengthen the external perception of your team, you weaken your opponent psychologically. By pressing home your image of power, you can make winning more of a reality. Your chance of success is what your opponent believes it to be.

Tell true stories of your strength, sincerely, to trustworthy neutrals. Promote what's good about you to your competitors. Sow seeds of doubt around any perceived weaknesses. Make any actual weaknesses seem like strengths, to deter

---

[350] LeBron James, four times NBA Champion and winner of two basketball Olympic Gold Medals.

your opponent from attacking them. Leave your opponent unsure what to do next. The more energy that's sapped away from them, by worrying about you, the less there is left to overpower you. You can gain control of a competition through dealing in perceptions and distractions.

~~~~~

In 2017, Natalie Fitzsimons from Northern Ireland won a UK & Ireland Championship title and earned the rank of sixth best player in the World. If like me, you didn't even know there was a UK & Ireland Monopoly Championship, you might think, so what? But like any other competition, there are controllables and uncontrollables to master in Monopoly. With a pre-set board, pieces and rules (all uncontrollables) there isn't much room for inventive play. For most of us, winning Monopoly means trying to mainstream better than our opponents. The smallest of margins can be enough to secure a win.

In a 2017 interview with the Mirror online[351], Natalie Fitzsimons shared her tips for winning Monopoly games. They are quite revealing, you might call them slipstreaming. Natalie's mantra is to get your hands on as many of sets of streets as you can and as soon as you can afford to, build houses on them. To achieve that faster than anyone else, Natalie's first three pieces of advice are inter-related.

The first is to "mortgage everything else and spend every penny on houses". By mortgaging the properties you own, you can buy more properties and more houses. Within this advice, Natalie believes that it's better to have houses on one location picking you up big rents, rather than having lots of different streets collecting lower rents. Secondly, Natalie advises players to stop buying at three houses and never buy hotels, as that's when "the amount the rent increases per house maxes out". Thirdly, Natalie suggests buying up to three houses per property as fast as you can, because "There are only a certain number of houses available in the pot for people to build with". Once you've monopolised the supply of houses, your competitors can't use them against you. Natalie deliberately creates a "housing shortage."

The fourth piece of advice is not to rush out of jail in the later stages of the game, once you've built your property empire. That's because you don't have to pay out any rents, from landing on other players' properties; and you can still

---

[351] The Mirror online on 24 December 2017.

collect all your rents. The fifth and final piece of advice is not to buy Park Lane. "It may be prestigious but Park Lane is actually the square in the game landed on less than any other." That's because of the pattern of squares leading up to Park Lane. The Community Chest and Chance squares can often push you further around the board.

Like Monopoly, every form of competition has its rules. How you adapt to them is what makes the difference between winning and being a runner-up. Natalie Fitzsimons has practiced the game so often that she knows which strategies are strong and which are weak. What skills and techniques can you create a monopoly of?

~~~~~

When we begin a task, we need to be fully focused and motivated, but we also need to be relaxed. When a task is challenging and pressurised, we need to find a way to handle it calmly, without stress. Otherwise we'll reduce our power to deliver. Priming ourselves for pressure situations helps us to handle them better. Priming allows us to produce the power we need, when we need it. Preparing ourselves to 'turn it on' can help us to do exactly that. Priming doesn't mean doing more last minute practicing for the task. We need to be fully-prepared for the task well before then.

Priming ourselves is a two-stage process. Firstly, it's about taking ourselves away from the build-up by switching to a familiar and unrelated routine, such as listening to music. Taking our minds off the task, with a positive and stress-free activity, helps us to relax and get to the starting line feeling mentally strong. Secondly, when it's time to compete, we use a trigger to refocus and remotivate ourselves to deliver the task. Full of energy, we can then bring out our power to do it.

"You're stronger and you're better and you're ready for whatever"[352]

Thinking positively in the build-up can definitely help us to produce a positive performance. Prepare your self-priming in advance. Analyse and rehearse the reasons for confidence. Then you are more ready to win. Thinking negatively has

---

[352] Singer-songwriter Alicia Keys, who has sold over 30 million albums and millions more downloads.

the opposite effect. If we're burdened with doubt, worry or stress, we won't be able to bring our positivity and inner-power. We have to be able to set aside our troubles before we perform. We have to start every competition as strong as we can be. Winners don't let themselves be side-tracked. Winners start-off believing that they can win.

An article in the Journal of Experimental Social Psychology called 'Power gets the job: Priming power improves interview outcomes' concluded that momentary changes in power can shift the outcomes of professional interviews. Two psychological experiments were carried out. One group of applicants was asked to recall a time they felt powerful and another group was asked to recall a time when they felt powerless. Both groups were then asked to either write a job application letter or be interviewed for admission to a business school. Independent judges, who were unaware of the applicants' experimental conditions 'significantly preferred' the written job applications and face to face interview performances of the applicants who recalled feeling powerful before they completed the task. How we feel can hugely influence our performance levels. Properly priming yourself, can add a great deal to the levels you can reach.

"Let your performance do the thinking"[353]

What we do for a living affects how much priming we need to do and what form it should take. We all want a relaxed and focused surgeon with enough passion to help us. But we also want that passion wrapped in a calm blue head, so that the surgeon can focus on carrying out the operation successfully. We want our healthcare professionals fully primed and in calm control. Without priming, we might get to see our newsreaders in a state of distress from the stories they read to us. We might get our doctors and nurses in tears when they are explaining our prognosis. We don't want angry police officers attending riots on the streets or panicking fire officers attending the scene of a major disaster. Everyone needs to properly prime themselves before they perform.

~~~~~

At a business dinner in 2013, I was on the same table as Michael Portillo. Michael was there to speak and present the awards. He arrived in good time and immediately spoke to the organisers, to familiarise himself with the format, facilities and staging. Then once all the guests were seated at their tables, Michael

---

[353] Charlotte Brontë (who had to publish initially as Currer Bell).

started to work the room. By the time he needed to take his seat again, Michael had spoken to over thirty of the forty tables. I've never seen any other speaker, at any other event, work that hard.

Michael's walk-about had a double purpose. Michael learned what kind of audience he would be speaking to and he got himself warmed up to speak. That was his priming. The walk-about also had an additional effect. Michael created a personal relationship with his audience, which primed them to enjoy the event and like his speech. He took people away from his television personality and politics (which could have divided the audience) and chatted to them in a charming and down to earth manner. Michael Portillo was in his element. When he stood up to speak, the whole audience was with him. The event went really well and afterwards everyone said how good Michael Portillo's speech had been.

~~~~~

A love of country can provide the devotion needed to fight in war. No one wants to be in that position, but if it comes, we need to be able to defend ourselves. The British Military is the defender and protector of the British people. It assesses its strength and ability to fight through what it calls the 'Measure of Fighting Power'. This is an assessment of its moral, physical and conceptual ability to fight.

The moral component deals with the human elements of leadership, motivation and troop morale. These are all vital management elements. Every team member needs to have clarity and belief in the mission and their roles in it. No leadership team can afford "to lose the dressing room".

The physical component is what delivers the fighting power, namely the people, equipment and materials. That physical component requires troops with the right qualifications, skills and abilities to operate the equipment provided. In terms of equipment, the three Services are very different. Generally speaking, the Army equips the soldier (relying on people to deliver the power), whereas the Royal Air Force and the Royal Navy man[354] the equipment.

All three services rely heavily on technology to help to deliver their fighting power. Without arms, ammunition, tanks, planes and ships our military wouldn't win many battles. The balance between people and equipment differs between the

---

[354] In a gender neutral sense.

three Services, for good reason. Military personnel always have to be optimised for their distinct roles.

The conceptual component is the glue that binds the whole together using common understanding and standard ways of operating. This component becomes increasingly relevant as the size and sophistication of battle groups increases. Within this conceptual component, all the individual competitors and teams must have a clear mission, approach (philosophy) and unwavering aim (will to win). The underpinning doctrine of fighting power cannot become fixed dogma. It is there to provide a framework for operating, within which the troops on the ground can work.

At the lowest level of the conceptual component, the military has set procedures and drills which remove the need to think about the intricacies of execution each time. In other words, everyone knows their roles and what their functions are. They also know what to do in the event that a fellow soldier, sailor or pilot is unable to fulfil their role. Our skills must become second nature.

"Every battle is won before it is fought" [355]

The three components of moral, physical and conceptual need to be simultaneously combined to create an effective fighting force. How that fighting force is led and engaged on the day will ultimately dictate the mission's success or failure, but the philosophy and preparation leading up to the fight will have a major impact.

The three moral, physical and conceptual components are pulled together through building closer relationships and training (lots and lots of training). Drills must be second nature, so as not to eat into the valuable mental capacity to 'out-think' the opponent. In essence if you are to win you must be one step ahead at all times, able to predict your opponent's next move and taking action before it can. The military calls this the 'decision-action cycle' or the 'OODA loop', which stands for Observe, Orient, Decide, Act. Linked to this is an adage designed to produce action, rather than analysis paralysis. That adage is 'An 80% solution in time, is better than a 100% solution too late'. Don't freeze and do nothing.

This whole approach works at every level whether developing a strategy in the MoD right down to the patrol on the ground. Out-thinking and then out-

---

[355] Chinese strategist, Sun Tzu.

manoeuvring your opponent is crucial to success. This requires the application of detailed planning and preparation, and the application of a plethora of other military principles. Excellent strategic planning and communication are absolutely vital in every mission. Without them there will be chaos and confusion.

> *"Forward, the Light Brigade!*
> *Was there a man dismayed?*
> *Not though the soldier knew*
> *Someone had blundered.*
> *Theirs not to make reply,*
> *Theirs not to reason why,*
> *Theirs but to do and die.*
> *Into the valley of Death*
> *Rode the six hundred."* [356]

~~~~~

A love of exploration and tackling new frontiers can drive people to take on brave and extreme challenges. In 2004, Dame Ellen McArthur set sail aboard the 75ft trimaran 'B&Q - Castorama'. She returned on 8 February 2005, 71 days, 14 hours, 18 minutes and 33 seconds later, having sailed over 26,000 miles to become the fastest person to circumnavigate the globe single-handed.

In September 2010, Dame Ellen launched the Ellen MacArthur Foundation with the goal of "accelerating the transition to a regenerative, circular economy". Ellen's new tack came as a result of her competition experience at sea. Being alone for nearly 72 days had shown her "what it means to rely on a finite supply of resources, as on the boat food, water and fuel were inescapably linked to success or failure."[357]

Dame Ellen's success depended on her ability to manage the finite provisions that she had with her. Making things last involves a focus on preservation, protection and self-restraint. All these involve personal discipline and self-control. It's a facile thing to say, but at sea you can't go to a hardware shop, get a supermarket

---

[356] 'The Charge of the Light Brigade' by Alfred, Lord Tennyson.
[357] The Ellen McArthur Foundation website.

delivery, or order in a takeaway. To keep herself fit and healthy, Dame Ellen had to eat and drink enough of the right substances every day. Otherwise her strength would have quickly reduced to a point she wasn't competitive. But she also had to go the distance. So Dame Ellen had to control the pace that she consumed her resources at. She created a process of sustainability and endurance to match her challenge.

"Strength comes from balance, as all bow makers know"[358]

As a yachtswoman, Ellen needed to generate enough firepower, every day. There were no days off. Dame Ellen could have eaten and drunk more early on to build more of an advantage (perhaps). But at what cost? When her supplies ran out would she have finished? Probably not. Would she have broken the World record? Almost certainly not. Dame Ellen's feat of setting the single-handed World record is an extraordinary win. It speaks of her inner strength. But perhaps the greatest win of Dame Ellen's career will be to help us waste less and regenerate more.

~~~~~

A desire to win cups and medals can be a strong motivator. But there is a stronger level of passion and power that comes from getting to play with your friends, for your club or country. Playing to the strength of teamship will make your organisation more appealing. More people will want to join it, bringing a competition for places. Getting into a good team should take effort. Any role worth having should be hard to achieve.

Rugby Coach Mike Ford encourages aspiring first-team players "to train harder and smarter than the players they want to replace in the team". The strength that gives them puts pressure on the current first team player in front of them. That, in turn, makes the current first-teamer train harder and invest more in developing their own game. Therefore everyone gets stronger.

~~~~~

Elvis Aaron Presley has sold an estimated one billion singles and albums. And that's just one of the records he holds for selling records. For the sales categories that he isn't in first place for, he is almost certainly in the top ten. Elvis's exact

---

[358] The Journey of Crazy Horse by Joseph Marshall III.

sale numbers are the subject of some debate (due in part to his double-A side singles) but Elvis has probably had 18 US number one singles. The Beatles are top with 20 (all between 1964 and 1970) leaving Elvis in joint second with Mariah Carey.

One record Elvis certainly does hold is for the number of albums charting in the Billboard 200 (the US album charts). The number of those charting albums? 129. Yes that's one hundred and twenty nine charting albums. Frank Sinatra is second with 82, nearly fifty less. Of those 129 albums, 101 of them went gold (selling over 500,000 copies) and 57 went platinum (selling over 1 million copies). The sales figures are truly staggering, especially when you factor in that two-thirds of all those sales have come since his death.

Elvis had a fantastic work ethic and a determination to succeed. There were certainly periods of self-doubt, especially during the 1970's, but when he performed live he gave it absolutely everything. Off-stage he was conservative and humble. Whereas, on stage his total commitment on stage changed live performances forever.

"In public, I like real conservative clothes, something that's not too flashy. But on stage, I like 'em as flashy as you can get 'em" [359]

Elvis was worth less than $5m when he died on 16 August 1977. Remarkably, Elvis's estate earned over $35 million during 2017 alone, forty years after his death. Many others have increased their own fame and fortune from having an association with Elvis. For example, Andy Warhol's 'Elvis Presley' series is the only known full-length silkscreen canvass that he produced. It is based on a still photograph of Elvis from the film 'Flaming Star' and sees Elvis as a gunslinger. These images are some of Warhol's most well-known. Every time someone revisits Elvis Presley, his popularity is restored. The 2002 Junkie XL's 'A little less conversation' went to number one in nine countries. The song featured Elvis's vocals from his 1968 hit. Every year that Elvis's sales seem to slip, a year or two later they bounce back, just like Elvis himself.

Elvis starred in thirty-one feature films during the 1960's. They were hugely popular for several years, meaning Elvis became the first film star to earn $1m a film. However, as the quantity increased, the quality decreased. The repetitive

---

[359] Elvis Presley.

formula began to fail. Cinema ticket sales dropped and so did album sales. The often forgettable film soundtracks were a pale imitation of the rock and roll star. By, 1968 Elvis hadn't performed live for seven years. His career was effectively over.

"Strength does not come from winning. Your struggles develop your strengths. When you go through hardships and decide not to surrender, that is strength" [360]

In a desperate attempt to re-start the career than made him exceedingly wealthy, Elvis's manager Colonel Parker agreed to make Elvis available for a television Christmas Special. The plan was to have Elvis sing wholesome Christmas carols and establish a new place in the market. Fortunately for his fans, the producers of the show had other ideas. They just needed to by-pass Colonel Parker to put them into effect. By including a partial rendition of Blue Christmas, they persuaded Colonel Parker that the show was a Christmas Special; and he allowed the programme to be shown, without seeing it.

As a result, the '68 Comeback Special saw Elvis back to his charismatic best, clad in black leather and surrounded by his closest musicians. There wasn't a hint of Christmas involved. With the shackles temporarily removed, Elvis was able to do his own thing once again. The programme marked the return of his high-energy, rock and roll persona. The '68 Comeback Special immediately re-launched his career. It led to a new contract for 56 shows in 28 days at the Hilton International in Las Vegas. All 56 shows quickly sold out. That started his Las Vegas residentials and kick-started his album sales. When he was free to be himself, he was great. When he was too closely controlled, he became a formulaic shadow of himself. Elvis was an instinctive performer. He needed to be free to do it his way. We all perform better when we have some control over our own destiny. We all need space to be instinctive.

"Ambition is a dream with a V8 engine"[361]

Elvis had a unique blend of looks, moves and voice. He had good manners and personal charm and a good sense of humour. To many people, he also huge sex appeal. It seems that teenagers and twenty-somethings, across the World, either wanted to be him or go out with him. Elvis was a recording star and a film star.

---

[360] Arnold Schwarzenegger.
[361] Elvis Presley.

His films offered audiences the chance to see Elvis sing and dance to a new album of songs. His music blended influences from gospel, blues, rhythm and blues (R&B), country and rock and roll (which he popularised). His voice crossed racial musical boundaries and opened up a national audience. No one else has been able to cross musical genres as successfully as Elvis. His personal characteristics were appealing, but it was his Super-tribe approach to music that produced his sound and gave him plenty of musical space to operate in.

"There'll never be another like that soul brother" [362]

Those collective influences produced a unique sound that appealed to everyone. Elvis's voice was a key strength, setting him apart from the likes of Bing Crosby and Dean Martin with their gentle, middle of the road sound. But the energy that he brought to his live performances was even more powerful. Those hips changed everything. They marked him out as a rock and roller. There had never been anyone like him before. Being the first person to do anything can set you apart. To say that now, in a single sentence, massively underestimates Elvis's impact at the time. And that impact was not without fierce opposition.

As Elvis 'the Pelvis' shook and gyrated his hips he thrilled many, but he shocked and unsettled many others. There was widespread fear and disgust at his performances. Whilst audiences loved him, the critics were all shook up. On 6 January 1957, Elvis was due to appear on a family variety television programme called 'The Ed Sullivan Show'. Following an outcry from priests, school teachers and terrified parents the programme's producers had a dilemma. Should Elvis be allowed on the show? They knew that he would guarantee large audience numbers, but they also felt a moral responsibility not to promote 'the devil's music'. The Ed Sullivan show decided on a compromise. They filmed Elvis performing, but only from the waist up. The programme drew over 60 million viewers, which was 82.5% of the national viewing audience at the time. The censorship of Elvis's hips didn't last for very long. Elvis was simply too popular. The strength of feeling was too strong. Rock and roll was what audiences wanted. The censors lost won the battle, but lost the war.

Elvis's musical and cultural impact cannot be underestimated. The combination of his blend of musical influences, universal voice and high-energy movement pulled all his strengths together. It popularised rock and roll. As the "King of

---

[362] 'The Godfather of Soul' James Brown.

Rock and Roll" Elvis Presley sits on his throne, whilst everyone that's followed him has given him a name check. As John Lennon famously said:

"Before Elvis there was nothing."

~~~~~

In any competition where you need a team of players or competitors, everyone needs to be available and ready to compete. Having a strong squad is always better than just having a strong team. That's because there's always a replacement who's good enough to come in and perform when illness, injury or personal crisis strikes.

Injuries aside, rugby coach Daryl Powell always gives his whole squad game time every season. That approach has three obvious advantages. Firstly, every squad player needs regular playing time in order to be "match fit and tuned in." Otherwise a player can't step in and perform at the level required. Secondly, resting players keeps them fresh and reduces the risks of injury and burnout. Thirdly, that means every player knows that they will lose their place at some point during the season. As a result, every player has to play well enough to get their place back, after their weeks off. These principles produce strength in depth.

~~~~~

Every mission brings a series of strategic and tactical decisions. The outcome of each decision will either get you closer to completing your mission, or further away. Your choices will make the difference between success and failure. And so do your opponent's. As well as having a clear head and good information, good decision-making requires an understanding of your relative strength and firepower. Where can you position your forces to achieve a decisive win? Where will your opponent try and overpower you?

Chess is a game of strategy and tactics. Players who are out-thought are outfought. Chess requires concentration, patience and a strong technical knowledge of the game. By choosing moves which put your opponent under pressure, you can bring your firepower to bear. The more you can influence and predict your opponent's moves, the more you can plan ahead. When you can produce pressure from two sources at once, you can force mistakes and manoeuvre your opponent towards defeat.

*"In order to improve your game you must study the endgame before
everything else; for, whereas the endings can be studied and
mastered by themselves, the middlegame and the opening
must be studied in relation to the endgame"*[363]

Chess has a series of established tactics and ploys to help you. Players need all the
help they can get. Taking your opponent's pieces is hard work, because as they
can move into a free square avoid being taken. That is as long as there's a free
square for that piece to move into. Trying to prevent an opponent's piece from
escaping, is a key part of the game.

A player can create a situation called the 'pin' by moving their piece into a square
where it can take the piece in front of it, or if that's moved, it can take a more
important piece hidden behind. The effect of a pin is that your opponent is forced
to take the lesser of the two evils and leave the less valuable piece where it is. As
the player trying to defend this situation, you're stuck unless you can take the
pinning piece. If you can't, you're damned if you move and you're damned if you
don't. Your only defence was to have moved one of those pieces earlier, but now
it's too late. Forcing your opponent to give up a piece is a powerful way to
increase your chances of winning. How can you position your team in a place that
pins your opponents?

A player creates a 'fork' where they move a piece into a square where it can take
two or more of your opponent's pieces at once. This move is most commonly done
with a Queen or Knight. The effect is that whichever piece your opponent moves, to
avoid being taken, at least one other piece is left vulnerable. A fork move can also
be used to put your opponent's King in check and line-up another piece at the same
time. Your opponent has to either take your piece, or move their King, to avoid
being in check. If your opponent can't take your piece, they will have to move the
King, leaving you free to take their other piece.

*"Chess is like body-building. If you train every day,
you stay in top shape. It is the same with your brain.
Chess is a matter of daily training"*[364]

---

[363] Jose Raul Capablanca, who became Chess World Champion in 1921.
[364] Vladimir Kramnik, the first undisputed World Champion, holding both the FIDE and Classical
titles in 2006.

The 'skewer' is where you move your piece into a position where it can take one of your opponent's more important pieces, or if it moves, take a less important piece directly behind it. By creating this skewer move, your opponent has to either take your piece, or that's impossible, move the more important front piece to safety and sacrifice the piece behind it. Once again your opponent is damned either way.

All these moves are examples of putting your opponent under pressure in two places at once. If you only take the competition to your opponent on one front, you have to have overwhelming strength and firepower, or you may lose. Even if you are more powerful, you might still lose if your opponent outflanks you. Taking the battle to your opponent on two or more fronts, will increase your chances of winning.

In every walk of life, planning ahead is vital. You need to make your best move and understand how your opponent will respond to it. Predicting what your opponent will do is a vital part of getting ready to make your move. This is a tough ask because, as we know, some people can think fifteen to twenty steps ahead. Practice improves your ability to think ahead and adjust your moves accordingly.

Advanced chess thinkers can be great assets for fast moving business roles and also pivotal sports roles. The same can be true for advanced musicians. Both chess players and musicians tend to have high-level skills in patience, concentration, dedication and perseverance. Both groups are able to quickly adapt to strategic changes. They also tend to be great at spotting patterns and mistakes in them. It pays to recruit and promote people who have these kinds of wider skills.

~~~~~

The seven Heptathlon events take place on two consecutive days of competition. On Day 1 there are the 100 metres hurdles, high jump, shot put and 200 metres. On Day 2 there are the long jump, javelin and 800 metres. The Heptathlon is an event involving multiple skills and exceptional endurance. Maximum physical performance is critical. Exceptional mental strength is just as important.

Katarina Johnson-Thompson became the World Heptathlon Champion in 2019. Before her, Dame Jessica Ennis-Hill was World Champion in 2009, 2011 and 2015. Jess was also Olympic Champion in 2012 and Olympic Silver medalist in

2016. Before Jess, Denise Lewis OBE was Olympic Champion in 2000, having been the Bronze medalist in 1996. Denise was also the World Championships Silver medal winner in 1997 and 1999. Denise, Jess and Kat are household sporting names.

What about the 2004 and 2008 Olympic Games? Were those barren years for Britain? The answer is no. Kelly Sotherton won the Bronze medal at both of those Olympic Games. That means that Great Britain has won a Heptathlon Olympic medal in the past six consecutive Olympic Games. We also have the favourite for a potential seventh in 2021. That's extraordinary success, especially when there are so few heptathlon competitions outside major championships.

Performing them of all consecutively in competition is not something that athletes can practice very much. So, practicing for the heptathlon involves taking part in the seven individual events separately, at different meetings on the European circuit. As a result, a hepthalete can't easily stay heptathlon ready. Why then has Britain been so dominant in this event, when our athletes can't complete in full competitions very often? How have our heptathletes continually risen to this challenge? The answer is a combination of physical strength, mental strength and planning.

Denise Lewis won her Olympic Championship through applying her ability with sheer determination. The injuries she suffered and her fluctuations in form didn't limit her. She fought back from injury and trained even harder. Denise's mental dedication and application made her become a winner. In the 2000 Olympics, Denise was lying in third place after day one, with strapping on a leg injury. She was on track for a Bronze medal. What got her up into Gold? The mental strength to fight for it with everything she had; and the physical resilience to achieve what her mind required of her. Her will to win was greater than any of her competitors. Denise has since given a 2019 interview to the Independent newspaper and was asked to summarise her life in six words. Her answer was self-reflective.

"Be the change you want to see"

Denise took her inspiration from her family. "Even when I was hospitalised twice, and when I lay in that bed thinking about what you're going through, my family and friends were the main reason I kept fighting." Wanting something can motivate you to try and get it. Wanting it for other people, who you care about, can power you to even greater heights. Denise used her family to give her the strength she needed. Finding what makes you strong is vital to a successful life. Being able to tap into it when you need to is critical to winning.

Jess Ennis-Hill was inspired by Denise. She was also determined to prove all the coaches wrong who told her that she was "too small to be a multi-eventer". Her response to the doubt and criticism was to turn it into motivational driver. "It gives you a push to show you can do it." Jess was naturally competitive and trying to prove she could beat the odds made her even stronger. That mental strength allowed her to train harder than her competitors and it allowed her to work on her weaker throwing and long-jump events in all weathers. When others would have given up or slacked off, Jess did more. She was able to become the best athlete that she could be. Her positive mindset put her body in its best position to win Gold. Jess learned what the winning standards were and then she chased them down.

"I learned what I need to do in the long jump, what I needed to do in the javelin and I've been able to rectify those events. It's been a bit of a learning curve, which is good"[365]

Both Denise and Jess have gone on to play active roles in supporting Katarina Johnson-Thompson. After missing out on an Olympic medal in 2016, Kat felt she had "imposter syndrome" and that she wouldn't ever win a major medal. However, Jess convinced her to keep going and Denise went with her when she relocated from Liverpool to Montpellier to support her training. By sharing their advice and guidance, Denise and Jess have given Kat the extra bit of self-belief that she needed. It was the last piece of her winning puzzle.

All three women are exceptional athletes and superb role models. But they would all acknowledge that none of them won their medals alone. They are all quick to thank their coaches and their family support network for their success. Every strong individual needs a strong tribe around them. These three champions were no different. Our teams offer us strength that we don't possess ourselves. Katarina relies on her coach for many aspects of her preparation, especially the art of being ready to win. We have to think and work as a team.

"When it comes to peaking at the right time, I have to thank my coach Mike Holmes. He is a genius"[366]

---

[365] Jess Ennis-Hill.
[366] Katarina Johnson-Thompson.

The next generation of British heptathletes now have three role great models to be inspired by. Hopefully Katarina Johnson-Thompson will add an Olympic Gold to her collection and then the next generation will go on to emulate the three of them.

~~~~~

On 20 May 2009, Sir. Ranulph Fiennes OBE reached the summit of Mount Everest, at sixty-five years of age and became the oldest British person to do so. At that moment, Ranulph also became the first person to have climbed Everest and crossed both polar ice-caps. These are just three of the lifetime achievements of Britain's greatest explorer.

Ranulph is fearless and driven from within. It's a drive that defies prudence and common sense. On one occasion, whilst trying to climb Everest, Ranulph had a heart attack that required hospitalisation and a double heart bypass operation. That only paused his adventures. It certainly didn't slow him down. Four months later, Ranulph completed seven marathons in seven days on seven continents as part of the 'Land Rover 7x7x7 Challenge' to support the British Heart Foundation. There is no denying his, bravery, fortitude and perseverance. Ranulph Fiennes is a winner because of his supreme inner-strength when it really matters.

"Success is not final. Failure is not fatal.
It is the courage to continue that counts"[367]

Sir. Ranulph Fiennes is an extraordinary adventurer. He is also an entertaining speaker, telling his stories with humility and dry wit. He is remarkably matter of fact about what are a series of exceptional achievements. There must have been endless opportunities to back out, stop, turn around and head for home, but whilst he could still stand, he refused to give in. He is built of the strongest of mental spirits. While his expeditions do not appear to have made him wealthy in monetary terms, they have certainly shown him to be rich in character; and that's what matters more.

~~~~~

When a player is sent-off the field of play, the strength of their team is instantly reduced. Sport is difficult enough to win with a full team. Weakening your own

---

[367] Winston Churchill.

team really helps your opponents and is incredibly counter-productive. You always need to have your maximum firepower out there on the pitch. No player should ever lose control and blow their own team's chances of winning. So many losing behaviours are avoidable.

In the 1998 FIFA World Cup, England played Argentina in the first knock-out round. During the game, David Beckham was fouled by Argentina's Diego Simeone. The referee moved in to award England a free-kick. Frustrated by the foul, David swiped his leg back up behind him, kicking Simeone. The referee now had a clear view of David's own foul and sent David off. England's best chance of getting the winning goal had left the field. England had to play the rest of the match with ten players. England eventually lost the game on penalties.

In 2005, Keiron Dyer and Lee Bowyer were playing for Newcastle United against Aston Villa. After 73 minutes, Newcastle were losing 3 v 0, down to ten men and struggling badly. Lee Bowyer reportedly went over and confronted his teammate Keiron Dyer about why he wasn't passing the ball to him. Keiron allegedly responded "Because you're shit". Lee didn't like what he heard and a grapple followed, leading to a full-on fight. The two players had to be physically separated by players from both teams. As a result, both players were sent off. Newcastle had to finish the match with only eight players, losing the game 3 v 0. In the tunnel, the Newcastle United Manager, Graeme Souness, allegedly challenged both players to a fight if they thought they were tough. Both players declined. Keiron was banned for 3 matches and Lee for four, robbing Newcastle of their services for several weeks afterwards.

The 2006 World Cup Final, between France and Italy, was finely balanced. The French captain, Zinadine Zidane, allowed Italy's Marco Materrazi to wind him up with offensive comments about a member of his family. With a rush of red-headedness, Zinadine lost his cool, headbutted Materrazi in the chest and was sent off. A tired looking France eventually lost the match on penalties.

In 2009, the Welsh rugby region the Ospreys played Racing 92 from France in the Heineken European Cup. In the first minute of the match, the Ospreys fullback Dan Evans jumped up to catch a high ball. Losing his balance mid-air, his flailing boot made contact with the head of Racing 92's Teddy Thomas. After thirty-seven seconds, Dan Evans was sent off. The incident was an accident and the sending-off incredibly unlucky, but it meant that the Ospreys had an uphill battle. Team discipline was absolutely vital. But sadly it wasn't there when it was needed. Scott Williams was sin-binned for infringing at a ruck. Then shortly afterwards, Aled Davies was sin-binned for a deliberate knock-on. So, for a period, the Ospreys had three players off the pitch. Despite a brave effort from the remaining twelve players, the Ospreys lost the match 19 v 40. Fourteen players won't often beat fifteen and twelve absolutely never will.

Your opponents will seek to damages your chances of success as much as they can. That's an uncontrollable. But self-inflicted wounds are very much a controllable to master and avoid. Your actions should never weaken you and strengthen your opposition.

Strength comes from togetherness, collaborative working and unity of purpose. On the back of the helmets worn by the Buffalo Bills American Football team, there are five words "It takes all of us". That shows mutual trust and humility. That work ethic strengthens the Bills and tells their opponents to fear their team spirit. The opposite effect is to be avoided.

In 1996, Liverpool wore white Giorgio Armani suits to the F.A. Cup Final. No one had veered away from classic dark grey or navy before. It was an instant talking point. Immediately on seeing the suits, the manager of Liverpool's opponents, Sir. Alex Ferguson, reportedly told his assistant manager that United would win the game "1 v 0".

Building a case for the arrogance of Liverpool's 'Spice Boys' in his head, Alex took it with him into United's dressing room and used it to motivate his players. Alex later reflected on Liverpool's decision saying "Arrogance or over-confidence, it was ridiculous. Absolutely ridiculous." Manchester United worked tirelessly, closed down Liverpool's attacking flair and won the game 1 v 0. Never willingly give your opponent the strength to beat you.

Takeaway thoughts:

- Strength comes in many forms
- Teams have to maintain their fighting strength and stay competitive
- We need the stamina and the will to win in order to endure
- We don't have to be strong 24/7 365, only when we are 'live'
- Strength comes from good decision-making
- Core strength and inner-strength matter enormously
- Manage the perception battle
- Be bold and take calculated risks
- Prime ourselves well
- Our skills must become second nature
- Be instinctive
- Think and plan ahead
- Work as a team
- Never be arrogant

3.11 WINNING FINISHING

The eleventh controllable is finishing. Whether it's closing a sale, reaching the summit of mountain or getting the ball down to score a try, winning takes a final stage, the finish.

Without mastering all the other controllables, we may never get the chance to finish off a win. But where we have mastered them, finishing is just the last natural step of our journey. How win ready we are dictates how well we take the opportunities when they come. With good positioning, preparation and alignment we will be ready and able to close out the win we want. We need to be ready for them, because there is no automatic end to a competition. It has to have been planned for and grafted for, long before that point comes. It's full of mental strength and character. It's made in the months and years leading up to it. Finishing means finishing off what's been long planned and delivered.

~~~~~

Finishing off a win can be very hard. It usually requires total focus and self-control in the key moments. When it comes to the moment of winning, some people find that they can't finish. When it comes to it, they can't focus or act. Under pressure, they sweat, tremble, shake and choke. This is not a permanent state, it's a human reaction to pressure. Being human, we have human flaws and human problems. Anxiety is just a red flag for an issue that needs to be overcome.

We cannot 100% cope, 100% of the time. Managing our anxieties allows us to finish when we need to. Winners have anxieties. They just find a way to manage them, by getting help and putting coping mechanisms in place. We need to substitute our inconsistent reactions with consistent processes. When we are stressed, we need to avoid strong emotional reactions and draw on winning processes to get us through the crisis.

We all need help and support. We all need to be honest with ourselves and our teammates. Managing health issues requires medical therapies and counselling support. Managing addictions requires medical therapies and counselling support. Not eating properly requires dietary advice, medical therapies and counselling support. Managing negative thoughts and self-loathing requires medical therapies and counselling support. Managing financial worries requires advice from a financial adviser and counselling support. Managing social anxieties (such as public speaking or networking) requires medical therapies and counselling support. Managing personal conflicts requires medical therapies and counselling support. All of these anxieties require professional help and support.

If you want your team to win, it's critically important to discover the anxiety triggers that you or your team have. Identifying those triggers is the first step in managing them. Controlling our anxieties allows us to finish when we need to. What puts you on edge? What gives you uncontrollable worries? What prevents you from concentrating or sleeping? What makes you irritable and unapproachable? What takes away your focus? What feels more controlling than the mission?

We can't operate at 100% maximum performance, 100% of the time. Expecting to, is flawed logic. Being expected to, is flawed management. Supporting ourselves and each other is absolutely essential. If we help each other, we can finish the mission together. Being human, we have human needs and we have human kindness. A team of people that truly cares about each other is a winning team. Don't rely on someone else to provide the finish, go and help them, or do it yourself.

In physical driving terms, being a Formula 1 racing driver is a solo-sport. It means driving a single-seater racing car for about 90 minutes, at speeds up to 233mph, with no one else on board to physically help you drive the car. However, that's where the solo references end. Off the track, there is a vast team of people managing, designing, preparing, promoting, analysing, repairing, re-fuelling and changing the tyres on the car. For every pair of drivers, there are at least 1,500 other people contributing to their performances. For every finishing position a driver achieves, there are thousands of inputs beyond the driving. Whilst only the driver makes it up onto the winner's podium, 1,500 other people are up there in spirit.

On Sunday 25 October 2020, Lewis Hamilton won his 92nd Grand Prix and overtook Michael Schumacher's long-standing race winning record. After the race, Lewis was very quick to credit his team for its support. "Everything we do together. We are all rowing in the same direction and that's why we're doing what we're doing." Every winner needs help to finish alone. Winners ask for help. Winners listen to help, Winners accept help. The fact that Lewis Hamilton sees himself a part of a team, and not as a solo performer, is exactly why less than a month later he won his seventh World Title, equalling Michael Schumacher's record haul.

~~~~~

Sir. Geoff Hurst was a footballer with West Ham United and England. Geoff's finest game was the 1966 FIFA World Cup Final, in which he scored a hat-trick to help England win the World Cup for the first (and so far only) time.

In 2018, I was grateful to be asked to co-host the South Coast Business of the Year Awards with Sir. Geoff. We spent the evening talking and doing our presenting duties. Geoff is clearly a thoughtful, humble person. That is his off the pitch persona. However, on the pitch he was a ruthless finisher. There have been many great goal-scorers over the decades, but Geoff remains the only male footballer to score a hat-trick in the World Cup Final.

In the dying moments of that famous game, England were winning 3 v 2. The clock was running out for Germany and England were only leading by one goal. The ball suddenly came to Sir. Bobby Moore in the England penalty area. Instead of booting it out into the stand, Bobby saw an opportunity and played a pass over the top of several German players. The ball dropped directly into Geoff's path and he started running towards the German goal. Sir. Alan Ball was free on his right and immediately called for the ball. Rather than pass it to him, Geoff took the ball on himself and shot with his less-favoured left foot.

I asked Geoff whether there was any hesitation in his mind before deciding to take the shot? He replied "None."[368] Geoff had no doubt in his mind. There was absolutely no chance of him passing the ball. He was a striker, he had scored two goals and was he full of confidence. The ball flew off his boot and went straight into the German goal. England won the match 4 v 2. Confidence brings focus and removes doubt.

Having the confidence to take the shot is one part of being a 'finisher'. Sir. Geoff Hurst had that. The other part of finishing is practicing your 'shooting' so much that your confidence is justified. Geoff had self-belief and a great strike. One fed the other, giving him the confidence to take on the shot. Whatever it is that we do, we all need to practice so hard that we believe we can 'score' every time. Then we can operate like we truly believe in ourselves.

~~~~~

Finishing is about taking your opportunities. It's about seeing and creating new opportunities too. Finishers see a bigger, better version of what they've been given and they deliver it.

Jacqueline Gold CBE is the Chief Executive Officer of the Gold Group, Ann Summers and Knickerbox. But that's not the level she started out at. Jacqueline began by doing work experience at Ann Summers. She didn't like the atmosphere or the way the shops were positioned for men to sell to men, for women. Jacqueline wanted women to be able to buy for themselves. So she created and launched the Ann Summers Party Plan, a home marketing plan for sex toys, with a strict "no men allowed" policy. It went on to be an enormous success.

When she was appointed CEO of Ann Summers, Jacqueline inherited a small, male run shop chain with an £83,000 annual turnover. By establishing a more female focus, a 70% female board and a more inclusive culture, Jacqueline transformed the business into a £140 million turnover national chain. With a sales force of over 7,500 women party organisers and 136 high street stores throughout the UK and Ireland, the brand has a national presence and identity.

---

[368] When Sir. Geoff speaks publicly, he tells a funnier version of this story which I won't spoil here.

Jacqueline is a very able, very personable leader. Having met her, I can say that she comes across as highly impressive, genuine and approachable. As a result, her success isn't at all surprising. There is an inner confidence to her, but there isn't a hint of arrogance. Rather than pull the ladder up behind her, Jacqueline has actively supported other women in business, through initiatives like her 'EmpoweredNotPerfect' twitter campaign. With statements like "Be the kind of women that makes other women want to up their game" Jacqueline has become a leading business role model.

Deep down finishers know their own strengths, they know that their success isn't just an accident. Jacqueline has advice for anyone who experiences any self-doubt. "Don't mumble your way through the discussion or apologise for even being there – put your case forward with conviction and pride and remember you deserve this."[369] Crediting her resilience as her great strength, Jacqueline Gold has used it extremely well and become an undoubted finisher.

~~~~~

Finishing has to be done without finishing off the winner as well. Assess the risks of damage to your own team or organisation before you fight a battle. Don't kill yourself winning. A Pyrrhic victory is a victory that inflicts such a devastating toll on the victor that it's tantamount to a defeat. The terms comes from an ancient battle.

"Whatever they were in life, here at the end, each man stood with courage and honour. They fought for the ones who couldn't fight for themselves and they died for them too. All to win something that didn't belong to them. It was magnificent"[370]

In 280 BC, King Pyrrhus of Epirus faced the might of the Roman army in Italy. Despite securing back to back victories at the battles of Heraclea and Asculum, his army reportedly lost the majority of its forces and almost all of its principal commanders. The Romans suffered greater casualties in both battles, but they had replacement soldiers ready to replace them. As a result, the Roman casualties had far less impact than the losses suffered by King Pyrrhus. After the battle, King Pyrrhus reportedly said "Another such victory over the Romans, and we are undone."

---

[369] Jacqueline Gold, reported in Marie Claire.
[370] Said by Emma Cullen, at the end of the 2016 version of 'The Magnificent Seven'.

"Only the farmers won. We lost. We always lose"[371]

More recently, a few historians have argued that Pyrrhus's losses were not as extensive as imagined and that the tag 'Pyrrhic victory' ironically shouldn't apply to him. Regardless of its accuracy, the saying 'a Pyrrhic victory' has stuck. A win needs to be a sustainable success. Don't get complacent or cocky as the finish approaches. Success means finishing the mission, without finishing off your organsiation. Keep the other ten controllables going, all the way to the end of the line.

~~~~~

However close a win might be, it can still elude you. There have been far too many examples of that to ever list them. How frustrating is it, to get incredibly close to winning something only to see it lost? We have already seen how Chelsea's missed penalties in the 2008 Champions League final could have won them the Cup, rather than Manchester United. There is always the need to close out a win. Keep going to the very end.

At the 1956 Grand National, Queen Elizabeth the Queen Mother was watching her horse Devon Loch from the Royal Box. Forty yards from the winning post Devon Loch was leading the race by five lengths. There was going to be a Royal winner. Without warning Devon Loch suddenly jumped into the air and landed on his stomach. Unable to get to his feet, he was beaten. No one knows exactly why it happened, but his jockey Dick Francis suggested that a loud cheer from the crowd may have spooked the horse. Ironically his collapse occurred right in front of the Royal Box. Queen Elizabeth the Queen Mother is reported to have said "Well that's racing!"

Very late on in the 1968 Rugby League Cup Final, Don Fox created a try which put his team on the cusp of victory. Having already been voted winner of the Lance Todd Trophy for the man of the match, Don merely had to kick the goal in front of the posts to win the Cup for Wakefield Trinity. He was on the brink of immortality. On a saturated pitch, Don slipped during his run-up and sliced the kick wide. As he famously sank to his knees in despair, Leeds celebrated an unlikely 11-10 victory.

---

[371] Said by Chris Adams, at the end of the 1960 version of 'The Magnificent Seven'.

In 1984, John McEnroe was on a year-long winning streak when he entered the French Open. John totally outplayed and dominated his opponent Ivan Lendl in the first two sets. By the time the third set was underway, the score was tied 1-1. Playing sublime tennis, John was on track to beat his opponent. But he became enraged by a distracting noise from a cameraman's headset, walked over and screamed at the cameraman during the match. He then couldn't refocus, going on to lose the match by three sets to two.

~~~~~

These heart-wrenching events show that losing can happen to anyone, at any time. Sometimes you have to accept them as an educational failure that teaches you how to win. Sometimes we have to accept that the uncontrollables were too great. But, whatever happens in the end, never accept defeat until it's all over. That's because if you've mastered the other ten controllables, you're always in with a chance of winning. Finishers find a way of finishing, however low the odds. Never give up.

In 1957, Charlton Athletic were losing 5 v 1 at home. They sixty minutes into a ninety minute match and the question was how many more goals would they concede? When the final whistle blew Charlton had won the game 7 v 6. Johnny Summers scored five of the Charlton goals and made the other two. Where did his second half performance come from? Johnny later revealed that he'd changed his boots at half-time. His old pair were literally falling apart. Badly prepared, his first half had been a struggle. Revived by a pair of new boots, Johnny Summers delivered one of the greatest comebacks in professional football.

In 1972, Lasse Viren found himself in Munich, at his first Olympic Games. Approximately half-way through the Olympic 10,000 metres final, Lasse stumbled and fell over. A Tunisian runner, Mohamed Gammoudi, tripped over Lasse and he fell over as well. The others were unaffected and ran on strongly. Two laps later, Mohamed Gammoudi gave up and stopped running. The shock and impact of the fall had badly affected him and he was too far behind to challenge. Lasse Viren was in a similar position, but he was not prepared to give up. He had come to win. Mentally prepared, Lasse got back up to his feet and gradually chased his way into contention. Eventually, Lasse caught the British race leader David Bedford and won Gold, in a new World Record time. Lasse Viren had come ready to win. His fall proved to be only a temporary distraction. When it mattered, Lasse Viren showed the mental and physical strength to deliver his mission.

In 1985, Dennis Taylor was playing Steve Davis in the World Snooker Final. Losing 7 frames to 0, Dennis couldn't control his nerves. Unprepared for the biggest occasion of his career, he was in danger of losing the match 18 v 0. When he finally won the eighth frame, he checked himself. He knew he could do better. As his form came back, he worked his way into the match. His increasing self-control gave him increasing self-belief. And as his self-belief grew, so did his performance level. Dennis Taylor finally got himself to 17 frames all with one to play. The 1985 World title came down to the very last ball, of the very last frame. By this point, Steve Davis was showing rare signs of pressure. Dennis Taylor's comeback had conquered his nerves and he potted the last black, to win his World Championship.

In 1981, at the 'Ashes' cricket test match at Headingley, Australia bowled England all out for only 174 and scored 401 for 9 declared in their own first innings. When Australia got England to 135 for 7 in their second innings, England were still 92 runs behind with only three wickets left. They looked down and out. Up stepped Ian Botham[372], who had scored the team's only 50 in the first innings. With no fear of anyone, 'Beefy' started hitting the ball as hard as he could, scoring boundary after boundary, for an unbeaten 145 not out. By the end of the day England had a narrow lead of 124 with one wicket left. After the day's cricket was over England had to relocate to a new hotel, as they'd checked out of theirs that morning on the assumption that they were about to lose. England added four more runs the next morning before losing their final wicket. They now had to defend a lead of 128. Australia were heavy favourites to win. Up stepped Bob Willis, who took 8 wickets for only 43 runs. England won by 18 runs and went on to win the Ashes. Thank goodness Ian Botham and Bob Willis believed what England's management did not.

In the 1999 Champions League Final, Bayern Munich were beating Manchester United 1 v 0 in the 90th minute of the match. Only a few short minutes of injury time remained. With tiring legs and minds, it was the two fresher United substitutes, Teddy Sheringham and Ole Gunnar Solskjaer who stayed alert and scored in the 91st and 93rd minutes. Manchester United won the match 2 v 1. The belief remained to the last seconds. The two substitutes were both win ready, which was part and parcel of the team's 'never-say-die attitude' under Sir Alex Ferguson.

---

[372] Now Baron Botham Kt OBE, after adding extraordinary charity work to his cricketing achievements.

It's my turn to finish now. My final message is this. If you master your controllables you will achieve at least a qualified success. If you haven't fully mastered them, you may not be win ready quite yet. But keep going. You can still win next time.

Takeaway thoughts:

- Mastering the other ten controllables makes us a better finisher
- Total focus is key
- Don't rely on someone else to provide the finish, help them or do it yourself
- Confidence brings focus and removes doubt
- Finishers see what else can be done and then get it done
- Success means finishing the mission, without finishing off your organsiation
- Keep going to the very end
- Never give up
- If you don't win this time, you can do next time

4. 'WIN READY'?

Winning is often difficult, subjective and dependent on the expectations and judgements of others. But it's also a controllable that we can influence. We need to define winning in a way that helps us to become winners. We need to set achievable winning outcomes and manageable winning standards. That will allow us to take control of the controllables around winning itself. They matter most of all. Then come the rest, the controllables we need for our mission, our competition. We need to give our full focus to the controllables that make the most difference to winning.

If we try and win anything on our own, we almost certainly won't win anything at all. Winning is about sharing responsibility, effort and achievement. Winning is a team game. Find your team, make it a tribe and then build a Super-tribe to power its winning.

Good luck with your mission. I hope you win.

Simon.

Printed in Great Britain
by Amazon

14965028R00224